CHICAGO

CHICAGO

A PERSONAL HISTORY
OF AMERICA'S MOST AMERICAN CITY

FINIS FARR

ARLINGTON HOUSE   *New Rochelle, N.Y.*

Permission is gratefully acknowledged to quote from the following books:

Herbert Asbury, *Gem of the Prairie: An Informal History of the Chicago Underworld.* Permission granted by Alfred A. Knopf, Inc.

Herman Kogan and Lloyd Wendt, *Lords of the Levee* and *Give the Lady What She Wants.* Permission granted by Herman Kogan.

Harriet Monroe, A Poet's Life: Seventy Years in a Changing World. Permission granted by Marguerite F. Fletcher (Mrs. Edwin S. Fletcher).

Top right book jacket photo by Kee T. Chang, Chicago Association of Commerce & Industry.

Library of Congress Catalog Card Number 72–78486

ISBN 0–87000–179–5

MANUFACTURED IN THE UNITED STATES OF AMERICA

TO
ROBERT DYER

Contents

CHICAGO

I

From the Glaciers

ACCORDING TO THE MARVELOUS STORIES OF GEOLOGISTS, THE CENTRAL valley of North America once alternated in climate, through an immeasurable period of time, between extremes of heat and cold. During warm spells that lasted some millions of years, the sea was boiling hot, covering everything. Then the sea went away, leaving a swamp that nourished hideous creatures, enormous flying insects, and walking fish, in steamy forests of exceedingly strange plants and trees. After that a few million years of cold would set in, and mountains of glacial ice would come creeping out of the north, grinding the land to prairie, and storing the energies of life far underneath the scarred and flattened surface of the ground. All this took a long time; about twelve thousand years ago, the last ice field in North America began to die. As it disappeared from northern Illinois, the melting glacier left the ancestor of Lake Michigan that geologists have named Lake Chicago. Covering what is now the metropolitan area to a depth of sixty feet, these waters burst their confining moraines, roared over prairies to form the Illinois River, and joined the drainage system of the middle continent. Some thousands of years later, a stretch of sodden ground came into view between the Des Plaines and the southern end of a small stream, one day to be called the Chicago River, which joined the lake through an inlet seven miles northeast of the swamp. The first men who came to this place were Indians. They crossed the marsh on foot, carrying their canoes, and so prepared the way for the first European visitors at the Chicago portage—Marquette and Jolliet.

Father Jacques Marquette was a Jesuit missionary, one of the "black robes" who went into the wilderness to bring Indians the good news about Christ, the Kingdom of God, and the possibility of salvation. Although six Jesuits had endured martyrdom at Iroquois torture stakes, black robes continued to appear in the remotest wilds, where they planted outposts like the mission of St. Ignace at the Straits of Mackinac, which Marquette established in the summer of 1671. These straits were narrows between Lake Huron and Lake Michigan; the chapel of St. Ignace stood on the bluff from which Marquette could study shades of blue in the water that reached beyond Mackinac Island to a limitless horizon. Here he was joined in December 1672 by a Canadian-born explorer named Louis Jolliet, who carried important papers from the French governor in Quebec. The documents authorized Marquette and Jolliet to lead an expedition in search of a great river said to be running somewhere west. They started out in May 1673 by way of Green Bay, the Fox River, and the Wisconsin. On June 17 they entered the upper Mississippi and claimed the stupendous discovery for France. By mid-July they had gone as far south as the Arkansas River, and learned that the Mississippi ran to the Gulf of Mexico. On the return journey they steered their canoes into the Illinois, and stopped near the future site of Peoria to visit an Indian village, where Marquette preached three sermons which so impressed the listeners that they made him promise to come back, and brought a dying child for baptism as he was boarding his canoe. Two hundred miles on, Marquette and Jolliet entered the Des Plaines, and talked with Indians who guided them through the Chicago River portage to the lake. Continuing up the west side of Lake Michigan, they reached Green Bay in September, having carried out one of the most important explorations in history. Both had recognized the significance of the Chicago portage, and Jolliet wrote in his report that "the cutting of one canal through half a league of prairie at this place" would allow boats to pass on a continental waterway reaching from the St. Lawrence to the Gulf of Mexico.

While Jolliet submitted reports at Quebec, Marquette rested near Green Bay, recruiting his strength and writing his journal. At the end of October 1674 Father Marquette went out to keep the promise he had given the Illinois Indians. On December 4 he reached the Chicago River, found himself too weak to go on, and settled in for the winter with two companions at a cabin near the fork. In early spring they crossed the portage and headed south, arriving at the village on Easter Sunday. But shortly afterward, Marquette's health broke; he grew worse rapidly, and

[12]

said he hoped to reach St. Ignace before the end. Much moved by his saintly bearing, the chiefs ordered a party of warriors to escort him home. Halfway up the east side of Lake Michigan, Marquette asked to be taken ashore. The place was near what is now Ludington, and the date was Saturday, May 18, 1675. They laid him on the beach where he could see blue water. There he died, aged thirty-seven years, eleven months, and eight days.

The next European to appear on the Chicago scene was a man whose character shines through the chronicles of his time. He was a soldier of fortune named Henry Tonty, cousin of Daniel Duluth and son of the Neapolitan banker who invented the Tontine form of insurance. Maimed in the service of Louis XIV, he wore a prosthetic device for which the Indians called him Tonty of the Iron Hand. Tonty was known throughout New France for his good heart and good manners, and he became a friend and lieutenant to Robert Cavalier, Sieur de La Salle. In June 1681 La Salle and Tonty met for a conference on Mackinac Island to plan a chain of forts that would secure the middle continent for France. Tonty came to the Chicago River to build cargo sledges for the expedition. La Salle followed in January 1682 and dated several letters "from the portage of Checagou," which he described as a place with good possibilities for the future. Ready at last to jump off into the wilderness, La Salle and Tonty went through the swamp with sledges, supplies, and men. They rebuilt a fort on the Illinois River that the Iroquois had destroyed, and then explored the Mississippi to its mouth. On April 9 they saw the Gulf of Mexico, and made the tremendous gesture of claiming the entire Mississippi valley, which they called Louisiana in honor of the king. Reporting his explorations in Paris, La Salle obtained a royal commission to plant a settlement on the lower Mississippi, and sailed from France in July 1684 with four shiploads of colonists. The future seemed bright, but his luck went bad when a navigator's mistake landed them on the coast of Texas. La Salle started across country for the Mississippi, but somewhere on the way his men mutinied and murdered him.

Left behind in charge of the Illinois settlements, Tonty went looking for La Salle in 1686, but did not get news of the murder until 1689. On hearing of it in September of that year, he started hunting the mutineers, but failed to find them. After that until his death in 1704, Henry Tonty gave able leadership to settlers while building the chain of forts that he had planned at Mackinac with Robert de La Salle. One may claim La Salle and Tonty as Chicagoans, with their magnificent ideas and their boldness and endurance, because they were the first to use the Chicago River as a base of operations for the whole great middle valley.

All students of Chicago have admired the dignity and decency in the early years of knightly soldiers and zealous missionaries, a class of people whose virtues stand in contrast to the greed, vice, and malice of many disgusting scoundrels who were to be prominent in Chicago's future history. Yet after La Salle and Tonty had gone, a hundred years went by and nothing happened at all, either for good or evil. The name "Chekagou," supposed to mean "wild onion," appeared on a map in 1684, but aside from an occasional trapper, no one passed through to hear the desolate sounds of wind in oak and cottonwood, surf on the shore, and sea gulls crying.

In the world outside, the strength of Spain had melted away, leaving France and England struggling over the furs and gold of North America. Several campaigns of the endless wars burned out along the east wall of Chicago's great valley, where Major George Washington marched in 1755 as colonial aide to General Edward Braddock, a typical military professional of his time. Braddock put his trust in firepower, maintaining that no enemy could stand before the British grenadier, the best equipped soldier in the world. No doubt Washington kept this doctrine in mind as he observed the tactics of French and Indian commandos while Braddock was suffering defeat at Fort Duquesne. The major got out alive, managing to extract his wounded general as well; still disdaining all provincial notions, Braddock died four days later. Eventually the British captured Quebec, and the treaty of 1763 closed out the French empire in North America. And so Chicago, along with the buffalo on its adjacent prairies, the monstrous five-foot muskellunge in its river, and the rattlesnakes in its swamp, attained a listing on the property rolls of George III. Then came a period when Chicago was part of Virginia, a geographical oddity caused by George Rogers Clark when he claimed the southern shores of Lake Michigan in 1778. And then at last in 1779 the founder of modern Chicago made his entrance. He was a French Canadian mulatto named Jean Baptiste Point du Sable, and he started the city's first commercial enterprise, a river trading post on the north bank east of the fork. Du Sable cleared white oak forest for a cornfield and worked a farm in addition to his trade in furs. His business was four years old when the North American colonies finally broke loose from England; he was prospering, four years later, when Congress passed the North West Ordinance, establishing the Territory of Illinois. In 1800 du Sable sold his property to another French Canadian, Jean Lalime. The bill of sale listed a main house with ground floor space of 22 by 40 feet, two barns, a mill that ran by mulepower, a bakehouse, a workshop, a dairy, and a smokehouse. In addition there were two calves, two mules, 28 hogs, 30 head of cattle, and 44 hens. Farm equipment included a number of carts, seven sickles, eight scythes, and the toolhouse containing nails, hammers, axes, saws, kettles, and other useful things. After concluding Chicago's first business deal, du Sable went to Missouri, where he died in 1814, a substantial citizen, and was buried in the Catholic cemetery at St. Charles.

In early spring of 1803 the first men wearing the uniform of the United States Army arrived in Chicago, under command of Captain John Whistler. This company of forty men had been on easy garrison duty at Detroit until orders came from high up to march to Chicago, and so they appeared one day in April, trudging along the shore, looking across prairie to their left, the lake with whitecaps to their right. When they crossed the tops of dunes, water in the lake and high grass on the prairie seemed to form two oceans, one blue, one brownish green; and the prevailing northeast wind made waves on both. The man who ordered them on this hike was the Secretary of War, General Henry Dearborn, whose name was to be given to a fort the men were sent to build on the Chicago River.

Sweating through the summer and fall, the captain and his men raised their fort on the south bank of the river where Michigan Avenue joins Wacker Drive today. Four corner towers made Chicago's first skyline, and behind stockades the soldiers prepared quarters for their families, who soon joined them. Among the children toddled the captain's infant son, George Washington Whistler, later to become railroad builder to the Czar, and father of James Abbott McNeil Whistler. Aside from soldiers and Indians, Baby George W. Whistler had a group of civilians to observe and wonder at. The colony included a French trapper and boatman named Antoine Ouilmette and his Indian wife; Dr. Smith, the contract surgeon; Jean Lalime, who had sold his business and taken the job of Indian interpreter at the fort; and the man who bought Lalime's property, John Kinzie.

Thirty-one years old when he bought out Lalime in 1804, John Kinzie was a man of parts. He had been born in Quebec, the child of a British army surgeon and the widow of a military chaplain. Young Kinzie left home early and ranged the lakes and forests, trapping and trading with Indians whose ways he found easy to learn. He also learned to work in silver, and the Indians along the Maumee River in Ohio Territory liked his rings, bracelets, and buckles so well that they named him Silver Man. When he came to Chicago, Kinzie brought with him his wife Eleanor who had been the widow of a British militia officer. The Kinzies were the leading civilian family in the settlement; they improved the main house at the trading post, spread bountiful hospitality before the visitors who occasionally came that way, and even provided musical entertainment when John played his fiddle in the evenings. One likes to imagine lighted windows and the sound of fiddling in the vast darkness of prairie and lake. So it undoubtedly was on holiday evenings; but life grew complicated; tensions arose in the relationship of civilians to the military that were to cause quarrels and violent death. The troubles had to do with fundamental questions that are not yet answered either in Chicago or the world at large.

To begin with, John Kinzie was banker to the fort; he supplied money to pay the bounties for men who re-enlisted when their terms ended. There was nothing irregular in this, for goldsmiths and silversmiths had traditionally served as bankers since the Middle Ages. Nevertheless, the handling of bounty money gave Kinzie more importance at Chicago—and in regional headquarters at Detroit—than he would have enjoyed had he been no more than sutler to the army forces. This he was also, supplying much of the food and all of the liquor the military people consumed. Kinzie seems to have liked to price supplies at half a dollar: he sold butter and tobacco at fifty cents a pound, and whiskey at fifty cents a quart. And one point of bitter disagreement between post and fort arose from Kinzie's policy of selling whiskey to Indians. Kinzie the businessman saw Indians as customers and sources of extremely high profit from the furs they traded to him; and he liked to serve out whiskey to make bargaining go well. And there is evidence that he had no objection to selling an additional supply, or using it as payment for the skins. His own accounts revealed this, for although the fire of 1871 destroyed Kinzie's books, reliable notes taken from his records and surviving the fire have shown that he dealt in whiskey by the sixty-eight-gallon barrel, and in a larger number of barrels than the people at the fort could have used, even if they had swigged the stuff day and night. Two attitudes toward an exploited race stood in opposition at Chicago. One was the view of army officers who went by the book and said the Indian was entitled to protection, even as they kicked him off his ancestral terrain; the other, a trader's approach holding the Indian as nothing more than a source of profit, who might be soaked in liquor if it suited the purposes of those who dealt with him.

An additional cause of tension at Chicago was the partnership that Kinzie maintained with John Whistler, Jr., the commandant's older son. Between the two factions stood Ouilmette, Chicago's first transportation magnate with his monopoly of freighting over the portage in sledges or boats; but he rented his largest boat from Kinzie, which probably inclined him toward the capitalist's side in the arguments that constantly went on. In 1808, Dr. John Cooper came to the fort, relieving Dr. Smith, and before he had administered his first dose of medicine, the physician saw that

[16]

relations between fort and village were ready to explode. A complicating factor was the presence of Lalime, former owner of the trading post. Better educated than Kinzie, Lalime was popular with the officers, who found him an expert interpreter. Cooper noted that Lalime was on bad terms with Kinzie, who had a violent temper, according to the doctor's diary. So matters went until 1810, when the partnership between Kinzie and young Whistler broke up, and charges and countercharges reached the authorities in Detroit. As always when underlings stir trouble, someone had to pay, and it turned out that the victim was Captain John Whistler, since the uproar resulted in his recall and the appointment of Captain Nathan Heald in his place. Kinzie had won—by superior clout, to use the term of a later day in Chicago. However, Jean Lalime still stood high at the fort, and his quarrel with Kinzie smoldered like a fire in a mine. It burst out in a fight at sunset on an April day in 1812, and Kinzie stabbed Lalime to death.

Kinzie was painfully wounded, and he took to the woods with the settlement's French Canadian blacksmith as his companion. A young girl saw the fight, tended Kinzie's wound, and helped him away to the woods. She was Victoire Mirandeau, the blacksmith's daughter, maidservant in Kinzie's house at the time. Seventy years later a local historian questioned Victoire, now the widow of John Porthier and believed to be the oldest woman in the city. Thinking back to what she had seen across the Chicago River in her thirteenth year, the old lady said:

"My mother was an Ottawa woman. My father was a Frenchman. I saw the fight in which Lalime was killed. It was sunset when they used to shut the gates of the fort. Kinzie and Lalime came out together and soon we heard Lieutenant Helm call out for Mr. Kinzie to look out for Lalime, as he had a pistol. Quick we saw the men come together. We heard the pistol go off, and saw the smoke. Then they fell down together. I don't know as Lalime got up at all, but Kinzie got up pretty quick. Blood was running from his shoulder where Lalime shot him. In the night we packed up some things, and my father took him to Milwaukee. I don't know where Lalime was buried. I don't know what the quarrel was about. It was an old one —business I guess."

Far away and long ago, the fight outside Fort Dearborn baffles any observer trying to bring it into focus through a haze of time like mist from the Chicago River. We know that "quick they came together," and a man lay dead. And we know that no one came from the fort to arrest or even question Kinzie. Perhaps the commandant wanted him to escape, and not come back, for it is obvious that Captain Heald had observed the weight of Kinzie's clout, and the downfall of Captain Whistler. Whatever the reason, there was no pursuit. Instead, the officers held a board of inquiry on the fight, and decided Kinzie was not to blame. They concluded that after shooting Kinzie, Lalime had pulled a knife. The men grappled and fell, and Lalime's death by his own knife followed either as an accident or the justifiable homicide of self-defense. By the time the woods-ranging blacksmith brought this news to Kinzie in Milwaukee, his wound had healed, and he returned to Chicago at once. Why had he run away, when it was a case of self-defense? The most likely answer appears to be that Kinzie thought he would not get a fair trial at the fort. The unbiased investigation and its favorable result must have come as a pleasant surprise, but it was the only good thing that would happen to John Kinzie and his family for a long time. Still unable to agree on whiskey, village and fort were to continue their quarrel until it met disastrous conclusion in the first great catastrophe of Chicago's life.

Many outside factors combined to bring on the ruin that now rolled over the people of this small and tentative town. One was a contribution from Napoleon Bonaparte, the Corsican dictator described by Edgar Lee Masters in his account of Chicago as "that great impresario of pain and trouble." Napoleon's gift to the world was universal compulsory military service, a doctrine of the French Revolution to which he gave enthusiastic continuance. In this matter the Napoleonic reasoning was clear: without conscription, we couldn't have big wars, and then where would we be? On their part, Napoleon's English enemies practiced a simple and direct form of conscription for the Royal Navy in the kidnaping of able-bodied men by street patrols called press gangs, ancestors of the modern draft board. Life in the English navy was so horrible that desertion became a problem to His Majesty's Government, and orders went out to stop ships of any nationality, search them, and remove suspected sailors.* Among the many objectionable aspects of this policy was the impressment of American along with British seamen, who would all look alike to the boarding parties. In addition, British merchants crowded hard in Parliament to cut off American shipping, which was prospering at their expense. We should bear in mind that the apparently eternal war between England and France was still going on; there were questions of neutrality to be invoked, and technicalities of transshipment to be used, in hampering American efforts to carry on trade while two empires fought a war. The point for Chicago was that the kidnapings at sea, plus the trade aspect of the matter, topped by the arrogance of many British officials and naval men, added up to the materials for war. But it is worth noting that the substantial New

*Recommended reading: *Sea Life in Lord Nelson's Time*, by John Masefield.

England traders opposed war with England; persons of this sort would play the leading parts in the swift building of mercantile Chicago at a later time. In 1811, the greatest pressure on President James Madison for war came from those who wanted to expand the northwestern frontier by conquering Canada, and from a powerful faction in the South. Of these Southerners, the most picturesque was Henry Clay, who sometimes added excitement to Washington life by hysterical shouting in the halls of Congress. As Speaker of the House, Clay led the final drive for declaration of war, which came in June 1812.

War talk had already cost lives in Chicago; the British in Canada had been encouraging Indians to harass American settlements, and two months before the declaration, a band of Forest Potawatami from Wisconsin burned the farm of Charles Lee on the south branch of the river, four miles from the fork. They left the mutilated corpses of Lee and another man to be brought in by a patrol from the fort. Kinzie's contacts among friendly Indians reported big trouble ahead, and a chief named Black Partridge came to the fort and said that his young men were taking to the war path. His heart was heavy, Black Partridge said, and he returned a medal he had received from General Anthony Wayne. Another general, William Hull, now had charge of American forces in the northwest. He was a veteran of the Revolutionary War, and had accepted command in 1812, his sixtieth year. Entrusting the security of the northwestern borders to Hull proved to be a mistake of epic proportions, which much blood and pain required to straighten out the mess he left behind him. At the outbreak of war, the general marched to invade Canada, but fell back on Detroit when he heard Fort Mackinac had surrendered. Early in August, Hull sent Indian runners to the frontier outposts, including Chicago, with orders to evacuate. These instructions reached Captain Heald on Saturday, August 9, 1812. It seems that military disasters, such as the charge of the Light Brigade at Balaklava and Custer's destruction by the Sioux, are usually accompanied by the issuance of orders so vague and imprecise that they appear to be designed to take the sender off the hook of historical responsibility. Hull's orders told Heald to close the fort and leave, "if practicable." And if it seemed practicable to abandon the fort, Heald was to distribute all supplies on hand to Indians as a gesture of appeasement.

On Sunday, August 10, Heald read the orders at morning parade. Then the bugle blew Officers' Call and the commandant asked for opinions. Some thought it best to fort up and await developments; the garrison numbered only one hundred men, and about twenty of these were sick and not fit to march. Another problem was the giving away of supplies to Indians. This would mean a big loss to Kinzie—complete ruin, as he saw it. Indians did not frighten Kinzie, in spite of the deaths at Lee's place. He was willing to chance it at his own house if the military would stay. However, he would be sworn in as militiaman with other able-bodied civilians and ride with the column if that was the way it had to be. One thing was certain, the whiskey must go. The provost guard came to Kinzie's store and knocked in the kegs, while at the fort the contents of all jugs except Dr. Cooper's medical supply went into the Chicago River.

On the following day there rose a stir of excitement and hope with the arrival of a famous Indian fighter, Captain William Wells, who had come from Fort Wayne at the head of thirty Miami braves to act as trail escort. Billy Wells had grown up in the family of the Miami chief Little Turtle, and Mrs. Heald, the captain's wife, was his niece. With this reinforcement at hand, there was no more talk of remaining huddled in the fort. Mrs. Kinzie and Victoire Mirandeau started packing and told the four children they were going on a trip. The first objective of the march was to be St. Joseph, and Kinzie decided to send his family by boat, while he rode with the column.

Meanwhile word had gone out that free supplies were available at Fort Dearborn, and Indians came to carry away food, blankets, and provisions. Many of them made no effort to conceal their anger when told that the whiskey had been thrown away. Sullen and resentful, they camped in the prairie south of the fort, waiting for something to happen. And on the night of Thursday, August 14, Heald gave orders that the garrison would march at seven o'clock the following morning.

When that time came, a hot sun had already burned off the mist as Mrs. Kinzie, her maidservant, the children, and a boatman went down the river and turned south between the shore and a sand bar that ran parallel to the beach in those days. From the fort came the thump of drums and they could see the column moving, Captain Wells and half his Miamis at the front, then seven wagons with the women, children, and sick, the soldiers marching alongside, the officers and civilians mounted, and the rest of Wells's Miamis as rear guard. Some accounts have said that the garrison fifes and drums were playing a dead march, which is hard to believe. However, Billy Wells had been talking with his Miamis, who gave him news that caused him to ride with a blackened face. Such was the custom of any Miami warrior who expected to be killed before the sun went down.

One has no trouble imagining how the column came to a point which is the corner of Sixteenth Street and Prairie Avenue today, bearing in mind that Burnham Park and the Meigs airstrip to the east are additions of a later time. A sand hill rose just ahead on the right. Wells galloped up the hill and saw many Indians—six hundred, maybe more—rising from the prairie and rushing to attack. He rode back, warned the column, and offered to lead a forlorn hope against the warriors streaming over the sand hill. Bugles blew, and Wells headed a charge through the attackers up over the dune to the prairie. Here the Indians surrounded the troopers, who might have done better, as any armchair tactician can see, had they stayed with the wagons. But Captain Billy Wells had fought many a fight, and he killed several braves before they cut him down, beheaded him, and tore out his heart, which some of them ate while others drank his blood in accordance with their belief that the virtues of an enemy could be acquired by cannibalism. With Wells down and the garrison surrounded, a detachment of young braves hopped in among the wagons and killed two women, twelve children, and twenty-eight soldiers. At the height of the butchery Black Partridge appeared, seized Lieutenant Helm's wife, and dragged her to the lake, where he hid her neck-deep until the killing frenzy died down. This rescue is commemorated in a work of sculpture that may be seen today at the Chicago Historical Society.

After the hand-to-hand fighting nine troopers in addition to Wells lay dead on the prairie. Captain Heald now saw that the Indians' commander was the bloodthirsty Potawatami chief Black Bird, not to be confused with the friendly Black Partridge. Black Bird stood at dune top, saw the captured wagons on one hand and the troops in a hopeless position on the other, and called Heald to a parley, offering the survivors' lives for surrender. Captain Heald accepted these terms, but in a few hours Black Bird decided his agreement did not cover wounded prisoners, and Heald was helpless. Mrs. Helm, crouching among the captives, saw an old squaw kill a wounded soldier with a stable fork. And all night long they were to hear the screams of five more wounded men as Indians tortured them to death.

When the fighting broke out, Mrs. Kinzie and her boatman came back to the river. She returned to her house and hid with her children under feather mattresses when Indians came looking for whiskey. The Indians had worked themselves into a violent frame of mind by the time Kinzie got back. They threatened to kill the trader and burn his house, but a rescuer appeared in the person of Billy Caldwell, whose Indian name was The Englishman (Sauganash), although he was the son of an Irishman and a Potawatami girl. A young man of thirty-two at the time, Sauganash was popular among Potawatami, and managed to persuade the intruders to leave Kinzie's place and join their colleagues who were burning the fort. Next day, the garrison survivors built coffins and buried their dead on the shore near the place where the wagons had halted. Three days later, all who had lived in garrison or village, with one exception, were on their way to Detroit, Kinzie and his people in their boat, the rest marching. Bad news waited ahead: the day after disaster in Chicago, General Hull had surrendered Detroit without firing a shot. The British jailed the Chicago people, military and civilian, for the rest of the war.

It was not too long an internment, for the war reached its end in 1814. An intolerable amount of incompetent leadership had bungled the opening American offensive against Canada and filled the country with gloom and discouragement for almost two years. The general architect of failure was ex-Secretary Dearborn, who had taken charge of field forces from Lake Erie to the Atlantic. He organized an expedition to capture Montreal, but did not get across the border. Defeated at Queenston, Dearborn carried on in such a feeble and indecisive manner that President Madison's new war secretary finally sacked him in July 1813. Still occasionally listed as a big man because his name appears 148 times in blue and white signs on an important Chicago street, Dearborn was one of the most ineffective leaders the nation has ever had to put up with. However, Henry Dearborn did not display incompetence so gross as to bring on criminal charges, which was the fate of General Hull, who experienced his best luck of the war in not being shot by a firing squad when it ended. A court martial convicted Hull of cowardice and neglect of duty, but found him innocent on an additional charge of treason. Nevertheless they sentenced him to be shot, an especially brutal thing because General Dearborn headed the court, and Dearborn's incompetence had been partly responsible for Hull's trouble in the field. President Madison signed the death papers, but then let Hull off in recognition of his good record in the Revolutionary War. William Hull has respectable apologists, and it appears that he issued some of his ill-fated orders because of regard for civilian safety, a doctrine of weight in military circles when Hull was soldiering. In spite of his concern, fourteen women and children occupied graves among the Fort Dearborn dead.

The man who stayed behind when all others left Chicago was Antoine Ouilmette. In the future, trainmen on the North Western line would call out his name thousands of times a week at the north shore suburb of Wilmette, but in August 1812 he and his Indian wife were the only inhabitants of Chicago, living in their cabin near the Kinzie place, and looking over the river to the ruins of the fort. Ouilmette still had sledges at portage and boats at dock, but there was no activity in transportation, or any other sort of business, while the war continued to its end. At Washington, an event of importance to Chicago took place in 1814 when President Madison sought Congressional authorization to cut a canal from the miry foot of the Chicago River to the Des Plaines and the Illinois, so linking Lake Michigan and the Mississippi River as Jolliet had suggested 131 years

[22]

before. The project made too much sense for immediate approval in Congress, and landed on the shelf, where it was to remain for thirteen years. And Antoine Ouilmette, who might well have been called as expert witness, continued to live with his wife beside the lake. Indeed, the area of the two-pronged river, the sand bar, and the swamp had seldom lain more desolate than during those four years from 1812 until the day in 1816 when John Kinzie and his family came home.

The Kinzies found their small wilderness estate about as they had left it. The main house which Kinzie had expanded from the original du Sable dwelling stood intact, with its long front porch under the shade of Lombardy poplars, and two giant cottonwoods towering over outbuildings and kitchen garden in the rear. White picket fences soon went up, enclosing a broad green space in front of Kinzie's house, while across the river Army men began to build a second edition of Fort Dearborn. After a few months, a competitor to Kinzie arrived in town and started building a house and store. He was Jean Baptiste Beaubien; his brother, known as Jolly Mark Beaubien, soon followed him to Chicago. A renowned fiddler, Jolly Mark made music side by side with John Kinzie at evening when the women lit bayberry candles and a man thumbed the jug on his elbow for a swallow he could feel right down to the floor. But during daylight hours, work was the main interest and activity in embryonic Chicago. On both sides of the river hens cackled, cows bawled, men sawed and pounded: something that archeologists will call Chicago One was on its way.

Illinois became the twenty-first state in the Union on December 4, 1818. Next year the legislators moved from Kaskaskia to Vandalia, locating the capital 230 miles from Chicago, which ranked as no more than a village of fur traders dependent on military post. Nevertheless, Chicago had already started to attract permanent settlers by the time Jean and Mark Beaubien made their appearance. And one of the most notable newcomers of the earliest years was Chicago's original New Englander, a young man who carried the resounding name of Gurdon Saltonstall Hubbard. Born at Windsor, Vermont, in 1802, Hubbard was sixteen when he signed on as apprentice to the Astor fur concern, and not much older at the time he first entered Chicago, his back bent under a parcel of furs, his long legs scissoring in the trail-devouring stride that earned his Indian name of Swift Walker. Gurdon Hubbard was the type of adventurous youth who came to the northwest with the intention of trading boldness and energy for profits that had the possibility of amounting to riches. Pioneers of another sort were those who brought along their women and children. Older than Hubbard, less wilderness-wise than the Beaubiens or Kinzie, these people looked mostly for a chance to establish homesteads on cheap

[23]

land, protected by law against creditors back east. For back there in the cities, acquisitive men had managed once again to outsmart themselves and stumble into panic. Here the greed of bankers, merchants, and superior tradesmen had caused inflation on an enormous scale that killed off jobs and sucked the value out of money. As always happens, financial disaster crashed on the heads of those least able to bear it. Imprisonment for debt had not gone out of fashion, and in New York City more than two thousand men lay in jail because they could not meet notes or pay bills. Creditors locked up more than a thousand in Philadelphia, and the jails of Baltimore held nearly a thousand more, half of them in for less than ten dollars, and only about thirty owing as much as one hundred dollars. Many a man dropped his traveling bundle quietly out of the back window and legged it for the outskirts of town when constables pounded at the front door with law papers to take away what little a man had left, or throw him into prison. And it is easy to understand that many a small farmer or working man found there was nothing to do but load the woman and children into a wagon, and head west. Some went part way by stage coach, or by deck passage to canalhead in upper New York, Ohio, or Pennsylvania. But mostly they came in their wagons, out the Wilderness Road through the Cumberland Gap; or up the Cumberland Road from Maryland across the mountains to the Ohio River; or over the Lancaster Turnpike from Philadelphia; or down the Genesee Road from Albany to Buffalo; and of those who came to Buffalo, some kept on by land and water to Chicago. But at first they were few.

Along with the native-born came a considerable number of new Americans, fleeing from European countries which Napoleon had made unlivable. However, the impresario of misery had done the United States one favor by selling to President Jefferson's representatives vast territories west of the Mississippi in 1803. This Louisiana purchase gave hope to pioneers, with a promise of room for expansion, the fresh start, the second chance, even the third chance, for it created what looked like an unlimited far western frontier beyond the trans-Appalachian middle valley into which they were already migrating. The pioneers—and future Chicago— had their patron in the man who made the purchase at $14,500,000 even though he doubted his strict constitutional authority to do so; and this agrarian Thomas Jefferson had written that "we have an immensity of land courting the industry of the husbandman. . . . Those who labour in the earth are the chosen people of God, if ever he had a chosen people, whose breasts he has made his peculiar deposit for substantial and genuine virtue. . . . Generally speaking the proportion which the aggregate of the other classes of citizens bears in any state to its husbandmen, is the proportion of its unsound to its healthy parts, and is a good enough barometer whereby to measure its degree of corruption. While we have to labor then, let us never see our citizens occupied at a work-bench or twirling a distaff. . . . For the general operations of manufacture, let our work-shops remain in Europe. It is better to carry provisions and materials to workmen there, than bring them to the provisions and materials, and with them their manners and principles. . . . The mobs of great cities add just so much to the support of pure government, as sores do to the strength of the human body."

Whether or not they proved to be supporters of pure government, the trans-Appalachian states in 1820 sent sixteen members to a Senate of forty-four, along with forty-three spokesmen to the House of Representatives. In Washington these westerners tackled a problem loaded with anger and death in the question of whether or not men might take slaves into new territories coming under government control. Morally there was no question at all, though preachers slapped the open pages of Bibles in southern pulpits while arguing that the region's peculiar institution enjoyed the blessing of their Lord. Perhaps so; but that still did not make it right, and many people felt it in their bones. Yet when it came to war that was supposed to settle the matter forever, there would be created a generation of undeserving northern noncombatant millionaires, including a large number of Chicagoans. And after that a hundred years would pass by with subterranean questions still unanswered, which would burst in rebellion to plague and scar the cities of the north, and most especially Chicago. The fact was that from the start, whatever concerned the nation's central valley had vital importance for Chicago; yet in 1820 it would have been hard to detect any grave significance for that small frontier community in the Missouri Compromise that was supposed to end the argument on how far slavery might go. As the reader knows, this compromise admitted two new states, Maine free, Missouri slave, while prohibiting slavery in Louisiana Purchase territory north of a certain line. There was politics in it, and big money in the value of the slaves that owners wanted to take across the wide Missouri.

Before the time Illinois gained statehood, the leading magnate of Chicago had carried on a certain amount of slave trading, or something close to it. The records indicate that John Kinzie sold "a negro wench, by indenture" to a man named Francis Bourbonne. Kinzie also bought black servants, as when he and Thomas Forsyth purchased a Negro named Jeffrey Nash "by indenture for their own use." One has no way of knowing the length of the indentures or the conditions of servitude; in any event the people who suffered the greatest injustice on the Illinois frontier were not the blacks, for they were few and had nothing worth stealing: the northern white man's victim was the Indian. Yet during the days of early Chicago and for a long time afterward, one could hear respectable voices say that driving forth from his ancestral country was no more than the Indian deserved.

Typical in vehemence and moral fervor was the condemnation of the Indian written by Joseph Kirkland, a Chicago historian whose parents, like those of the infant George Washington Whistler, had brought him as a baby to the Midwest frontier. His mother, Caroline Stansbury Kirkland, was the first important woman author in Illinois, bringing out in 1839 a book of pioneer sketches called *A New Home—Who'll Follow?* which earned praise from Edgar Allan Poe. Mrs. Kirkland was the granddaughter of Joseph Stansbury, the American Tory agent who made contact between Benedict Arnold and the British, and served as go-between until General Arnold was safe on the other side. Stansbury wrote a volume of satirical verse describing this feat of underground warfare, and bequeathed literary talent to his granddaughter and her son; and although Joseph Kirkland grew up a lawyer, he also became Chicago's first writer of work that merited critical attention from William Dean Howells back east. Indeed, Joseph Kirkland stood among the founders of American realistic fiction with his novels *Zury, the Meanest Man in Spring County, The McVeys,* and *The Captain of Company K.* Bearing all this in mind, it is interesting to read what Kirkland wrote about Indians when he compiled his two-volume *Story of Chicago* in the 1880s. Kirkland began his estimate by stating that the Indian "was proud yet vain; indefatigable in destruction and ineffectual in conservation; cruel to the pitch of insanity; greedy; where he went there was terror; where he passed there was devastation. As either master or servant no more perfect failure ever existed. He acknowledged no superior, and he controlled no inferior except his own helpless, enslaved womankind. He was a natural drunkard, and self-denial was beyond his utmost mental and moral scope. In short, the most indocile, intractable, unlovable, unmanageable of the tribes of the sons of men, was the American Indian. Nothing of the Indians' past, worth knowing, can be known. Their present shows no progress, their future, as Indian, no hope." Joseph Kirkland rounded off the indictment with a further reference to the Indian custom of torturing prisoners. "All other wrong things can be forgiven," he wrote, "but not cruelty."

During the 1820s, as Chicago gradually grew to be a hamlet of 150 residents, little attention went to Indians except as producers of valuable furs. Sometimes there would be a camp of them south of the fork on the ground where Billy Wells had died. But Kinzie, Ouilmette, and the

Beaubiens knew how to deal with these people; other than a few minor thefts, there was no trouble. As the decade began, the ethnologist Henry Rowe Schoolcraft came through Chicago on the fact-gathering expedition that was to result in his six-volume *Historical and Statistical Information Regarding the History, Condition, and Prospects of the Indian Tribes of the United States.* This work is a monument in American scholarship, and its author spoke well of Chicago and "the hospitalities of Mr. Kinzie." Other travelers stopped by from time to time during the years from 1820 to the early 1830s that historians call a period of somnolence in the young town's life. But in carrying one's mind back to those days and nights, one should not think of a village in hibernation. There was continual building, a fence here, a barn or cabin there. And numerous travelers reported on the merrymaking that accompanied Beaubien's or Kinzie's hospitality— the fiddles mewing and the boot soles scraping as callers lined out "Money Musk" or "Leather Breeches": *I lit on a stump when the jinny shied, But leather breeches save my hide.* . . . From its beginnings, Chicago always felt an obligation to show the visitor a good time.

In addition to dancing and drinking, Chicagoans and their visitors had a selection of field sports—hunting the wolf on horseback, the bear on foot, and the aquatic fowl who fed on rice at the edges of the portage swamp. The small dark wild geese known as brant went into the hunters' bags, along with swans and ducks, while sportsmen with hook and line found plenty to interest them in the river. Here the choice game fish was the giant pike, the muskellunge. This armored creature, with his spatulate snout and powerful tail, looked like something that had started to develop into a walking fish that could live on land with the prospect of turning into a big reptile after a few more million years. It did live out of water long enough to die hideously, snapping the long teeth in its jaws, and the broad bands of teeth on its palate and tongue. On the banks of the north branch, one of the creatures seized and killed a farmer's cur-dog that came too close to its death throes. An appropriate mascot for Chicago, the muskellunge disappeared when the town grew large enough to contaminate the river.

Throughout Illinois in the decade of the 1820s, more serious than any sport was the business of taking land that had belonged traditionally to Indians. After most such expropriations, a moralizing tone could be detected at the councils of the settlers. Kirkland was to write it as undeniable history that the Indians practiced horrible cruelties; but whether or not they outdid Europeans and white Americans in cruelty, they lacked the organizing power to keep invading pioneers from settling on their land. The greatest Indian leaders never succeeded in persuading the tribes to stop fighting each other and unite against the white man. A chief named Tecumseh had tried, failed, and met death in battle with the rank of major-general, British army forces, in the war of 1812. And the last chief to cause trouble for Illinois and Chicago was Tecumseh's lieutenant, Black Hawk, the leader of the Sauks. He said that white men honored their treaties with the Indians only when convenient. All through the 1820s, the Sauk tribesmen looked on at the diminishment of their holdings in Illinois while the government at Washington kept promising them thousands of acres beyond the Mississippi. Some of the Sauks moved out, and some refused to go, but wherever they vacated land, settlers immediately moved in, often ploughing up Indian burial-grounds in haste to get the corn crop started. Black Hawk appealed to Washington, and there was powwow in Congress, with nothing accomplished. In 1832, Black Hawk marched into Illinois at the head of some five hundred followers, not intending to make war, but heading for Wisconsin where they hoped to find planting room. Troops fired on these Indians carrying a flag of truce, and the so-called Black Hawk War began. After leading his original column and tribal reinforcements in several bloody fights, Black Hawk retreated to the Mississippi, hoping to get his people back to Iowa. Disregarding a plea for truce, U.S. soldiers and Illinois militiamen attacked in what is called the Battle of Bad Axe, one of the least glorious in our military annals. Firing from a gunboat, troopers killed a number of women and children on rafts crossing the river. They also slaughtered more than two hundred men, bringing the total kill of Indians to about six hundred in the short war.

The soldiers captured Black Hawk, and President Andrew Jackson released him after a brief imprisonment, never to fight again. Black Hawk died in Iowa a few years later, and during those last days he may have reflected, on some long prairie afternoon, that he did at least succeed in shaking up Chicago by his expedition into Illinois. For when word came in the spring of 1832 that Sauks were on the warpath, a mob of refugees hastened to Chicago and overwhelmed the village's first hotel, which John Kinzie's son James had built in 1828 on the west side of the north bank near the fork. Some others found lodging in the town's two dozen houses, but most lived at the wagon parks or under tents. Although they escaped the Indians, many of these people died in Chicago from the ravages of cholera, brought to town by Federal troops, and exploding among the refugees when hot weather hit their unsanitary camps. The disease would attack without warning: the suddenly nauseated victims would fall to the ground with excruciating pains in their legs and backs, sometimes dying at once, sometimes living through two days, eaten by fevers of such

[28]

voracity that body temperature would continue to rise for several hours after death. No doubt the preachers thought of the text in Scripture concerning the arrow that flieth by day and the pestilence that walketh in darkness: either could strike with blinding speed on the Illinois frontier.

Like many leaders of lost causes, Black Hawk became a figure of romance, and today his name appears at several places in Chicago, perhaps most notably on the shirts of a professional hockey team. For years the writer of this narrative held the erroneous notion that the statue on the Board of Trade building was supposed to represent Black Hawk, with his blanket on his back, gazing forever up La Salle Street toward the Wisconsin hills where he had hoped to lead his tribe. As the journalist eventually discovered, the statue represents Ceres, goddess of agriculture. But there is a connection: at some distant time before they were driven out, Black Hawk's ancestors planted the seeds of maize, or Indian corn, in the soil of Illinois. No one knows how long ago it was that a special kind of men called seed hunters went out on a trail that ended among the communal pueblos of New Mexico. Here they heard drums, and saw medicine men covering snakes with grain. Then the seed hunters filled their pouches and turned toward home, where they scattered new living energy on the tribal lands. Since that day the energy has increased beyond estimation in recurring crops of Indian corn, and corn-fed animals. And whether the credit belongs with Ceres, or with a manitou residing in the rain clouds, Chicago's agricultural hinterlands were to enrich Chicago in a way that could not have been predicted by the boldest pioneer or the most acquisitive trader.

Time now moved the little town on into the 1820s, and a special Chicago kind of time it turned out to be, going by more quickly than in those places where the future, when it came, might just as well have been the past. This would never be said of Chicago. Somebody once foisted a chamber-of-commerce kind of motto on the place: "I Will." But that is wrong. The true watchword of Chicago is "What Next?"

2

Birth of a City

CHICAGO BECAME SURE OF ITS FUTURE ON THE DAY IN AUGUST 1827
when news arrived that Congress had finally authorized the Illinois and
Michigan Canal. Two more years were to pass before the State Legislature
set up a commission to carry out the plan, which included the making of
a survey and map of Chicago. Published on August 4, 1830, the map
showed an area three-eighths of a mile square bounded by Halsted, Kinzie, State, and Madison streets. These street names and nine others—Des
Plaines, Jefferson, Canal, Wells, La Salle, Dearborn, Lake, Randolph, and
Washington—were chosen by the commissioners and James Thompson,
the surveyor. Lots went on sale immediately at the Federal land office, and
the first investors in Chicago real estate paid no more than seventy dollars
each for parcels of ground measuring 100 by 80 feet. The building of a
bridge near Randolph Street added value to these holdings in that same
year, and the town also gained the distinction of being named county seat.
The new County of Cook covered more ground than it does today, as the
Legislature afterward carved from it Du Page, Will, and McHenry coun-
ties. But Chicago was its seat of government and the three members of the
Court of Cook County Commissioners met there on April 13, 1831, to
announce a schedule of taxes at one-half of one percent on a property list
that included watches, clocks, cattle, horses, mules, distilleries, and building lots. Another important matter came under discussion when the commissioners granted tavern licenses to Samuel Miller, Russel Heacock, and

Elijah Wentworth, the last named licensee having taken over from Archibald Caldwell, who had been partner with James Kinzie in the village's first hotel. In addition to granting licenses, the commissioners ordered the following scale of prices:

Each half pint of rum, wine or brandy	$.25
Each pint do	.37-1/2
Each half pint of gin	.18-3/4
Each pint do	.31-1/4
Each gill of whiskey	.06-1/4
Each half pint do	.12-1/2
Each pint do	.18-3/4
For each breakfast and supper	.25
For each dinner	.37-1/2
For each horse fed	.25
Keeping horse one night	.50
Lodging for each man per night	.12-1/2
For cider or beer, one pint	.06-1/4
For cider or beer, one quart	.12-1/2

The commissioners at their first meeting authorized Mark Beaubien to run a ferry across the Chicago River, the privilege to cost him fifty dollars a year. This transaction broke Antoine Ouilmette's monopoly, and emphasized Beaubien's emergence as the leading enterpriser of Chicago after John Kinzie's death in 1828. Beaubien also got into the tavern business, and early in 1831 built what is regarded as Chicago's first purely commercial structure in the two-story frame Sauganash Hotel, named in honor of Billy Caldwell. Through the years, Chicago hotels have come in two traditional kinds, either excellent or very bad. The latter tradition got the earlier start. For this we have reliable word that serves also to illustrate the natural law that when an American community takes form, an English author immediately turns up to give a lecture, see the sights, and point out shortcomings.

The first English author in Chicago arrived at the early date of 1833. His name was Charles Joseph Latrobe. It is remarkable that Chicago at this time in its life had already been heard of enough to attract a traveler of Latrobe's type, for he did not waste money examining unimportant places. Wearing top hat and muffler in the Swiss Alps, Latrobe had recently made some of the most important climbs in the history of mountaineering. In contrast to the Alps, the country on which he now looked out was flat as a banknote, with prairies stretching like an extension of the lake. Upon arriving in Chicago, Latrobe had gone to the Sauganash, where Mark Beaubien hurried forward to greet him. The innkeeper had grown stout

[31]

from good living, and Latrobe noted his jolly red face set off by a blue brass-buttoned swallow-tailed coat. This was to be Latrobe's last favorable impression at the Sauganash, which he described as noisy, filthy, and vile. Everything was left to the confused ministrations of a fat, wheezing, gin-soaked housekeeper, while the servants did nothing but run up and down stairs with trays of drinks, for liquor could be ordered and consumed in any part of the establishment. It does not sound restful, but there was life at the Sauganash, and it provided facilities for every sort of public meeting, including the sessions of a debating society that considered both sides of such questions as which was the more dangerous element, water or fire.

Latrobe could not make himself eat at the common table, which reminded him of a hog pen. He observed that when platters came from the kitchen, their contents instantly disappeared before the dexterity of eaters who must have seemed all arms, elbows, and whiskers. Indeed, Latrobe's reaction to manners in the American west was that of Martin Chuzzlewit a few years later; but he did admit the excellence of Beaubien's roast fowl, and he liked the hunting and shooting. As master of the wolf hunt, Mark Beaubien felt an obligation to show sport, and gave Latrobe a good mount from the Sauganash stables, on which the top-hatted Englishman pursued a wolf over the prairie, ran him down, and killed him with an axe. Charles Latrobe was probably Chicago's first visitor who might be described as a distinguished foreigner, or at least a celebrity; he published several books about his travels, and became Governor of Victoria, New South Wales.

Greatest of Chicago happenings in the year of Latrobe's visit was the signing of a treaty with the Ottawa, Potawatami, and Chippewa Indians who infested the region. Although they came in thousands for the pow-wow, these Illinois and Wisconsin tribes had forsaken the warpath and caused no panic among the white inhabitants of Chicago. As some farseeing chiefs had predicted in Tecumseh's day, long association with settlers had caused deterioration among the Indians. A sense of defeat, loss of purpose, and weakness for liquor had combined to bring the savages into a state that white men regarded as contemptible, though the shrewder among them had exploited it for years as a way of making money without risk. Catering to the Indian's taste for alcohol, John Jacob Astor's American Fur Company had reaped enormous profits, and his Chicago agent Gurdon S. Hubbard had a hand in the business. Hubbard knew Indians—somewhere on the Swift Walker's back trail was a common-law Potawatami wife and two half-breed children. John Kinzie's son was an Astor agent, and the government charged him with selling liquor to Indians, but nothing came of it beyond the filing of complaints in Washington. Through the years military men and civilian officials who had been sent to guard the Indian's rights wrote thousands of reports in protest against a system that produced nothing but debauchery and misery in the face of an extremely cool kind of theft by the traders. These gentry charged the Indians up to fifty dollars a gallon for the whiskey that made them too drunk to get fair value in trade goods for the skins they harvested year after year. The easy money bred corruption, and sometimes found its way into the pockets of men who might have considered themselves bound in honor to protect the Indians. A striking example of such money in official hands came to light years later when the account books of the American Fur Company went on sale to collectors at the Anderson Galleries in March 1909, and scholars discovered an entry for 1821 showing a boodle of $35,000 paid to Lewis Cass, then Governor of the Michigan Territory and afterward Democratic candidate for the Presidency against General Zachary Taylor. The ledger entry was unquestionable, but failed to show what service Governor Cass had rendered to John Jacob Astor and his traders on the Northwestern frontier.

Whatever the Astor money may have bought from Cass, the fur industry that had centered on Lake Michigan began to fade away when the Indians signed over their lands around Chicago. Astor himself sold out and retired in 1834 to cherish the twenty million-dollar fortune he had acquired from his operations in the fur business, in real estate, and in lending money to the U.S. Government at a high rate of interest. But Gurdon S. Hubbard had not grown rich in furs, and he showed an understanding of Chicago's immediate resources as early as the winter of 1829, when he marched into town with a procession of 400 hogs trotting ahead of him. Assisted by half a dozen vicious, long-toothed herd dogs, who snapped along the flanks of the column, Hubbard cracked a whip in the air and yelled curses at dogs and swine alike in a voice that carried above the barking, grunting, and squealing. The procession halted at a slaughterhouse that Archibald Clybourne and his sons had built four years before, and after the butchering Hubbard stored the carcasses in snowbanks by the river, selling at a profit the following spring. In a few years Hubbard built a packing plant and warehouse of his own, so big that rivals called it Hubbard's Folly. And though he did not found a great Chicago fortune, Gurdon Hubbard remained among the recognized first citizens until his death in 1886. For all the importance of the butcher's trade in connection with Chicago, coming to mind as it does with Sandburg's inevitable line, this industry was not the main foundation of the city's wealth, and in years to come, the packers would move most of their business elsewhere without doing any lasting damage. The true significance of pigs to Chicago lay in their early demonstration of how the town could process and package a primal raw material and send it to consumers anywhere in the world. Before the digging of canals and the laying of railroads, each pig represented fifteen to twenty barrels of corn, with the motive power of four legs. Thus fundamental energy could walk itself to market, with sometimes as many as a thousand hogs in a single drove, living off the country as they came. Illinois hogs relished farm slops and corn, including the leaves and cobs, but going overland they also devoured acorns, roots, bark, frogs, crawfish, and snakes of every kind. Admiring farmers called the pigs land sharks, land pikes, and alligators for their voracity, and prairie racers for their speed in going to Chicago at the rate of ten miles a day. The hogs' flesh made prime eating, and by the late 1830s, Chicago-dressed pork was in demand at Liverpool and London. What Chicago had done with meat it also could do with lumber, wool, minerals, and metals; it would be ready when the age of distribution arrived.

In the same year that the Indians assembled for their land treaty, Chicago became a self-ruling municipality, no longer under the control of county commissioners. Incorporation as a town was enacted on August 4, 1833, and five days afterward the voters elected a board of trustees, direct ancestors of the present city government. These first town fathers immediately ordered the building of a jail and the appointment of a constable. On November 6 the trustees increased the area of Chicago, making Ohio Street the new boundary on the north, Jackson Street on the south, the lake on the east, and Jefferson Street on the west. And at the same time, there rose a pother about Chicago's future in Washington, where Congress had appropriated $25,000 to create a harbor for the new town. This project was not to be carried out before a dispute took place between Stephen A. Douglas, Chicago's first politician of national stature, and Jefferson Davis, then a young lieutenant in the Army engineers. Douglas wanted the harbor built fourteen miles south of town where the Calumet River ran into the lake. In winning his argument that the harbor should be placed at the mouth of the Chicago River, Jefferson Davis rendered an inestimable service to the future city, where one looks in vain for his monument today.

It took two years to conclude all business with the Indians at Chicago. Their future portion of the country was to be on reservations beyond the Mississippi; meanwhile, they accepted payment in money and goods for their claims to the midwestern hunting grounds. According to an honest official named Thomas L. McKenney, who for a time was U.S. Superintendent of Indian Affairs, the total of lands acquired from all tribes in the country cost the government only two cents an acre. But so far as Chicago was concerned, the Indians would be out of mind the moment they went out of sight. And on a day in August 1835, while government agents distributed blankets and pots, along with the last cash payments, the last detachment of Indians emptied hundreds of whiskey jugs and danced howling through the streets, pausing here and there to look in at windows or to execute a knife dance at a cabin door. Twenty-three years before, the members of this same Potawatami clan had killed and tortured white men on the ground where they now capered and tumbled, or lay in muddy gutters sick from their last debauch of Chicago booze. Then they were gone.

During the year 1833, in which trustees entered office and Indians came to judgment, a number of events took place that held importance for the future. Encouraging to all who saw it, for example, was the prompt action of Jefferson Davis and his engineers in dredging away the sand bar that lay parallel to the shore. If that sand bar were still there, one would look out across it today from the Reference Reading Room of the Chicago Public Library; its removal for practical reasons turned out to be also the first aesthetic improvement of the lakefront.

Another noteworthy occurrence of the same year was the arrival of the Rev. Jeremiah Porter, a young Presbyterian minister who went from Princeton Seminary into service as an Army chaplain, and came to Chicago with a detachment of troops assigned to Fort Dearborn. Mr. Porter organized the town's first church and preached its opening sermon on June 26, 1833. Within two years Episcopalians and members of other Protestant denominations had founded churches, and Roman Catholics also came early to the field, not forgetting that Jesuits had been the original Christian missionaries in the region many years before. The pastors of Catholic and Prostestant churches alike could read local religious news from the time their doors first opened, for the *Chicago Democrat*, the town's first newspaper, started publishing in November 1833. At year's end the *Democrat* reported that 150 new buildings had gone up in Chicago during the past twelve months, and that over 20,000 visitors had passed through town.

Most of the visitors were settlers hoping to find farmland not too far from the marketplace that Chicago offered, and the civilized life the town afforded even in those early days. Two hundred wagons a week would pull in at the campgrounds between Halsted Street and the river; the memories of all Chicago children in that period included the fascination of the wagon parks at night when the supper fires and lanterns dotted the darkness. By day, the travelers revealed themselves to be lanky and bearded men, their wives worn-looking and drably dressed, the children peering from wagons, cur-dogs slinking beneath. A few sunsets and sunrises in the wagon park, a few tools bought in town, some seed, maybe a piece of bright cloth for the woman, and they moved out. Many of these people were good human material, the strong and patient salt of the earth; but after settling in their homesteads, a noticeable class among them would sink to the level of peasants because of bad farming practices, or lack of stamina in body and brain. Men who were both able and lucky got on, and sometimes prospered; and the day of "social Darwinism" was moving toward its dawn when none would question the doctrine that only the fittest should survive. A Chicago boy stared in wonder at a scarecrow figure on a wagon box and the man leaned down, showing brown stumps of teeth in a wolfish grin: "What you looking at, sonny? Tough times make tough people."

Not all who came into Chicago, riding the wagons or huddled on the decks of sailing vessels or hiking the trails and roads, went on to take up farmland. From the beginning, certain men on first arrival looked around at the muddy streets and the shacks and shanties—the "buildings" of the *Democrat's* report—and then, perhaps, looked farther and saw the blue lake under its infinite sky. At this point a newcomer might begin to feel within himself the instincts of a townsman who has found his town. Among those who felt this way, one of the most remarkable was John Stephen Wright, a young man from Massachusetts whose gentle manners exposed him to starvation in the midst of plenty when he took his place at the public table in the Sauganash dining room. Here the youth found himself competing for the flapjack platters and dishes of meat with the most formidable eaters of the entire Middle Border, the Hoosiers who brought in droves of swine from Indiana. For a week he got nothing but cold tea and potato peelings, until his plight drew the attention of Latrobe's gin-soaked housekeeper, Mrs. Mark Beaubien. The woman recognized that Wright was a decent young fellow, and arranged for him to get his meals ahead of the voracious Hoosiers. John Wright was grateful, for he had come to Chicago because of an extraordinary set of circumstances and was alone in the town, sleeping at night under the counter of a store. His maternal uncle was Professor Chester Dewey of Williams College, a Congregational clergyman who also ranked as one of the country's most versatile scientific investigators. In tutoring his nephew, the professor had found that he had a genius on his hands. Instead of entering the youth at Williams or Harvard, Dewey advised him to go west and join some rising community on the country's edge, in expectation that those who profited most from the new economy would be those who owned the land on which it grew. The professor's reasoning convinced not only his nephew but the boy's father as well. It happened that the father had become seriously sick some years before, and had prescribed for his own case, maintaining that long rides on horseback would have him fit again. Accordingly he took a ride all the way to St. Louis, and returned the following year in perfect health. On the trip Wright had seen western land lying ready for development, a sight which made him agree with his brother-in-law's predictions. In 1833 father and son started for Chicago, traveling first on a flatcar behind a primitive locomotive that covered their faces with soot and burned their coats with sparks that stuck like wet snowflakes. Then came a long pull on the Erie Canal, and the last lap on a lake schooner out of Buffalo. Old Man Wright had a stake of eighty $50 gold pieces strapped under his shirt in a leather bag. To protect the money he carried a knife and pistol; John stood watch when his father took a nap. At Chicago, Mr. Wright left John at the Sauganash while he went up into Fox River country to spy out the land. When he got back a month later, he found that his seventeen-year-old son had opened and stocked a store on credit and was selling a line of goods at 150 percent over New York prices. Moreover, it turned out that John had moved his pallet from the Sauganash to a nook under the counter, not so much to save room rent as to sleep without interruption by the drunken yells, swearing, and fighting of barbarous Hoosiers from the Wabash River country, who caroused day and night in the hotel taproom. A respectable Chicagoan reported to Mr. Wright: "Never you fear for John. The boys tried their best to get him into their frolics, but he was no go." Instead of associating with rowdies, John had been among the first to help the new minister start his church, and served as Sunday School librarian, carrying the collection of books wrapped in a red and blue bandana. Some eastern Sunday School had sent these second-hand books as a gesture of home missions to form Chicago's first public library. But this was not all John S. Wright had been up to; like the servants in the parable who increased the talents during the owner's absence, the young man had made a profit buying and selling a lot on Lake Street near Clark Street, and had taken option on 160 acres west of town, pledging his father's credit on the deal. Although he had already bought 150 acres along the Fox River, Mr. Wright took up the real estate optioned by his son, depositing the remainder of his grubstake for title to the land. Then the Wrights ordered more merchandise from Buffalo, and announced that they had permanently settled in Chicago.

At this time Miss Eliza Chappell of Mackinac came to town with the intention of teaching school, and the Wrights provided a schoolhouse by giving Miss Chappell their store, after dividing it into two rooms, one for instruction, the other for the teacher's living quarters. This gesture made them the first patrons of education in Chicago, to be followed by many others through the years. Wright had progressive ideas on education, and before long he would begin to publish them, with the remarkable array of mystical theories about the American West that would make him nationally known as Prophet of the Prairies.

Many another Chicago speculator made money during those two years, and the smell of money reached back east, where men of business sniffed at it like gourmands waiting for a dish to emerge from some great cook's kitchen. Among these financiers was one whose interest would have a lasting effect on Chicago; his name was Charles Butler, and he came out from New York City to see what was going on with his own eyes. Chicago in turn looked at Mr. Butler, and even the tobacco-spitting loafers in front of the Sauganash could see that he was no farmer, for one could not imagine him in the position of having to belabor mules or oxen to make them pull a Conestoga wagon out of the mud. Charles Butler was a wealthy Wall Street lawyer, and he had a brother, Benjamin Franklin Butler, who held two jobs in Washington under President Andrew Jackson, drawing salaries as Secretary of War and Attorney General at the same time. Wearing a plug hat and swallow-tailed coat from the reliable firm of Brooks Brothers, which was to establish a Chicago beachhead 117 years later, Mr. Butler pulled hip-length waders over his varnished shoes and nankeen trousers before making several tours of inspection around the town. He liked the look of things, and decided to invest $100,000 of family funds in Chicago real estate. Mr. Butler was too important a man to stay out west and oversee the playing of the money after it was down; he was both pious and wealthy, and he had to get back to New York and help found Union Theological Seminary. He needed a trusty relative to ride the market, one who could manipulate the family investment while bearing in mind the Chicago slogan of buy low, sell high. The Washington pluralist was too busy; but there was an available brother-in-law, a bright young man who had recently served a term in the New York State Legislature, where he had pushed the building of railroads with public money. The young man was William Ogden, and Charles Butler did the future city of Chicago a favor by bringing him there in 1835 to look after the money he had ventured on purchases of land. Writing and reading in a time of gross inflation, it is hard to conceive the value of the $100,000 that William Ogden took in charge, but in 1835 such a sum was real money. Ogden had been a sharp hand in the counting house since he was fifteen years old, and had promoted land sales in his native New York State, but when he first looked over the Chicago property, he suffered a loss of nerve. Most of the Butler purchase west of town seemed little better than a swamp. This might prove hard to unload, and Ogden wrote to Butler that a generation would have to pass before they could pull their money back, and for the present the enormous investment of $100,000 must be carried as a loss. And there was no tax advantage here, for in those days there was no income tax.

William Ogden had to pass another week in Chicago before he realized that he was on a seller's market, perhaps the greatest ever seen. Ogden then surveyed the tract, cut it into lots, and within ninety days had recouped the original stake and still held two thirds of the property riding the market. The completed deal, for the entire parcel, yielded profits of over a quarter of a million dollars with very little work for William Ogden. One could wonder what the stump-toothed man on the Conestoga might make of it, but it is not at all surprising that Ogden closed his New York office, and set up permanent headquarters in Chicago. It was a good place to be if one liked money, for the rocketing prices of land caused money to multiply with dazzling rapidity. One parcel of ground that went for $5,500 in 1833 brought $100,000 in 1836, and this was outside town limits. Within the town, forty acres priced at $400 for the entire parcel in 1833 sold for $200,000 three years later. In 1835, a plot of ground increased 500 percent in value to $100,000 in three months. Gurdon Hubbard cashed in, holding $66.66 worth of ground on La Salle Street for six years, to sell at $80,000 in 1836. In another deal, he rode the market to $75,000 profit in ninety days. It was breathtaking, and population kept pace with profits as the town clerk counted 4,000 permanent residents in 1836—sixteen times as many as had lived in Chicago only three years before.

Although the land speculators regarded the Lake Michigan-Illinois River Canal as a sure source of wealth, William Ogden said that railroads were the coming thing, and that Chicago would benefit beyond anyone's imagining when trains could run east and west, carrying products from the hinterland. It took courage to preach this doctrine in 1836, with Chicagoans crowding aboard two schooners and a steamboat on July 4 to go down the south branch to the portage swamp—now called Mud Lake— where work was officially started on the great canal. Cannon crackers exploded, the bank played, and liquor flowed down citizens' throats while politicians yelled and sawed the air in exhibitions of the folk art which was called spreadeagle oratory.

Undeterred by the uproar over the canal, William Ogden examined the map of Illinois, and found in its northwest corner the prosperous town of Galena that outranked Chicago in real wealth because of the lead mines around it. After brooding on the possibilities for a time, Ogden set out to link the two towns on a Galena and Chicago Union Railway, and soon completed the line on paper with the help of Jonathan Young Scammon,

[39]

a civic leader whose fifty-five years of useful contributions to Chicago had begun twelve months before on his arrival in 1835. Like a majority of the founding citizens, Scammon was a New Englander—indeed, one of the most formidable sort, a State of Maine man. In promoting the railroad, Ogden needed such an associate, whose unimpeachable probity matched his own, for at that time there were hundreds of railroad schemes in the planning stage all over the country, some of them under dubious sponsorship. One thinks of Mark Twain's Colonel Mulberry Sellers, and his proposal to run a line through Slouchburg and Doodleville, Belshazzar, Catfish, Babylon, Bloody Run, Hail Columbia, and Hark From the Tomb. As William Ogden now found out, hustling money for the Galena and Chicago Union was harder than selling real estate to speculators. But he never doubted the result, and a few more years would prove him right. Meanwhile, Ogden became aware that there were cultivated people in the small muddy town. For example his associate Scammon was a lawyer, but not the type who was unable to function without a cud of tobacco in his cheek. Like the Wrights, J. Y. Scammon took an interest in public schools, and he started founding study groups and charitable societies, many of which he served as president. On his part, Ogden made a substantial contribution to the higher life of Chicago by bringing in the town's first professional architect, John Mills Van Osdel, to design a spacious two-story frame house for the center of the block bounded by Rush, Erie, and Ontario streets and North Wabash Avenue, thus giving the near North Side its start as a good residential section. John Van Osdel was to practice in Chicago until his death in 1891 at the age of eighty. His first Chicago building was the Ogden house, a commission he received on his arrival from New York City in June 1837; his last work was to be the Monon Building which went up in 1890 as the first modern building in the world to reach a height of thirteen stories. The architect started his Chicago career under the best auspices, for the State Legislature had incorporated the town as a city on March 4, 1837, and his first client, William Ogden, had been elected mayor on May 2, defeating John H. Kinzie, the pioneer trader's son, by a two-to-one margin.

The new mayor had at his house distinguished guests whose collective eminence offered further proof that one could sense a special destiny about Chicago, even in 1837 when its population of 4,117 stood in comparison to 15,000 in St. Louis and 40,000 in Cincinnati. Population did not tell the whole Chicago story, and the poet William Cullen Bryant found it necessary to satisfy his curiosity by seeing the place, as did Ralph Waldo Emerson. Like Charles Latrobe, Emerson believed in visiting important places and people, for in his role of all-purpose popular oracle he had to stay abreast of the times; he had recently gone to England and paid his respects to Landor, Coleridge, Wordsworth, and Carlyle. Now Emerson must have his look at Chicago; he lived for a week as Ogden's guest, and enchanted the townsmen with the steady charm of his serene personality. Then the sage returned to his Concord study and wrote about the emotional effect of the "sea-wide, sky-skirted prairie." Emerson and Bryant understood Chicago, and passed their understanding on; but another writer of high reputation had preceded them with a visit the year before. That distinguished traveler was Harriet Martineau, an Englishwoman who had become one of the world's best-known authors with the success of a book entitled *Illustrations of Political Economy.* Miss Martineau had given this forbidding title to a collection of extraordinarily readable short stories, and had come to the United States in search of additional material. When Harriet Martineau visited Chicago in 1836, she saw a heavenly blue on the lake, and the prairie shining with flowers, a scene like nothing she had encountered anywhere else. Moreover, Harriet found a number of "educated, refined, and wealthy persons" in the town, a welcome discovery though a surprise. Her two books written after visiting the United States were *Society in America* and *Retrospect of Western Travel.* In these works Miss Martineau revealed herself a sympathizer with the New England abolitionists already demanding an end to slavery in America; and the books showed that the author believed in emancipation for women, as well as for black slaves of either sex. It must have been both as abolitionist and feminist that this small, plain, deaf woman captured the hearts of her sisters in Chicago; a group of them brought her a bouquet of prairie flowers, not knowing that Miss Martineau had lost not only her hearing, but also her sense of taste and smell. When the ladies presented their gift, Harriet said, "It is beautiful. I thank you with all my heart."

Harriet Martineau was a good journalist, and she got out on the streets of Chicago, even though jets of liquid mud shot up from between the sidewalk boards at every step. She saw streets crowded with loud speculators hastening to sales conducted on every corner by promoters who mounted ladders and bellowed at the crowd. Some of the dealers hired sandwich men who paraded with placards calling attention to the bargains and huge profits available. Others sent mounted Negroes dressed in fantastic liveries up and down Lake Street and State Street, bawling their employers' addresses and promises of wealth. Still another form of advertising was a man on stilts who somehow kept a footing in the mud; and through all the wheedling and huckstering and shouting, nobody seemed to have any curiosity as to why the sellers would part with such valuable properties. But it is always like that in a boom market, whether of land

[41]

titles, stock certificates, or Holland tulips. "It seemed as if some prevalent mania infected the whole people," Miss Martineau observed. That was a just remark, for the land gamblers had by now gone far beyond the lots around Chicago, which did have value, as Charles Butler and others like him had observed. But now they were buying and selling markers—mere scribbled notes like a receipt in the betting ring at an English racetrack —which they took as representing titles to an incredible number of acres in all parts of the Northwest. It would seem that Colonel Sellers had colleagues who put towns as well as railroads on paper. Timberland, farmland, areas warranted rich in minerals or as sources of water power—all were offered in large parcels and one could buy direct from freshly drawn though unofficial maps, receive a marker, rush to the street, and sell at a profit in less than an hour. In other words, these frenzied men were buying and selling paper, without the slightest interest in the Michigan dunes or Wisconsin forests the paper was supposed to represent. Nobody seemed to understand that the boom was bound to reach a crest, or to have any idea of what might happen when they went careering down the other side. They found out soon enough, in the national panic of 1837. The quickest way to describe this catastrophe is to say that big men in Paris, London, Philadelphia, Boston, and New York suddenly came awake and saw that they had tied up money in railroads that ran only on paper, canals that were not yet open, and lots in towns that existed only as suburbs of Cloud-Cuckoo-Land. Every investor pulled back at the same time, and as usual, the little men were trampled in the rush. Eastern bankers called in the funds they had happily pressed on their outland colleagues only a few months before, and the western and southern banks either blew up completely or started paying depositors in homemade money that had no purchasing power. Shops and factories shut down, and men begged in the streets for scraps of food.

The hard times hit Chicago in the spring of 1837, and knocked the land boom out of existence in a single business day. Within a month all notes of the Illinois Bank became worthless, the state having disowned its financial obligations. In Chicago the speculators began to call for cancellation of all deals past and present, and a general dishonoring of markers. At this point William Ogden went into action: supporting the local banks with his fortune, the new mayor gave the losers a breathing spell by persuading the City Council to issue scrip, a local paper money that kept business limping along and was accepted for taxes, theoretically bearing interest of one percent a month for the public till. According to the historian Herbert Asbury, Chicago now acquired its nickname of the Garden City because each householder planted a vegetable patch in order to ensure a few greens and potatoes for the table. The high-hatted barkers and stilt-walking sandwich men disappeared; and Chicago's population increased by only a little over three hundred from 1837 to 1840.

There was no doubt about it, Chicago had taken a hard blow and landed in its own mud. But now in the early 1840s the town began to show recuperative powers. The homesteaders in their thousands had continued to pass through during all the excitements of the boom, and kept on coming afterward, sometimes with cash to spend for tools or animals. And here and there among the visitors would be another founding citizen, like Matthew Laflin, the third of his name, who saw no reason to pull out even though he had arrived in 1837, with the panic at its worst. A Massachusetts man, Laflin was interested in supplying powder from his father's mills for blasting the line of the Lake Michigan-Illinois River canal; he also owned a device to be used in crushing bark for tanneries, and had manufactured axes in Saugerties, New York. Finding himself in agreement with William Ogden about Chicago's prospects, Laflin bought land, laid out the city's first stockyard, and set up a Bull's Head Tavern for the convenience of cattlemen. Some forty years later he was to give this tavern as a home for alcoholics undergoing treatment; by that time he had organized the city's first bus line and its first waterworks, and had founded a durable Chicago family. Today Matthew Laflin's name is memorialized by the building on North Clark Street that houses the Academy of Sciences and the Illinois Museum of Natural History where one can see, in startling realism, the walking fish that once crawled around Chicago, and the tropical rain forest that covered the Middle West before the glaciers came.

Another newcomer in the same period was John Wentworth, a youth who walked up to town from Calumet Harbor, carrying his shoes to save leather, or so he always told the story. Destined to become mayor and Congressman and editor of the *Democrat*, young Wentworth came to Chicago immediately after graduating from Dartmouth College in June 1836, and his nickname of Long John was inevitable because he stood something over six and one-half feet tall. Distinguished by fondness for the jug, and grossly overweight in later life, Wentworth was the first of Chicago's picturesque politicians. He was editor in charge when the *Democrat* became a daily paper in 1840, and got credit for making it the leading voice of the Northwest. In Congress on the Democratic ticket from 1843 to 1851, and from 1853 to 1855, Wentworth was to serve two more years, as a Republican, after the Civil War. Whether or not John Wentworth first stepped on it with bare feet, he learned soon enough that the most prudent thing to do with Chicago real estate was hold it for a while; and on this principle he made a comfortable fortune. It is a truism that no one gets through life entirely free of trouble. And one disaster that overtook Long John descended on him when he had been drinking in a saloon and came across Allan Pinkerton, the Scotch roughneck and organizer of the private detective and industrial guard agency that still exists under his name. The men quarreled and started fighting at the corner of State and Lake streets. Though he had superior height and reach, Wentworth was out of condition, and Pinkerton caved him in with punches to his prominent belly, kicking him into the gutter. This Allan Pinkerton was to conduct the newly elected President Lincoln to Washington by a circuitous route in order to foil an assassination plot he claimed to have uncovered; and in the Civil War, Pinkerton had charge of spies and counterspies.

Students of Chicago history should not infer from the Wentworth-Pinkerton fight that such brawls between leading citizens were ordinary occurrences. On the contrary, from the earliest beginnings of human life along the Chicago River, the magnates left rolling in the mud to the rough element. And it must be recorded that the criminal classes of the frontier had started to settle in Chicago as soon as the town took shape, along with thugs and hoodlums expelled from the eastern cities, and blackleg gamblers from the South. In addition, a scandal of whores and their pimps had gone into Chicago residence as early as 1835, when the town council decreed a twenty-five-dollar fine for anyone convicted of keeping a brothel. The city fathers found it necessary to impose a larger fine less than three years later. By that time, unsavory persons of every kind were established in Chicago, and they hung on through the depression following the boom just as respectable people did. Rowdies, sneak-thieves, horse-thieves, burglars, and muggers populated the Chicago underworld, and along with the gamblers, brothel-keepers, and prostitutes, drank so much beer and whiskey that the town's reputation as a "universal grog-shop" spread through the country. When the town became a city in 1837, six wards were laid out, and the council appointed one law officer for each of these divisions, serving under a high constable. John Shrigley was the first in this position, and Samuel J. Low, who succeeded him in 1839, obtained a grant for two assistants in addition to the ward constables. From then until 1854, says Asbury, the police force never had more than nine men, although the population increased to over 80,000 during those years. The rogues and rascals of Chicago took advantage of their strong position, and every morning the *Democrat* had new outrages to report. Honest men found the presence of hundreds of loafers in front of the hotels and tippling houses exasperating; and this hostility may have cost one loafer his life. He was a young Irishman named John Stone, according to Asbury's account, who arrived in the United States when thirteen years old, and died on the gallows at the age of thirty-four at the first legal execution in Chicago's history. As a notorious loafer, Stone passed most of his time in dramshops or walking around the billiard table in Couch's tavern at Lake and Dearborn streets, when he was able to snare a pigeon in the crowd of idlers, ruffians, and drunkards. It was said that Stone had threatened the virtue of Mrs. Lucretia Thompson, a Cook County farmwife; when this woman was found raped and murdered, the authorities put him on trial for the crime. The jury convicted Stone on circumstantial evidence, although he asserted his innocence to the end. The death sentence was carried out at once, with the High Constable and the sheriff heading the cavalcade of two hundred citizens and sixty militiamen that rode beside the cart bringing John Stone chained and manacled to the gallows on the lakeshore three miles south of the courthouse. Here he was hanged in the presence of a large crowd that had followed the military and civilian escort. The day was Friday, July 10, 1840, and the trap fell at 3:15 P.M., after which two Chicago doctors took away Stone's body for dissection.

If John Stone's end had any admonishing effect on the inhabitants of Chicago's underworld, nobody saw outward evidence of it; and few drank to his memory in the boozing dens along Adams Street. Devil take the hindmost was their watchword; and their brutal manner of life stood in contrast to that of a group whose members had set out to introduce social graces in Chicago. Late in 1837, a number of young men decided it was time Chicago had a formal dancing-party; they made themselves a committee, arranged the ball, and sent out invitations. Among the documents of early Chicago that survived the fire of 1871, these invitations exert immediate enchantment on the student who takes them from their fragile envelopes in the Historical Society, the fascinating attic of Chicago. There is gilt, like an old-fashioned valentine; at the top in octagonal borders, an eighteenth-century ballroom scene, with ladies curtseying while gentlemen bow; the printing is clear, in a handsome typeface, not at all florid, something on the order of J. B. Bodoni's design, and one's company is respectfully requested at a Social Cotillon* Party to be held at the City Hotel on January 1, 1838, by the managers, who are Messrs G. S. Hubbard, H. G. Loomis, R. A. Kinzie, James Allen U.S.A., J. H. Walker, and J. T. Sprague. Something comes through here, faint but compelling, young men organizing a party, women dressing for it, the hopes, the hesitant ones, the floor committee pledged to see that each wallflower gets at least one dance—it is faint, yet singularly touching as it comes across the years.

On January 11 another dance took place, and a Washington's Birthday

*Correct spelling at the time.

[45]

Ball lit up the new Tremont House in February. Its managers were H. I. Tuller, E. A. Mulford, B. E. Dodson, C. H. Blair, and Frederick Walker. Among other young men who danced and went to parties were G. C. Harris, Buckner Morris, Isaac Harmon, M. A. Kimball, and Joseph Naper from the nearby prairie settlement of Naperville. This type of young man usually was looking for a wife; when the local marriageable girls were spoken for, he would try to pledge a visiting young lady, for there were always several in town, brought there by female instincts that told them these enterprising young Chicago men were good husband material, the sort who could protect a woman and her children. And if all the visitors were taken, the young man would go east and find a girl who did not mind setting up housekeeping in Chicago. A young man of this kind was Walter H. Burley, who wrote in the winter of 1838 to his half sister back east that he had "attended a ball and danced until two o'clock in the morning with the elite of Chicago." It appears that the elite had physical endurance as well as elegance, for if the dance started at three in the afternoon, like the Social Cotillon Party, it had lasted to the equivalent of ten or eleven in the morning for a ball of the 1970s. The nimble Walter Burley remained a bachelor dancing man until 1845, when he brought a wife to town. She wrote to a friend, "I have gained twelve pounds in six weeks, and my weight is now 116 pounds, *just think of it!*" After describing some velvet she had admired in a Lake Street shop, the bride continued, "I am almost to the end of my plain sewing. I have my cloak to make and then I shall go at my quilt, and that is all I expect to do this winter. I mean to go out and enjoy myself, study French, etc. I have a great many plans laid out for the winter. I have just got an extract book to try to improve myself in writing and I shall practice on my guitar all I can. The piano is sold." Mrs. Burley concluded her letter by remarking, ". . . we have been married eight months and two days." Two years later, Mrs. Burley commented on the developing social life of Chicago by writing to describe the successful Fireman's Ball, with two bands and three supper rooms. The thirty-five managers had sent out 1,050 invitations. She reported that the mud was so deep outside the hall that men in hip boots had to lift the women from their two-wheeled carts and carry them to the doorway; for all that, it was a fine party. We would like to hear more, but there is not to be much further communication with this nice woman; although Mrs. Burley had gained weight so well on her arrival in Chicago, she now began to find herself unable to summon the strength for parties where a pretty woman danced every dance, and started the decline which was then called "fading away with consumption." Mr. Burley became a widower on May 23, 1852.

There are so many of these pleasant women, whom one would like to have known. Another gentle voice that comes to us through letters is that of Mrs. Leander James McCormick, whose husband's brother Cyrus had opened a Chicago factory for his patented reaping machine in 1847. The McCormick brothers came from Virginia, but made no pretensions of aristocracy, being of the sound, plain, Scotch-Irish Presbyterian stock. Around Chicago some said that Cyrus McCormick was so mean that if you boiled him to broth, the devil wouldn't sup him; but his wife and sister-in-law met with general approval. In return, these ladies approved of their new homes, as Leander's wife showed when writing to her sister in the early winter of 1848. Young Mrs. McCormick reported, "We have beautiful red and green carpet in the hall and dining room, and are going to put a sofa and pretty lamp in the parlor." She wrote that there were many Yankees in Chicago, and in order to hold up their heads among them "Leander & myself have brushed up considerably. He has bought a new suit, overcoat and all, and I bought a small cloak the other day." Mrs. McCormick added a significant item, relating to a feeling of civic inferiority which occasionally becomes evident even now: a milliner had said that her $3.50 New York velvet bonnet would cost $8.50 in Chicago.

Business got better in the five years following 1843; John Van Osdel designed and built a house for Archibald Clybourne, who had continued to prosper as a butcher, since people had to eat, even though they could get along without buying lots in Wisconsin, Michigan, and Indiana. The packer's mansion crowned a low hill northwest of town, where Clybourne Avenue now starts. It had tall white columns, and around it grew maple, cottonwood, oak, and elm. In town F. C. Sherman, later a mayor, had built his City Hotel three stories high at Clark and Randolph Streets, where seven years later he would add two stories and change the name to the Sherman House, ancestor of today's twenty-three story structure. To compete with the Sherman, some of the other innkeepers began improving their accommodations; but visitors of importance usually received an invitation to stay with William Ogden, and gratefully accepted it. In addition to Emerson and Bryant, the mayor entertained Vice President Martin Van Buren, the Irish novelist Charles Lever, and Samuel J. Tilden, who was to gain the distinction of losing the Presidency of the United States even though he got a majority of the popular vote. Another guest was Daniel Webster, loaded with honors and fame, who had the presence of a great actor. He had fascinated Carlyle with his "mastiff mouth and eyes like dull furnaces of anthracite waiting for the spark of oratory to fire them." Mr. Webster was not so formidable as all that over a glass of toddy; a New Englander, he understood Chicago very well. The list of notable visitors at William Ogden's house also included Charlotte Cushman, the tall, deep-voiced leading actress of the American stage, and two New England aboli-tionists, the Boston orator Wendell Phillips and the Transcendentalist critic and reformer Sarah Margaret Fuller. Thirty-three years old when she made her visit in 1833, Margaret was a sharp-looking little woman with a nasal voice and a habit of incessantly opening and shutting her eyelids. The unfavorable impression would last for only the briefest time, as Margaret could captivate anyone with the charm of her personality. Emerson said that a conversation with Margaret was a joyous event, and Chicagoans agreed with him after meeting this remarkable woman. What she meant to Chicago was not immediately apparent, for no one could then know how the arguments for abolition of slavery would eventually be answered; and her other message of Transcendentalism also lingered undefined in the air, imprecise but influential. Today one can see how large a part in Chicago's life the Transcendentalist ideas have played: high-minded basic notions of idealistic individualism and self-reliance, together with the theory that human perfectibility can be coupled with civic improvement—these ideas have inspired every man and woman in the noble company of Chicago's planners, teachers, reformers, and social-service workers. Like any discerning visitor to Chicago, Miss Fuller ap-preciated the beauty of prairie and lake, often riding out under a July moon and seeing the lines of wagons parked around their fires, and the ships' lights giving an effect that was "very majestic." By day the spectacle was even more moving; she would ride in the later afternoon looking for a certain "flamelike flower" among others that "gemmed and gilded the grass near the blue lake." Then came a serene moment when the sun set "with that calmness seen only on the prairies."

By 1844, the year after Margaret Fuller's visit, Chicago had recovered its commercial tone and spirits, and the population had grown to a little under nine thousand. A city directory which appeared in that year makes instructive reading, filled as it is with names and addresses, statistics, advertisements, and remarks by James Wellington Norris, its publisher. Only seven years after the land boom collapsed, he was writing that the present "sudden and unexampled prosperity of Chicago had caused the most strenuous exertions to be made, in other places, by misrepresenta-tion and downright falsehood in regard to our circumstances and condi-tion, to enduce emigration to stop short or to pass by us, and to direct capital and enterprise into other and foreign channels." Norris did his part in keeping capital from flight, and encouraging local enterprise, by con-ducting an employment agency where he offered jobs for clerical workers, domestics, laborers, foremen, cooks and waiters. In this office he kept the

"corrected register of all inhabitants, at all times available to the public."
Norris reported occupations along with names, listing the trades of team-
ster, laborer, carpenter, clergyman, shipwright, mason, shoemaker, tailor,
sailor, blacksmith, wigmaker, milliner, men's hatter, physician, farmer,
waiter, grocer, attorney, dress and cloak maker, saddler, pawnbroker,
musician, porter, wagon maker, millwright, milkman, gunsmith, water-
borer, bricklayer, auctioneer, cradle-maker, barber, bookbinder, printer,
butcher, and dealer in iron and nails. Norris also listed one citizen as a
vagrant, another as an idler.

Among the advertisements was a notice of the new Tremont House that
now stood five and one half stories high at Lake and Dearborn streets,
surpassing the City Hotel in comfort and elegance. It is significant, too,
that hotels in New York and New Orleans bought space in which to put
their claims before Chicagoans, and that commission merchants and
brokers in those cities solicited Chicago business. Among local advertisers
were several physicians, like Dr. Egan, who anticipated colleagues of the
present day by stating that he "could be consulted in private cases at his
Residence or Office, but could not attend out-door practice." Patients not
able to get the physician to attend them might go to the City Drug Store
on Lake Street and buy Dr. Egan's Sarsaparilla Panacea, which had "long
been celebrated for its restorative and renovating effects in Chronic Diseases." Not only patients but apprentice doctors found matters of interest
in the directory's paid space: a full-page advertisement announced the
resources of Rush Medical College, ancestor of all Chicago's medical
teaching and research. This institution had been authorized by the state
in 1837, but the panic stopped the money, and it was now just getting
under way. William Ogden headed its board, and Grant Goodrich, an early
citizen active in good works, was secretary. Among other trustees sat John
H. Kinzie and Walter Loomis Newberry, member of a rich Detroit family,
who had recently centered his lumber business in Chicago and built warehouses on the river. Chief of the four-man faculty was Dr. Daniel Brainard,
professor of anatomy and surgery, and fees for the sixteen-week lecture
and demonstration courses were set at $20 for Dr. Brainard's specialty;
chemistry and *materia medica,* $20; theory and practice of medicine, $10;
obstetrics and diseases of women and children, $10; dissecting ticket, $5;
and for graduation, $20. To graduate at Rush, a young man had to undergo
three years of study "with a respectable physician," and take two courses
of lectures, "one of which must be in this institution," two years of practice
being acceptable for the other course. The announcement ended by stating that the candidate must be at least twenty-one years old, and of good
character, that he must present a thesis on some medical subject of his own

composition and in his own handwriting which must be approved by the faculty, that he must "pass an examination in all the branches taught in this college," and that "good Board and Room can be obtained in Chicago at from $1.50 to $2.00 a week."

Education for women was the subject of an advertisement calling attention to the Chicago Female Seminary which had been established in the previous year by the Reverend A. W. Henderson, A.M., a Presbyterian clergyman. He announced that "the object of this Institution is to give young Ladies a thorough practical education, to develop and mold character, cultivate the manners, and form correct habits." Looking up Mr. Henderson's address, one finds that he boarded "with Mrs. Green at the corner of Clark and Washington." This was a select house and other young men starting in Chicago gave it as their home address, or lived at one of three or four similar places, such as Mrs. Post's, Mrs. Haight's, and Mrs. Wright's. The head of the Female Seminary had big men on his board: the pastors of the First and Second Presbyterian Churches, Grant Goodrich, attorney W. H. Brown, and Isaac N. Arnold of Arnold & Ogden who lived north of the river at Ontario and Dearborn Streets. Much has been written about past rivalries of the North, West, and South Sides of Chicago, because each in its time had an individual flavor and separateness, and a colony of loyal residents, both rich and poor. But it appears to be undeniable that the near North Side was the first neighborhood in which men like Isaac Arnold gathered other substantial citizens around them, for the directory shows that in addition to William Ogden's nearby house, there was Walter Newberry on Illinois Street between Rush and Pine (now North Michigan Avenue), Mahlon D. Ogden at Dearborn and Walton Streets, attorney S. Lisle Smith on Rush Street, and Grant Goodrich not far away. Along with scores of others they were the typical prosperous North Siders of the time, often occupying an entire block with trees, an ample vegetable garden, and a family cow. Norris listed these leading citizens in various ways; he also gave a statistical abstract of the population, prefiguring the University of Chicago's immense studies of the city around it which would store up information in years to come. The directory of 1844 arranged people under these headings:

Females, ten years old and under:	1,017
Females, ten years to 21:	630
Females, over 21 and under 45:	1,393
Females, over 45 and under 60:	116
Females over 60:	34
Males, ten years old and under:	1,008
Males, ten years to 21:	562

Males, 21 to 45:	2,067
Males, 45 to 60:	128
Males over 60:	27

Then came a statistical second class cabin, with 65 colored, 773 Irish, 816 Germans and Norwegians, and 667 people born in other foreign countries. The total was 7,580, and perhaps the first thing to catch the modern reader's attention is the small number of people over sixty; then one thinks of those 2,025 little boys and girls and sees how things would be in fifteen years.

James Wellington Norris must be rated a good reporter with a feeling for his town, who made this early directory a still valuable book. However, he is to be suspected of employing irony when he writes that "Brawls and affrays are extremely rare in our streets—and it may be justly said, that a more peacable and quiet population can nowhere be found." The newspapers did not agree; during the 1840s they told of a constantly increasing criminal element, and reported that Chicago had replaced St. Louis as the country's gambling capital west of the Alleghenies and north of New Orleans. Norris left a clue to the realities of the time when he wrote that his total of 7,580 population was too low, and that the actual figure should be over eight thousand. The difference represented the people in Chicago who did not care to have their names and addresses on a list. In their dens along Clark, La Salle, and Water streets, and in cockfighting roadhouses on the plank-paved highways leading southwest of town, and in shacks and shanties huddled behind the warehouses on the river, the outlaw population had flourished for years while busily promoting every sort of vice and crime. One is entitled to ask where the customers came from to support the gamblers, tapsters, and brothel-keepers; for answer we should bear in mind those 20,000 visitors who went through Chicago in as early a year as 1835; and in the 1840s, canal diggers, lumberjacks, and sailors were always on hand. It is true that boozing dens got some opposition from the Mariners' Temperance Society, headed by Grant Goodrich; but the usual Chicago recreation of sailors and other men with pay in their pockets was to spend that pay on liquor, women, cards, dice, and betting at cockfights and dogfights. Along that line they found a novel and popular favorite in Pape, the celebrated fighting pig. Trained and managed by a renegade Hoosier who made headquarters at a roadhouse near Naperville, Pape would take on any dog in a match to the death. In action the pig would go for the belly, and draw the dog's intestines, to the great joy of spectators who occupied benches around the fighting pit.

On the side of law and order, the constables, by all accounts, were hardy men and quick to use their clubs; but most crimes, including manslaughter, never came to the authorities' attention. A derelict might disappear after a fight in some dingy taproom and no one be the wiser. For among the shady characters in this early Chicago underworld there lurked the resurrection men who raided cemeteries to furnish cadavers for the medical school. On occasion the resurrectionists might deliver a subject that had not undergone the formality of burial; if they and their customers agreed on anything, it must have been that dead men tell no tales.

Such was the underside of Chicago life in 1847, when an important event took place for a population that had grown to nearly fifteen thousand. In Washington as Congressman, Long John Wentworth organized a River and Harbor Convention that brought three thousand delegates from eighteen states into Chicago to see and learn how money could be made in all sorts of dealings centered on this town. The convention proved to be the most profitable piece of civic promotion in the nineteenth century; and as we know, in that same year of 1847 Cyrus McCormick had already selected Chicago to be the manufacturing and distributing point for his reaping machines.

In the following year, the Lake Michigan-Illinois River Canal officially opened on April 10 when dignitaries rode the freighter *General Fry* on the first trip down to Lockport, along with a brass band and a continuous exploding of oratory that reached a climax with an address by the champion windjammer of the Middle West, Congressman Daniel Wolsey Voorhees, the Tall Sycamore of the Wabash. Six months later, William Ogden enjoyed a triumph when the first train ran over the tracks of his Galena and Chicago Union Railway. A short run for publicity purposes only, it nevertheless marked the start of what would one day be the great Chicago and North Western line. Looking to the future, the Mayor and Council pushed out the city limits to North Avenue on the north, Wood Street on the west, and 22nd Street (now Cermak Road) on the south. It soon became obvious that they had not expanded merely for the benefit of snakes and prairie dogs; in the following ten years, people and buildings would cover all Chicago's ten square miles. And that decade of 1848 to 1858 would prove to be the decade that made Chicago a city in the modern sense of the word.

3

Chicago's War

CHICAGO HAD BEEN GROWING AT A FASTER RATE THAN ITS POLICE
force until February 1855, when the authorities increased their corporal's
guard of watchmen to three precinct organizations, each numbering
thirty men plus a captain and four lieutenants. This force came into being
just in time for the first bloody confrontation on Chicago streets between
police and crowds of angry demonstrators, in the disturbances known to
history as the Lager Beer Riots of April 21, 1855.

The trouble started with the election of a City Council and mayor from
the anti-foreign Native American or Know-Nothing Party; these men had
scarcely taken office before they raised the annual saloon license fee from
fifty to three hundred dollars. The lawmakers said they intended their
ordinance only to discourage low taprooms, but it appeared to be aimed
at foreign-born workingmen's relaxation and pleasure. The Germans were
especially indignant; they were an industrious, orderly sort of people, and
more than thirty thousand of them had come to Chicago by 1855, fugitives
from their own country after the suppression of the liberal-nationalistic
revolution in 1848. More skilled than their fellow immigrant Irish at trades
commanding good pay, Chicago's Germans had set up a colony on the
North Side, where they established newspapers, shops, and churches,
along with taverns which they visited in evenings and on Sundays to play
cards, talk politics, eat sausages, and drink beer. When the German saloonkeepers refused to pay increased license fees, Mayor Levi D. Boone or-

dered enforcement of the Sunday closing law. The Germans refused to close, and Boone sent police against them armed with pistols and heavy canes. The police dragged some two hundred publicans and their employees to jail, clubbing those who showed fight. Setting April 21 as the trial date, the judges granted the saloonkeepers and bartenders release on bond, and rumors of civic uprising began to circulate throughout Chicago.

On the morning of April 21, a crowd of more than four hundred Germans marched behind fife and drum over the Clark Street bridge to Court House Square at Clark and Randolph Streets. There they drew up in ranks before the combined Courthouse and City Hall which John Van Osdel had designed and built two years before. A deputation entered the courtroom and announced that any decision against the saloonkeepers would start a riot. These leaders then went outside and deployed their people so as to stop traffic on Clark and Randolph Streets. The yelling and cursing Germans held this position until a platoon of policemen led by Captain Luther Nichols rushed from the City Hall basement and fell upon them with metal-weighted clubs. The police also struck a number of Germans with handcuffs used as brass knuckles, and some officers fired pistols, one shot narrowly missing Allan Pinkerton among the spectators. Taking nine prisoners, police drove the crowd north over the Clark Street bridge. As they retreated, the leaders shouted, "We'll be back!"

Mayor Boone ordered the chief of police to bring in every man off duty, while the sheriff swore in 150 deputies from docks and warehouses. In the early afternoon, spies brought word that five thousand North Side Germans had armed themselves, planning to burn the City Hall and hang the mayor. The reports were exaggerated, but at least a thousand men had organized, and they marched down through the near North Side at three P.M., armed with shotguns, pistols, swords, butcher knives, hammers, and clubs. The generals of this army had brigaded two detachments, which they led over the bridge to confront two hundred police and deputies who stood in three ranks across Clark Street.

Gunfire on both sides opened the battle, in which twenty men received serious injuries. The only death at the scene of the fight was that of a German who blew off a policeman's arm with a shotgun blast, and then fell dead, killed by a shot from a deputy's revolver. After nearly an hour of fighting, the rioters withdrew, carrying a number of wounded men, some of whom died in the following week, during which a number of extremely private funerals took place on the North Side. After this affair, fourteen men went on trial for rioting, two were convicted, and none went to jail. And the authorities shelved the question of enforcing Sunday closing laws. A few months later, a majority of the city's voters helped defeat a state prohibition law, and there was no interference with liquor sellers or their customers in Chicago for a long time to come.

Two years after the Beer Riots, the authorities again deployed a body of police against citizens, in the battle of the Sands, a neighborhood of shanties north of the river and east of Jean du Sable's first cornfield. Doubt had arisen as to the ownership of these few acres, and title litigation was slowly clearing the courts. Meanwhile, a colony of squatters had moved into the Sands and erected forty or fifty hovels in which the lowest of Chicago's rum-sellers, gamblers, and prostitutes transacted business. There were reports that sailors and canalmen had been drugged, beaten, and robbed in the Sands, but it was no use complaining to the law. The police had declared the Sands an Alsatia to be ruled by thieves and cut-throats, where criminals could take refuge, and all others must proceed at their own risk. Under this arrangement, things went along comfortably enough, at the price of several unsolved murders; but the inhabitants of the Sands at last caused their own downfall when they violated the basic principle of Alsatias by issuing forth from their evil neighborhood, in the spring of 1857, and making a public scandal.

The trouble arose when the manageress of a Sands brothel accused the virago known as Mother Herrick, who conducted a house of prostitution called the Prairie Queen, on State Street, of luring away one of her girls. Supported by a gang of ruffians, the Sands brothel-keeper marched to the State Street establishment, broke in, thrashed Mother Herrick, tumbled the piano down the front steps, and took the girl back, along with several star boarders from the Prairie Queen. The invaded premises were so centrally located that the sound of cursing and fighting offended respectable ears, with the result that complaints went up to Long John Wentworth, who had succeeded Levi Boone in the mayor's chair. The blame fell entirely on the Sands contingent, rather than to Mother Herrick, who was respected as a capable executive. But in spite of the justice in Mother Herrick's cause, and the decent citizens' indignation, the police wanted no trouble with the terrible residents of the Sands, and it took the clout of William Ogden himself to get action. Ogden had marked the Sands for future development, taken over some disputed leases, and offered to buy out the remaining squatters at a reasonable figure. A few accepted Ogden's terms, but the majority refused to sell, and defied anyone to move them. Ogden thereupon put pressure on Long John Wentworth, which sealed the Sands' doom. However, the Mayor and police moved with caution, waiting for a time when they could count on the element of surprise. On April 19, word came over Wentworth's intelligence network that on the following day every man in the Sands would be out of the district from morning until late afternoon, attending a program of dog fights at a roadhouse west of town. In the morning of April 20, 1857, Long John Wentworth and his men peered from behind barrels in the rear of a warehouse and saw the entire male population of the Sands march out, accompanied by vicious dogs, all under command of the neighborhood's two most formidable bullies, Dutch Frank and Mike O'Brien. Half an hour later, Wentworth entered the Sands at the head of thirty policemen, along with the sheriff and Ogden's agent carrying law papers. They brought teams of dray horses, and wagons loaded with chains, hooks, and crowbars. They also attracted a crowd of idlers, who joined the police in helping themselves to liquor and pulling down the flimsy houses with tackle from the wagons. This combined force of police and loafers soon had the shanties burning, and Long John summoned the fire department. But instead of trying to save the hovels, the firemen turned hoses on the occupants and drove them shrieking away, so that when the men of the Sands returned from the dog fights, they found the whole neighborhood wiped out. The Sands never again had any importance as a vice district; its inhabitants continued their activities in other parts of the city.

The thieves and prostitutes of Chicago might as well have been on another planet, so far as the residents of the new houses north of the river and south of Oak Street were concerned. In this neighborhood around the mansions of William Ogden and Walter Loomis Newberry the police gave diligent service, and at many houses coachmen and gardeners were on duty in addition to Pinkerton's private watchmen. Because of this protection, burglars avoided the near North Side, and loose women never paraded there; the young people who grew up in this part of town lived in an atmosphere from which ugliness was excluded, leaving serene happiness and beauty.

Among these fortunate young people Julia Newberry was born on December 28, 1853, at her father's house at the corner of Rush and Ohio Streets. On reaching the age of fourteen, Julia began to keep a diary, whose first entries show that her mother and aunts, with their friends, were types of Victorian sheltered womanhood. And later on, when the years had passed to turn these women into grandmothers, and the money piled to make them dowagers in society, they remembered the simplicity of childhood days. Said Mrs. Joseph Frederick Ward, "The Chicago of my childhood was a green and flowery place—a place of gardens and trees and birds and grass and charming homes—of sandy beach and dashing waves, with a sense of youth and the beginnings of things all about us." The girls of the privileged near North Side who were Julia Newberry's companions went to Miss Whiting's School on Ontario Street, or downtown to Professor

Sawyer's establishment, before going east for "finishing." They also attended a private dancing class in rooms provided at 156 Rush Street by Mrs. W. W. K. Nixon, whose colored butler Richard was the pride of the neighborhood.

Some of the leading citizens patronized the public high school, whose first class had graduated by the time Julia became a young lady. A member of the class wrote, "We received our diplomas in great glory at Metropolitan Hall at the corner of Randolph and La Salle Streets. There never was a grander occasion—there never could be a grander occasion—than that was. The city fairly crowed over us." It is important to note that on the whole these young people and their parents provided their own entertainment—that is, they entertained each other. Sheltered girls and women had appeared at subscription dances and concerts, and at the theaters which had been part of Chicago life since 1843, but they expressed themselves most fully at private theatricals in which they were performers. One winter the parlors of William Ogden's house, for example, served as stage and auditorium for an opera called *The Lovers*, starring Signorina Eleanora Wheeleretta, Signor Guglielmo Emersonio Strongini, Signor Samuellino Jonstonio, and Signora Elizabetta Drummondino. In addition to home productions of opera and drama, the quality folk enjoyed charades, and conversation parties that required no rehearsals and ended with refreshments at half past ten, or eleven at the latest.

The North Side had no monopoly on Arcadian social life. Over on the West Side, a boy named Hobart Chatfield-Taylor, later to be one of the city's most valued memoirists, as well as a novelist and biographer, was beginning to notice what went on around him in a big house on West Washington Street between Halsted Street and Union Park. A colony of Kentuckians lived out there, inhabiting the tranquil neighborhood around Jefferson Park, a little green square bounded by West Monroe and Adams Street, near shady cross streets called Ada, Elizabeth, Ann, and May. Perhaps because of southern influence, the West Siders claimed to provide better refreshments than one got on the North Side. Hobart remembered lake trout and perch, prairie and domestic chicken fried or in salads, scalloped oysters, pound cake, and ice cream made by turning hand freezers as God intended. No wonder West Siders thought themselves the best people in town; and they had manners too. As Chatfield-Taylor when he was old and famous reconstructed a vanished scene, recalling a dance at his house which he observed from the stairway, the young people who skipped over the crash-covered floors in the Virginia Reel, or moved more formally in cotillion figures called by Johnny Hand, the Viennese orchestra leader, seemed wonderful to his eyes. Here was Huntington Jackson, the

[57]

handsomest man in Chicago, dancing with Mrs. John M. Clark, recently a bride, still a charmer; and as the music stopped, Miss Susie King, red-haired and the reigning beauty, stepped into the hall to catch her breath before the polka. Her gloved hand rested on the arm of Archie Fowler, a young man known to travel in fast company and frowned on by many of the older people. Susie's fan was carried by Scott Keith, while her bouquet of roses had been given into the care of Lieutenant Sandy Forsyth, a cavalry officer. Little Hobart hoped to be noticed on the landing beside his governess, but at this moment his uncle Wayne Chatfield stepped up to Miss King, paying his respects with a graceful compliment. Uncle Wayne did not join the lovely girl's train of admirers, but passed into the main room, to dance with the plainest wallflower there. Hobart wrote of this uncle, "Never have I known his equal either in courtesy or thoughtfulness, or in kindness of heart without ostentation." If Wayne Chatfield had a fault, Hobart said, it was an excessive reverence for birth. This observation shows that family connections had become important in Chicago while many of the family founders were still alive—the most rapidly developed aristocracy in the history of American social classes; with certain disappearances, and a few additions, the original structure of upper-class Chicago has continued in existence to the present day.

The great days of the South Side were still to come when Dr. William Bradshaw Egan bought a tract three miles below town in the wilderness through which Marquette and Jolliet had struggled. The region got the name of Cottage Grove from a stand of trees near an abandoned cabin, the only building to be seen for miles around when Dr. Egan took possession of his land. A sociable bachelor, the doctor built a fine house and entertained patients, friends, and prospective buyers on a grand scale. "One-third down, balance in one, two, or three years," the doctor would say as his butler poured wine at dinner, or the male guests lit cigars and sipped brandy in his library. He soon sold enough lots to found the community known as Egandale, and when he cashed in his holdings toward the end of the 1870s and moved to England, Dr. Egan left behind the nucleus of Hyde Park as well as the memory of hundreds of superlative dinners. Early Hyde Park had the same straightforward quality as the rest of town. At the start of things one building served both Episcopalians and Presbyterians, and for heating purposes the two denominations maintained separate woodpiles. The Anglican sexton found it necessary to put up a sign: "EPISCOPALIAN WOODPILE—HANDS OFF."

Almost always the houses of substantial Chicagoans had wide porches where young people talked and sang on summer nights. And in the grounds around the houses, the vegetable garden continued as an institution, from memory of panics when a man liked to feel that at worst he could still provide food for his family. Hobart Chatfield-Taylor recalled seeing peas on the table that had been picked by his own small hand, "for I had been taught to be useful instead of ornamental, even though I dwelt in a mansion surrounded by lawns in the midst of which a fountain spurted from a conch-shell poised upon a smudge-faced Cupid's palm." One often saw fountains, and sometimes they were unconventional, as in the Isaac Arnold garden where a stream of water issued from the mouth of a Silenus-like face carved on a granite rock known as the Waubansee boulder. The face was said to be the work of Indians, or possibly by some artist of a prehistoric people living near Chicago before the Indians came. Perhaps the carving was only a practical joke in sculpture, committed by soldiers at the fort and left in the woods to astonish its discoverers; but a stroll through the Arnold garden to marvel at the strange face never seemed to lose interest as a way to close one of those long late Indian summer evenings under that tall and cool Chicago sky with the orange color of the prairie sunset off in the west and perhaps the feeling of fog in the air, or a wisp of it trailing from the lake. Now the Arnold garden is gone, but the Waubansee boulder remains at the Chicago Historical Society to the delight of every visitor, with its archaic smile as though thinking of a simpler day. A Chicago woman recalling those times in old age said they might be summed up in the recollection of neighborhood cows making their leisurely return each afternoon from nearby pastures. Down Rush Street they would come, each animal turning into its own barnyard. "There was the Henry King cow, the Skinner, Ogden, and Newberry cows, and if one hurried quickly up to Huron Street, the Rumsey cow could be seen sauntering to the west, the Arnold cow to the east—all obedient to habit and direction."

That pleasant sort of Chicago life doubtless had its effect in attracting Carter Harrison there. He came from Kentucky where he was connected with the well-known families indicated by his names. Born in 1825, Harrison was a graduate of Yale and a widely traveled young man when he first saw Chicago in 1850. After looking the town over, he returned home, took a law degree, and married a Kentucky belle. In 1855 he came back to Chicago, and three years later bought the Henry M. Honoré house on Ashland Avenue in the Southern colony on the West Side. No one ever came to chicago better equipped to deal with the place than its future Mayor Carter Harrison, and he started by acquiring real estate, even though another national panic had burst out the year before he bought his West Side mansion. It seemed as though these panics were timed to explode every twenty years, but the ladies of the near North and West Sides felt no inconvenience in 1854 other than that which came from the unreliability of Illinois banknotes. Every morning the Chicago clearing house listed banks in three classes, according to whether their notes were worthless, redeemable at discount, or good for par value at the shops on Lake and State streets. Gold and silver were welcome but there was so much counterfeit in circulation that each merchant's cashier kept a bottle of nitric acid on his tall desk, for testing coins. However, the shop owners gave established customers every courtesy, including credit, for in Chicago the age of the carriage trade had arrived.

Lake Street merchants of the better type followed the lead of a New York State man named Potter Palmer, who had opened his dry goods store shortly after coming to Chicago in 1852. Although born a Quaker, he associated with sporting people in his leisure hours. But in the shop, where he closely watched every detail, Potter Palmer showed that he knew how to wait on the quality, and appreciated their trade. Always elegantly dressed, he stood inside the main entrance and bowed low when lady patrons entered the place, his manner a sincere indication that his sole purpose in the world was to see that they were pleased with whatever they chose to buy. It was Palmer who first based commercial conduct on that now abandoned slogan, The Customer Is Right. That was the way Palmer did business, and in 1856 he hired a like-minded assistant when young Marshall Field arrived in Chicago from the bleak village of Conway, Massachusetts. At this time Field was twenty-two, the product of a farm childhood and a few years of clerking in a general store. When he came to Chicago, he had a little money in his pocket, and a passionate desire for more money in his soul. And if there was a New England frostiness about the young man, he also had New England virtues, including the belief that no dollar may be pocketed without first giving the customer good value for his money. Marshall Field would have rejected the doctrine of selling obsolescent products, or automobiles with wheels that came off while the family was speeding on its way to visit grandma, and he would have collapsed in a fit of the blind staggers had anyone told him the makers would call back *eighteen million* horseless carriages in need of vital repairs. For where Potter Palmer liked quality in customers, Marshall Field had a holy feeling about quality in goods. To understand that feeling, one must carry one's mind back to the honest materials selected by the Deacon when building the one-hoss shay.

A few months after hiring Marshall Field, Potter Palmer advanced him to head salesman. It was a well-deserved promotion, for young men of Field's intelligence and superior bearing were scarce in the retail trade. The owners did not employ women at the time, and many of the salesmen were insufferable asses, with ridiculous affectations, and something bordering on impertinence in their attitude toward customers. Marshall Field made a better impression; where his colleagues offended with oiled hair, fake jewelry, and exaggerated tailoring, Field dressed like a preacher or gambler in plain black, and cut a self-respecting figure in a semi-menial occupation; and while the counter-jumpers laid out bolts of fabric with swoops, thumps, and flourishes, Marshall Field worked in a controlled style, bringing up merchandise without fuss or flurry, civil and attentive, and never allowing a mound of rejected goods to accumulate on the counter. Ladies appreciated the elegance and refinement of his controlled style, and they liked it as much as they detested the mud through which they had to make their way on shopping tours.

Mud on the streets had become such a nuisance that people began to joke about it. One humorist sank a pole in a puddle and hung up a sign, "This way to China." Men repeated the story of a farmer pulled from mud up to his neck on State Street, who told his rescuers that he had been standng on a mule. Wells Street loafers found it amusing to stone small dogs in puddles where they drowned and floated with swollen bellies. All agreed that an amount of mud which the young frontier town had endured as unavoidable could no longer be tolerated in a city with a population of over one hundred thousand. Accordingly, a number of projects to eliminate mud got under way, one of them an attempt to pave Wabash Avenue with stove lids, which proved a failure. The city fathers admitted at last that something must be done about drainage, for the center of town was a marsh. To this great question they gave a tremendous answer: they would raise the entire business district and all its streets and buildings to grades of six to twelve feet above prevailing levels. Then began a series of typically Chicagoan labors, the city's first intentional alteration of its environment. They attacked the task in 1855 and continued for ten years at varying rates of completion, so that a sidewalk ten feet in the air might connect with adjoining block at the former level by means of steps going down. Or one might turn at a street crossing, walk up a wooden stairway, and continue several feet above where one's head had been before rounding the corner. Buildings also rose to new levels with sidewalks and streets. Contractors accomplished this by the power in jackscrews turned by hand, a fraction of an inch at a turn. One of the first lifting operations raised an entire block of four-story buildings at Lake and Wells streets, then the busiest corner in town. Another remarkable lift took place when all five stories of the Tremont Hotel rose six feet without a crack in the brick walls. In this job 1,200 engineers turned the jacks under direction of an enterprising young man from New York State named George Mortimer Pullman. He was a sturdy, deep-chested fellow with a chin beard like Uncle Sam's and a head the shape of a bowling ball, twenty-four years old when he came to Chicago and set up as contractor in 1855. A few years later Pullman left town, failed in a Colorado mining venture, and then returned for his great success in building railroad cars.

During the time the city was raising streets and sidewalks to uniform new levels, their erratic heights caused some odd spectacles. For example, a young shoe drummer named Dwight Lyman Moody, who was also a zealous Christian evangelist, might often be seen pursuing a sinner up steps and down, until he caught up with his quarry and made an urgent plea to consider the opportunity of salvation. Like Marshall Field, Dwight Moody had come of Massachusetts stock. Having been exposed to liquor, gambling, and evil ways, Moody had undergone conversion at a prayer meeting just before he came to Chicago seeking his fortune in 1856. First employed at Wiswall's boot and shoe store, he took to the road as salesman for the wholesale house of C. N. Henderson, boarding in Chicago with the well-known Mother Phillips on Clark Street. An entirely different sort from Mother Herrick, this woman catered to select commercial gentlemen, providing a home for such newcomers as Edward Isham, the future Civil War generals George V. Smith and John L. Thompson, and the peppery Levi Z. Leiter, who was to become a partner of Potter Palmer and Marshall Field. In this ambitious company, Dwight Moody could get out and push with the best of them. Described as a "portly, bustling, Simon Peter sort of man," Moody rented four pews at Plymouth Church and went into the highways and byways hunting people to occupy them. Once he spotted a young girl who had dropped out of Sunday School, and hurried after her, the girl scudding up and down plank sidewalks, the corpulent Moody showing good staying power in the rear, and gradually closing in. To his horror, the child entered a saloon and ran upstairs through the barroom. It turned out that her widowed mother owned the place; Moody eventually persuaded the woman to attend church regularly and leave the liquor business. Moody took a special interest in children, and prided himself on a Sunday School class of homeless boys who earned their living at odd jobs and carrying messages. These urchins lived in packing boxes or under bridges, and had a limited life expectancy, because of starvation, disease, gang fights, and the danger of being assaulted and murdered by homosexual tramps who threw their bodies into the Chicago River. Originating as foundlings on the steps of police stations, or escapees from orphanages, these waifs carried no names in the ordinary sense; instead they went under such monickers as Red Eye, Smikes, Madden the Butcher, Jacky Candles, Giberick, Billy Blucannon, Darby the Cobbler,

Butcher Lilray, Greenhorn, Indian, Black Stove Pipe, Old Man, and Rag-Breeches Cadet. As they looked up on Sunday at Dwight L. Moody, the complete knowledge of evil written on the street-Arabs' wizened faces perhaps made the preacher realize, if he had not discovered it before, that Chicago had indeed become a city.

Dwight L. Moody was the most famous evangelist of his time, but during the early Chicago years he often faced mockery on entering newspaper offices in search of free space for notices of revival meetings. These encounters taught Moody the value of a tactful approach, but the reporters did not get an equal benefit from the association, and in Moody's view they remained a crew of gin-sodden wretches. It was true that many Chicago reporters took comfort from gin and whiskey after their long hours of work, for which the proprietors paid miserable salaries. Nevertheless, by 1857 Chicago had become a center of competitive publishing. It was easy to see why journalism had begun to flourish: in the twenty years since the city's incorporation, a dozen banks and eighteen railroad lines had come into being; there were over fifteen hundred business establishments, and a Board of Trade; Chicagoans now could read the news of this activity, along with comments on topics of the day, and several kinds of political editorializing, in ten local newspapers and thirty magazines.

Among the publishers John S. Wright had achieved a conspicuous place, and as usual his motives were mostly unselfish. When his first fortune vanished in the panic of 1837, Wright had continued to describe the future of Chicago with the zeal of Dwight Moody telling what Heaven would be like. Preaching is easier than practicing, but in the early 1840s Wright backed his prophecies by inducing a capitalist named Frederic Bronson to sell him an option on a business block. When real estate prices rose again, Wright borrowed $29,000 from his two brothers, who had followed him to Chicago, and took possession of the Bronson block, which sold for $450,000 ten years later. No longer the skinny boy starving in the midst of plenty at the Sauganash, Wright had become a handsome man whose blue eyes sparkled with interest in everything about him. He married a red-haired Southern beauty who may have thought she had gone beneath her station in becoming a Chicagoan's wife, since she was connected with the high quality in Virginia, not only to the Byrds of Westover, but to the Washingtons of Mount Vernon. A grand-niece of George Washington, and orphaned at the age of nine, Kitty Turner had been taken in by the John Augustus Washingtons who inherited the Mount Vernon estate. Mrs. J. A. Washington had a mother's hopes and ambitions for Kitty, and approved of her betrothal to a Southern army officer of noble descent. This man turned out to be a drunkard, and they had to send him away. Shortly

[63]

afterward, John Wright went East in search of investors for Chicago, met Kitty, and the two young people fell in love.

In Chicago as a bride, young Mrs. Wright found out that her husband's interests ranged beyond those of an ordinary businessman. One thing, that came close to an obsession, was his feeling about the low salaries of school-teachers. Wright had taken an interest in the work of Henry Ward Beecher's sister Catherine, who had brought teachers to the West under the promise of better wages than they could earn in New England, where the State of Maine, for example, paid only $15.40 a month to male teachers, and as little as $4.80 to females. In Illinois the pay ranged from the men's $18.00 a month to $10.00 for women. This fell far below any reasonable and decent standard, according to John S. Wright. Like all Chicagoans of his time, he had seen the sale of school lands after the first mapping of the city. The legislators had reserved 640 acres for the benefit of the school system and sales in 1835 and 1836 had yielded $38,619.47; then the authorities realized that they should have held the school lands for rentals. Had this been done, the Chicago public school system would be landlord today for most of the Loop and the railroad yards below, collecting rent from every foot of ground between Madison, Twelfth, State, and Halsted streets.

Though this opportunity was gone forever, John S. Wright got a bill past the State Legislature, creating county school boards throughout Illinois to be supported by property taxation. After this achievement, Wright linked public education to another of his enthusiasms, the encouragement of scientific agriculture. When only twenty-five years old, he had started a Union Agricultural Society, and in the following year he had opened a Farmers' Reading Room at 112 Lake Street. Wright said that with reading and study, farmers would understand the value of education, and fight for a system of free rural schools leading to a State Agricultural University. City people also would benefit, especially in Chicago, the place that gathered energy from prairie grain and sent it to the world along the lines of transportation.

In January 1843 Wright brought out the first number of The *Prairie Farmer, Devoted to Agriculture, Mechanics, and Education,* serving as editor without pay, and advancing money for printer's bills, although he was financially pressed during the paper's first two years of life. As in many of his ventures, Wright was justified by results, and the *Farmer* proved to be one of the best among Chicago's lively publications. So sanguine was Wright's temperament, both in publishing and in land promotion, that he never seemed to worry when confronting what might look like an altogether hopeless situation to a lesser man. Only three years after the founding of *The Prairie Farmer*, he had taken the responsibility of a wife, and Kitty was no girl to hunt bargains or turn collars and cuffs. In 1852, Wright was able to commission the portraitist George P. A. Healy to paint Kitty in a dark green habit and a hat with plumes, riding an Arabian horse. A portrait by Healy meant high social and financial standing in Chicago, perhaps more important to Kitty Wright than to her husband; nevertheless, the business community rated him "a man worth six hundred thousand dollars as he stood" in 1856.

Soon after launching *The Prairie Farmer*, Wright found a colleague in Professor Jonathan Baldwin Turner, a Yale man and an abolitionist who had recently left the Congregational ministry. Jonathan Turner promoted the famous "horse-high, bull-strong, pig-tight" fencing of Osage Orange hedge, the most effective single contribution to the prosperity of Illinois and the basic wealth of Chicago, aside from McCormick reapers, in the years before the Civil War. Hedge fencing was but one of many problems *The Prairie Farmer* solved for its readers. The paper showed its resourcefulness, for instance, in the question of rat control. Grain spillage and table leavings on rich Illinois farms had fed generations of rats, the creatures breeding by incalculable millions throughout northern Illinois, and invading and occupying Chicago. The rats had begun to cause alarm as early as 1840; one hundred and thirty years later, in the 1970s, Chicago rats exceeded Chinese rats in size, intelligence, and ferocity. But the northern Illinois-Chicago breed would have died out before the twentieth century if everyone had used the methods of extermination that Wright and Turner recommended. While starvation was the basic strategy of their war on rats, the editors suggested many additional methods of attack. One was to salt the feeding grounds with powders that exploded inside the animals. Another was to beat drums near the holes and burrows so that the rats would rush out into nets lined with fish-hooks. If this failed, one might put a Chicago commercial product called Fairy Compound into rat holes. The compound came in pellets of lard containing phosphorus and whiskey; after swallowing a pellet, the rat would run in search of water, which suggested an advertising slogan, "They Go Outside to Die." And it might be possible to frighten rats off premises if one rat could be captured and equipped with a belled collar, or so *The Farmer* said. Although pet raccoons and weasels destroyed rats, the paper reported, it was hard to keep them from killing chickens as well; and a correspondent wrote that guinea fowl drove every rat off the place, which seems incredible, yet *The Prairie Farmer* printed the letter as an item of interest. But the editors may not

[65]

have been serious when they published a subscriber's statement that if a trapped rat were placed on a floating block in a barrel of water, other rats would answer his cries, fall in the water, and drown.

Another valued contributor to *The Prairie Farmer* was its horticultural editor John Kennicott, known as the Old Doctor because he had been one of Chicago's first physicians. Unlike the doctor who advertised in the city directory, John Kennicott had called on patients in their homes, a cheerful small man riding a big horse and carrying medicine in his saddlebags. After retiring from practice the doctor entered journalism, enlisting with Wright and Turner in the cause of establishing a professional school of agriculture to rank with colleges of medicine. He urged readers of *The Prairie Farmer* to grow fruit, and eat plenty of it, a life-prolonging improvement on potatoes and fried pork. The doctor thought of everything: he suggested a device called the Baby Jumper, a boatswain's chair at the end of a limber pole, which "allowed the infant to bounce up and down most happily while the mother turned to other duties." Manufacturers stole the idea and made large profits, which they refused to share with the doctor. This was not surprising, for inventors had a hard time of it in this period prior to the war. The McCormicks, for example, had long been fighting among themselves over the question of who invented the reaper. All that could be said with certainty was that *somebody* had invented a reaper, back on the farm, but by the time Cyrus and his brothers got their product to market, they faced a number of rivals in the making of mechanical harvesters. One of the competitors was John S. Wright, who added reaper manufacturing to his other ventures in 1851. Going into business with a man named Obed Hussey, Wright used a design supplied by Jearum Atkins, a self-taught mathematical prodigy, crippled in a farm accident and confined to his bed. The promoters carried the bed into a field so that Atkins could watch a reaper in operation, and after twenty minutes he saw what was needed, a new kind of mechanical rake that worked on the principle of the human arm. In contrast to the manufacturers who stole the Baby Jumper, Wright put Atkins's Automaton on the market under an equal partnership deal. Cyrus McCormick took up the challenge by ordering his drummers to tell everyone that the Automaton was dangerously unsound. Lashing the livery-stable horses that drew their buggies over country roads, McCormick's men hurried through the hinterland, disparaging Wright's product at every stop. After them came the Automaton drummers, making equally damaging accusations against the McCormick machine, and sometimes fighting rival salesmen with their fists. Wright sent a challenge to Cyrus McCormick, offering to bet $98,000 to $30,000 that his machine could beat McCormick's in clearing a measured field, stakes to be held and paid on the spot by a politician or saloonkeeper. McCormick was well aware of the Automaton's superior speed, and he backed away from the attractive odds. Everyone took this to mean that Wright had overcome powerful and unscrupulous competition, and he did good business until the summer of 1856, when green wood in a number of Automatons warped in the unusually dry heat. Wright made repairs at the cost of fifty dollars per machine, a drain on his resources in worsening times. Defying personal misfortune, Wright predicted good conditions a year later when he wrote that the West could expect one million new citizens in the next few months, each with one hundred dollars cash for immediate spending. One week later, on July 9, 1857, the Chicago Bank of Commerce closed its doors. By the end of the month word was out that crops had failed, and another national panic began. John Wright took some hard blows; his $600,000 fortune melted away; he had to sell land, assign property to his brothers and other creditors, and give *The Prairie Farmer* to its printers. Undaunted as always, Wright seized his pen and began issuing pamphlets, circulars, letters, and articles. He wrote that "The money panic has brought a most favorable time to buy Chicago property." Three years later, he was still distributing optimistic circulars although by that time it appeared that civil war could not be avoided, and here again Wright got at the heart of the matter: "No earthly power, not even the dissolution of the Union, can divert from Chicago the business and traffic of the great Northwest."

What was to become one of the most successful institutions in the Northwest had appeared for the first time in Chicago on June 10, 1847 with the opening number of the *Daily Tribune.* Its first editor was John T. Scripps, who founded a newspaper chain in later years. Not a success at the start, the *Tribune* had barely managed to stay alive until Joseph Medill of Cleveland entered the paper's managing group. Medill had been born in Canada of Scotch-Irish stock, and had come to Ohio, where he called for the founding of a new national party in his *Cleveland Leader.* Moving to Chicago in 1855 at the age of thirty-two, he made himself the most forceful among the partners, including "Deacon" William Bross, who bought control of the *Tribune,* and he saw to it that the paper held its own against the competition of nine daily rivals on Chicago streets.

From their beginnings, Chicago papers tried for liveliness and readability, a tradition they have followed to the present day. There was plenty to write about: the underworld supplied accounts of vice and crime; the numerous dishonest politicians were targets for editorializing and partisan reporting; and the immigrant communities, seething with violent excitements, provided many a sensational story. Then too, it seemed that the bursting natural energies of Chicago and its territories would sometimes go rushing out of control and provide an especially horrible public disaster. One of these natural calamities involved an immigrant group when a political club of Milwaukee Irishmen chartered the sidewheeler *Lady Elgin* for a cruise to and from Chicago on Friday September 7, 1860. All went well on the trip down, and three hundred men, women and children of the Independent Union Guards looked forward to a moonlight voyage back to Milwaukee when they set out, along with fifty passengers picked up at Chicago, for the return trip. The German band was playing and couples were dancing at midnight when a storm broke and seas began rolling high. This in itself was no danger to the *Lady Elgin*. But her captain was not prepared, at two-thirty in the morning, for the sudden appearance of the schooner *Augusta*, which loomed out of the murk, rammed *Lady Elgin* with her sharp prow, and vanished in the darkness. The *Augusta*'s Captain D. M. Malott reported the collision when he arrived at Chicago early in the morning. His own ship was leaking and he had barely made port; whether he knew it or not, *Augusta* had given *Lady Elgin* a fatal wound.

Immediately after the crash, the *Lady*'s port rail had gone under, her engines had fallen through the bottom, and as she went down, huge rollers had smashed the upper works and carried them away, leaving one section of the hull afloat as a raft for about three hundred people. Until a wave knocked him under, Captain John Wilson stood on a floating bulkhead and encouraged the survivors to hang on as they drifted toward the shoreline of Winnetka, sixteen miles north of Chicago and about ten miles from the spot where the ships collided. Clouds obscured the moon and the only illumination came from flashes of lightning, as men and women began to lose their grip on wreckage, or their hold on children, and families together would slide into the water and drown. About a hundred and fifty still clung to floating wreckage when the sun came up and they found themselves close to Winnetka shore, where an implacable surf was pounding. A large crowd watched many of these people drown as the surf took them. Although little could be accomplished, some of the onlookers plunged in and did what they could. Among them was a divinity student from Northwestern University named Edward Spencer, who struggled through surf fifteen times, pulling out a drowning man or woman in each attempt. On his sixteenth try he brought in a husband and wife. Then Edward Spencer collapsed with exhaustion and in his delirium kept asking, "Did I do my best? . . . Did I do my best?" Edward Spencer lived to the age of eighty-one, and is memorialized by a bronze tablet on the campus.

At the official investigation, Captain Malott admitted that he had seen the *Lady*'s light twenty minutes before the collision, but delayed changing course until too late. The price of the *Lady Elgin* disaster came to 297 lives; Captain Malott and his crew went into another ship, the schooner *Mahor*, which broke up in a storm a few months later and went to the bottom of Lake Michigan with all on board. Under a changed name, the *Augusta* met a similar fate, running into her last storm in 1894. By that time generations of Midwestern youth had learned a ballad by the Chicago songwriter George F. Root, with its haunting chorus:

> Lost on the *Lady Elgin*,
> Sleeping to wake no more,
> Numbered in that three hundred
> Who failed to make the shore.

Shipping news often combined business and disaster, though not on the scale of the *Lady Elgin*, and editors of Medill's sort knew how to make the most of it. They also looked out from Chicago across the country and saw an opportunity to take power through the new Republican party, whose first national platform had denounced "those twin relics of barbarism, polygamy and slavery." After losing the national elections in 1856, Joseph Medill found the man he was looking for in the ablest jury lawyer at the Illinois bar, Abraham Lincoln. After a disappointing term in Congress that ended in 1849, Lincoln had gone to work rebuilding his career with diligence and courage of a sort that the builders of Chicago could appreciate. One evidence of Lincoln's standing came when Grant Goodrich of the inner circle offered a law partnership, but with characteristic wry self-denigration, Lincoln said it was beyond his powers to make good in Chicago, and he would feel more comfortable maintaining an office at Springfield with W. H. Herndon and traveling the circuit courts. In fact, Lincoln had a large Chicago practice of banks, insurance companies, and railroads, including the Illinois Central. He appeared at every session of the Chicago Federal Courts, and took Medill along on his travels around Illinois, so that the editor could report all he said and did. It soon became clear to Medill that Lincoln was a persuasive speaker who possessed additional assets in his height of six feet four inches and his unforgettable face —the "plain ploughed face" that riveted the attention of Henry Adams a few years later. And it interested Medill to note that when arguing before a jury or addressing a crowd from the stump, Abraham Lincoln worked in a controlled style like that of Marshall Field behind the counter. It was a new way to approach the public with something to sell, and Medill recognized its effectiveness the moment he saw it.

Confident of the power in their man's unassuming but competent approach, Lincoln's Chicago backers sent him against a master of the elaborate style in the late summer of 1858, when the seven Lincoln-Douglas debates began. In these discussions Lincoln was challenging the incumbent Stephen A. Douglas for his seat in the United States Senate, the outcome to be determined by a vote of electors at the State Legislature, as the law specified in those days. Lincoln and the *Chicago Tribune* also sought a national audience, with the coming Presidential campaign of 1860 in mind. Through the years Senator Douglas had made a good impression in Chicago by his support of measures to use taxpayers' money in building privately owned railroads. But Douglas went off the track in the fight over extending slavery into new U.S. territories. Using his matured political skill, the Senator had pushed through the Kansas-Nebraska Act of 1854 which repealed the Missouri Compromise, and provided that settlers in new territories should decide for or against slavery by vote at the time they applied for statehood. Passage of this Act was the greatest single legislative factor in bringing on the Civil War, which was not, of course, the intention of its sponsor. A firm touch on the wrong note was the Douglas specialty at the height of his career. In achieving his vast and costly errors, Stephen A. Douglas used large talents as a speaker, and although unusually short in stature, he bore himself in such an authoritative manner that men called him the Little Giant. He went in for old-fashioned arm-waving oratory, and often fueled in a barroom before delivering an address. The liquor had no outward effect except to deepen the booming sonority of a voice so powerful that it could move leaves on a tree 300 feet distant when he mounted the stump.

Considering Lincoln and Douglas as folk artists, one understands the power of their appeal to a public starved for shows and craving dramatic entertainment of any kind. It is not surprising that more than ten thousand people came to see and hear their first encounter on August 21, 1858, although the visiting crowd was more than twice the population of the town in which Lincoln and Douglas were opening the series of debates. Joseph Medill headed the corps of Chicago newspapermen who made the seventy mile trip to Ottawa, along with reporters from cities back east, and the journalists witnessed an amazing spectacle in the host of people who had come to town by railroad, wagon, and canal. Hundreds were drunk, and fell unconscious from liquor and heat before the contestants appeared. Small boys and yapping dogs raced through the crowds, marshals wearing sashes and top hats bustled on official errands, hoodlums threw cannon crackers, constables struggled to stop fights, militia companies paraded, bands blared, drums thumped, peddlers bawled at every corner, and the delegation of Chicago swindlers and pickpockets toiled at a frantic pace to harvest the takings spread before them, while politicians gathered factions to heckle and applaud. The debaters entered like prizefighters, each followed by an entourage of bottle-holders and seconds. The debates made first-rate drama since each speaker launched a personal attack, Douglas painting Lincoln as an abolitionist, while Lincoln accused Douglas of being a pro-slavery man. They rated evenly as entertainers, Douglas in the grand manner, sometimes raging up and down the platform, Lincoln working in the new plain style, with his elbows close to his sides, and limited gestures. The seventh and last debate took place at Alton on October 15, and by this time Medill and his *Tribune* people were sure that Lincoln had split the Democratic party when he forced Douglas to equivocate on the question of slavery in territories before application for statehood.

After the speechmaking subsided and the voters went to the polls, Joseph Medill rejoiced at what he took to be a clear-cut victory for his man when Lincoln tallied 190,000 votes to 176,000 for Douglas. However, the state apportionment law took away the victory, and on February 5, 1859, a joint session at Springfield returned Douglas to the U.S. Senate by 54 votes to 46. Disappointed but only momentarily discouraged, Medill and Lincoln pulled themselves together and looked ahead: there was little time left to prepare for Chicago's first national party convention.

The place of meeting stood at Lake and Market Streets, an enormous wooden building with seats for ten thousand people, which the Republicans named the Wigwam to suggest a council house for political braves and chieftains. They gathered in Chicago during the week previous to May 16, 1860—the 466 Republican delegates plus countless job-seekers, sightseers, petty criminals, and newspapermen from all over the country. The proprietors of the Tremont, the Briggs, and the two or three other first-class hotels indulged in the practice known nowadays as overbooking, so that every room was full, extra beds stood in hallways, and clerks took pleasure in turning away late comers who thought they had reservations. The hotelmen raised bar prices, which did not deter patrons who ordered the fashionable new gin cocktail as an eye opener before breakfast. The grasping innkeepers inspired hackdrivers, who tripled their fares and openly robbed drunken passengers, and the gambling houses put on extra shifts of steerers to bring visitors for fleecing by the croupiers at the wheels and the stickmen who handled the dice, all drawing overtime wages so that no dollar should escape. Newspapers reported that the city had been declared "open" through the courtesy of Mayor Long John Wentworth. This meant that any delegate was free at any hour of the day or night to be cheated in a gambling house, sickened by bad liquor in a deadfall, or infected with disease in a brothel.

At first the biggest man in town was Senator William H. Seward of New York, whom the Eastern papers touted as a sure bet for the Presidential nomination. Uneasy about rowdiness in Chicago, Seward had brought along two bodyguards from the New York prize ring, a sensible precaution for a gentleman of fifty-nine who did not wish to be jostled by hooligans or have his hat pulled around his ears. Medill and his friends were ready for the distinguished Mr. Seward. They planned to let him break in front and make the pace; they would then run him down on the second ballot, and pass him on the third. Medill and the other Lincoln managers held their man under wraps at Springfield, but there were plenty of colorful figures to be seen on the Wigwam floor, among them the fearsome radical Republican Congressman Thaddeus Stevens from Pennsylvania, who suggested a Shakespearian villain as he dragged his lame leg around the hall, and glared at the crowd from burning eyes in a thin-lipped parchment face under a coarse black wig. Less terrifying though odd enough in its way was Mr. Seward's appearance: with his narrow shoulders, penetrating little eyes, and projecting beak, he looked like a wise macaw. No one had ever seen W. H. Seward without a fuming cigar in hand or mouth; he smoked forty a day. A plume of smoke followed him as he moved from the New York seats to other parts of the floor, bargaining with the chiefs of state delegations. At the same time Medill had unleashed a corps of political hacks, under command of a downstate judge named David Davis and a Chicago railroad lawyer, Norman B. Judd. There was some question as to their competence when the convention climaxed on the morning of June 7, 1860, and the third ballot showed Lincoln one and one-half votes away from the necessary 233, with Seward still alive at 180. Seward's agents were canvassing the crowd, offering money and jobs, and there remained a chance that New York could rally on the next ballot, and send Lincoln back to a political log cabin instead of the White House. It was a breathless moment; the only sounds were the tapping of ladies' palm-leaf fans and the scratching of reporters' pencils. Then a deep-voiced Ohio delegate rose and addressed the chair: *Ohio—wishes to announce—the change of four votes—to Abraham Lincoln!*

That announcement in a shed on the Chicago River settled the country's fate for years to come, and all present recognized the importance of the moment. The delegate's voice had echoed for only an instant when Medill's henchmen burst into cheers according to instruction, while rowdies fought for state banners and a hellish din broke loose. Up front, the chairman flailed away with his gavel until the heavy lignum vitae head broke off, flew into the crowd, and knocked a delegate cold.* The band started blatting out a polka and the Lincoln delegates went capering around the hall in a victory dance. Cannon thundered from the Wigwam's roof, and that night there were torchlight parades in every town and city of the Middle West.

When the national election was over, it could be observed that the total vote for four candidates had run about three to two against Lincoln, but he had a majority in the electoral college because of his strength in the Northwest and Northeast. Medill, Isaac Arnold, Charles Ray and the other Chicago Republican strategists had united the North and divided the nation. When he got to Washington, Lincoln had to deal with the most rapacious gang of spoilsmen ever seen, many of them presenting bills for services at Chicago. The worst specimen in this crew was old Senator Simon Cameron of Pennsylvania, who had grown rich through graft, having gained special notoriety by cheating the Winnebago Indians on a colossal scale in 1828. At Chicago, Cameron had received the pledge of a cabinet post in return for delivering his state delegation. Republicans of the better sort deplored the necessity, but Lincoln made Cameron Secretary of War, resisting the old man's original bid for the Treasury. At the War Department, Cameron began to take an extraordinary interest in contracts for equipment and appointments of officers in the Quartermaster Corps, for there had come a permeating sense that war might start tomorrow, and a smell of blood and money in the air.

When shells landed in Fort Sumter on April 11 and 12 of 1861, Chicago reacted with intense excitement, and after the President's call for militia to serve three months, the city led the nation in a debauch of patriotism. And there was more than flag-waving involved: it was easy to see that Federal armies must take control of the Mississippi, and Chicago stood at the head of the valley, obvious center of distribution for goods, weapons, and men.

The first week of war established the business pattern, and figures crawled rapidly down ledger columns as the money came in. Chicago's books showed every cent of profit, but no record has been found that a member of the inner commercial group went to war, though many were of military age: Potter Palmer was thirty-four, George Pullman was

*This originated the joke in which the victim comes to and says, "Hit me again, I can still hear him."

twenty-nine, Marshall Field was twenty-six; but these were men of the counting house, not men of the sword. Here and there the younger brother of a dominant family volunteered and marched away, and some of these died fighting or from sicknesses that ran through camps as dirty as those which had brought cholera to Chicago in the 1830s. The typical Chicago soldier in the ranks was a young clerk, student, or workingman, and the officers usually had been plant superintendents, teachers, small merchants, or professional men. Dwight Moody went out as an unofficial chaplain and hospital attendant, came under fire several times, and comforted the dying by promising to take their last words to parents and wives. He soon had enough of it, and returned to civilian life. Back in Chicago, no one except an occasional veteran of Mexican campaigns had any idea of the product that battles leave behind them, and thousands of young men stepped forward for short-term enlistments as though signing on for an extended picnic or patriotic camping trip.

There was no need for press gangs at the start; orders to join the colors came from an even higher source than the great man in the White House. Frances Willard's sister Mary wrote in her diary about a "war meeting" at the Evanston Methodist Church on the rainy ninth night after the surrender of Fort Sumter: "When the 'Star-Spangled Banner' was sung, as I joined in the chorus, I was half wild with enthusiasm, though I stood there so quietly. Above the pulpit hung the national flag, arranged in graceful folds around a portrait of Washington, who looked serenely down upon us, as if confident that we would not desert a cause in which he thought no sacrifice too dear. Several speeches were made, and then was a call for those who were willing to volunteer to come forward and sign the muster roll. I shall never forget the scene that followed. Rapidly they went; young men whom we all know and esteem; students in college and in theology; men who had wives and daughters looking after them with smiles of pride on their lips though there were tears of sorrow in their eyes; and beautiful boys, with their slight forms and flushed young faces. Cheer after cheer went up from the excited audience as each one took the pen and wrote his name as a volunteer in the army that goes to save the Union. God pity the man who is not prepared to die before he joins the army. Oh! if we could have known the agony that will result from what was done in the church we love so much, and where we have worshipped so peacefully together, I know we should have filled the house with sobs, and tears would have fallen like the rain that beat against the windows as though Nature herself were grieving."

A gallant Chicago officer was Colonel Robert G. Ingersoll, known as the Fighting Atheist, though to be precise he was a fighting agnostic. Captured by rebels, the colonel suggested that he might entertain his guards with a lecture. Now it happened that Robert Ingersoll was one of the age's great spellbinders, the equal of Lincoln or Douglas; mounted on a stool, he had almost hypnotized the rural Southern soldiers into releasing him when an officer came along and ordered him to stop talking before he persuaded the entire detachment to join the Union side. Shortly afterward Ingersoll was exchanged, in accordance with military custom. Later on, Lincoln stopped the exchanging of prisoners when he saw that the practice favored the South, with its smaller population. From this came one of the ugliest evils of the war, as prison camps on both sides turned into death camps because of starvation, filth, and lack of medical care. Chicago had an especially deplorable place of detention in Camp Douglas on the South Side, where 6,129 Confederate prisoners died during the last three years of the war out of twenty thousand confined. Dwight Moody did what he could in frequent visits, but one day encountered a young sentry at the outer gate who did not recognize him. "Stand back!" cried the excited farm boy, pointing his bayonet at Moody's chest and hoping for an excuse to ram it through him. The evangelist roared, "I am Moody, of the Young Men's Christian Association! Let me pass, for the work's sake!" Astonished by the powerful voice, the boy lowered his weapon and Moody went on in.

It was appropriate that this place of death and sickness should be named for one of the chief architects of the war, Senator Stephen A. Douglas, who abandoned partisan opposition to Lincoln when shooting started, and had gone out across the North calling for blood. He died on April 25, 1861, and the city placed his name on its list of heroes. In the speechmaking at the funeral, some went so far as to say that the Little Giant had worn himself out in a great cause and died like a soldier.

Be that as it may, there was no lack of impassioned oratory in Chicago for any occasion from the interment of a politician to the gathering of loafers in Court House Square or in front of a taproom. During the first months of the war, a continuous rolling of drums resounded, summoning citizens to rallies or beating time for detachments of Home Guards, older men who had organized to defend Chicago from invasion. It was an unusually fine spring, with days when the lake reflected American blue from cloudless skies. And in this spring of 1861, with the *Tribune* blaring like a Roman war horn, the fostering of martial spirit became the responsibility of a Union Defense Committee that included James H. Bowen, Thomas Hogue, Grant Goodrich, a dozen judges and preachers, and the governor of Illinois. Chicago and Illinois also furnished the Union a number of highly ranked military men. In addition to Ulysses Grant, who rose from discredited retirement to become a four-star general, the state provided nine permanent and 53 temporary major generals, together with no less than 125 of the little buck generals or brigadiers. Today the most interesting thing about this list of officers is that nine of the sixty-two major generals were named Smith: Giles A., Arthur A., Franklin C., George W., Gustavus A., John C., John E., Robert F., and Robert W., a statistical impossibility yet there it is.

Both future generals and privates felt the power of the oratory that the Union Committee provided by day and night. Favorite speakers such as Long John Wentworth, Senator Lyman Trumbull, Benjamin F. Ayer, Wirt Dexter, John L. Hancock, the Hon. S. K. Dow, the famous "War Democrat" Matt Carpenter, and Robert Ingersoll before he left for active service, could always draw a crowd, and Isaac N. Arnold, now a Congressman, frequently yelled before large crowds to whom he brought the latest word from Washington, where he stood near the Presidential chair. Among all these men of the mouth, only Fighting Bob Ingersoll had first-rate talent. The rest were bullshooters in the old Daniel Webster tradition, each man the sort of speaker, as George Ade later remarked, who arrived at a meeting with his Voice wrapped in a Shawl Strap. But some were good entertainers, folk artists of the minor sort, even though the performance on critical analysis amounted to nothing more than waving the bloody shirt and making the eagle scream. For that matter, an instance of a speaker actually arousing an eagle's wrath occurred when Old Abe, the bald eagle who served as mascot to a Wisconsin regiment, appeared at a Chicago rally. Chained to his perch, Old Abe folded his wings and seemed to be in good humor until the orator worked himself into a frenzy and emitted a yell that could be heard in Benton Harbor, whereupon the eagle began flapping his wings and screeching, and tried to get at the fellow. Old Abe compiled a combat record of twenty battles and sixty skirmishes, and retired to the Wisconsin State Capitol, where Jane Addams saw him in 1870. Jane thought this was the veritable American eagle about which she had heard from her father at home in the small town of Cedarville, Illinois. Old Abe lived until 1881, when he died in a fire. The bird's body, stuffed and mounted, remained on exhibition until it burned to ashes in another fire on February 27, 1904.

Along with flags and fireworks and living symbols of bellicosity such as Old Abe the war eagle, Chicago loved the singing of a quartet led by the Lumbard brothers, who frequently appeared at patriotic rallies. Jules Lumbard sang bass, while his brother Frank took the lead tenor part, with a voice that had "a triumphant heartiness" according to Frederick F. Cook, star reporter of the *Chicago Times*. The Lumbards often sang songs by George F. Root, who had written about the *Lady Elgin*; singers and composer gave help to the Northern war effort when they introduced "The Battle-Cry of Freedom."* Root's inspiration came from Lincoln's second call for troops and he wrote the song overnight. The Lumbards rehearsed next morning and gave the first performance at a mass meeting on Court House Square. The crowd went wild when Frank's voice soared in the chorus, *We'll rally round the flag, boys, we'll rally once again. . . .*

Chicago began to learn the cost of rallying round the flag when early casualty lists brought in the name of the first well-known Union officer to die. He was a young Chicagoan from New York State named Elmer Ephraim Ellsworth, a military theorist and amateur soldier of wide repute immediately prior to the war. As a youth of twenty-one in 1858, Ellsworth studied law at Abraham Lincoln's Springfield office, and in his spare time gave military instruction to volunteer companies at Elgin, Rockford, Lake Forest, and Chicago, and also to Wisconsin University students at Madison. Elmer Ellsworth was the leading authority on Zouaves, the Berber troops of the French army. He had sent to France for all the books on Zouave tactics and drill, teaching himself the language in order to read these texts. The Oriental uniform of wide trousers, fez, and loose jacket got a powerful grip on Ellsworth's imagination, and the young men in his companies took up the fashion. Ellsworth and his Zouaves exhibited their intricate marching throughout the country, appearing before President Buchanan on the White House lawn, and in the drill hall of the United States Military Academy at West Point. When war broke out, Lincoln made his pupil and friend a colonel, and Ellsworth led a regiment of Zouaves recruited from the New York Fire Department to Washington on May 14, 1861, meeting his death the following day while hauling down a Confederate flag in Alexandria, Virginia. There was sadness in Chicago at the news, for a number of local youths had trained as Zouaves at Lake Forest Academy, and now awaited orders to move out in a unit called the Ellsworth Guards. And there was mourning in Washington, where Ellsworth's body lay at the White House, and the President and his wife wept as though at the loss of a son, Mrs. Lincoln placing a wreath of artificial flowers in the coffin. Their grief must have been especially poignant since their eldest son, though of military age, was not in the army, but very sensibly pursuing his studies at Harvard College. When Medill and other Chicagoans complained to Lincoln about it, the President said there was nothing he could

*George Frederick Root, originally from Massachusetts, also composed "Tramp, Tramp, Tramp, the Boys Are Marching," "Just Before the Battle, Mother," and "The Vacant Chair."

[77]

do: two of his four boys had died in childhood, and if Robert were placed in danger, Mrs. Lincoln would go crazy. Mary Todd Lincoln was indeed a pitiable woman, frequently tortured by migraine, and ultimately destined to go out of her mind. The thing about her husband that puzzled her friends was his ability, in the face of Robert's privileged position, to commit such an outrage as the pious and unctuous letter to Mrs. Bixby, whose five sons had been reported dead in battle.* A politician is a man who can do things like that, and then wonder why people are looking at him in a thoughtful way.

Lincoln's friends in Chicago entered a time of euphoria as the war gathered pace and they began to see the extent of profits to be reaped. They had more than one reason to feel fine: having nominated and elected a President, they were taking a hand in running a war at a safe distance, and every day they read about their greatness in the home town papers. But on the streets there was another story: Mayor Long John Wentworth had so mismanaged the police force that the State Legislature passed a law early in 1861 to put the direction of Chicago police in the hands of a municipal board. Long John took this as an insult and discharged every member of the force at two o'clock in the morning of March 21, 1861. The city had no official protection for the next twenty-four hours, during which the Board met and put the force together again. With the police under new management, optimistic Chicagoans hoped for some abatement of crime, but soon observed that politicians still controlled the force and gave honest officers small chance of promotion.

A poorly led, undermanned, and corrupt police force was exactly what Chicago's sporting and criminal elements wanted as the town began to boil with war activity and money started to flow. It is true that the denizens of low resorts on Wells, Monroe, and Clark streets respected a certain few officers such as two-fisted Simon O'Donnell of the traffic detail, or the dreaded Captain Jack Nelson, whose name made crooks and bullies turn pale. But the Chicago underworld flourished with almost no interference from the police in the boom times brought on by the spending of army and industrial payrolls, along with the large sums profiteers threw away at gambling tables, and paid to brothel-keepers.

The more money there was to spend, the more numerous grew the army of panders, whores, rum-sellers, swindlers, and robbers who gathered to harvest it. Herbert Asbury has written that "the human scum of a hundred cities swarmed into Chicago from all over the country." Bawds

*Lincoln had received an erroneous report. Two Bixby sons were killed, one was discharged, and two deserted.

[78]

and criminals arrived in such numbers that they overflowed into the suburbs, giving the community of Cicero, for example, its first ill repute, while within city limits they strengthened and enlarged the outposts established by vicious persons driven from the Sands. On the South Side below Madison Street from the lake to the river, where almost every house was disreputable, the worst of all was the emporium of depravity conducted by Roger Plant, at the northeast corner of Monroe and Wells streets. Plant was a jockey-sized Englishman, born in Yorkshire and schooled for violence and crime in Liverpool and New York. He had come to Chicago at about the time Marshall Field arrived, and resembled the merchant in his devotion to business, which he carried on with strict attention to customers' requirements. An excellent fighter, though small, Plant kept knives and pistols handy, but could use his teeth if necessary, and when grappled by an opponent would try for a thumb in the eye. At the time Plant took over at Monroe and Wells streets, a tree grew in front, giving the name of Under the Willow, which might make one think of geisha girls, lutes in a garden, and the tea ceremony. On the contrary, Under the Willow was "a refuge for the very nethermost strata of the underworld—the refuse of the Bridewell," according to Frederick Cook of the *Times*. As war continued, Plant enlarged his establishment by building houses at the sides and rear; some said he had dug an underground passage from his cellar to other resorts in the neighborhood, for the convenience of fugitives from the law. The tunnel was a myth, as the law never caused enough trouble to create need for such a thing; and Plant did so well in the first two years of the war that his additional rookeries reached a total of sixty rooms, in which he transacted business twenty-four hours a day. Among the activities was a school for thieves, with a class for girls under twelve. Plant also rented rooms to the procuresses who frequented railway stations in the guise of trustworthy old housekeepers looking for domestic help. These creatures brought country and immigrant girls to a room at the Willow, where gangs of rapists assaulted them in preparation for sale to neighboring panders. In addition to providing services by staff harlots, Plant rented space to free-lance whores and male degenerates. He also produced shows in which men and women made sexual contact with animals, the entertainment concluding with an exhibition by a coprophagist. Roger Plant eventually sold the Willow at an enormous profit, retired to the country, bought a stable of race horses and set up his carriage, but failed to gain acceptance in good society.

One Chicagoan in every ten was a bawd or thief when the city entered the war decade of 1860 with a population of 110,000. This was more than three times the population of 1850, and by 1870, the city would be ten

[79]

times its size of twenty years before. From 1861 to 1865, Chicago grew from day to day too rapidly for accurate estimates, but nobody worried about that in the stimulating atmosphere of war. It was wheat against cotton: increased use of McCormick's Chicago reapers released enough young farmers of the Middle West to win the war, assisted by men from the State of Maine and other places, who learned the soldiering trade by surviving a succession of horrible battles like that at Cold Harbor, where Lee and Grant haggled over protocol for three days while wounded men died begging for water. In ugly contrast to the sufferings of soldiers stood the greed of moneymen in the North, and the bickering of state politicians in the South. Belligerent emotions carried nearly everyone away; but even at the height of fury there were those who saw the war as a national disgrace for which two overrated leaders must take final blame; and there would be plenty of blame left for the advisers and manipulators, like Isaac Arnold and Joseph Medill of Chicago. As Henry Adams saw it, the government itself had been "the agent of a near-lethal rupture in domestic society. . . . It was a degraded act of which nobody had cause to be proud." Adams went on to say that "The bitter essence of it is all in Francis Parkman's reflection on what he thought the failure of universal suffrage. It was a nation's shame, he held, that the American people had not virtue, temperance, and wisdom enough to abolish slavery peacefully and harmlessly."

As one might expect, Chicago had a clear-eyed student of war in John Stephen Wright. He observed that just as he had predicted, a stupendous boom had come to Chicago and lesser industrial strongholds of the North. And the loss of Southern markets was forgotten in Chicago when Congress passed the Homestead Law of 1862, which practically gave away two and a half million acres of Western farmland to all comers. Government contracts went into receptive hands, and Chicago manufacturers did not always resist the temptation to enter a grafters' paradise of selling shoddy goods to the Army: uniforms that dissolved in the rain; shoes that fell apart; sugar that was half sand; coffee mixed with sweepings of rye; rotten meat; and defective weapons. Rear Admiral David Dixon Porter said that he saw deployed in addition to the regular forces a host of "speculators commanded by General Greed, General Avarice, General Corruption, General Speculation, and General Breach of Trust, with all their attendant staff of harpies, who were using the Army and Navy for the vilest purposes." Headquarters for these tacticians of theft and bribery was Chicago, and there John Wright began a remarkable effort to think the matter through, and find out how it could be that a handful of politicians could order up armed forces and send them to destruction, torturing millions of people with incalculable anguish. Wright's question was, where did these minis-ters of fear and pain get their authority? He saw that the answer must also settle the question of sovereignty, and with this objective in mind, he began burrowing into libraries to remedy his lack of information on the history of governments among men.

Wright went East in search of material and consulted Samuel F. B. Morse, the portrait painter who had turned his mind to problems of com-munication, and produced the electrical sending and receiving apparatus, together with the Morse code, which made him known as father of the telegraph. The seventy-three-year-old artist and inventor publicly op-posed the war, although he had embarrassed his followers by issuing a pamphlet that cited Scripture in support of slavery. The truth was that the old great Morse had turned into something of a crank, but this did not deter John Wright of Chicago in his characteristic pursuit of enlighten-ment. And Morse listened attentively when Wright revealed his grand design to read everything written on the nature of the state from antiquity to the present day. Wright's problem was translating and Morse solved it by introducing a learned clergyman, the Rev. J. Holmes Agnew, who could read any known language at sight. By early 1863, Wright and Agnew were deep in research, tunneling and mining in libraries, and laboring at a mountain of books in Wright's Chicago study. Outside, the war went on, and as always the wrong people got killed, the wrong people got rich. Indeed, it became evident that most of the bleeding and dying was being done by men with nothing at stake, and little benefit in prospect, whatever the outcome. The Confederate cause was hopeless from the start, since the North possessed a greater share of national manpower and most of the industrial resources. It had seemed for a while that the Northern working-man might benefit from high wages at war plants. But prices ran ahead of workmen's pay, as the cost of living shot up to 125 percent of pre-war levels, and wages rose only 20 percent in buying power. In Chicago, industrial workers had to take pay in unsecured "greenbacks" printed by the government to finance the war, which rapidly lost purchasing power as additional hundreds of millions came off the presses. But Chicago work-ingmen preferred even this dubious paper to the bills of Illinois banks. The spectacle of this economic injustice caused Wright to drive his pen across page after page in outlining a philosophical and political study that was to fill five volumes, and define the social contract and the state. This work would teach nothing less than how to bring about conditions under which the state might be rendered harmless, and made the servant of the people, never again to inflict blind cruelty as master. By January 1864 he had completed his prospectus, including a sample of the work to be called, in its entirety, *Citizenship Sovereignty, Published for American Citizens, the True Maintainers of State Sovereignty.*

Wright called this preliminary statement *The Compend*, and sent it to editors, teachers, ministers, and politicians in Chicago and the Eastern cities, soliciting subscriptions so that he could finish the work. His reasoning in *The Compend* on the immediate causes of the war was interesting, for it assigned moral responsibility to both parties: according to Wright, the South was wrong in seceding, the North in refusing to allow secession. One of the disappointments in Wright's life ensued when only a handful of subscribers showed interest in the proposed five volumes of political philosophy. Nevertheless, Wright scored an important point in *The Compend*, by his remarks on Abraham Lincoln's conduct of the war. Wright said that Lincoln impressed him as an honest man and a patriot, but that the President's suspension of constitutional civil liberties and imprisoning of critics, and his interferences with freedom of the press were "the most infamous, outrageous usurpations of modern days."

In that remark John S. Wright touched something of direct concern at Chicago. As fighting went on, the working people of the city became disillusioned, and many voices joined in demanding an end of war. The German and Irish workers had native-born allies in making protests: these included the Copperheads, as Medill called the Confederate sympathizers on the West Side; the blacklegs, Southern gamblers who had come to town to escape military service and to assist in fleecing the dupes who crowded Chicago's gambling dens; the Virginian Cyrus McCormick, who ran for Congress as a Democrat, for which the *Tribune* called him a traitor and said he had stolen the idea for the reaper; and the publisher of the *Chicago Times*, Wilbur Fisk Storey. A typical upper-class Chicagoan of his day, Storey had come out of Vermont, and considered himself too old for combat at the age of forty-two when war broke out. He was nevertheless a competent street fighter, one of the few men of standing not too proud to mix it in a public brawl, whereas his rival Medill left such activity to the *Tribune's* hired bravos. There is no question that someone like Roger Plant could have taken Storey apart, but he defended himself capably against the sort of assailants who ordinarily beset a newspaper publisher. For example, when Storey and his wife were attacked on the street by a party of actors from a burlesque show, he sidestepped the leading lady's claws and stretched the troupe's advance man senseless with several well-aimed punches, while Mrs. Storey, a motherly-looking woman with gray hair, stunned the actress with a blow of her handbag, which was weighted by a Bible and prayerbook that had heavy metal clasps. It is easy to see that such a man backed by such a wife would not tolerate censorship, even when ordered by a government in Washington that had locked up civilians for protesting about the war, and had shot and hanged soldiers for military offenses, in spite of the widely advertised pardon of the young sleeping sentry by the kindly old man in the White House. By 1863, Storey and his free-spoken *Chicago Times* had penetrated official skins, and orders that the paper should cease publishing on June 2 came from the military governor of Chicago. This officer, who ruled over the Military District of Ohio, which included Illinois, was the hirsute Major General Ambrose Everett Burnside, a failure in business and war, deposited in a rear-echelon job to save face for the brass who had been foolish enough to trust him. Nobody took Burnside seriously, and it is certain that so important an order as that which closed a Chicago newspaper must have originated above him, and with highest approval. Wherever the order started, it exploded like a mortar shell in Chicago, and when word got out that a military edict had suppressed the *Times*, thousands of men rushed into the streets looking for trouble, egged on by blacklegs and Copperheads delighted at a chance to start riots. The first action of the day came when a drunken soldier invaded the *Times* office and Wilbur Storey knocked him through a window. All over town, Copperheads mounted boxes and barrels to yell at excited crowds, "If the *Times* is not allowed to publish, there will be no *Tribune!*" And at the *Tribune* plant, the lean red-haired Joseph Medill loaded a rifle and stared at the crowd beginning to form on the street below his window. At his side stood the Kansas desperado Colonel Charles Jennison, whose long hair and fringed buckskin jacket proclaimed his Western origin. Jennison headed the *Tribune's* army, and he put sharpshooters on the roof, their guns commanding every approach to the place. "If anyone tries to keep the *Tribune* off the streets," said Joseph Medill, "those streets will run with blood."

On the following morning Burnside surrounded the *Times* building with troops, and a muttering crowd stood throughout the afternoon and evening just beyond reach of the bayonets. Next day, June 4, dawned hot and sticky—good weather for bad temper and impulsive action; by eleven in the morning, rumors ran that twenty thousand armed men planned to turn out as Copperheads at a protest meeting called for eight P.M. on Court House Square. But Joseph Medill and General Burnside had been making use of the Morse telegraph all the preceding night, and shortly after one P.M. orders arrived from Washington to call the whole thing off. The crowds around the *Times* building howled in triumph when the clank of machinery came from its pressroom; and throughout the remaining months of the war, Colonel Jennison and his crew of ruffians remained on guard at the *Tribune.*

What happened now in Chicago? More of the same—silks and satins for the profiteers' women, diamonds and pearls, champagne foaming in the glasses, diners gorging on rich meats and well-aged game served at fine hotels by deferential blacks, the only Negroes Chicago really liked. Wright's friends thought it quaint when his wife's maid heard she was free and cried in alarm, "I don't want to be free! I want to stay with Miss Kitty!" Freeing the Negroes meant nothing to the average Chicagoan, and was not the reason why he went to war. And when it was over, worse than the cruelty, worse than the coarsening, worse than the enthronement of gross materialism was the damage the war did by making Chicagoans, along with the rest of America, self-worshiping citizens in a self-praising land. Self-worship took them all, for winners had victory to gloat over, losers defeat to explain. But they were all losers—including the President, killed by a bullet from the gun of a ridiculous man who should have been firing blank cartridges, or putting a hump on his back and calling himself Richard the Third.

They brought their President back from his mean death, and in Chicago the apotheosis began. The coffin on its caisson, draped in black, rolled from the railroad station to the City Hall. General Fighting Joe Hooker rode ahead, and twenty generals followed him, their horses sidling against each other. Next came fifty clergymen in frock coats, carrying their tall hats wound with mourning ribbons; one hundred young ladies followed, robed in white; and a procession of citizens brought up the rear, their heads bowed, the tramp of their feet an accompaniment to the tolling of bells and the thudding of muffled drums. Frederick Cook reported that the bands played "a solemn dirge, now subdued to a sobbing cadence, and now rising in heart-moving lamentation" as the coffin was carried to the center of the City Hall and Court House rotunda, the most impressive enclosed space in Chicago. They opened the coffin and thousands of men and women, and their wondering children, lined up to get a look at the dead face. These mourners packed the streets outside, marshalled into double lines by soldiers, police, and committeemen wearing funeral rosettes on their lapels. It was a long ordeal to stand in those waiting lines: women fainted, children yelled and wailed, and dogs trotted sniffing, or sat back and howled, disturbed by the strange atmosphere. Police and cursing soldiers drove peddlers away, and the long lines shuffled on. Instead of using his press credentials, Frederick Cook stood in a public line, and reported that when he finally got into the rotunda, there was an impression of semi-darkness, somber draperies, and dim light from a can-

[84]

delabrum at the head of the casket. It was all hurried in the candle light: "At every step, was heard the whispered 'Move on!' and before you got a proper look, you were out in the street again." In the momentary glimpse, Cook thought the face had looked "exceedingly small." He stood in line a second time, and after an hour and a half again passed the coffin. Then he went to the *Times* office and wrote, "My original impression was confirmed, the face appearing much smaller than one would expect from the unusual length of body. And upon inquiry I found that others had come away with a similar impression."

The Lincoln funeral train reached its last stop at Springfield, where they buried him, long to be worshiped as god and hero in the American myth. At Chicago, the emotions aroused by Lincoln's death and transfiguration soon began yielding practical results. One of the first beneficiaries was George M. Pullman, alert to all possibilities in promoting his railroad sleeping-cars. Some days after the burial, he heard that Mrs. Lincoln still lay prostrated by shock in Washington, afraid that the trip to Springfield would be more than she could face. He dispatched a palace car for Mrs. Lincoln's use, and soon received word that the widow appreciated his thoughtfulness and would come West in the Pullman car. There remained only a few days before Mrs. Lincoln planned to start, and during this brief period Pullman somehow got enough men working to prepare the special track necessary for the passage of his car from Chicago to Springfield. This feat of engineering drew attention wherever people read newspapers. It would be unfair to say that Pullman thought only of publicity: his was an act of kindness, as well as the greatest commercial promotion of the age. All over the earth, men told each other this was Chicago style—brushing obstacles aside, getting results. And basking as they were in the admiration of the world, it is no wonder that George Pullman and his friends became convinced that they could do no wrong, a belief they were to hold until death took them too.

4

Barriers Burned Away

IN THE EVENING OF OCTOBER 8, 1871, GEORGE ADE SAT ON A FENCE
outside an Indiana town and looked northwest at a glow on the flat skyline
that was not the glow of sunset. People said Chicago was burning, and
since George was only five years old, the news delighted him, and in his
mind a toy city smoked and crackled. His elders did not feel such joy and
satisfaction, but to many of them the glare on the horizon represented just
punishment like the fire called down on the unrighteous by Elijah of old.

Had the barons of Chicago been in the habit of reading the Old Testament, they might also have taken warning from the Thirty-seventh Psalm,
with its observation of the wicked man in power, "yet he passed away, and
he was not: yea, I sought him, and he could not be found." The book
having most influence on Chicago in the late 1860s was not the Bible, but
Charles Darwin's *Origin of Species by Means of Natural Selection, or the
Preservation of Favored Races in the Struggle for Life*. This book had a
profound effect in England and the United States because of a slogan that
Herbert Spencer coined from it: the survival of the fittest. The phrase of
five words entered the language to give prosperous citizens assurance that
both poverty and wealth existed in obedience to biological law. The doctrine applied to past, present, and future: in a million years the muskellunge might crawl from the Chicago River, and in another million years
might succeed in turning himself into a big lizard; meanwhile, the Chicago
capitalist remained free to exploit his environment and his fellow men,

an evolved type performing his natural function here and now.

Writers called these ideas Social Darwinism, which was grand stuff in the minds of the rich, the able, and the lucky, but scarcely comforting to the average man, particularly in Chicago. Of course things looked good on the surface, for there was money in town after the war, and the tide of luxury gave no sign of receding; but prices continued to rise, while some wages went down, and some jobs disappeared altogether. The McCormicks still paid good money, but a man had to take what was offered at the plant gate, with no discussion about hours and conditions of work. And there was something wrong with money itself; even the supply of wretched Civil War greenbacks became smaller as Washington retired the paper. Hard times struck again in 1867, and some of the people living in those little frame houses on the far West and South Sides began going hungry. This was not the result of anyone's greed or mismanagement, nor did it come from founding immense Gilded Age fortunes. It was all natural. Professor Darwin said so, according to universal belief; and in Chicago, Joseph Medill said so. He wrote in the *Tribune* that unhappy working people had only themselves to blame, for the "cause of the impecunious position of millions of the wage classes in this country is due to their own improvidence and misdirected efforts. Too many are trying to live without labor and too many squander their earnings on intoxicating drinks, cigars and amusements, who cannot afford it."

This doctrine failed to charm the working population of Chicago, which numbered more than 175,000 German, Irish, Swedish, Polish, and other sorts of European born men and women as the year 1867 reached its end. McCormick, Pullman, Palmer, and Field knew that Socialists were preaching an entirely different doctrine to the "wage classes." Most numerous among the skilled and intelligent Germans, these agitators worked at trades by day, and edited seditious pamphlets in dusty little printing shops by night. Pinkerton detectives kept the big men informed of what the little men were up to; and the reports grew so alarming that Palmer and the rest raised a fund and started negotiations with the government at Washington for the establishment of Fort Sheridan, and the Great Lakes Naval Station, eighteen and twenty miles north of City Hall. The men in the counting houses felt safer with the Army and Navy close at hand, because in 1870, when the population of Chicago passed 300,000, two thirds of the people worked for wages, and 95 percent of the wage earners were foreign born. The average annual pay of industrial employees came to $405.64. Supposing the usual workman to have a wife and three children, this allowed $81.14 per year for the support of each person. Medill was right, there was little here for entertainment and cigars.

[87]

Julia Newberry lived in a different world, for although her revered father occasionally showed his associates the signs of a neurasthenic anxiety over money that was to darken his last days, he kept this emotional disturbance from his daughers and wife. The great men of Victorian Chicago sometimes lost their way; it was Newberry's tragedy that in the year preceding his death in 1868, while his womenfolk were traveling in Europe, he found himself unable to believe that he remained what he had been for many years, a rich man in possession of extensive properties derived from a lifetime of successful trading. He set out for Europe, and died on board ship, unattended and alone because of his conviction that he could not afford a nurse or companion.

Outward sign of Walter Newberry's prosperity, his wide-porched house stood in spacious grounds at Rush and Ohio streets, with the carriages ready, the horses, the coachman and helpers, and inside the house spacious halls and rooms with books, statues, and pictures. Purposely a good way short of magnificence, this kind of living still went considerably beyond the mere comfort of those said to be "in easy circumstances." Margaret Ayer Barnes and Janet Ayer Fairbank wrote in the 1930s that cultivated Chicagoans of sixty years before kept close ties to the Eastern seaboard, but lived a delightful life with a flavor of its own. Generation handed down to generation such heirlooms as grandmother's Lowestoft tea set, father's first editions of Thackeray, the seed pearl brooch and earrings which were presents of the groom, and always the family pictures, because these people sat for portraits, and often the portraits were by the same Healy who had painted Mrs. John S. Wright in her green riding habit. No American city of the period could have found a better semi-official protraitist than George Peter Alexander Healy, a Bostonian who had met with encouragement from Thomas Sully, made a success in Paris after studying with the Baron Antoine Jean Gros, and placed the impressive canvas "Webster's Reply to Hayne" among the historical works in the Capitol at Washington. In Chicago, Healy painted merchants and bankers in an appropriately institutional style, occasionally making background more interesting than face and figure to the eye of the present time. But Healy painted Chicago women in a personal way, and one loves them on sight. For example, rich and warm beauty lives in his portrait of Mrs. Frederick Dent Grant, daughter-in-law of the President, born Ida Honoré. And Mrs. Edward Tyler Blair, daughter of William McCormick, is a woman one would give a great deal to know, as Healy shows her, with short dark hair and a bouquet in her hands, on the verge of smiling as she sits in her pink Worth gown. And what is the meaning of the haunted look on the lovely face of Mrs. John deKoven? One would like to join these women, if only it were possible, on one of those breezy porches with somebody playing a piano nearby. Most of the diaries and letters by which one might come to know these ladies burned in the fire of October 1871; Julia Newberry's diary survived because she had it with her on a trip to Europe at the time of the fire. But on the blue Chicago ninth of June in 1869, Julia was at home and writing:

"Here I am in the old house where I was born, & where I wish I could always live; it is the dearest place on earth to me, & worth all London Paris & New York put together; Sister & Mother may talk, & say what they like, still I shall persist in my opinion, that there is no place like home."

Julia knew that by the end of summer she would be gone with her mother and sister on another trip to Europe. And she felt an emotion that has troubled all wandering cultivated Chicagoans from that day to this— the desire to be in two places at once. Travel they will, with the money and style and personal confidence to make their way wherever they wish —and yet—"I am writing in what (to me) is the most perfect room I ever was in. My Studio. It fronts South and East, with the most beautiful view of the lake, & the most delicious window, so wide and deep. It is irregular in shape also, & just the right size, with a genuine sky-light, & private stair-case leading down into my dressing room. There are two book-cases, and the loveliest closet; indeed it is just perfection. . . . I don't believe there is another girl in the United States, or even in the world that has a real studio room built for *her*; it really breaks my heart to think of leaving it and going to Europe again. . . . I like Chicago so much, so much better than any other place, & we have such a beautiful home, & it is all associated with Papa, & now to go & leave it all! . .

Two miles south of Julia's old home a different sort of city residence had become fashionable in the Marble Terrace that faced the lake on Michigan Avenue opposite the present site of the Illinois Central station. A block of four-story town houses with party walls, the Terrace provided spacious drawing rooms and libraries on each "parlor floor" behind tall arched entrances at the top of high stoops. In contrast to the Newberry mansion with its big yard, this design would become the standard city house of the late nineteenth century, and although the marble of the Terrace was sandstone, the plan proved satisfactory to such eminent Chicagoans as J. Y. Scammon, P. F. W. Peck, Deacon Bross of the *Tribune*, Tuthill King, John L. Clarke, and Judge Hugh T. Dickey, who stood out as an honest and competent jurist of a sort not always encountered on the Chicago bench. Looking at the Terrace, one missed the feeling of hospitality that emanated from the wide-porched houses on the near North Side, and the *Handbook of Chicago,* published in the early 1860s, reported that "the lofty front had a glittering, heartless appearance, and a stern, unifying grandeur, but no warmth, no geniality." The Terrace caught the attention of a writer named George S. Phillips, who recorded his impressions in 1866: "On one of those dreamy Indian summer afternoons of late autumn, while standing in the elegant salon of one of those palatial residences in Marble Terrace, before a grand French plate mirror, extending from the ceiling to the floor, reflecting the beauties of the lake and sky, and looking like a sea of glass surrounded by a golden shore, we involuntarily exclaimed, If this be not the highest ideal of domestic luxury, where shall wealth or fancy go to find it?" The quotation comes from an advertisement that he wrote for the Wiggers picture frame and looking-glass shop on Randolph Street. Inviting customers to the A. H. Miller jewelry store on Lake Street, Phillips called its doorway "the crystal entrance to some Aladdin's palace where the treasures of earth and sea, refined and polished by cunning workmanship, are all flashing forth their intense splendor." He wrote that patrons might examine "a coronet of pearls, inwoven with a starry way of brilliants, and lying as though it had just fallen from the brow of a princess. . . ." Phillips described the essence of a diamond in Emersonian diction as "the ultimate effect, the idealization, the spiritual evolution of coal, the butterfly escaped from the autumnal touch, the realization of the coal's highest being." And he wrote that opal was "the moonlight queen of the kingly diamond." In 1867 Phillips published the best piece of verse written in Chicago up to that time. He called it "Silence":

> Old Time was dead, and the pale hours lay
> In his tomb around him solemnly,
> And earth, like a vision, had passed away,
>
> And not a wreck of its beauty stood;
> For mountain and meadow, field and flood,
> And all that was bright and fair and good
>
> Had turned to a shapeless void again;
> And Death, whose arm had its thousands slain
> Had broken his sceptre and ceased to reign.
>
> And there was none o'er this scene to mourn
> Save one pale maiden whose locks were torn,
> And whose tearful eyes and looks forlorn
>
> Spoke more than her voiceless tongue could tell
> Of all that the lovely earth befell,
> Ere she heard the voice of its funeral knell.

And she did weep, though her lips were sealed,
And though naught she felt could be revealed,
And though her heart with its grief concealed

Was ready to burst! She wandered on
O'er the fields of space, all sad and lone,
For *Silence* knew that she wept alone.

Early one morning in December 1868 Frederick Cook of the *Times*
found Phillips unconscious in front of his boarding house on Wabash Avenue. The doctors at Mercy Hospital said Phillips had two broken ribs and
a case of chronic undernourishment complicated by acute alcoholic poi-
soning. He became delirious and died two hours later in a straitjacket, with
Cook the one friend at his bedside to speak an epitaph, "He was always
the gentleman."

The death of this talented hack caused little comment in Chicago,
where persons in less trouble than Phillips were known to climb the railing
of the Clark Street bridge and drop into the oily river. Members of the
banking and mercantile aristocracy, however, had lived free of ordinary
anxieties and troubles throughout the Civil War. And in the years that
followed, these men became convinced that if Chicago lacked any
amenity of civilized life, the town could supply it as soon as the need
identified itself and means to meet it could be defined. One desirable thing
that Chicagoans had observed on trips to New York was the Union Club,
an all-male social organization modeled on older institutions in London,
and supplying a meeting place for members with an ample number of
deep leather chairs, whist tables, fireplaces, newspapers, and deferential
attendants who would quickly fetch drinks, tea, toast, or sandwiches to any
part of the building. The grill room offered a hearty menu plus inexhaustible stocks of wine, liquor, and cigars. Furthermore, the governors of the
Union carefully limited membership to good safe fellows of high commercial and social rating, though a cad named James Gordon Bennett* did
manage to get in. But on the whole, the Union listed a well-behaved and
like-minded membership who found it a strong tower against women,
foreigners, cranks, and process-servers. Having been entertained at the
Union Club often enough to see how it worked, a number of Chicagoans
decided it was time their town had such a place. A nucleus existed in
something called the Dearborn Club, a loose organization of fifty or sixty
men who had started meeting toward the end of the war to play cards in

*Bennett was ostracized for using the drawing-room fireplace of a prominent family as a
urinal during a New Year's reception.

rooms on State Street opposite the Palmer House. This group moved to the Portland Block on the southwest corner of Washington and Dearborn streets, where the club went bankrupt and closed in the fall of 1868. Those who had visited the Union saw that Chicago needed something more than a few hired rooms for the founding of a gentlemen's club; and in June 1869, forty men of standing appointed a committee to invite one hundred citizens to contribute $100 each as founding members of a new organization. After some missionary work the idea caught on and 101 men signed the roster, the last place going to Samuel L. Keith. A small group including David and George Gage, Wirt Dexter, George Pullman, General Anson Stager, and C. B. Farwell met preliminary expenses by lending $500 each, the money later returned with interest. With this capital in hand, the club historian Edward T. Blair recorded that subscribers met on May 1, 1869, "to settle any doubt as to the new organization's character by electing as president a gentleman who was considered representative of all that was refined and elevated in the community." He was E. B. McCagg, who had married a daughter of William Ogden, entered law practice with J. Y. Scammon, and built up one of the largest real estate fortunes in town. A world traveler, Mr. McCagg was the owner of a fine private library, and "a type not too common in Chicago at that time."

For its first home the Chicago Club rented the Farnam mansion on Michigan Avenue between Adams and Jackson streets. Operating on a policy of "no dogs, Democrats, women, or reporters," with membership doubling within a year, the governors established a branch for quick lunches at Washington and La Salle streets, while at the main house, a number of those beings only described as clubmen soon materialized. These men habitually played whist in the afternoons, and it was remarked that Chicago like older cities now could boast of male idlers other than tramps and derelicts. But most of the whist players looked in at countingrooms on the way home between five and six. Among the dignitaries of the card room Granville Kimball stood out with his courtly old-fashioned ways and long-tailed coat that almost swept the ground. Colonel Lucius Tilton of the Illinois Central came frequently to the club and welcomed every chance to drink a toddy with a fellow member, or to cap a story by Colonel Henry Farrar, a former Bostonian. Surprisingly frank in tales told outside the clubrooms, Edward Blair recorded that Dr. Cornelius S. Eldridge could become bad-tempered when booze took him, a failing that members excused because he had seen horrible slaughter in the Civil War. Members avoided the crockery merchant Arthur Burley, a mean drunk. Levi Leiter could become contentious, and his voice was loud. George Pullman insisted on winning all arguments; perhaps because of his $500 underwriting,

Pullman habitually allowed his club bills to run overdue, and he saved the printed notices from the treasurer calling on him to pay or be suspended, which are still to be seen among his papers in the Manuscript Room of the Chicago Historical Society. The founding committee offered to admit General Phil Sheridan without charge, but he insisted on paying up like the rest, not knowing that Blair had subjected him to an inspection as keen as Julia Newberry's. The club historian observed that Sheridan had a short thick body and neck, a bullet-shaped, disproportionately large head, and a complexion scarlet from good living. The general had a heavy jaw under high cheekbones and little squinty eyes—all in contrast, wrote Blair, to an agreeable and modest manner. Julia had been severe in her judgment of Sheridan's "Um—yes," for he was patient with bores, and the automatic small murmur was nothing more than his signal that he was listening. Early in his career as a clubman, General Sheridan established a favorable reputation for being quick to sign drink chits, and became known as a good touch, ever willing to extend a small loan to one or another of the moochers who had managed to gain entrance at this well-heeled fraternity. Blair left a number of memorable snapshots, such as his picture of the sawed-off, pugnacious Samuel Johnston, the Samuellino Jonstonio of home opera; and the characterization of an unnamed founding member whose urbanity may be estimated from his reprimand by the committee for drawing a pistol at the card table. This argues a certain heartiness and innocent virility, which continued for some time, as there is no denying that heavy-duty spittoons are to be seen in photographs of the clubrooms taken in 1910. But on the whole, the atmosphere of the Chicago Club was gracious, in the style of its New York model, and if the inmates needed an example of conduct, they could always find it in Edward J. Minot, noted judge of food and wine and the scion of an old Boston family, whose faultless manners testified to his membership in the Somerset Club and the Boston Anthenaeum. Another example of good form was set by Henry R. Pierson, president of the Chicago & Northwestern Railway, who had come from Albany and was one of the few college graduates on the club's first roster.

John S. Wright had little time for club life, and in the late 1860s he faced the most severe financial troubles of his career. The tightness of money that came in 1867 forced Wright to assign valuable holdings to his brothers, and he no longer commanded respect in the counting houses; he began to pass hours along the riverside, disregarding the noisome conditions of the water, and meditating on larger meanings in the scene of lumberyards, honest shapes of warehouses and grain elevators, and chimneys pouring black smoke into the air. And soon, as always when caught in a corner, Wright grasped his pen and set it marching across paper, planning to write what was intended to be another promotion circular, but growing, as a frenzy of work gripped its author, into a volume of 432 closely printed pages in small type. The tempo of the town had moved him, for he could see the city growing all around with the speed it had shown in the 1850s. Businessmen more conservative than Wright predicted that at least 300,000 citizens would be counted in the census of 1870; but he thought the total might well be 50,000 more. In any event, Wright was correct in theorizing that the rate of growth was the most important statistical factor, and in this Chicago had surpassed St. Louis by 35 percent since 1860, and during the same period had grown nine times as fast as Cincinnati, fading Queen City of the West. In writing this work, Wright needed no learned collaborator, and scratched away alone at a mound of business reports, railroad timetables, stockholders' bulletins, financial publications, letters, atlases, maps, manufacturers' catalogues, shipping schedules, records of public proceedings, and statistical abstracts of every kind. What came out was a hymn to the city that Wright loved, with a title page announcing:

CHICAGO
PAST, PRESENT, FUTURE
relations to
THE GREAT INTERIOR
AND TO THE CONTINENT

Wright addressed this account of the past and vision of the future to the Board of Trade, and wrote in his preface that "Nature never makes a city, and no human institution is more artificial, depending upon a conjunction of causes, which, however liberally bestowed by nature, lies dormant until operated by human effort and ingenuity. . . ." Referring to an epigraph in which he quoted the passage from the Sermon on the Mount about the city set on a hill, Wright continued, "The superficial observer, it is true, considers the notorious flatness of site only emblematic of the flatness awaiting Chicago, when the exuberance of adolescence shall have spent its power. . . ." But the surrounding prairie supplied something, Wright pointed out, that did not strike the eye, for out there lay the exact spot where a drop of rain might fall and "half of it run its ocean-course to the Gulf of St. Lawrence, the other half to the Gulf of Mexico, indicating the propriety of the idea that we here unite the Great Valley of the Rivers with the Great Valley of the Lakes in indissoluble bonds." Wright besought the Board, therefore, "to invite Consideration of the Obligations of City and Citizens in view of the unparalleled Benefits Showed by God and Country."

Though sincere in his lofty approach, Wright took a realistic tone when he said "To make money, not to improve our morals, every man of us came to Chicago." He added that too much puffery had been written; in contrast, Wright avoided bragging and tried to make even his criticisms practicable suggestions for improving the city. He thus earned the distinction of being the first publicist to suggest the linking of boulevards and parks which resulted in the belt of green Chicago wears today. "I foresee a time not very distant," said Wright, "when Chicago will need for its fast-increasing population a park, or parks, in each side of the city. Of these parks I have a vision. They are all improved and connected by a wide avenue, extended to and along the Lake Shore on the north and south, and so surround the city with a magnificent chain of parks and parkways that have no equal in the world." Impressed by this splendid conception and the array of facts and figures, the Board of Trade promised Wright to subsidize several thousand copies of *Chicago, Past, Present, Future,* but soon backed out of the deal and left him holding the unsold books. Without the promised help in meeting printers' bills, Wright suffered the pain of seeing his work neglected. Fifty years would pass before Wright received credit for his vision of parks and boulevards; recognition came when Hobart Chatfield-Taylor directed attention to the forgotten Wright in 1917 and named him prophet of the prairies.

It may be that even more gratitude for the Chicago park system should go to alderman Laurence Proudfoot, savior of Lincoln Park. When Proudfoot joined the City Council in 1865, he found that boodlers had introduced a resolution to sell a large piece of land north of and adjoining what is now known as North Avenue. Nearby since 1835 had lain a sixty-acre cemetery; in 1860, the council had prohibited further burials there, and relatives had taken most of the bodies away, leaving a cultivated tract among sand dunes and pine forests sloping up from the shore. An additional 120 acres was to be bought by the city, and Lake (now Lincoln) Park made its appearance on the map. It still existed only on paper when Proudfoot came to the council, for most of the aldermen had succumbed to greed and bribery, and the land which made the park we have today, with its blend of landscaping and wilderness, almost fell into the grasp of butchers who wanted to chop it up and crowd it with streets and houses. Proudfoot understood how land prices could explode once the pressure started, and he knew that at a certain point the additional acreage marked for Lake Park would become too expensive for the city to buy, which was what the boodlemen counted on to lend a semblance of practicality to their scheme of unloading the cemetery site which had already been acquired. In opposition Proudfoot rallied the newspapers to support the policy that "We must set up our parks now, before the land becomes too dear to be bought." The boodlemen outvoted him in Council, but celebrated victory too soon, for Proudfoot went to Springfield, where legislators had been known to pass laws simply because the Cook County bosses opposed them. As many a Chicago reformer learned to do, Proudfoot manipulated downstate prejudice to good ends, and on February 18, 1865, brought back a bill establishing the North Park Commission and protecting public land from Oak Street Beach to Montrose Harbor for all time to come. The councilmen later gave the park its present name during some transport of idolatry for Lincoln; but it is a monument to Laurence Proudfoot.

Many blocks of buildings five stories high gave the handsome effect of metropolitan uniformity to large parts of the city by 1870, while numerous church spires and the romantic Water Tower on Chicago Avenue set off the skyline. With their elegant stone or cast iron fronts, the larger business blocks reminded visitors of Paris, and forests of masts at the heads of downtown streets brought comparison with Liverpool and Limehouse to mind. Among other new structures stood the Opera House on Washington Street, built by a promoter named Uranus H. Crosby from plans drawn by William W. Boyington, who also designed the Water Tower. Crosby invested $600,000 and saw his Opera House completed in the last year of the war. He postponed the opening performance in April 1865 because of the murder of President Lincoln, but when they finally entered the place, all members of the first night audience agreed that in Crosby's Opera House, Chicago had the finest theater in the country. On the ground floor, Kinsley's Restaurant and the salesrooms of the W. W. Kimball Piano Company set off the two-story arched entrance to the Grand Promenade which led to the auditorium. This interior had been built on so large a scale and had such an air of richness that the city rocked with astonishment a year after the opening when Crosby announced a plan to offer the building as first prize in a lottery. The promoter explained that he had put so much money into making his Opera House the most superb on earth that he had run out of cash, and a lottery appeared to be the shortest and quickest way back to solvency. Some wondered why Crosby did not consult bankers or such capitalists as William Ogden or Potter Palmer, who was turning his attention to the development of downtown Chicago. Crosby stated that Chicago had always liked to take chances, and he now proposed to offer the sporting and business public a chance such as would never come again—the possibility of owning a magnificent Opera House for an investment of only five dollars, the price of a ticket in his lottery. In addition to the building itself, Crosby promised to give 305 other prizes from the works of art with which he had adorned the place. These included the famous bust of Lincoln by Leonard Wells Volk, a Chicago sculptor who rivaled Healy in portraiture, and had also produced the colossal Douglas monument. Two landscapes by George Inness appeared on the list, but for the most part the prizes were works of genre painting in a familiar style such as "Scene in the Tyrol," "Selecting the Bridal Dress," and the companion pieces "Strawberries" and "Raspberries."

Many syndicates of sporting men took shape in the saloons, a senior bartender or the owner himself acting as manager, to make substantial buys in Crosby's lottery. The pools formed in this way would take as many as a thousand tickets in one order, under such names as Bottom Dollar, Bohemian Club, Kiss Me Quick, General Sheridan, General Grant, Dead Broke, and Bloody Tub. On January 21, 1867, a crowd of syndicate men and individual ticket buyers filled the Opera House to witness the drawing. The *Tribune* claimed to have information that Crosby had sold $850,-000 worth of tickets representing 170,000 chances for the grand prize. Crosby refused to tell how much he had taken in, but said he retained ownership of 25,000 unsold tickets. A committee of businessmen supervised the proceedings, which continued with increasing suspense as winners claimed the 305 art works. At last came the drawing for first prize, and the Chairman announced that the winning ticket was No. 58,600. Certain newsmen had predicted that whatever its number, this ticket would prove to be held by Uranus H. Crosby, but they were wrong. Referring to the master list, the chairman told the audience that the winning number and the grand prize belonged to a gentleman who was not present, Colonel Abraham Hagerman Lee of Prairie du Rocher, Illinois. Reporters could find no one who had ever heard of Colonel Lee, and there was no telegraph office in Prairie du Rocher, 275 miles downstate. Next day, Uranus Crosby announced that he had telegraphed instructions for a St. Louis lawyer to send a messenger spurring out on the wintry roads to Colonel Lee's village. Crosby's next piece of news revealed that the winner was coming to Chicago, but under secrecy as to his movements. When reporters caught up with Lee a few days later in a Chicago hotel, they found him to be a picturesque former riverboat pilot and war veteran, with startling news to impart: he had sold the opera house back to Crosby for $200,000 in cash. The report of this deal aroused skepticism, and some of the syndicate men began to discuss the technical problems

[97]

that might be encountered in hanging Uranus Crosby to a lamp-post. The promoter thereupon turned the theater over to his brother, and left town.

A short time before the raffling of Crosby's Opera House, another impressive building had come to completion nearby, at the northeast corner of State and Washington streets. This structure, the marble-fronted new Field & Leiter store, testified to the progress of its operators in commercial Chicago, and also showed the financial genius of Potter Palmer. Both Field and Palmer had come a long way since the days in the 1850s when they had bowed and scraped before the quality on Lake Street. Indeed, Palmer had made so bold as to declare that Lake Street should no longer be the choice shopping street of the city. He decided that State Street could be developed into the most important retail and general business thoroughfare in town, and began to buy property along its length, taking William Ogden and other financiers into some of the deals as he planned and bought. Meanwhile, Field had been prospering in a wholesale and retail drygoods house as an associate of John Villiers Farwell, rich and pious patron of Dwight L. Moody and the Young Men's Christian Association. Marshall Field then established the retail store as a separate concern in partnership with Levi Leiter, capitalized at $890,000, of which Palmer added $450,000 to Field's $260,000, the balance supplied by a few favored investors, thankful for the opportunity to come in. This was no five-dollar raffle; Palmer had paid for the building, with its 145 feet of State Street frontage, and he rented it to Field and Leiter for $50,000 a year. When the store opened on October 2, 1868, the three enterprisers betrayed no anxiety as to the outcome of the investment, each behaving as usual—Leiter barking at underlings, Field in a beautifully cut Prince Albert coat watching the main floor with the coolest look in Chicago. People had already noticed that young Mr. Field's left eye seemed absolutely without expression and some swore it was glass. Not so: it was merely the colder of two cold eyes. As for Potter Palmer, he stayed in the background as he did in all situations that did not directly involve his name.

Palmer's name, however, came to prominence in another enterprise, a seven-story hotel at the southeast corner of State and Monroe streets. Opening after extensive remodeling in March 1871, the "new" Palmer House recognized no rival in luxury and attention to guests' requirements, except perhaps John B. Drake's Tremont House. Potter Palmer was a familiar figure to sporting circles in Chicago; he enjoyed whiskey and cards, drove fast horses, and appeared with good-looking women at racetracks and shows. His manner of life drew little criticism, for like his friends Field and Leiter he had acquired wealth in a way that seemed to benefit the entire community. It was true that riches had come to these men "through the dark iron gate of war," as Joseph Kirkland wrote. But Major Kirkland meant no offense. He himself had gone under fire many times. Nevertheless, he wrote in a deferential tone about rich men who had kept themselves out of the fight while waving flags, cursing rebels, and pocketing gold. The greed and cowardice were obvious, but for some reason the Major never attacked the question of the magic in money, that could transform a profiteering civilian into a personage of authority and dignity, while the penniless combat veteran, unless he went into politics, found himself like Falstaff's broken troopers at the town's end, to beg during life. It was the magic of money that purified the gamy atmosphere around Potter Palmer and made him eligible to court a young lady less than half his age, daughter of a leading family from the West Side. This girl, whose name was Bertha Honoré, combined Southern charm with Chicago vivacity in irresistible style. Her father was the real estate operator Henry M. Honoré of Kentucky, and like all white Southerners not otherwise titled, he bore the rank of colonel. Previous to bringing his family from Louisville to Chicago in 1855, Colonel Honoré had conducted a small hardware business. He made money trading in Chicago lots, and by the time Bertha had passed her twentieth birthday in 1870, people from all three sides of town crowded the Honoré reception on New Year's Day. At this function Bertha and her younger sister Ida made delightful hostesses as they saw to it that everyone got plenty of scalloped oysters, roast turkey, chicken salad, Madeira, and eggnog, while bourbon flowed in the colonel's library. On her return from an Eastern convent school two years before, Bertha had enchanted the guests at her debut. Since that occasion, the girl had sparkled with beauty and charm at the Bachelors' Assembly Balls and the Tremont House concerts, always under chaperonage. She had a large number of admirers, among whom one might have thought the bewhiskered Mr. Palmer unsuitable with his aura of cigars and whiskey, his pouched eyes, and the undeniable rough mileage behind him on his passage through life. With this in mind, Chicago guessed that Palmer must have passed some sort of private scrutiny to gain his place among Bertha's followers, for certain it was that if an improper person had approached the girl, Colonel Honoré would have shot the scoundrel dead. At any rate, the family announced Bertha's engagement to Palmer early in 1871, and they were married on August 11, the bride aged twenty-one, the groom forty-four. It was a fine day in the rainless summer, and not too warm. The seven hundred guests who ate the wedding feast catered by Kinsley formed the first of many large companies that were to assemble for fifty years to honor one of the most appealing characters in the Chicago story, the celebrated, the world-renowned hostess, Mrs. Potter Palmer.

After the Palmer-Honoré wedding, the fine summer of cloudless days and brilliant nights continued, the dry air occasionally moistened when fog rolled in from the lake, to disappear before prevailing westerly winds. Since early in July through the month of September only an inch of rain had fallen on the city of Chicago. By the first days of October, men had begun to speak about the danger of a big fire, and disturbing reports came in from the Northwest. In many places, Chicago drummers traveling in their buggies along country roads had seen grass fires rushing across prairies, and had jettisoned sample cases and lashed horses to escape the storm of fire. In the Michigan and Wisconsin lumber country, millions of blackened stumps on thousands of ruined acres showed where forest fires had burned. There was a great deal too much dry wood in Chicago, masked behind stone and cast iron along the business streets, openly used from floor to roof of most houses in the residential districts.

Joseph Medill warned in the *Tribune* that the city had reached a dangerously combustible state with its "everlasting pine shingles, shams, veneers, stucco and putty." In addition to the danger of pine shingles catching fire, the tarred roofing invited disaster: at noon the pitch would bubble in the sun, seemingly just a degree or two under the level of explosion. Guarding the city, an undermanned fire department had only 48,000 feet of hose, eighteen ladder trucks, and seventeen fire engines. A considerable amount of this equipment was damaged and out of use waiting repair, and under that handicap the fewer than two hundred firemen turned out for thirty alarms in the first week of October, which ended with a fifteen-hour battle on the West Side, where $750,000 worth of property burned in a fire that consumed several warehouses. On the following morning, Sunday, October 8, the watchmen in the Court House tower knew that the men of the department had almost exhausted their strength, without making the city any less likely to crack into flame.

The New England settlers on the near North Side were not the only Chicagoans to maintain cows. Moreover, theirs have been mostly forgotten, while the cow kept by Mrs. Patrick O'Leary of the West Side has become without question the most famous cow in history. The O'Learys were a respectable working family, living on the ground floor at No. 137 DeKoven Street, seven blocks south of Harrison Street and a little under a mile west of the Illinois Central station and the lakefront. Although Lincoln Park lies due north, DeKoven Street qualifies as a West Side address because the Chicago River runs east of it. In the barn behind the

O'Leary cottage, the cow supposedly kicked over a coal-oil lantern and started the great Chicago fire, on the evening of October 8, 1871. The O'Leary family never ceased to deny the story that their cow had been responsible. One of the five children grew to prominence as Big Jim O'Leary, gambler and politician; he said it was true the fire started in the barn, but as the result of tramps or neighborhood boys smoking, a common cause of fires in those days. His mother blamed the carelessness of a neighbor, known to have entered the barn before the fire broke out. There were other explanations, some highly ingenious like that of Ignatius Donnelly, the Wisconsin reformer, who said the entire Middle West had been made combustible because of elements formed in the soil by the passage of a comet thousands of years before. But among all possible causes advanced, Mrs. O'Leary's cow had the strongest appeal to popular imagination and became immortal.

Whatever set it off, the fire covered DeKoven Street in a few minutes; the watchmen at City Hall saw flames in the early dark and immediately signaled out an engine company. Hundreds of citizens also saw the flames and heard the roaring, snapping, and cracking that characterized the fire throughout its course. Some of these men ran to the police telegraph alarm boxes that the authorities had recently installed on a number of corners. You opened the box and confronted a sign reading *Pull Lever, If Gong Does Not Answer, Repeat Call* and a metal arrow on a dial with points marked CALL WAGON—THIEVES—FORGERS—RIOT—DRUNKARD—MURDER—ACCIDENT—VIOLATION OF CITY ORDINANCE—FIGHTING—TEST OF LINE—FIRE. The citizens' alarms reached the tower too late to correct an error the watchmen had made on spotting the fire when they misjudged its location and dispatched a company that had to come more than a mile, although others were closer. But it made no difference in the end.

At eleven-thirty P.M. fire leaped the river and began to devour the South Side. It now seemed likely the entire city would burn and refugees fled west. Little George Ade on his fence eighty miles away in Kentland was not the only child to be wakened because of the fire. Hobart Chatfield-Taylor heard people running in his comfortable West Washington Street home and came downstairs at midnight to find the adults so busy that nobody ordered him back to bed. The eight-year-old boy looked out and saw hundreds of people struggling past, some trying to control frantic horses, others staggering under bundles or helping children and old people along. The gas works had blown up with a sound like all the thunderstorms in the world; the only light in the streets came from red skies to the south and east. Like many in the prosperous neighborhood, Hobart's mother and father opened their house and dispensed food and clothing all night long. They continued this generous work throughout the following day, giving away among other things their son's entire wardrobe including his new velvet party suit, and finally the remaining clothes on his back, wrapping Hobart in a blanket until additional clothing was obtained.

One of Hobart's neighbors was a twelve-year-old girl named Cora Murray, who also enjoyed the boon of avoiding bedtime Sunday night. Cora recorded that her father hurried to his office, and her three big sisters "went to see what they could of the fire with a minister who was visiting Father, and how I longed to go, but I was not old enough to have any fun. But I didn't go to bed anyway. Father came home and said he got his key into the office door, but his clothes caught, and he got out of there with coattails on fire." At her request he gave Cora the office key to keep as a souvenir for her own little girl when she had one. After breakfast the sisters came home and set to work with Cora and two younger brothers digging a hole in the back yard for the piano. They abandoned this work to pack bundles in case they should have to leave in a hurry. Cora took her pillow out of its case and put in her "dear little writing desk," first removing the ink. She added "some books and some tin models for making wax fruit that I thought my sisters would like again some day. It felt pretty knobby, but I was determined to have it ready. Everyone said it would be cold sleeping out on the prairie, so I put on seven petticoats and three dresses."

Cora and her family did not have to join the refugees, for the fire stayed east of the north and south branches of the river except for twenty blocks around its point of origin. The South Side and the business district took the first shock of it, and then early Monday morning fire jumped the main stream of the Chicago River and started up the North Side as fast as a man can run. One may ask how flames could jump water: they did it easily enough because the heat at the core of the fire amounted to more than three thousand degrees Fahrenheit, and generated a gale that hurled burning planks and timbers hundreds of feet to fall on dry, well-tarred roofs that set off the houses by spontaneous combustion.

As they fled, many North Siders made quick decisions about what should be taken along. Children clung to pets and carried birdcages, women snatched up jewel boxes, and men would sometimes take heavy, framed pictures from walls and carry them away. With such an idea in mind as they prepared to leave their house on Illinois Street near Chicago Avenue, Mrs. Dwight L. Moody begged her husband to take his Healy portrait with him. Moody said, "I can't do that, my dear. Suppose I am met on the street by friends in the same plight, and they say, 'Hello, Moody, glad you have escaped; what's that you have saved and cling to so affectionately?'—It would not sound well to reply, 'I've got my own portrait.'" Dwight Moody took his favorite Bible with his personal commentary scribbled in the margins. Another minister compelled to run for his life on the North Side was the celebrated Dr. David Swing of the Fourth Presbyterian Church where the McCormicks worshiped. The Swings retreated in good order, one daughter taking a cat, the other a canary; Dr. Swing entrusted his manuscript case, with several undelivered sermons, to one of his students. Soon the theologue met a young lady who needed help, and abandoned the papers, which were never found. The minister told the young man not to worry about it, for a gentleman must always aid a woman in distress.

Isaac N. Arnold was at home on the near North Side, and gathered his family for flight after a horseman had clattered up Cass Street yelling "The water works are on fire! Run for your lives!" Arnold's young daughter Frederica never forgot the scene, for as the broad piazza where she and her friends had so often played began to burn, and sparks started flying, here came their neighbor Samuel Johnston carrying a tray with decanter and glasses. Johnston said, "We must take one more drink together, Mr. Arnold, before we go."

"It would be most welcome," said Arnold.

"Here's to your very good health," said Johnston, and then everyone had to leave. Frederica spent the following day and night on the beach, pleased at sharing an adventure with grown people, and thankful that she had been able to carry two pet kittens to safety.

Looked after by parents, neighbors, and servants, the children of prosperous North Side families escaped many of the terrors that overwhelmed adults and children alike in the densely populated blocks downtown. Along with crowds of grown people, street boys like Dwight Moody's Rag-Breeches Cadet and Darby the Cobbler joined in looting, and one of these urchins gained immortality by catching the eye of a visitor in town named Alexander Frear, whose account of what he witnessed during the fire has been used by most subsequent writers. As he walked through the tumult on Lake Street, Frear saw "a ragamuffin on the Clark Street bridge who had been killed by a marble slab thrown from a window, with white kid gloves on his hands." Another child impossible to forget is the little girl Frear saw among hundreds of lost children wailing for the parents "whose golden hair, worn loose on her back, caught fire. She ran screaming past me, and someone threw a glass of liquor upon her, which flared up and covered her with a blue flame."

Alexander Frear had been staying at the Sherman House, and his particular concern was the safety of his sister-in-law, as his brother had gone out of town. The sister-in-law had become separated from her children; somehow Frear got her a cab in front of the Sherman House, in which she drove to the house of a relative on the far South Side, where the children turned up in good condition, having been taken to safety in a boat. But Mrs. Frear had been so distracted with anxiety that she lost a satchel containing two gold watches, a medal given to her husband as an officer in the First Wisconsin Volunteers, and two hundred dollars in bills and currency stamps. After sending his sister-in-law to safety, Frear remained in the business district until fire drove everybody over bridges north and west. He noticed that the fire was almost smokeless: when the flames had licked over a building, there was nothing left to blow away. Thousands of rats poured along the gutters, and horses screamed as burning fragments fell on them, breaking from control to stampede in the streets. Gangs of ruffians and their women rushed from dens in neighborhoods below the business quarter, raided saloons and liquor shops, and began systematic looting of the big retail stores, sometimes backing up wagons and filling them as though on legitimate business. The toughs also attacked citizens removing valuables from their homes, and tore cherished clocks, pictures, and articles of apparel from the owners' arms. Frear got a detailed view, for the light was pervasive: "The air filled with the falling embers, and it looked like a snow-storm lit by colored fire." By this light he saw a woman kneeling at Wabash Avenue and Adams Street "with a crucifix held up before her and the skirt of her dress on fire." Around her the mob fought over liquor and merchandise, while an Irishwoman calmly walked through the crowd, leading a goat that was big with young. On the same corner Frear saw "a fellow, standing on a piano, who declared that the fire was the friend of the poor man. He wanted everybody to help himself to the best liquor he could get; and continued to yell from the piano until someone, as drunk as himself, flung a bottle at him and knocked him off it." A few yards away, Frear saw a fireman bathing his head in whiskey while the shouting of terrified or drunken people blended with the sound of disaster—"explosions that followed each other in quick succession on all sides, to the accompaniment of a crackling noise as of an enormous number of dry twigs burning."

Everyone in the business district and adjoining neighborhoods had heard another sound continuously since the first alarms came in just after nightfall. This insistent noise was the tolling of the bell in the Court House tower, which had continued through the fire's uproar. And as the bell beat on, John Van Osdel gathered his plans and ledgers, and forced his way to the newly remodeled Palmer House. Having been construction boss on this job, the architect knew every hall and stairway, and he hurried by the shortest route to the hotel basement, while fire thundered from street to street, closing in on the building. Van Osdel dug a hole in the earth of the basement, put the documents down there, then covered the pit with layers of damp clay.* The matter of preserving records was vital to a city that existed on commercial credit and the ownership of property. Essential Chicago might live on without houses and business blocks, so long as there remained records of its mortgages, borrowings, lendings, suits, titles, deeds, and ownerships. But lacking this paper, the material city could hardly be rebuilt. This made significant the moment at five minutes past two in the morning of October 9, when the tolling from the Court House tower stopped, and the bell came crashing to the ground. Within half an hour, the Court House itself had disappeared, and as Major Kirkland wrote, "every scrap and vestige of the Public Records of Cook County had vanished into thin air and ashes."

The business structure of Chicago survived because of private records in the keeping of specialists known as abstract men or conveyancers, most of the business being handled by Chase Brothers, Jones & Sellers, and Shortall & Hoard. Each of these firms had a set of books, with indexes of property owners, lot records, and most important of all, the title abstracts which were brief statements of the deeds relating to each piece of property, copied from the official records. The conveyancers maintained their offices near the Court House, and by eleven o'clock it could be seen that they would be destroyed in a few hours. And it was John G. Shortall of Shortall & Hoard, with a few loyal employees, who met the emergency in a way that put most of the city's businessmen in their debt beyond any payment of money. Hurrying uptown from his home on South Michigan Avenue in his velveteen house coat, Shortall found the awnings on fire at the windows of his ground floor offices at Washington and Clark Streets. Unlike Mr. Murray, he had forgotten his key, and had to kick the door open. Then he ripped down the awnings, and began to stack ledgers on tables, as several faithful clerks ran in through the burning door and joined him. Realizing there would be no use in taking further risks without a horse and wagon, Shortall went into the street to look for a drayman, for a few liverymen were still cruising the business district, offering their services at piratical prices to looters and honest men alike, first come first served. At this point J. Y. Scammon came along on horseback, and Shortall said, "Mr. Scammon, I am afraid we are all going to burn up." "I fear so,"

*The records survived, and Van Osdel's method of preservation suggested a system of fireproofing that is still in use.

[105]

Scammon replied, and galloped up the street. The next man Shortall recognized in the crowd was James W. Nye of the Hibbard & Spencer hardware firm. Together they hauled down the reins of a horse whose driver had an empty wagon. The man objected to picking up a load until James Nye drew a revolver. The clerks rushed out with their arms full of ledgers, and when they had filled the wagon they saw that it held only one fifth of the records.

"We'll get this much away anyhow," said Shortall, and Nye jumped on top of the books and put the revolver against the driver's neck. Then a transfer man named John L. Stockton appeared, driving a large, double-teamed wagon, which he put at Shortall's service. Again the clerks flew at the smaller wagon, this time to unload it; Shortall called off the volunteer gunman and dismissed the driver with five dollars for his trouble. The Stockton truck afforded room for every book and file in the offices of Shortall & Hoard; as they piled on the last ledger, they heard the crashing of the Court House bell from floor to floor. With Shortall, Nye, and the clerks hurrying alongside to beat off drunkards and looters, and to extinguish sparks, the wagon moved out. The men worked their way east and south, and at last reached Shortall's house, where they unloaded the records and stacked them in the hall, library and parlor.

Meanwhile, Shortall's partner had been trying to reach the office, but had not been able to get within three blocks of it. He then headed for Shortall's house, where his partner's wife opened the door. She said, "Mr. Hoard, won't you step inside?"—and an overpowering emotion struck him when he saw the records stacked along the walls. In one sense, Chicago was there, safe and sound.

John Shortall had gone back to the business district to do what he could at Hibbard & Spencer in return for James Nye's help. Worn out by his efforts here, Shortall finally started home on foot, again heading toward the lakefront before turning south. He stopped for a moment at the doorstep of the Western News Company on State Street, and later recalled that "there it was, for the first time, that I lost my nerve." Only a block away, he saw "walls crumble with heat, that seemed to melt, slowly, steadily; one could see them moving in the process of disintegration, and presently sink helplessly down. . . ." The energies released with such terrifying force raged up the city for almost four miles, and on the North Side only the Walton Street house of Mahlon D. Ogden remained standing. Rain came late Monday night, and by Tuesday afternoon the ruins had cooled sufficiently for officials and curiosity seekers to enter the burned districts. And Alexander Frear observed that "standing on a slight elevation at State and Madison Streets, say the height of an omnibus, one could see the trees in

Lincoln Park, two and one half miles away, with everything in the intervening space utterly destroyed."

The burning of Chicago supplied a topic for hundreds of books, articles, lectures, and sermons, and preachers told congregations that the fire had been a visitation aroused by the wickedness that flourished in the city. One minister on whom the disaster made a memorable impression was the Rev. Dr. Edward Payson Roe, who found inspiration for one of the largest selling novels ever published, *Barriers Burned Away.* The fire had scarcely cooled before this novel appeared, which makes one suspect that Roe had started his tale some time before October 8 and added the fire, which does not break out until page 395 of a 487-page book. But the author makes good use of the fire after he gets it started. In one scene Miss Brown, daughter of a rich brewer, offers money to a truckman for the rescue of her maid from a burning house. " 'Who wants yer thousand dollars?' replied Bill Cronk's gruff voice. 'D' ye suppose we'd hang out here over the bottomless pit for any such trifle as that? We want to save the gal!' " Next, Miss Brown recognizes Cronk's companion as Dennis Fleet, hero of the novel, and asks, " 'How can we ever repay you?' "

" 'By learning to respect honest men, even though they are not rich, Miss Brown.' "

Shortly after this Cronk raids a liquor shop, and Fleet knocks the bottle from his hand. Cronk is furious until he sees a falling wall kill a drunkard too besotted to get himself to safety, and soliloquizes, " 'What a cussed old mule I was to kick up so. Look here, Bill Cronk, you just p'int out of this fiery furnace. You know your failin', and there's too long and black a score agin you in t'other world for you to go tonight.' "

The heroine of this novel shared Miss Brown's error of failing to recognize honest merit. She was Christine Ludolph, niece of a wealthy German, and she had looked down on Fleet for being nearly penniless, though an artist and of good family. In spite of Christine's haughtiness, Fleet hurries to her North Side mansion on the night of the fire. He finds her unable to leave because a servant has run away and there is no one to help her get dressed; and in a daring scene, the hero plays lady's maid and puts the heroine into a costume suitable for fleeing from a holocaust. During the rest of the night and the following day, Christine's eyes are opened to Dennis Fleet's good qualities: he thrashes ruffians, comforts children, reassures old people, and finds the exhausted heroine a bed in an abandoned grave in the old Lincoln Park cemetery. Next day Christine turns into a Florence Nightingale among the homeless people, and reveals that her uncle, who has died in the fire, had exaggerated the family's importance. When Dennis asks if she still intends to claim her European title as the

Baroness Ludolph, Christine replies, " 'All that nonsense has perished as utterly as this my former home. My ancestral estate in Germany is but a petty affair, and mortaged beyond its real worth by my deceased uncle. All I possess, all I value, is in this city. Mr. Fleet, you see before you a simple American girl.' " Dennis then asks if there is hope, and "With a little cry of ecstasy, like the note of joy that a weary bird might utter as it flew into its nest, she put her arm around his neck and buried her face in his shoulder and said:

" 'No *hope* for you Dennis, but perfect *certainty*, for now EVERY BARRIER IS BURNED AWAY!' "

For all the success of Roe's novel, no barriers between rich and poor, or separating one class from another, can be said to have come down in the Chicago fire. Brick and wood were the walls that fell, turned to rubble across four square miles, making 100,000 persons homeless, and destroying some eighteen thousand buildings, including all the hotels, theaters, and commercial structures of the business district. The authorities found two hundred and fifty bodies in the ruins, and in addition, about that number of people died without trace, vaporized at inner parts of the fire. The Board of Trade estimated property loss at $200,000,000—in those days an almost inconceivable amount of money—which was not all covered by insurance. In some cases, fine-print contracts absolved the insurance companies, or they went out of business rather than pay. Nevertheless, the Chicago mercantile community seemed to find something bracing and stimulating about the disaster, as though clean slates came with empty cash boxes, and for once in history a city had a chance to reap a profit in the future from errors of the past. That was how John S. Wright reacted, and he saw it all; he was at his office on Washington Street that Sunday evening. With his wife visiting in the East he had taken the opportunity to work all day, and around half past eight he propped up his shoeless feet for a nap, which was disturbed by unusual noises outside. He then set out to follow the fire, marveling at "the grandeur of that immense sheet of flame." Early next day Wright met D. H. Horton, the publisher, and impressed him by "walking through the ruins like a man in a garden on a morning in June."

Horton said, "Well, Wright, what do you think *now* about the future of Chicago?"

Wright replied, "I'll tell you what it is, Horton. Chicago will have more men, more money, more business within five years than she would have had without this fire."

"Half of Chicago is in ashes," wrote Julia Newberry in her diary, "it is too awful to believe, too dreadful to think about." She was in Rome and the date was October 13. Julia wrote, "Not a thing was saved from our house, not a thing. . . . Who could have dreamt that when I drove away from the house on that beautiful June morning in 1870, that I saw it, & all my Chicago for the last time; if but one or two houses were burned, but they are all gone, all! . . . Papa bought the land, Papa built the house, Papa planted the trees, Papa lived there . . . he died far away from us in mid ocean, with no one to care for him when he needed it utterly, no one to learn his last wishes, no one to love him; & now with all that the few traces of him are swept away for ever."

Julia Newberry never came back. Lingering in Italy, she caught the treacherous Roman fever and died on April 4, 1876. By that time her native city had rebuilt itself on such a scale that Julia would have had a hard time recognizing the place. And so perhaps it was better, after all, that this gentle Chicagoan died in Rome, like Daisy Miller.

5

Field, McCormick, Pullman, and Palmer

THE ENERGIES CHICAGO PACKED WITHIN ITS BORDERS HAD EXPLOD-
ed in the great fire, and the rebuilding came with equally dramatic swift-
ness. "The city smolders," wrote Ella Bradley Ward to her brother at
Dartmouth College, and while she wrote, her husband was resuming
banking operations in a tent. Obtaining money in this emergency presented less of a problem than some had feared. A week passed before cash
money came in from Eastern banks, but the kind of money that is represented by marks in ledgers continued to exist, as did the notional money
that men created when they shook hands on deals and trusted one another
for payments in the future. The famous "baked banknotes" made their
appearance when businessmen broke open the few safes that had not
oxidized, and found something that had been paper money, a material
between ash and dust. They boxed up this detritus, which approximated
what the paper would have turned into after the passage of three or four
million years, and sent it to Washington. Working like archaeologists of the
future, Treasury experts estimated the baked money's value, and sent new
bills to Chicago in return.

Although nearly everything of value in the burned area had turned to
ashes, men of property feared looting after the fire had ended. Allan
Pinkerton reflected their feelings in a memorandum to watchmen and
private police: "Any person stealing any property under my charge, or
attempting to break open the safes, as the men cannot make arrests at the

present time, they shall kill the persons by my order. No mercy shall be shown them, but death shall be their fate."

The ferocity of Pinkerton's manifesto helped to sow a crop of rumors that criminals had invaded Chicago, arsonists had started more fires, and vigilantes had hanged incendiaries and looters. Newspapers printed the sensational stories, and some contemporary historians followed the press in recording outbreaks of lawlessnessesss and lynching that did not take place. In the present day Robert Cromie, most reliable modern historian of the fire, tells of the one street shooting and death known to have resulted from the catastrophe. This affair grew from the calling of troops to the city, a measure instigated by General Phil Sheridan, who suggested to Mayor Mason that federal forces should be summoned to protect public works and reassure the citizens, although the people were calm now that there was little left to steal and no fire to run from. Nevertheless, Sheridan wired for troops to the Secretary of War, William Worth Belknap, a man who was to resign from office a few years later under charges of malfeasance. Sheridan told Belknap that the fire was a national calamity, and in the Secretary's name proceeded to call out Army detachments from Omaha, Jeffersonville, and St. Louis. After a week, Mayor Mason put the city under martial law with Sheridan commanding. On the previous day Governor John M. Palmer had received a message from General Anson Stager, an executive of the Western Union Telegraph Company, to the effect that Chicago lay at the mercy of thieves and hoodlums. Palmer also heard the rumors that citizens were shooting arsonists in the streets, and he dispatched militia to Chicago, arriving early Wednesday five hundred strong, with a battery of field guns. Meanwhile, seven hundred federal troops had entered the city, and General Sheridan reported to Mayor Mason: "I am happy to state that no case of outbreak of disorder has been reported. No authenticated case of incendiarism has reached me, and the people of the city are calm, quiet, and well-disposed."

Carpenters had been hammering and sawing night and day to complete enough temporary shelter by October 17 for all homeless families not taking refuge with relatives, friends, or volunteer hosts, and the city appeared to be in good order. The Governor at Springfield now addressed Mayor Mason with acerbity. "It has occasioned me the profoundest mortification," said Palmer, "that you failed to inform me of the necessity, in your judgement, for the employment of military force for the protection of the city; and it has pained me quite as deeply that you thought it proper, without consultation with me, to have practically abdicated your functions as Mayor. Happily there is no necessity, either real or imaginary, for the longer continuation of this anomalous state of affairs. The U.S. troops are now in Chicago in violation of the law. Every act of the officers and soldiers of the United States Army that operates to restrain or control the people, is illegal, and their presence in the city—except for the purposes of the United States—ought to be no longer continued." On the night of October 18, Colonel Thomas W. Grosvenor, the public prosecutor, was walking home at midnight after visiting Judge Augustus Banyon at his house on Harrison Street. Grosvenor had reached University Place and Cottage Grove Avenue when a nineteen-year-old sentry called on him to halt and declare himself. The young recruit, whose name was Thomas Treat, had been signed for twenty-days' service in an outfit with the anomalous title of First Regular Chicago Volunteers, and had never handled a gun before. He shot Colonel Grosvenor dead after words passed between them. Firemen from a nearby engine company took Grosvenor home, and next day the news caused tremendous indignation in Chicago. The *Times* denounced Sheridan as an "imperial satrap" and the Police Board protested to Mayor Mason that there were too many armed patrols marching around the city. The *Tribune* defended Treat as a soldier doing his duty, but this editorial stand had no effect on Governor Palmer, who said he would seek indictments against Mason, Sheridan, and Treat. Although the coroner's jury brought in a verdict of murder, Treat went free and nothing further was done about the killing of Thomas Grosvenor on Cottage Grove Avenue by a trooper, however temporary, in the United States Army. The incident brought martial law to an end, even though Medill and some others urged Sheridan to keep four companies in battle array, and the General bucked their request up to President Grant. Governor Palmer also appealed to Grant, who replied that Sheridan had been ordered to do nothing that violated either the Constitution or the laws of Illinois. Sheridan's soldiers remained in town until just before Christmas. Apparently they behaved like troops anywhere, for a committee of legislators reviewing acts of violence arising from the results of the fire, during the soldiers' occupation, found that only one disturbance had *not* been instigated or committed by the U.S. troopers. However, an influential group among the rulers of Chicago wanted the soldiers at hand, and supported them even when they made things unpleasant for ordinary folk. In a typical occurrence, a policeman arrested four troopers for terrorizing citizens, only to find himself hauled up on misconduct charges; he was acquitted when the main witness for the prosecution, Sheridan himself, failed to appear.

Chicago needed the financial help of Eastern bankers on her account books rather than the military hindrance of drunken soldiers in her streets. And this help came promptly enough to the leading businessmen, who kept their credit and their holdings of land beneath the ruins and ashes unimpaired, thanks to John Shortall and the others who saved the records of Chicago real estate. But the city did not recover by its own efforts alone: the story of destruction touched generous impulses, and contributions for the relief of Chicago began coming in from all over the world. Gifts of money reached a total of five million dollars, the equivalent of perhaps a billion in the currency of one hundred years later. Of this sum, people in foreign countries gave nearly $1,000,000—half of it from England, and $145.91 from Russia. In addition to cash, donors sent food, clothing, and supplies, including tools for men and sewing machines for women. A gift indicating sensitivity in its originator came in the form of five hundred books for the Chicago Public Library; the project was started by the English writer Thomas Hughes, a member of the Christian Socialist party, and author of *Tom Brown's Schooldays*. In Chicago some found themselves uncomfortable in the presence of generosity and said that poor people enjoyed undeserved benefits after the fire. It was true that relief payments continued until 1876, when the money finally gave out. And no doubt the administering of relief brought its problems. A Chicago businessman wrote to a lady in Philadelphia, suggesting that she send dresses only to people known to her who would "give them to needy persons rather than to relief committees who are unduly influenced by the poorer classes, [including] those who are not deserving, were not burned out, the scum of society, who always push themselves forward in such cases." There was a feeling of guilt in the air: and it oppressed many Chicagoans such as the merchant James W. Milner, who wrote on October 14 to an Eastern friend that "the fate of Gomorrha has come upon the city."

Despite the anxieties that statements like Mr. Milner's implied, the rebuilding of Chicago took place with great rapidity: within three years the scars had disappeared, and the business district stood new and complete within twelve months. Even before the restoration of gas lighting, and the construction of new theaters and concert halls, Chicagoans again were satisfying their esthetic hungers; and early in the winter of 1872, Mrs. Edward Blair joined the audience that packed a hall on Twenty-Second Street "where the stage alone was lighted and that with candles." They had gathered to hear the Norwegian violinist Ole Bull: "With his grand figure, his noble head and beautiful white hair, he came forward, gave us a bow of old-fashioned courtesy and a benign smile, lifted his violin to his shoulder, laid his cheek against it, and filled the world with music."

John Van Osdel dug up his ledgers before the earth could cool in what had been the Palmer House basement. Those books remained in use until Van Osdel died in 1891 at the age of eighty, and today they give a clear idea of architectural costs in the rebuilding of Chicago.

[113]

Van Osdel's fee for preparing plans, specifications, and detailed drawings for "Plain Wholesale Stores and Warehouses" was one and one half percent of the total cost, plus another one and one half percent if he was to superintend construction. For "Retail Stores, Plain Dwellings and Public Buildings," he charged the same superintending fee, but asked two and one half percent for the designs. If the job was a "Court or School House" the client could choose between the Greek and Italian styles at two percent, but for plans in the Gothic, Norman, or Romanesque manner the designing fee rose to three percent, a price that also applied to "First Class or isolated dwellings requiring elaborate details." Van Osdel's accounts show that he subcontracted the carpentry, painting, wrought and cast iron work, plumbing, gas fitting, roofing, draining, masonry and brick work, plastering and stone cutting. Campaigning on a platform of stringent fireproofing regulations, Joseph Medill won election as Mayor. However, Van Osdel's observation of the way baked clay protected his records had more to do with preventing another big fire than anything Medill accomplished at City Hall. And when his term ended, Medill went back to the *Tribune,* where he bought full control on the strength of a loan from Marshall Field; meanwhile, Van Osdel continued to study the properties of terra cotta (cooked earth) and found that the material had engineering as well as esthetic values. Van Osdel called for floor arches of hollow tile in his plans for the new Kendall Building to replace the burned structure at the southwest corner of North Dearborn and West Washington Streets; and terra cotta partitions were used here for the first time. Ahead of the Kendall Building in completion, and typical of the swift rebuilding to follow, the structure known as Central Union Block 1, at the northwest corner of West Madison Street and Market Street (now North Wacker Drive), opened its doors to tenants and visitors a few days over two months after the fire, on December 16, 1871. Even more remarkable was the opening of the Nixon Building at the northwest corner of South La Salle and West Monroe streets, which received tenants one week after the fire. The building had been under construction for some time and was nearly finished when the fire came, and to the credit of an architect named Otto H. Matz, had a number of fire-resisting elements in its plan: the joists were wrought iron, supporting brick arches; the halls and main rooms had marble floors; concrete covered the tops of beams, and the ceilings carried an inch of solidified plaster of Paris as a protective coat. There may have been also a good deal of luck in this partially completed building's escape from destruction; at any rate, for years afterward the Nixon carried a plaque stating "This fireproof building is the only one in the city that successfully stood the test of the Great Fire. . . ." For whatever reason, it was not the only building to escape: over by the South Branch, in an isolated position on West Randolph and Market Streets, the Lind block survived when the fire turned north and leaped the main stream of the Chicago River.

The city had not fully recovered from the fire before disaster struck again, in the form of another of those money panics that no one seemed able to explain or forestall. A calamity across the nation as well as in the Middle West, the depression and panic of 1873 had among its discernible causes inflation of currency, vast thefts by underwriters and brokers such as Jay Cooke of Philadelphia, whose failure started the landslide, over-building of railroads, and knavery in Washington. Five thousand firms went bankrupt, the figures in the books totaling $228,000,000 that no longer existed, though it was impossible to explain why. The greatest hardships fell as usual on working people, who had to live not by hen tracks in ledgers, but coins on the grocery counter. In Chicago, breadlines could be seen, and the lines stretched long; farmers had grain to feed the hungry, but went into debt at the market, where prices continued to fall. The most prudent course was to go short in corn and wheat on the Chicago Board of Trade; but not everyone was in a position to do that. And out on the prairies, a new way of looking at things began to take form, while down at Salem, 230 miles below Chicago, William Jennings Bryan attended high school, did chores, earned spending money at additional odd jobs, and planned to go to college, become a lawyer and amount to something in the world. He was a tall, good-looking youth, always present at the debating club, and he liked to memorize long pieces from Scott and Shakespeare for the elocution class.

In spite of the business failures in the Middle West, Chicago continued to grow through the hard winter and discouraging summer of 1874. Though thousands lived in shacks, just as they had before the fire, many thousands more came into town to scratch a living. The city reached 400,000 population by this year of 1874, and looked back across forty years to its incorporation—forty years of Chicago time that apparently held more happenings and discharged more energy than time could encompass in any other place. The older citizens, therefore, stood in high regard, though some of them, like Gurdon S. Hubbard, had taken harder blows from the fire and the panic than they could absorb with dignity. Such was the experience of John S. Wright, who had identified the fire as the most important placemark in Chicago history. But it also marked a turning point in his own life, after which everything went wrong. He began to suffer spells of excitement, and his brothers had a doctor sign papers to shut him away as a lunatic. His wife got him out, and he hurried to the

Eastern money markets, as he had hurried so often in the past, advising all who heard his voice to put their funds in action at Chicago. The city, Wright said, would always survive bad times because it was founded on the realities of ore, lumber, livestock, and grain. He started writing a circular that called on citizens to replace the common law with natural law: "To ease the path of man in the glorious years to come—the future, the future, always the future!" But by 1874, Wright's mind failed, the family put him in an asylum near Philadelphia, and there on September 26 he died. They brought his body back to Chicago for burial in Rosehill Cemetery on the North Side, with Indian Summer coming, and farmer's sons entering the State Industrial University that Wright had planned for in his busiest years. And so, said Bross of the *Tribune*, there closed one of the most useful lives ever lived in Chicago.

On December 31, 1876, the Rev. Dr. Abott E. Kittredge rose in the pulpit of the Third Presbyterian Church at Ashland Boulevard and Ogden Avenue, to review the past year. What he had to say revealed that the fashionable Chicago clergy no longer saw divine retribution in the fire that had flattened the town five years before. His talk was an example of pulpit oratory in the style of the day, and five hundred communicants expected no less as they looked up at the stern, handsome features of the forty-two-year-old pastor, and after hearing his description of some troubles in the outside world, turned their attention back to Chicago:

"But here in our midst," said Dr. Kittredge, "has it not been a wonderful year? Tell me, you who have watched the growth of this wonderful city from its cradle, have you ever seen such marvels as have met our eyes during these hallowed months? The Lord of Glory has visited Chicago. . . . Oh! what wonders he has wrought in our midst!" After continuing briefly in this vein, the minister turned to the roll of the dead:

"We are not all here who, a year ago, greeted one another with a Happy New Year. I have stood in twenty-seven of your homes, by the casket which held your precious dust, and have mingled my tears with yours. The Shepherd has folded nine of the lambs to his arms in Heaven, and the empty cradle and the little shoes no longer needed make your parental hearts very heavy as these festival days return. But remember, 'It is well with the child' . . . Many have gone home from the membership of this church, a larger number than in any previous year of my ministry among you. The first to hear the summons was one of our young men—George Holbrook—who, after sewing seed in our Campbell Park Mission, removed to a neighboring town. . . . But God wanted him in a still grander field, and with the harness on, he fell asleep in the Beloved, and today we can almost hear the voice which led the children in the hymns of the Sabbath school, leading some division of the choir that stands ever before the throne. Then from the sisters of this church, the summons came for one—Mrs. Forsythe—who had not worshiped with us for many years, but whose love for this church of her early day forbade the severing of her connection. In the morning of the first day of the week, she passed into the eternal rest of the unending Sabbath, and a more faithful wife, mother, or sister never went in through those pearly gates. Two months flew by and then the angel came to the bedside of one who had suffered long and patiently—Mrs. McGregor—and at his gentle touch, the spirit was released from the worn-out tenement, and husband and children wept on earth, while she began to sing the song of Moses and the Lamb. . . . Another —Mr. William Bryson—fell on the field of intense business activity, but his religion and daily toil were never separated, and so, though death came suddenly, he was ready—the lamp was trimmed and burning. One moment hard at work for the city, whose faithful servant he ever was, the next moment Jesus was saying to his glorified spirit, 'Well done, good and faithful servant.' Many of you know and loved that sweet, patient sufferer —Mrs. Susie Welles—who for years had been helpless as a little babe, unable to take a step, but lying day after day on a couch of pain. Susie is helpless no longer, she is walking with firm step the golden pavement, and pain and infirmity are buried forever in the grave. . . . Mr. Henry M. Ketchum . . . left this city more than a year since, in search of health, but the Master had for him a higher service, and among the mountains of Vermont he fell asleep to wake on Mt. Zion, where weakness and pain are never known.

"Who would call one of these cherished ones back again? Back to the changes, the disappointments, the temptations, the hungerings, the tears of this pilgrim life? No, no! . . . They will be waiting and watching for us, until we, too, reach our home of perfect love and perfect joy, where the seats are never, never made vacant by death. . . ." At this point the speaker paused and looked over his enthralled audience, while the organ began playing the hymn "One by One." Then the pastor continued, "Whose seat will be vacant a year from now, of those who now sit before me? Some of us, beyond a doubt, will not be here when 1877 has taken its flight. But who? God only knows." And the choir began singing:

> We too shall come to the river side
>   One by one;
> We are nearer its waters each eventide
>   One by one . . .

The ensuing year of 1877 brought the sorrows Dr. Kittredge predicted, and some that he had not thought of. Among those who died was the founding financier, William Ogden, who had seen Chicago grow from a mud village to a city with more than half a million people in its metropolitan area; and just as Dr. Kittredge's oratorical style demonstrated a favorite form of spoken art, Ogden's last will and testament showed the development of a literary art which had just entered its high period. It was a New England trait to venerate a will and relish its wording, and Chicago, Boston's sister, was New England's child. The Ogden will ran to more than twenty thousand words, and a glance at the eighth section of its third clause will give an idea of the mood these documents could induce for an admiring reader:

"To such charitable uses as I shall hereafter designate, without the solemnity of a will; or, in default of such designation, as a majority of my said Executors and Trustees select and appoint, the remaining one and a half shares, or seven and one half per centum of said income and distributable moneys. But in this connection I authorise and empower my said Executors and Trustees, or a majority of them, in their own discretion and not otherwise, to apply not exceeding the said one-half share at any time or from time to time, in case or so long as it may not have been applied to such charitable uses, to the use of all or any of my heirs who they may deem in need, or worthy and entitled to receive the same." The measured words applied to the *income* from the estate, and in a later part, the eighth section of the sixth clause, Ogden made a similar disposition of one and one half shares in the *principal* of the estate, and in each case his relatives fought over the money.

Deaths of rich men were not the only startling occurrences of 1877: the year also saw the worst outbreaks of violence, except for war, that had yet occurred in the United States. The trouble began in the New railroad systems, recently extended from coast to coast, and built by public money and the sale of public land. Although they had reaped enormous profits, the owners of these lines paid scanty wages to the train crews, and reacted with horror when the men asked for more. Instead of a raise in pay, the crews got an increase in the amount of work required; in some instances the bosses doubled the number of freight cars to be handled for a day's pay. The struggle to correct abuses of this sort led to excessive power for organized labor in the mid-twentieth century; but in 1877, employers had the greater strength, and used it without mercy. The railroad workers formed a national union and struck the major lines; and as the transportation center of the country, Chicago saw some of the bloodiest battles between owners and laborers that took place in the spring and summer of 1877. Hobart Chatfield-Taylor heard that the militia had killed "eighteen ragged commune wretches," as Mayor Monroe Heath called them, on the Twelfth Street bridge. The boy slipped out and saw the militiamen load cannon at the bridge, and later in the day he saw a citizens' patrol ride by—stern-faced men with revolvers at their belts and Civil War sabers slapping the bony flanks of the street car horses they had seized for mounts. Then came four companies of Regular infantry in their slouching route march, fresh from battles with Indians, or so Hobart thought. He reasoned that conditions must be very bad to make men burn freight cars and fight soldiers; but he read in the *Tribune* and elsewhere that strikes and boycotts were un-American.

Opposing "America" in any way would be a sin, for patriotism had become the secular religion of the United States in the last quarter of the nineteenth century. The old American stock was good enough for Chicago, and what they most looked up to in that city was the Yankee or Southern name, combined with money. But gatherings sometimes took place to which just the old name was a ticket of admission. Such were the annual pioneers' receptions at the Calumet Club, a men's social institution on the South Side that once had the appearance of being a fortress of wealth and privilege founded to last as long as the city itself. Organized in 1878, the Calumet built a fine clubhouse at Michigan Avenue and Twentieth Street for the use of an impressive roster of substantial men who paid the $100 entrance fee and $80 annual dues, including Marshall Field, George H. and Louis E. Laflin, George M. Pullman, six members of the Wheeler family, W. R. Linn, Levi Z. Leiter, and Solon Spencer Beman, the architect who designed the W. W. Kimball mansion on Prairie Avenue and the Grand Central railroad station. There could now be no doubt the club idea had caught on, for the Union on the North Side and the Illinois on the West Side came into existence along the same lines as the Calumet, and a man might belong to one of those, according to where he lived, in addition to the Chicago Club downtown. On the 18th of October in 1878, the Calumet combined an exhibition of paintings loaned by members with a reception for early settlers of Chicago. It was an elegant affair, made all the more notable by the attendance of a military hero who had recently been President of the United States. Chewing the stump of a cigar and blinking his little red-rimmed eyes, Ulysses S. Grant appeared to be suffering discomfort until the committee escorted him to a side room where whiskey tables stood in readiness. In addition to liquor, the green-coated Calumet waiters offered galantine of turkey, boned partridge and quail, sliced buffalo tongue, breast of chicken à la Parisienne, Gulf shrimp salad, filet of salmon in mayonnaise, sandwiches, wine jellies, confectionery, bisque glacé, Nesselrode pudding, Charlotte Russe, cakes, fruit, and coffee. It was by no means too fine a feast to offer "persons who were residents of Chicago and of age prior to the year Eighteen Hundred and Forty," for as an old spry lady remarked, "We were here at the begunment." On the whole, the old names had prospered: Adsit, Armour, Dickey, Peck, Patterson, Laflin, Scammon, Goodrich, Warner, and Wood; Caton, Clybourne, Dole, Gale, Loomis, Manièrre, Skinner, Harmon, and Judd—all these names had appeared in the directory of 1839. And then there were Fullers and Wentworths, Meekers and Newberrys and Magees: when they first came to town there had been no liveried club servants with trays of dainties, and yet it had been but forty years before.

At about this time Mrs. Touchett of *The Portrait of a Lady* remarked with certainty that there were only twelve American names. She might have added that four of the twelve were Chicagoan: Field, McCormick, Pullman, and Palmer. Yet no member of these ducal families could have attended the old settlers' reception as a guest. On the other hand, the largest picture on display in the loan exhibit at the reception—Meissonier's "The Outpost"—had come from the collection of Marshall Field.

Along with a number of his close friends and fellow rulers of the city, Marshall Field lived on the South Side. Richard Morris Hunt had designed his house at 1905 Prairie Avenue, which resembled the owner with its air of correctness and austerity—and no slightest suggestion of exuberance or warmth. Field's first wife had become a semi-invalid, taking many trips abroad for her health. In Chicago, some people knew that Field had a friend in Delia Caton, the wife of Arthur Caton, a prominent lawyer. The Catons lived on the South Side, as did George M. Pullman, who could part the draperies and peer out from the tall windows of a mansard-roofed house near the Field residence. One got an impression of heaviness and solemnity in that part of town; and at the top of Prairie Avenue stood a house that gave the weightiest impression of any in Chicago—the Glessner mansion, designed by H. H. Richardson, the best known architect in the country. Henry Hobson Richardson had come out from his Boston office to build for Marshall Field a huge wholesale store and warehouse that set the tone of a Romanesque Chicago which weighted the earth and climbed the sky during the decade of the 1880s. An architect so bold, so decisive in his ideas, and so sure of his intentions would find enthusiastic clients in Chicago, and Richardson might have put more of his personal mark on the city had he not died at the age of forty-eight in 1886, before the Field building had reached completion. As it was Richardson built a remarkable red sandstone house for Franklin MacVeagh on the North Side in addition to the Glessner stronghold on Prairie Avenue, which sheltered a founder of the International Harvester Company. Both plans influenced local domestic design for years, and an observer can still spot romantic Richardsonian detail in the stonework of many a Chicago house in the kind of decaying neighborhood where old mansions seem to be inhabited by a race of palmists, instructors on the electrical guitar, renters of dress suits, and sad-looking elderly persons who sit on the stoops all afternoon in felt slippers and keep large vicious dogs. The MacVeagh house on Schiller Street near Lincoln Park went down before the iron ball of the wrecker in 1927, but the Glessner house, now owned by the Illinois Institute of Technology, continues to stand on Prairie Avenue, with 150 feet of granite wall extending west on Eighteenth Street. The architectural critic Montgomery Schuyler said of this house, "The whole aspect of the exterior is so gloomy and forbidding and unhomelike that but for its neighborhood one would infer its purpose to be not domestic but penal." Behind those walls a group of ladies met with Mrs. Glessner each Sunday to read aloud, and membership in this company indicated high social standing; so also did any invitation to be entertained across the street at the limestone chateau that Solon Spencer Beman had designed for W. W. Kimball, the piano manufacturer. Fine carriages and horses passed in front of these houses and the two or three hundred equally imposing establishments along South Michigan Avenue and Drexel Boulevard. Curtis Jadwin, the grain speculator hero of *The Pit*, lived down that way, and liked to drive two horses hitched to his double-seated buggy, with his Negro groom beside him, and the spotted coach dogs Rex and Rox trotting under the rear axle. Jadwin did not go in for show, nor make his team conspicuous with boots, bandages, and similar fittings; but men who knew horses invariably stopped to watch when Jadwin's turnout went by, the team going "heads up, the check rein swinging loose, ears all alert, eyes all alight, the breath deep, strong, and slow, and the stride, machine-like, even as the swing of a metronome, thrown out from the shoulder to knee, snapped on from knee to fetlock, from fetlock to pastern, finishing squarely, beautifully, with the thrust of the hoof, planted an instant, then, as it were, flinging the roadway behind it. . . ." Going to call on Lucy Dearborn, Jadwin wore a black slouch hat, a gray dustcoat with a black velvet collar, and tan gloves that he twisted and crumpled in holding the thoroughbreds to their work. With such controlled elegance at the doorsteps, the South Siders gave a girl in another part of town the impression that they thought themselves the only pebbles on the beach. But Curtis Jadwin and his haughtiest neighbors eventually moved to the North Side, for the social demise of their area became certain in the mid-1880s, when the Potter Palmers built on Lake Shore Drive.

Before looking north of the river, Potter Palmer had done big things downtown. The fire had destroyed thirty-five buildings that brought him nearly $200,000 a year in rent, and there was no denying that this was a staggering blow. But Lyman Gage of the First National Bank stood by, and the building of another new Palmer House continued, although it took two million dollars to bring the grand hotel to completion, from the plans of John Van Osdel. Potter Palmer continued as an active hotelman, working in a small office that had a large window commanding the entire main floor, so that the owner could be out in a jiffy to greet an important guest or upbraid a careless employee. After the Palmer House settled down as the best known hotel in Chicago, holding its own against the two other large and splendid hotels, the Sherman and the Tremont, and the small but first-class Richelieu, the proprietor began to look for another challenge. Palmer had gone as a guest to the houses of the magnates who colonized the South Side, and thought it all very well to live in a fine house on Prairie or Michigan Avenue, except for one thing: the tracks of the Illinois Central went by so close at hand that they spoiled the lakefront and caused an incessant nuisance of noise and soot. What good did one get from being a millionaire if one had to put up with the clangor and dirt of railroad trains day and night? Thus Palmer spotted the basic error in the near South Side—for all its weight and grandeur—and he looked up across the Chicago River, and decided to invest in land that lay north and east of the pleasant neighborhood that had taken its tone for a long time, as time went in Chicago, from the Newberrys, the Ogdens, the Arnolds, and their unexceptionable neighbors. For years the boys of these families had ranged a semi-wilderness along the shore, climbing dunes, splashing through pools where the surf had run in, fishing, hunting ducks, and camping in scrub growths of pine and willow. Potter Palmer's idea was to make solid land of this marsh, and he sent machinery and men to draw sand from under the lake and pile it on shore, blotting up swamps and extending the beach. Palmer bought most of the reclaimed and new land at reasonable terms from the city, keeping in mind the Chicago saying, "Buy by the acre—sell by the foot." The city then put through a street which was to be called Lake Shore Drive, and on the eastern half of the block bounded by Schiller and Banks streets, Palmer set the architects Henry Ives Cobb and Charles S. Frost to work. They started their task in 1882, designing a house for which Mr. Palmer said he would like to pay about ninety thousand dollars. It rose in Ohio limestone and Wisconsin granite, and the costs rose also through three years, while an imported village of Italian artisans worked to complete the castle that the architects had drawn for a princely client who at last said, "Do not show me the final reckoning." In the end the house cost more than $1,000,000, but Palmer got his money's worth in undeniable magnificence. The house also served as an advertisement for the Lake Shore Drive development, and attracted so much attention that Palmer could pick and choose among the applicants for property. He sold to none but those he considered his peers, and thus founded the Gold Coast, which is the Drive from Pearson Street to North Avenue, with certain adjacent territory, and still the most elegant part of town, although the castle has been gone for many years. Bertha Palmer was a lovely woman, blooming at thirty-six, when Potter conducted her to the finished house in 1885. Although Palmer had reached his sixtieth year, he got out of the carriage as nimbly as a young man, and held out his arm for Bertha to touch as she stepped to the driveway. Now they stood in the porte-cochère of a towered structure in the English battlemented style that some preferred to call castellated Gothic. The contrasting stonework looked far from ancient, and they could see that the grounds would need planting, along with a growth of ivy on the castle walls, before that look of newness softened away. They walked up red sandstone steps and entered an octagonal space three stories high, hung with Gobelin tapestries. Under their feet lay Oriental rugs and tiger skins, setting off the gigantic fireplace of this entrance hall, and they saw above the mantel the Honoré coat of arms. Broad stairways led upward past stained-glass windows that lit the landings with a ruby glow. On the second floor they entered a white and gold drawing room, the first completely authentic Louis XVI salon in Chicago, for all the furniture came from the time of Louis, and some of it from his palace. As a personal touch Palmer had ordered the tile floor inlaid with a pattern of Bertha's favorite pink roses. Then came the dining room, panelled in San Domingo mahogany and big enough for fifty guests; and Palmer's library and billiard room, with everything necessary for ease and comfort. By now the general effect had made itself felt: much magnificent carving in wood and stone; mural paintings wherever tapestries did not hang; archways leading to cavernous rooms in which waited constellations of chairs, sofas, and side tables; a great deal of gold and silver filigree; Venetian mosaics; onyx set into the heavy doors; and in each room a huge fireplace of marble and oak. Mrs. Palmer's room was done in Moorish style with an oak floor, paneled wainscotting, and carved ceilings; blue taffeta curtained her bed, a Louis XVI museum piece, and there was a dressing room in black and gold, with bathroom to match, featuring a basin decorated with mother-of-pearl in a floral design—pink roses. Nearby the architects had placed a small French sitting room where Mrs. Palmer could work with her secretaries and receive intimate friends.

At the top of Palmer Castle the ballroom and art gallery stood ready for the first big dance the owners cared to give. Chicago had to wait only a short time for this event, at which Hobart Chatfield-Taylor, now twenty-two years old and a Cornell graduate, looked with approval on the rose-red velvet hangings and the chandeliers which had been designed by Louis Comfort Tiffany of New York. The catering and music offered no surprises —as usual at fashionable parties Kinsley waiters served supper and poured champagne, while Johnny Hand and his orchestra played for dancing. What rivetted the attention of the guests, aside from the grandeurs of the house, was the vitality and charm of the hostess, for Bertha Palmer on that evening took her place in the public mind as leader of Chicago society.

The conception of society in the sense of the refined and well-mannered people of a given community was not new, but the idea of *high* society, with its display of wealth and elaborate rituals, was something of a novelty. Once it got well started, nothing could stop this idea, which flourished and grew now that the passage of two decades had softened the raw edges of Civil War money, just as the fog rolling up over Lake Shore Drive from the newly made beach would soften the outlines of the Palmer mansion. For better or worse, the years of the cultivated carriage trade gave way before the arrival of the gilded age. From now on a recognized high society in big American cities would develop as an organized force, an army on the march with a supply train of great houses like the Palmer palace, clubs, hotels, smart churches, boarding schools, colleges, and resorts. The social army would give employment to a host of sutlers—milliners, tailors, headwaiters, headmasters, games coaches, hairdressers, preachers, orchestra leaders, dancing instructors, portrait painters, grooms, coachmen, chefs, footmen, lady's maids, and newspaper people. As public relations officers of high society, these journalists had an important task to perform, because the attitude of social leaders toward publicity changed almost overnight. As recently as 1880, Frederick Cook of the *Times* had drawn an assignment to bring in the guest list of a party on the South Side. The hostess received him politely, but showed signs of distress when he asked for names. It could not be done; the family had merely gathered a few friends for the evening and there was no news in that. Feeling that the young lady was right, Cook returned to his office, where the editor said not to worry about it, for it really made no difference whether or not the list of names got into print. But even then the society column as we have known it was struggling to be born in the *Times* and other Chicago papers. At about the time that Cook drew blank as a society reporter, a woman newspaper writer covering a children's party on the West Side had given names under disguise that must have been easy to penetrate: "Dressed as Little Eva, Florence Grace P——r was taken up to Heaven on wires, wearing white, all crimped, and puffed, with blue boots, and gloves, and over-skirt, and was the pet and delight of at least two people there, and the admiration of all." Another girl named Lucille W——d drew the reporter's attention by "wearing the tiniest pink boots edged at the top with gold lace." Then the reporter wrote, "And the boys! Oh how near I came to forgetting them! They did not wear any ruffles or laces, but they danced well and had each particular hair in place, and wore tight gaiters and white kids. Two little fellows with bright eyes and supple limbs, who have the most beautiful mother imaginable, wore knickerbockers of black velvet, white waists, blue sashes, blue boots and gloves, and blue neckties. The smallest one was about as large as a doll, and I lost my heart to him early in the evening. Then there were Masters H——ss and C——s, and C——k, who were gotten up exquisitely, and made sad havoc among the ladies, especially Master C——s, who carried his left arm in a sling, and was very pale and interesting. Then came supper, and the little ladies who were mamma cut down, and the little gentlemen who were miniatures of papa, were carried off ingloriously and were shawled and great-coated, and taken home to bed, surfeited with the early sweets of life, and quite sure it would always be just like that, in the world. But we whose *couleur de rose* hies back, when theirs is beginning, wisely shake our heads, but keep our croaking to ourselves."

The boys who charmed the lady reporter with their graceful movements on that evening long ago had no doubt received instruction from the fashionable dancing master Alvar Bournique or his rival, J. Edwin Martine. As enforcers of a minimum standard of manners among upper middle-class children, the dancing masters of Victorian America exercised a civilizing influence in the Gilded Age, and Bournique had opened his first Select Dancing Academy as early as 1867, at the southwest corner of Randolph and State streets. Nine years later, he branched out on the South Side to teach "Fashionable Style in Dancing, with particular attention to Deportment." Martine established his academy at Clark and State streets, and also made instruction available on Ohio Street in the near North Side and on Ada Street, one of those byways near Jefferson Park on the West Side. Bournique and Martine held the lead, but many other dancing masters advertised as the 1870s came and went. For example, Professor A. Fisher announced himself as Tutor of the Terpsychorean Art, competing among others with Monsieur Mirasole, Mr. Sullivan of Boston assisted by Mrs. Sullivan, and Professor A. M. Loomis, who came from Springfield, Massachusetts. Though they competed for pupils, the masters met in councils where they decided what new steps to introduce, and how to meet attacks by the hellfire preachers of the city, who denounced dancing as immoral. It can be proved that press agentry existed as early as 1876 by citing a piece of copy the masters planted in a Chicago paper: "DANCING —Its Advantage for Sanitary Purposes—A Physician's Evidence in Its Favor." The story was told by an unnamed doctor who had examined a neurasthenic sixteen-year-old girl and informed her parents that "Very vigorous measures must be used, if you expect to restore her to health. Divorce her from anything mental, so far as memorizing anything is concerned; then send her to dancing school, that she may combine exercise with order and melody.' The child, her large eyes open with wonder and delight, interrupted with 'Dancing school! Oh! how I've longed to go! But Mother says it's wrong, and leads to wickedness.' What a dilemma for a physician! What a dilemma for a child! 'Did you ever intend your daughter to play the piano, guitar, or other musical instrument?' said I to the mother. 'Oh, yes,' was the answer. 'Why,' I continued, 'show such partiality to the upper extremities? The hands are rendered happy as a medium of melody; the feet are rendered equally happy in the same way.' " The parents accepted the doctor's prescription and the girl recovered her nervous tone in the course of dancing lessons.

Private dancing classes for which one had to pass an admission committee became important, because they furnished the element of exclusivity, an indispensable ingredient in creating a formal society with leaders, followers, and outcasts beyond the pale. Some said that Bournique's private dances on the South Side were the most desirable, while the partisans of Professor Martine made similar claims for the North and West Sides. Martine furnished the hall used by a group of young North Side men who had called themselves the Cinders when they started a membership class immediately after the fire. The people attending such "classes" already knew how to dance: what it amounted to was hiring the professor to act as master of ceremonies at a small ball, where one knew everybody from childhood. Such groups produced the Assembly Balls in later times, the most important gatherings in the society year until after World War I. The Assembly guest lists received annual editing by a committee wielding power to cast into outer darkness, so far as official social recognition was concerned.

The three or four most important Chicago dancing masters of the 1880s not only planted newspaper stories like that which told of the doctor's dilemma, but managed to appear in frequent interviews. For example, Martine received a reporter on September 27, 1888, and answered questions such as "Do you find any difference in the styles of dancing on the South Side, say, and the West Side?" Martine answered, "Well, I can't say that there is much. The better classes, I think, do not dance so well as what you might call the bourgeoisie, the middle classes. The reason is that the better classes, the wealthy and aristocratic people, do not wish to mingle with middle-class people on the floor of a dancing academy, and so they learn in private classes at their homes, where they dance upon carpets, which are fatal to a smooth gliding step." The reporter asked, "Have you noticed the West Jackson Street Glide in any of your pupils?" Martine said, "I never heard of it. What is it?" The reporter said, "Young people in that neighborhood, from habitually putting their right foot forward in stepping down from the sidewalks of the alley crossways, have developed a sort of one-sided crouch." "No," Martine said, "the young people I teach in the West Side are as refined and elegant as any in the city, and hold themselves better than most."

If dancing teachers furnished good copy in the newspapers, the owners of fine horses, like Curtis Jadwin, put on the best free show in the streets. Out beyond Paul Cornell's Hyde Park development on the South Side, a syndicate of rich men had established Washington Park Race Track, with grandstands, a landscaped infield, and a clubhouse for fashionable patrons. Driving up the circular roadway to the clubhouse on a racing day—most especially on American Derby Day in the late spring—was the acknowledged public showing of skill for any Chicagoan who wished to give an impression that he had sporting blood. Or, if he did not himself handle horses, the moment when his coachman drove his turnout past the critical onlookers served to prove whether or not the owner had taste and a sense of style. Hobart Chatfield-Taylor always felt confident under this inspection, for his uncle and father had brought him up to know good horses, correct equipment, and proper riding and driving. And on the morning of the American Derby in 1888, Hobart adjusted his gray top hat, strolled around the clubhouse circle, and reported to his friends that Potter Palmer had turned out both a coach and a char-à-banc, with leopard skins spread over the seats of both vehicles, which failed to win approval from sticklers for good form.

Despite the attention paid to horses and the different kinds of carriages, Chicago listed only four genuine, full-dress private coaches in 1889. And then, Chatfield-Taylor recorded, "The fifth coach to appear on Michigan Avenue was my own yellow-wheeled Kimball drag, drawn by a team of golden chestnuts, and I confess that I took particular pride in the fact that both coach and harness were made in Chicago." And so Chicago had five coaches. It was also true, Chatfield-Taylor admitted, that "General Joseph T. Torrence of the Illinois National Guard sometimes appeared driving a drag, but somehow the rest of us never quite accepted him as a member of the coaching set." Chatfield-Taylor also recorded that in addition to the genuine coaches, one might see Marshall Field in "a highly respectable stanhope phaeton with long-tailed horses." And there were several four-horse brakes, "and at least a score of tandem carts to add their sportive zest to the Derby Day parade, along with dog carts, tilburys, gigs, and stanhopes, and a goodly sprinkling of smart victorias with pretty rosettes on the head-stalls of their sleek-coated horses, and pretty women within them conscious that the eyes of friend and enemy alike were on their newest gowns. Even the husbands beside them were, if they happened to be wearing white spats for the first time in their lives, painfully conscious too, I fear, of the scornful glances of their business associates, the Derby being an occasion of ordeal rather than joy for many a citizen of our budding metropolis. Nevertheless, it was a notable event in the life of the city."

All men who achieved standing in Chicago, or aspired to it, recognized the symbolical value of owning fine horses, and showing that one was aware of taste and style in such matters. And although a man as certain of himself as Hobart Chatfield-Taylor might be pleased that his carriage and gear had been made in Chicago, nobody questioned the final authority of England in everything having to do with fashionable display. So it was that a large number of English grooms and coachmen came to Chicago in the 1880s, and many attempted, with varying success, to exploit and bully their employers. Some of these insolent, cheating servants were not even Englishmen, but Yankees posing as British in order to draw higher pay. One of the impostors got a job with Victor Fremont Lawson, the hymn-singing proprietor of the *Chicago Daily News*. The man called himself John Tilbury, and came to Lawson with forged credentials to back a manner of assurance and competence. Tilbury was a scoundrel, and no Englishman, having been born James McGraw in New York City. He later became known to the police as Phonograph Jimmy because he made a specialty of stealing those instruments; he also worked as a dog-stealer, general thief, and blackmailer. While employed by Lawson, Tilbury made the barn behind the publisher's mansion at 1550 Lake Shore Drive a center of dogfighting and cockfighting, betting, and carousing for a gang of drunken grooms and coachmen who looked to him for leadership in any avenue of criminality that might be open to them. Tilbury founded a Rich Men's Coachmen's Club, with headquarters in the Lawson barn, to take advantage of members' opportunities to steal valuable dogs which they would sell, train as fighting animals, or return to their owners for ransom. They also engaged in blackmail, and rumors ran through the city for years concerning the intelligence network these rascals operated, pooling information as to who went where at what hours, and what they said, forgetting that coachmen have ears. Respectable servants held Tilbury's gang in horror, and wrote anonymous letters to the police, accusing various coachmen of having been deserters from the British army, or former inmates of English and Irish jails. Tilbury himself showed how the blackmailers worked, some time after leaving Lawson, when he got into the employment of Mrs. Hollis M. Thurston, daughter of the wealthy commission merchant John T. Nash. Tilbury had managed to convince Mrs. Thurston that he was a former Guards officer and the black sheep of a titled family. After a few months, Tilbury told Mrs. Thurston that his charge for not revealing certain family secrets would be $12,500. The lady agreed to pay, and when Tilbury entered her room to collect, Mrs. Thurston said in a carrying tone of voice, "Here is the money you demanded. Now give me the letters and photographs in your possession." Tilbury made for the door, whereupon private detectives leaped from closets and seized him. They searched his room, found two pistols and a dagger, and questioned him for hours before turning him over to the regular police. Next day when the story got out, the *Times* reported that "Chicago society has turned white with dread." Mrs. Thurston came heavily veiled to testify before the grand jury, which sent Tilbury to trial on charges of extortion by threat. Tilbury gave his case to an expert criminal lawyer, and Mrs. Thurston had to endure public embarrassment when the judge allowed this attorney to launch an attack on her character and conduct. The blackmailer went free on grounds that arrest and detention by private detectives had violated his rights. But the police then made Chicago so hot for Tilbury that he left town, and dropped from sight.

The case of Mrs. Thurston showed how the underworld could reach and damage a respectable Chicagoan. Only a few could feel safe, and honest men or women, when well advised, avoided court action because both crooked lawyers and crooked judges would be arrayed against them, and in most cases justice could not be obtained except by arrangements outside the channels of courtroom law. At this time, a great deal of the recognized and accepted corruption in Chicago was administered by one of the ablest thieves ever to follow his calling in the city. His name was Michael Cassius McDonald, and he deserves credit, like other bold Chicagoans, for the way he recovered losses and rebuilt his business after the fire. One might forget that the fire had been as hard on sporting people as on anyone else—the brothels, dramshops, shady hotels and gambling rooms had gone up in flame as irrevocably as the premises of merchants, lawyers, and bankers. Indeed, McDonald *was* banker—a faro banker, who had presided over that game in many a choice location since he first worked his way up from minor swindles and crooked card manipulations on trains running in and out of Chicago. Thus he developed great dexterity as a monte-thrower, and had no equal at tossing out three cards, apparently crimping the corner of the pay-off card, which a confederate would point out to the victim, but the folded corner always turned out to be on another card. Founded on the basis of all confidence games—cheating a would-be cheater—three-card monte still yields a good income to swindlers around airports and bus stations. Mike McDonald well understood the greed that inspired the victims in their efforts to beat his game by suggested dishonesty, but he had respect for those who refused to swallow the lure of three-card monte and other such rigmaroles, and uttered the phrase, one of a number that Chicago has added to the language: "You can't cheat an honest man."

During the war McDonald had recruited hoodlums to go as soldiers in the Union army; when they got their enlistment bounties, from which McDonald collected a commission, the men deserted, then enlisted again, collected another bounty, and so on until the South caved in and the lucrative racket ended. Profits from this business helped establish McDonald as proprietor of several gambling houses, and by the decade of the 1880s, he had taken hold in Chicago politics as well. After becoming boss of the city, McDonald assigned locations for houses of prostitution, granted licenses for gambling, and distributed money from criminals and brothel-keepers to police officials, court employees and judges. In the early 1880s McDonald got on good terms with Mayor Carter Harrison, and had the satisfaction of seeing the honest police chief Simon O'Donnell reduced in rank. Harrison appointed William J. McGarigle in O'Donnell's place and all went well until the new chief changed jobs, taking appointment in 1882 as warden of the Cook County Hospital. In this berth, he bribed Chicago aldermen to pay McDonald's contracting firm $128,500 to paint the courthouse with a mixture of chalk and water. Lawson uncovered the scandal in his *Daily News*, and several aldermen stood trial. Mike refused to put in the fix and they drew jail time, while McGarigle left town without delaying to pack a bag; nothing happened to McDonald.

As an executive of vice and crime, McDonald ranked with Jonathan Wild of eighteenth-century London. Both men held that there must be an unvarying tariff on all sales of stolen goods, proceeds of gambling, and returns from prostitutes and blackmailers. McDonald always split the money forty percent to the thief, sharper, or pander, twenty to the police, and the rest to a kitty from which only Mike himself could extract funds. Out of this treasury McDonald paid judges, aldermen, and city officials, and supplied money to use in fixing juries. He parceled out territory and interviewed crooks and confidence men at his office in a large four-story building which stood for years at the northwest corner of Clark and Monroe streets. A first-class saloon occupied the ground floor, and gambling rooms took up all the second floor except for McDonald's office, where he sometimes tested prospective croupiers, dicemen, and blackjack dealers, sending them directly to work if satisfied as to their experience and skill. Needless to say, it was no good trying to fool Mike McDonald about the handling of cards, and in this office McDonald added another phrase to the American language when he told a successful applicant, "Never give a sucker an even break."

On the upper floors McDonald's wife rented furnished apartments to a select clientele of croupiers and bunko men. The list of paying guests included such highly regarded sharpers as Kid Miller, Dutchy Lehman, Snapper Johnny Malloy, Black-Eyed Johnny, the Traveling Kid, Appetite Bill, Jew Myers, and Tom O'Brien, a virtuoso who earned the title King of the Bunko Men. Mary McDonald also welcomed the swindler known as Hungry Joe Lewis, who had taken Oscar Wilde for several thousand dollars during the poet's visit to the States in 1882. In that same year it turned out that Charles Francis Adams, Henry's brother, had larceny in him: Adams was taken for $7,000 by Red Jimmy Fitzgerald, who always stayed with the McDonalds when in Chicago.

A reform mayor named John A. Roche got in when Carter Harrison finished his fourth term in 1887, and word went out that discretion would now be advisable in the gambling, swindling, and pimping industries. Mike pulled back $2 million from the kitty and went into semi-retirement in a fine house on Ashland Avenue. But the McDonalds did not settle to the peaceful domestic life they had earned by years of hard work. In a few months Mary ran away with an actor. Mike brought her back and they were reconciled until Mary again eloped, this time with a Catholic priest. Meanwhile, Carter Harrison had regained office, and Mike McDonald returned to business, remaining active until he died in 1907.

Complaisant politicians, steely acquisitors, and industrious doers of Satan's work were by no means the only makers of the future in the Chicago of Mrs. Potter Palmer, Cyrus McCormick and Mike McDonald. In suburban Evanston a woman lived and worked whose influence on the nation, as well as on the city, would be more than that of any other Chicagoan in her time. She was Frances Elizabeth Caroline Willard, one of the first feminists of the world; as founder and leading spirit of the Women's Christian Temperance Union, Miss Willard had a large share in bringing about the passage of the National Prohibition Act, which had as great an effect on Chicago as any piece of legislation ever passed by Congress. But Frances Willard might never have entered the feminist movement, and founded the Union, had it not been for the influence of her father and two other men, President Charles Grandison Finney of Oberlin College and a Chicago clergyman named Charles Henry Fowler.

When Frances was a girl of five on a Wisconsin farm, her father took her to the house of a neighbor who had died, led her to the open coffin, and lifted her for a good view of the dead face. Mr. Willard meant well, thinking this would impress Frances with the seriousness of life and inevitability of death, but the only result was to give the child a feeling of anxiety and dread, which increased shortly afterward when Willard took his daughter to hear Dr. Finney preach on hellfire and damnation. Finney had modeled his speaking style on that of Senator Douglas; he raged in the pulpit, and frightened sinners into fits. Besides terrifying Frances, the sermon fixed in her mind Finney's objections to the use of alcohol, tobacco, coffee, and tea.

Willard had emigrated from Ohio to the Wisconsin farm where Frances passed eleven years of harsh existence before she escaped to start her education at Milwaukee Female College. She became a teacher, and in 1871, at the age of thirty-two, took the position of dean at the Ladies' College of the North West, which had just merged into Northwestern University in Evanston to become its women's department. And it was here that Frances Willard met Charles Henry Fowler, the handsome young Methodist preacher who was pulling every wire within his reach to obtain the presidency of Northwestern.

A future bishop of the Methodist Episcopal Church, the Rev. Dr. Fowler had a brilliant mind, and a mastery of pulpit oratory that acted powerfully on his hearers. He could talk for hours in perfect sentences and balanced paragraphs, with an underlying rhythm that drew shouts and moans from camp meeting audiences when he chose to hit them with the full force of his voice and personality. A widower in search of a wife, Fowler became engaged to Frances Willard at the time she entered on the deanship of the Ladies' College. It had the look of a good match, but Fowler's conviction that women should stay out of public life disturbed Frances, and he also gave her the impression of not being a whole-hearted advocate of higher education for girls. Nevertheless, the engagement lasted eight months, until the night that Fowler announced that he had decided to go to China as a missionary. "You must go with me, Frances," he said, "are you willing?" Here he sounds like Mr. St. John Rivers, decent and well-intentioned; therefore one can understand Frances Willard's surprise when she said, "Yes, Charles, wherever you go I will go"—and he answered, "Good! I am delighted that you said that. I have no intention of going to China —I was only testing your love."

The vanity of a man who presumed to test her love produced a feeling of revulsion in Frances Willard, and she broke off the engagement. This jolt to Fowler's self-esteem touched a mean streak in him, as Frances would find out soon enough. The trustees of Northwestern appointed him president in October 1872, and after that she had nothing but trouble in the women's college which she was supposed to control. Reporting to the trustees at the end of his first academic year, Fowler said that the "matter of the Ladies' College had become anomalous and embarrassing."

Fowler kept up pressure throughout the following year, and at the next board meeting persuaded the trustees to recognize a faculty committee that brought in a list of twenty-one rules for the government of women in the university. Offensive in their pettiness, the rules covered such matters as the driving of nails and emptying of waste baskets; even so, Miss Willard had been given authority over the women in all things, including the emptying of baskets, and the list of regulations was an invasion of her territory. Fowler justified this by the legalism that while most of the women had come as members of the Ladies' College when it allied itself with the university, still there had been a few women at that time already in the university, and when Fowler put them under Miss Willard's care, he reserved to himself the right to enact regulations governing their conduct. The trustees adopted the rules that the committee had brought in, and so Frances Willard suffered public mortification.

Miss Willard could not stay under these circumstances. She said, "The world is wide and full of elbow room; this atmosphere is stifling—I must leave it." Her letter of resignation went to the trustees the same day. Two days later, when the board reconvened to consider Miss Willard's resignation, reporters from the downtown papers were on hand. Some trustees had not voted to accept the humiliating rules, and others hoped to persuade Miss Willard to stay. At the start there was a feeling of conciliation in the air, until Mrs. A. J. Brown rose to say that the women of the community wanted the dean of the women's college to have even more authority than she had exercised before the new rules had passed. At this, angry shouts rang out, and men leaped yelling to their feet. In those days the question of economic and educational equality for women generated high emotional pressure, and some men went temporarily insane when confronted with it. The chairman whacked away with his gavel like a man chopping wood, and quieted the meeting so that Mrs. Brown could go on to say that the Ladies' College had been built up by women, and was under their management when it became the women's department of the university, but many unnecessary troubles arose after Dr. Fowler's arrival, even though it had been agreed that the Ladies' College would take the women already enrolled in the university, and that these women would be under the authority of Dean Willard. All manner of annoyances had arisen, and they were the work of Dr. Fowler. Again the yelling broke out, and Fowler cried above the uproar that Dean Willard had not discharged her duties in an efficient manner. This made Frances burst into sobs and hurry out of the meeting hall. Her brother had been waiting at the campus gate. He took her home to the small house they occupied with their mother, and Frances went to her room, where she cried alone in pain and shame. At this low point in her life, the influence of three men solidified a lifetime distrust of the male sex in Frances Willard's mind and spirit; and the results turned out beyond computation. Frances had courage, and when the tears dried, her eyes were able to see a great work to be performed, for which she had indispensable qualities of imagination and leadership.

"Drink and tobacco are the great separatists between men and women," Frances announced. "Once they used these things together, but woman's evolution has carried her beyond them." And now, along with her friend Kate Jackson, a teacher of French who had resigned in protest against Dr. Fowler, Frances Willard set out to organize the world into a better place. She was a small woman, five feet three inches tall and weighing scarcely one hundred pounds, and she made up for her lack of physical impressiveness by an intensity of spirit that burned through her writings and public speeches. A Woman's Christian Temperance Union had already been formed, and its presidency offered to Dean Willard, who had put it aside because there was not enough time to be both an official of Northwestern University and the head of an organization with the potentialities of the Woman's Christian Temperance Union. Frances now was able to give full time to the WCTU—the acronym already recognized throughout the country—and accepted its presidency in 1879. That was the year in which Frances led a delegation of fifty women into the Illinois State Capitol, along with porters who carried a huge role of muslin, bound in blue and white ribbon, on a wooden platform. Glued to the cloth were ruled pages on which 110,000 men and women had written their names, in the longest petition ever presented to a legislative body. The signers asked passage of a law allowing women to vote whenever questions of regulating the liquor traffic came before the electorate. This proposition typified Miss Willard's manner of working, aiming as it did in one thrust for two objectives, the prohibition of drink, and the granting of suffrage

[134]

to women. Sympathetic legislators wrote a bill to Miss Willard's specifications, but it failed to pass.

Nevertheless, she had shown her followers the meaning of her slogan for the WCTU, which was "Do Everything." To act upon this motto, Miss Willard set up forty departments, each one agitating for a specific reform, such as the limitation of child labor, and increasing the penalties for assaulting women. Frances Willard had her mother as adviser for many years, and a faithful friend, secretary, and biographer in Kate Jackson. Miss Willard did not marry, and it appeared that when she addressed audiences, she was bringing into focus emotions that might have been expended for the benefit of a husband and family. Deep friendships with women brought Frances the sympathetic support she needed in her life of incessant travel, writing, speaking, and acting as moderator among the factions that grew in the Union as it became an international organization, the most influential group of women the world had seen. With WCTU encouragement, the Prohibition Party developed bargaining power, polling 271,058 votes in the presidential campaign of 1892; from this grew the Anti-Saloon League, which finally succeeded in obtaining a national prohibition law in 1919. And prohibition brought on a period of profitable activity in the Chicago underworld, thus linking by a clear chain of events the session of Methodist trustees in pious, bone-dry Evanston, and the doings of Irish and Sicilian gangsters fifty years later on.

The other spinster saint of Chicago, Jane Addams, was a fourteen-year-old schoolgirl at the time Frances Willard went out from the academic world. Jane had a strong-minded father: years before her birth, John Addams on his way to Chicago had written in his diary that Canada, through which he was passing, made a feeling of derision cross his mind because "all this country is subject to the government of a *woman,* and for republicans, this will not do." Then he reached Chicago, a young man with $4,000 in his pocket, looking for a good proposition; after a week, he decided "too many businessmen are already here." Straight across the prairie John Addams rode for three days, until he came to the village of Cedarville in the hills six miles from Freeport, and the same distance south of the Wisconsin border. Here he settled in 1844, and as the years went by, Addams acquired a grist mill, a saw mill, and a thousand acres of land; he became rich; he planted Norway pines on the hillsides; he helped found the Republican party; he served seven terms in the state legislature; he stayed in safety during the Civil War; and he worshiped Lincoln. In turn, Mr. Addams received worship from his daughter Jane. Her mother had died when Jane was two years and four months old, and from that time on her imposing, successful, and masterful father was the center of the

[135]

world. Jane was an odd little thing—frail, pigeon-toed, and carrying her head on one side because of spinal curvature, which gave her a bird-like look; but the child's questing spirit could be felt by any sensitive person who looked into the large intense eyes that dominated her small anxious face. The anxiety came from fear that she might fail to earn her father's approval, or might shame him in some way. Years later, Jane wrote that on walking to and from church with Mr. Addams, she would drop several paces behind, so that "strange people should not know my handsome father owned such a homely little girl."

At the age of six, Jane noticed the shanties of the mill workers, and failed to get a satisfactory answer to her inquiries as to why some people had to live in little houses. When she grew up, said Jane, she hoped to have "a big house in the middle of the little houses" where people might come if they wished. At the age of ten, she started reading her way through the Addams library, getting up an hour early in the morning to consume Pope's translation of *The Iliad*, and a four-volume *History of the World*. By this time Jane's father had married again, giving her a loving stepmother, and a satisfactory stepbrother, George Haldeman, who was six months her junior. The boy made a good playmate for a girl whose back had not yet grown strong, and the two children had all outdoors as a playground, a privilege that Jane remembered through adult life in a way that kept her heart open to street children, so constantly and dangerously interrupted in their play. By contrast Miss Addams recalled the joys that she and George took for granted as "free-ranging country children," climbing hills, exploring caves, tramping through woods, and eating box lunches. Jane and George sometimes had trips to Chicago, but they enjoyed the best day of their lives on a trip to Madison where they saw Old Abe, the living war eagle. A few years later, Jane's father subjected her to another sort of experience by sending her, a girl of fifteen, to attend the deathbed of her old nurse. Jane drove four miles through a snowstorm and found the farmhouse in the gray dusk, with one light showing. Inside, she heard the feeble call of "Sarah," her mother's name. The girl entered the bedroom, no more words were uttered, and the old nurse died. Jane lifted the lamp, and in place of the familiar face saw "strange, august features, stern and withdrawn from all the small affairs of life." Driving home through the snow, Jane "felt the riddle of life and death press hard."

In June 1877, Jane passed entrance examinations for Smith College at Northampton, Massachusetts. Her father decided not to allow her to enter an Eastern college, for he was a trustee of the Rockford Female Seminary, thirty miles from Cedarville, and it occurred to him that it would look better for Jane to obtain her higher education there. Jane was disappointed at not entering Smith, but there was much to be said for Rockford, which had been chartered as a junior college in 1847. The institution came under control of Miss Anna Peck Sill two years later, and started a senior college department which had 50 students among a total enrollment of 180 girls when Jane entered in the autumn of 1877. Among the other entrants in the freshman class, Jane met Ellen Gates Starr, whose future life would be important to Jane Addams and Chicago. Ellen Starr put in only one year at Rockford, but her wit and intelligence caught the interest of students and teachers alike, though the faculty disapproved of her statement that in religion, she sought more than "casual Presbyterianism." Still the English department applauded her essays, "Poetry" and "Art in Florence," written for the college magazine.

After Ellen Starr's departure, Jane became the most interesting student at Rockford. Her appearance was "quaint," as her nephew and biographer James Weber Linn recorded: she stood at Frances Willard's height of five feet, three inches; she still carried her head a bit forward and a little to one side, so that her eyes conveyed an expression of unusual earnestness, Mr. Linn says, "even at that abode of earnestness, Rockford Female Seminary." But as her health improved, through the four years at Rockford, and her back grew strong, the earnestness became lightened by a sparkle of enthusiasm which never left her. That sparkle drew an audience to Jane's room, a center of public discussion except when she hung out the sign "ENGAGED," which meant that she had tasks of study or writing to complete. A pillar of the *Rockford Seminary Magazine*, she contributed essays in faultless Emersonian English, and an eloquent piece on the character of Macbeth, which showed the influence of Coleridge.

It was inevitable that Jane should get into disagreement with Miss Sill, who placed heavy emphasis on Christianity and training for the mission field; each Sunday morning, Jane met with Miss Blaisdell of the classics department and read the New Testament in Greek, for its literary value, as Jane explained to her friends. Miss Sill disapproved of this approach to Scripture, yet how could one forbid the reading of the New Testament in Greek? Battle would have to be joined on some other issue, which turned out to be the pronunciation of Don Quixote in the course on Spanish literature. Jane advocated "Kehotay" against Miss Sill's "Quixxott." Refusing to accept the ruling, Jane drew a two-day suspension from classes. The pedagogues Fowler and Sill seem fated to live in history mostly for the trouble they caused Frances Willard and Jane Addams; but Rockford Seminary, at least, afforded benefits that Miss Sill could not take away. One advantage lay in the nearness of co-educational Beloit College, some of whose men came down to Rockford every Saturday night for a visit at the

Seminary. There were sleighrides in winter, ice-cream suppers in the spring, mandolin concerts, and male voices in the choir on Sunday mornings. Rollin Salisbury was admittedly the brightest young man in the Beloit crowd, and he had a special liking for the big-eyed little Addams girl. At the end of his senior year, Salisbury asked Jane to marry him. She refused the offer, and he remained a bachelor all his life, and throughout a career as one of the world's leading geologists at the great Dr. Harper's University of Chicago. In that same spring, Jane competed against Rollin at the Interstate Collegiate Oratorical Contest. Another speaker among the nine finalists was William Jennings Bryan of Illinois College at Jacksonville who impressed the judges with his platform presence. Neither Bryan nor Salisbury came in first, although to the chagrin of Rockford they both finished ahead of Jane.

On graduation, Jane Addams decided to become a doctor. It meant going east to study, and this time Mr. Addams did not alter his daughter's plans. Jane entered the Women's Medical College in Philadelphia, and during her first year suffered a collapse that sent her back to Cedarville for rest and quiet. Agreeing with the doctors that medical school was out of the question, Mr. Addams suggested that Jane should travel abroad to recover her health while adding to her general education. Off she went then on an extended tour of the sort that prosperous Midwesterners delighted in; like Julia Newberry, Jane planned to travel for two or three years, and she meant to do more than see the usual sights and enjoy social sponsorship of the sort available to a rich American girl in European cities.

While Jane Addams was traveling abroad in search of health and enlightenment, Mrs. Potter Palmer had advanced to her place of unquestioned eminence at home. It would be unfair to Bertha Palmer to think of her only as an ornamental personage. From the beginnings of her career as chatelaine on Lake Shore Drive she aspired to be more than merely a society queen, to be in her own way a thoughtful and useful citizen. It was true that Mrs. Palmer had a well-developed sense of display. But she also had a sense of propriety which told her that a great lady must be a real lady, whose character showed in the way she behaved toward those who could do nothing for her. For Bertha Palmer, this classification of humanity included nearly everyone in Chicago, for Mrs. Palmer, secure in her castle with her personal beauty, her many marvelous possessions, her wonderful clothes, her jewelry and works of art, seldom found herself in the position of having to ask a favor. Even before the days on Lake Shore Drive, she had seen her sister Ida marry Frederick Dent Grant, the President's son, on October 20, 1874. At this time, Bertha's son Honoré Palmer made his first public appearance, at the age of eight months, carried on a satin pillow and wearing a long embroidered dress with a pale blue ribbon sash. Honoré watched the ceremony with perfect calmness, for which he received compliments as his Scotch nurse took him away through the crowd at the reception. Such a lucky woman Bertha Palmer seemed, by the later 1880s, with Honoré a big boy and his younger brother Potter coming along, and the great house to fill with guests, not only fashionable folk, but interesting people, men and women of achievement who lived in Chicago or passed through the place, as everyone was sure to do sooner or later. Personifying the best side of the city—its respect for art and literature, its desire for improvement, and its hearty welcome to strangers—Bertha Palmer entertained politicians and reformers, labor leaders and shop girls, eccentrics, cranks, and zealots of many kinds. And in the cavernous kitchens of the mansion, Mrs. Palmer conducted a cooking school for society girls. Why should a rich girl learn to cook? There were several reasons, according to Bertha Palmer: for one thing, a young woman needed practical knowledge to direct a husband's household properly; for another, a society girl might marry a poor man; it had been known to happen, for if the young man was obviously on his way up, some things could be overlooked. But suppose the young couple should be so pushed for money they could afford *only one servant*. Then it would be a good thing if the bride could prepare meals, on that servant's twice-monthly day off. Mrs. Palmer refused to grant a diploma for anything so easy as chicken salad, or a chafing-dish concoction. Society girls were not the only young women to be taught at Mrs. Palmer's house; Bertha held meetings for factory girls, and provided space for the Woman's Trade Union League, helping the millinery workers to organize a successful strike. Nothing could possibly be more different from the policies of Mrs. Astor, the New York and Newport society queen. Mrs. Astor had a councilor of state named Ward McAllister, who put a phrase into the language by decreeing that only four hundred people, whom he named, met Mrs. Astor's social standard. The nearest thing to a Ward McAllister around Mrs. Palmer was her young friend Chatfield-Taylor, and he was neither a snob nor a fool, nor did he try to lay down the law in the social world, where he was gathering material for his first novel, *An American Princess*. His heroine, who resembled some of Henry James's young ladies, was a delightful girl from Lake Forest, well-mannered and rich, who married a titled Englishman, as American girls were beginning to do in those days. Bertha Palmer deprecated such marriages, and many years later, as a widow traveling in Europe, tactfully got rid of an elderly alcoholic peer for whom Edward VII was acting as matchmaker. Chicagoans including Joseph Medill's granddaughter, along with other Americans, were to find wife-hunting European nobility a bad lot, all too likely to gamble, run after other women, mix morphine with brandy, and wind up in private Swiss hospitals complaining of snakes and spiders on the sheets.

Bertha Palmer had a better husband than most available examples of European nobility, and now in the last years of the 1880s he was still in good health, though beginning to show signs of wear, and not too proud to murmur to a friend at a party, "My feet hurt." Potter Palmer's presence at the hotel inspired employees to watch over the patrons' comfort in a way that can only be guessed at nowadays. For example, the Negro in charge of the cigar counter had a prodigious memory, and if he had sold a drummer a certain brand of cigar, and the traveler returned a year later and stopped at the hotel, out would come a box of the same brand, along with plenty of *yassah, yassuh,* plus a grin from white teeth, and a deferential bow. "I remember *you,* certainly, suh." The drummer would go away walking on air, and Potter Palmer would allow himself a smile. But woe to the employee about whom a complaint was lodged. In the guest's presence Palmer or a hotel official would upbraid the culprit and fire him from his job, though sometimes merely until after the guest had gone. It was easy to find help, with few so skilled and valuable as to have the temerity to argue with Mr. Palmer. The same conditions existed in other lines of work: Phillip D. Armour, George Pullman, and Marshall Field fired employees high and low, when displeased or in a mood for retrenchment. Indeed, Field had a yearly custom that chills the blood as we think of it today. During the Christmas season, he would invite a dozen executives to dinner at the house on Prairie Avenue. There would be plenty of wine and liquor, though the host took none. After dinner, when the cigars were fuming and the brandy lay in the glasses, Field would announce the bonuses, and praise those who had performed well during the year. He would also announce the firing of one man, with the remark that "After January first, Mr. So-and-so will no longer be with us." And that dead-looking left eye reflected no more sympathy than its fellow.

Another typical large employer was Victor Fremont Lawson of the *Chicago Daily News,* who had been moved to conversion at a revival meeting by Dwight L. Moody, leaping to his feet and staggering down the sawdust trail to the mourners' bench with cries and groans of deepest emotion while the golden voice of Ira Sankey sang "Just As I Am, Without One Plea." Sincere as he had been in his response to Christian preaching, Lawson refused to study the passages in Scripture having to do with generous treatment of employees. Granting a raise seemed to cause him physical anguish; his personal papers now to be seen at the Newberry Library contain files of correspondence from the publisher, vacationing in

Egypt, and fighting the bestowal of a two-dollar raise on a reporter in Chicago. Lawson had never been short of money. His father, a prosperous merchant, had sent him to boarding school at Exeter and then instead of entering college young Victor had gone into business with such solid backing that he was able to take control of the *Chicago Daily News* and make it a great newspaper. In many ways Lawson was a good employer, except for the difficulty over salaries; yet when men left for higher pay elsewhere, he called them ungrateful and took it as a personal hurt.

Lawson did not fraternize with Palmer, Pullman, and Field, pillars of the millionaires' table at the Chicago Club. As a daily lunch companion the millionaires preferred Robert Lincoln, now a Chicago lawyer and figure of importance in the city. He held a big job at Washington as Secretary of War from 1881 to 1885, mostly in the Administration of Chester A. Arthur. Thereafter, except for six months as Minister to Great Britain, Robert Lincoln devoted himself to Chicago enterprises, serving for a time as president of the Pullman Company. Most people thought him starchy and hard to talk wtih, but the regulars at the millionaires' table did not go in for idle chatter. They enjoyed a good discussion of debentures, with a brisk exchange on preferred stocks to follow. They could count on Robert Lincoln for such information, and he seldom missed lunch at the table, which was round, and always afforded room for John Crerar, a director of the Pullman Company who was an old Scotch bachelor with a red face, white hair, and sharp nose, famed for piety, devotion to his ancient mother, and unfailing attendance at all social events in Chicago. They reserved a seat at all times for Henry W. King, "the Mayor of Rush Street," an elder of the fashionable Fourth Presbyterian Church. King's unassailable probity had made him head of the Relief and Aid Society which distributed millions of dollars to victims of the fire. He tried not to sit next to John deKoven, director of banks, railways, and trust companies, who became irascible if anyone questioned his opinions. A more agreeable companion would be Franklin MacVeagh, wealthy wholesale grocer, patron of H. H. Richardson and one of the Club's "college-bred men" as its historian was proud to point out.

Reverenced for their power and wealth by the other members, the companions of the millionaries' table never joined the hard-drinking group that congregated in a stuffy barroom on the second floor of the club's second home on Monroe Street. This room was known as the café, and it made up for any lack of magnificence by being snug and comfortable, not only for human members of the club but for Charley the rat, who sometimes ventured out to sample the cheese and biscuits. Charley was a fine rat of the good Chicago strain, adding intelligence and a sense of just

[141]

how far he could go to native quickness and alertness. Members admired the bold yet deft way with which this small animal helped himself at the buffet, and they used his presence in playing a joke on any visitor who might say, "I do believe I see a rat over there" by replying, "Rat? On the sideboard? Impossible, old man. Are you sure you're quite all right?" It is likely that there were several Charleys, for hundreds of rats swarmed in the walls. The club remained in its decrepit house until 1893, when it bought the building vacated by the Chicago Art Institute at Michigan Avenue and Van Buren Street. Long before the move, the governors discussed the need for taking in new members, especially younger men. At the annual meeting in 1889, a committeeman proposed offering membership to fifty young men at a reduced fee; the proposer said that of the young men already in the club, "many had died, left town, married, or made other arrangements," a statement that brought down the house, as the historian recorded.

Whether or not they had trouble paying an entrance fee of $100, young men achieving membership at the Chicago Club found the charges reasonable enough once they got in. The wine list made good reading with Pommery or Cliquot Yellow Label at $2.75 a quart and Mumm's Extra Dry at $2.50. Old Oscar Pepper rye whiskey came to $1.25 per quart, while Russian caviar brought twenty-five cents a generous portion. Clubmen were equally comfortable two miles north at the Union on Dearborn Street, where the entire staff of servants waiting on 462 members 24 hours a day received total wages of $3,852 for the year 1882. They probably received an equal additional sum in Christmas gratuities, but the steward's annual salary, not included in the figure for servants' wages, was only $1,000, although he took pride in having sold 100,000 cigars during the year, and 6,000 quarts of wine and liquor. President of the Union was Henry Bishop, known for his tact and courtesy, who also sat at the millionaires' table downtown.

Despite the comforts and privileges they enjoyed, Henry Bishop and his friends had a gnawing worry, from which their minds were never entirely free. The census tabulations kept their nerves strung tight: in the years between 1884 and 1886, the population had grown from 630,000 to 830,-000, but only one in every four Chicago residents was white American born. The rest were German, Irish, Bohemian, Polish, Swedish, and Norwegian. And although the magnates of native American birth had money, land, stockyards, and factories under their control, these rich men knew that Chicago was the center of a revolutionary movement of the foreign born, notably the Germans, that might grow to be powerful and dangerous. The movement was no secret, for in addition to the *Times*,

Herald, Post, Daily News, Mail, Tribune, Record, Journal, and *Inter Ocean,* Chicago had half a dozen anarchist, communist, and socialist papers that persistently called for drastic redistribution of American wealth. However logical the arguments for this change might be, men like Field and Pullman regarded them with horror, and understandably refused to consider such proposals in a philosophical frame of mind.

Credited with inventing the sleeping car, Pullman in fact had patented, with another man, an idea that a number of experimenters had worked on. The Pullman Company had grown because of his organizing talent, and his flair for promotion as shown in providing Mrs. Lincoln's car, and his perception that the American public was going to demand comfort and luxury in railroad travel, and would find the money to pay for it. In 1879 George Pullman commissioned Solon Beman to lay out a model town for workers, near the plant on the far South Side. Landlord as well as employer, Pullman attempted to regulate the men's lives in a way that they resented. Strife was to ensue, the first large installment of trouble arriving in 1882 when Pullman cut the transportation allowances for men not yet accommodated in the company village from twenty to ten cents a day. One thousand men struck, but others took their jobs, and they never again drew carfare or any other form of pay from George M. Pullman. The same thing happened to the 150 men in the freight car department who struck against a wage cut in 1884. Pullman continued cutting pay, in one department at a time, so that his people did not suffer the plant-wide grievance that might have organized them as a unit, but in the early spring of 1885 the militant Knights of Labor called out 1,400 Pullman workers in the movement for the eight-hour day, something their employer regarded as wicked and insane. He carried his point, with the help of strikebreakers and armed guards; for the next eight years no known union man worked for Pullman, and it may be that his intransigence during that period did more for the labor movement than Eugene V. Debs, the organizer who went to prison for it. One can understand, at any rate, how George Pullman felt when an underling placed before him a copy of a radical Chicago paper, *The Alarm,* and pointed out a letter to the editor:

"Dynamite! Of all the good stuff, this is the stuff. Stuff several pounds of this sublime stuff into an inch pipe (gas or water pipe), plug up both ends, insert a cap with a fuse attached, place this in the immediate neighborhood of a lot of rich men who live by the sweat of other people's brows and light the fuse. A most cheerful and gratifying result will follow. In giving dynamite to the downtrodden millions of the globe, science has done its best work. The dear stuff can be carried around in the pocket without danger, while it is a formidable weapon against any force of militia, police or detectives that may want to stifle the cry for justice that goes forth from the plundered slaves. It is something not very ornamental but exceedingly useful. It can be used against persons and things, it is better to use it against the former than against bricks and masonry. It is a genuine boon for the disinherited, while it brings terror and fear to the robbers. It brings terror only to the guilty, and consequently the Senator who introduced a bill in Congress to stop its manufacture and use, must be guilty of something. He fears the wrath of an outraged people that has been duped and swindled by him and his like. The same must be the case with the 'servant' of the people who introduced a like measure in the Senate of the Indiana legislature. . . . Dynamite is like Banquo's ghost, it keeps on fooling around somewhere or other in spite of his satanic majesty. A pound of this good stuff beats a bushel of ballots all hollow, and don't you forget it. Our law makers might as well try to sit down on a crater of a volcano or a bayonet as to endeavor to stop the manufacture or use of dynamite. . . . From thought to action is not far, and when the worker has seen the chains, he need but look a little closer to find near at hand the sledge with which to shatter every link. The sledge is dynamite."

The writer of this letter signed himself "T. Lizius." Nothing further being heard from or about T. Lizius, the industrialists always maintained that the letter, which appeared on February 21, 1885, was a disguised editorial, and they usually presented it as such when quoting it to show the danger of revolution in Chicago. There did exist a threat of civil war, with white-collar clerks and junior executives organized into rifle companies, while German Soicalists on the North Side armed themselves and drilled in hunting clubs and shooting societies. The *Tribune* had laid down the challenge: "If the Communists of this city are counting on the looseness of our police system and the tendency to proceed against crowds by due process of law, and hope on that account to receive more leniency than in Europe, they have ignored some of the significant episodes in American history. . . . Judge Lynch is an American institution. Every lamp post in Chicago will be decorated with a Communistic carcass if necessary to prevent wholesale incendiarism . . . or any attempt at it." Mrs. Cyrus H. McCormick could hardly have been an advocate of hanging troublemakers out of hand; like her husband a benefactor of the Presbyterian Church, Nettie Fowler McCormick had seen Cyrus die in 1884, worn by his struggles with men who demanded not only an eight-hour day, but ten hours' pay for it, which he called an intolerable increase in the wage rate. For the time being Mrs. McCormick was regent of the vast factory on the West Side. Thinking of the future, she sometimes enclosed newspaper clippings about labor troubles in letters to her son at Princeton. "I hope you discuss these matters with your classmates," she would write, "for you and young men like you will some day soon have charge of this country." It well might be that the younger Cyrus McCormick thus received his first information about two fellow Chicagoans, Albert R. Parsons and August Spies of the Socialist Labor Party; for during the eight-hour disputes, the *Chicago Mail* featured these agitators on its editorial page:

"There are two dangerous ruffians at large in this city; two sneaking cowards who are trying to create trouble. One of them is named Parsons; the other is named Spies. . . . These two fellows have been at work fomenting disorder for the past ten years. They should have been driven out of the city long ago. They would not be tolerated in any other community on earth. . . . They are looking for riot and plunder. . . . Mark them. . . . Keep them in view. . . . *Make an example of them if trouble does occur.*"

On May 1, 1886, it appeared that Chicago was thoroughly prepared for any trouble that might take place on this traditional holiday of labor organizations. The police had gone on an emergency schedule and 1,350 militiamen stood to arms; indeed, the police, guardsmen, and private forces from Pinkerton's and other agencies had been alerted early in the year. The police had frequently broken up workers' meetings, and had themselves sustained injuries in the fighting. The resulting enmity between working men and police had come to focus late that winter at the McCormick works. Here the management had ended a dispute about unionization by closing the plant on February 16, locking out 1,400 men. A strike followed, but on March 1, 300 men reported for work under guard of police and Pinkertons. No violence occurred, but the big employers continued to fear an outbreak of terror on May 1, which turned out to be a peaceful day of picnics, parades, and sign-carrying demonstrations that resulted in no extra work for the police. The Chicago Trades and Labor Assembly ended the day by holding a grand ball.

That was Saturday night, and Sunday passed quietly, but on Monday an outburst of violence ended the truce and ushered in a time of trouble that would sacrifice human lives to the bomb, the gun, and the gallows. On the afternoon of Monday, May 3, the lumber handlers' union called a meeting near the McCormick plant, and although they were a small minority of the McCormick labor force, almost six thousand men turned out for their rally. August Spies was the principal speaker, assuring the workers that they would win their fight for shorter hours if they would close ranks and stand together. Just as he ended his speech the McCormick plant whistles wailed, and 500 members of the audience rushed off to attack the men issuing from the gates. The strikebreakers retreated into the factory, where windows crashed to the ground as union men hurled stones against the glass. The police fired pistols, and answering shots came from the crowd. In a few minutes Captain John Bonfield appeared, at the head of 200 additional officers, who routed the crowd with clubbing and pistol fire. August Spies hurried over to the factory, arriving in time to see the crowd running from the police, who killed one demonstrator, seriously injured six, and inflicted minor injuries on about fifty others. The police suffered injuries to six men, two of them badly hurt. Spies now went to the office of his paper, the *Arbeiter-Zeitung*, where he read an erroneous report in a late edition of the *Chicago Daily News* that the police had killed six workers. He then wrote a manifesto calling all laboring men to arms.

Next morning the papers carried praise for Captain Bonfield, and quoted him as saying, "We have perfected arrangements for prompt and decisive action in all cases. There will be more or less rioting, a few sanguinary conflicts, some blood spilling perhaps. But I do not anticipate anything like a repetition of the riot of 1877." And the *Inter Ocean* editorialized, "It was demonstrated yesterday that the men who follow the lead of Spies and Parsons are a menace to society." Crowds of working people took to the streets, cursed the police, attacked them when it seemed advisable, sacked and burned saloons believed to be resorts of informers, and twice fought large police detachments near the McCormick works. There might be worse to come: the *Arbeiter-Zeitung* distributed handbills calling for a mass meeting that night in the Haymarket, at which speakers would denounce "the shooting of our fellow workmen yesterday afternoon." Printed in English and German, the leaflet concluded: "WORKING MEN, ARM YOURSELVES AND APPEAR IN FULL FORCE!—THE EXECUTIVE COMMITTEE."

Haymarket Square was an open space formed between Halsted and Desplaines streets by a widening of Randolph Street, four blocks west of the South Branch. About 1,300 people turned out, although the square could hold many times that number; the proximity of the Desplaines Street police station may have accounted for the smallness of the crowd. But those who did attend got a bonus in the appearance of Mayor Carter Harrison, who rode up and doffed his big black hat to enthusiastic applause. Harrison had the reputation of being the working man's friend, and although he had grown rich from prudent handling of real estate, he did not kowtow to those who had grown even richer. Marshall Field once rebuked the mayor for being too liberal, remarking in the names of his colleagues at the millionaires' table, "Mr. Harrison, we represent great interests in Chicago." Carter Harrison replied, "Mr. Field, any poor man owning a single small cottage as his sole possession has the same interest in Chicago as its richest citizen." Carter Harrison had no hesitation in addressing a labor crowd, for he had provided many jobs for union leaders in the city administration. Before the Haymarket meeting, he had ordered Captain Bonfield to hold a reserve force at the Desplaines Street station house; then he rode out to observe the situation, stayed through August Spies's remarks, and almost to the end of the speech by Albert Parsons, which the mayor understood would bring the program to a close. With cloudy skies threatening rain, and about 900 people still in the Haymarket, Mayor Harrison went home; everything seemed peaceful and under control. After Harrison's departure, Parsons ended his speech, but instead of calling for adjournment, introduced another speaker, Samuel Fielden, who hardly got going before it started to drizzle and the crowd melted to about 400. Fielding saw it was time to wind things up and at twenty minutes past ten he was saying, "In conclusion—"when a column of 180 policemen, led by Captain Bonfield, came marching across the square and halted at the speakers' platform. Bonfield called out, "In the name of the people of the State of Illinois, I command this meeting immediately and peaceably to disperse." He pointed at some bystanders and continued, "I call upon you and you to assist." Fielding said, "We are peaceable" and the speakers filed down from the rostrum.

There was a pause, in which no one seemed to know what to do next. Then something came through the air and struck the ground near the middle of the police column, and the shock of an explosion knocked people to the sidewalk fifty yards away. At the point of explosion, men went down not to rise again—one policeman killed, and six fatally hurt. The uninjured officers charged into the crowd, hitting with clubs and firing pistols, killing one and wounding twelve. About sixty people vanished into dark alleys, hurt but still able to run. And the bell in the City Hall tower began ringing, as it had for the great fire, to warn all citizens that revolution had come to Chicago.

6

"We Have Been on the Brink of a Volcano!"

AS A RESULT OF THE EXPLOSION IN THE HAYMARKET, EIGHT MEN CAME
to trial. These defendants were the sifting of two hundred suspects whom
the police had questioned; the State charged them with conspiring to
murder Mathias J. Degan, the officer who died at the scene. In the six
weeks between explosion and trial, six more policemen died of injuries
inflicted by the bomb, and a second spectator died from the effects of
police gunfire. State's Attorney Julius S. Grinnell led the prosecution, and
although the defendants had good lawyers working for them, everybody
knew they would be convicted. During the trial Grinnell shifted ground,
telling the jury he would show them who had thrown the bomb, but later
asserting that it did not matter who threw the bomb, for the defendants
had advocated revolutionary violence, and if people were killed by any
action of the sort recommended, then the defendants were all guilty, as
accessories to murder in the first degree. This argument had the logic of
a war crimes trial: after the killing starts, be sure not to finish on a losing
side. The judge hammered home this point, curbing the defense, smiling
on the prosecution, and at last instructing the jury either to convict, or put
the whole nation in terrible danger. Accordingly, on the morning of Friday June 20, 1886, the verdict came in that August Spies, Michael Schwab,
Samuel Fielden, Albert R. Parsons, Adolph Fischer, George Engel, and
Louis Lingg were to be hanged; and the eighth defendant, Oscar E.
Neebe, was to spend fifteen years in jail.

Every big newspaper in the country echoed the satisfaction and relief that the Chicago editorialists immediately expressed. The *Inter Ocean* stated, "Anarchism has been on trial ever since May 4; and it has now got its verdict. . . . The verdict is unquestionably the voice of justice, the solemn verdict of the world's best civilization. . . . It now comes to be understood that such issues as anarchism are of the nature of treason, and that, in order to secure the public safety, it is necessary that those who seek to propagate them be treated accordingly and summarily." The *Tribune* said, "The verdict has killed Anarchism in Chicago, and those who sympathize with its horrible doctrines will speedily emigrate from her borders or at least never again make a sign of their sentiments." But it was to be regretted that the "murderers, communistic conspirators who sought to throttle the constitutions and laws" would undoubtedly appeal to the Supreme Court at Washington. This they did, but the High Court let the sentences stand. The pardoning power of Governor Richard J. Oglesby now became the anarchists' last hope, and there was pressure in favor of commutation from death to imprisonment. One of the most striking expressions of belief in the anarchists' innocence came from a young woman named Nina Van Zandt. The daughter of a Chicago businessman, Nina had attended the trial, and fallen in love with August Spies, although she had never met him. His attorneys allowed a marriage by proxy to take place, so that Nina Van Zandt Spies would be a martyr's widow if the State of Illinois carried the sentences out. Major Kirkland reached the conclusion that at least three should have their sentences commuted, and that Oscar Neebe ought to be released. Henry Demarest Lloyd, son-in-law of Deacon Bross of the *Tribune*, also raised his voice for clemency, which caused the Deacon to alter his will so that the Lloyds would inherit no *Tribune* stock. And Lyman Gage at the First National Bank attempted to use his influence as a financier to convince his fellow magnates that the trial wouldn't do: granted that anarchists were bad men and belonged in prison, one shouldn't hang seven men as accessories to a murder without showing some connection to the crime. The trial looked bad, said Gage, and would haunt them later on, after the executions created martyrs for the revolutionary cause.

Early in November, a week before the scheduled hanging day, Lyman Gage learned that the governor might spare the lives of Neebe, Parsons, Schwab and Spies if big men in Chicago requested that he do so. Along with Demarest Lloyd, Gage thereupon called fifty Chicagoans to a private meeting at which he hoped Marshall Field would take the lead in recommending that they all go on record in favor of mercy for the anarchists. As soon as the men took seats in a conference room at the Board of Trade,

Field rose and said that since he made no claim to be a speaker, he had brought someone along to speak for him—State's Attorney Julius Grinnell. As Field's spokesman, the prosecutor said that the trial had been fair and the sentences justified. At the end of Grinnell's speech, most of those present got up and left, making it obvious to Gage and Lloyd that Field's clout was greater than theirs. Nevertheless, the governor continued to receive pleas for clemency signed by union members, teachers, and other citizens, including Benjamin F. Ayer, Lyman Trumbull, and Marvin Hughitt of the North Western railroad.

Hanging day was November 11, and as it came closer an unbearable anxiety gripped Chicago. Thousands were asking the governor to spare the anarchists' lives, but at least an equal number had let him know that they wanted the prisoners to die. Everyone admitted that the Haymarket bomb had come from somewhere among those people in Chicago who called for the city's industrial structure to be drastically changed, and this was a proposition that the defendants had endorsed. And one of the men on trial, Louis Lingg, had been a maker of bombs, though it was not established that he had made the Haymarket bomb, and acceptable witnesses placed him two miles from the Haymarket at the time of explosion. But a bomb had burst, seven policemen had died, sixty-eight more had been wounded. So then it was a fact that radical revolutionaries, or at least one such person, had struck at conservative Chicago and drawn blood. Therefore it was easy to believe, if one wished to, that the seven anarchists facing death had formed the general staff of revolution, and must be exterminated before they destroyed the country. But if one granted this much, who could say what might happen when the anarchists' followers took their revenge?

Extraordinary events on Sunday, November 6, served to strengthen the argument that the anarchists represented organizations that wielded dangerous power even with the leaders in jail. At ten o'clock that morning, warders searched Lingg's cell and found four dynamite bombs. Six hours passed before Sheriff Matson announced the discovery, and cried to the reporters, "Merciful God! We have been on the brink of a volcano!" Then he added, "What a revolution in public sentiment this will produce." The news brought a swift change in public opinion that weakened the clemency movement just when final appeals were going in. William M. Salter of the Chicago Ethical Culture Society, for example, had worked side by side with Lyman Gage and Henry Demarest Lloyd, but now said he hardly had the courage to visit Governor Oglesby for one last plea. He added that the bomb discovery was "the worst thing that could have happened."

Despite this discouragement, delegations appeared at the governor's hearing on Wednesday, November 9, 1881, handing up petitions which more than 200,000 people had signed in Chicago, New York, and other large cities. The conservative, craft-union element in the labor movement made an appeal through its leader Samuel Gompers, who spoke from the floor. Oglesby heard them all, and closed the meeting with a promise that he would announce his decision on the following day.

That day was November 10, and shortly after nine in the morning news came from Cook County jail that plunged Chicago and Springfield into wild excitement. The jailers had heard what they described as a muffled explosion in the cell occupied by Louis Lingg. Rushing to investigate, they found that Lingg had blown his face off with some kind of explosive which he had managed to detonate in his mouth. He lived for six hours, conscious to the end. The authorities theorized that someone had smuggled dynamite in a cigar, or that Lingg had managed to hide a fulminating cap from the bombs found in his cell. Some said the jailers had killed him; people believed what they wanted to believe. And many Chicagoans now said that the anarchists would escape the hangman, not as a result of action by the governor, but because the proletariat would rise and treat Cook County prison as the sans-culottes had treated the Bastille. Anxiety in some circles became acute; the owners of one large wholesale house distributed 150 breech-loading rifles to the employees, with unquestioning faith that their people would defend the established order.

At seven that evening, Governor Oglesby made his decision known. Reading an official communication to newspapermen crowded around the desk in his study, the governor said he was satisfied that all the condemned men were guilty; however, it would be possible to "modify" the sentences of Fielden and Schwab to imprisonment for life. The others must hang. With Lingg already dead, that left Parsons, Fischer, Spies, and Engel to die on the following day, and at fifteen minutes past noon on Friday, November 11, the four men stood in their cells to greet the party of clergymen, officials, and executioners that came to get them. Only in dreadful nightmares can one have an idea of what it must be to walk out of a room knowing that one's life is to be suddenly stopped in a few minutes' time. Whatever their inward horrors may have been, the anarchists remained calm, and encouraged one another, walking to their deaths with composure beyond praise. A hush had fallen on the city, where police, deputized citizens, militiamen, and Army troops stood alert, not knowing what to expect when the long tension was released. At the last moment, each anarchist uttered a bold farewell, and Parsons cried, "Let the voice of the people be heard!"

Every Chicago newspaper had installed a special wire to the prison, and an instant after the trap fell, telegraph keys crackled in the city rooms and copyboys ran downstairs to fasten up signs already prepared in black type: THE ANARCHISTS ARE DEAD. Upon reading this news, the citizens who had stood in crowds around the bulletin boards turned away and went about their business. Calm descended on Chicago; no communes rushed from the streets where the workers lived; the soldiers stacked arms. Whatever their beliefs about the guilt or innocence of the anarchists, almost every man and woman in Chicago felt more comfortable now that they were dead. Forgetting the men still in prison, prosperous Chicago believed the case irrevocably closed; there would be no more trouble, and it was even possible that the city and nation had witnessed the dawn of a golden age.

7

Saint Jane and Others

THERE WERE A FEW CHICAGOANS WHO SAW THAT WHAT HAD DAWNED was only a gilded age, and they developed the city's social conscience, which lay in the keeping of such men as Henry Demarest Lloyd, Lyman Gage, and Dr. David Swing. This erudite clergyman, who came from historic Lane Theological Seminary in Cincinnati, had raised up a fearsome enemy in Dr. Francis Landey Patton, chaplain to Cyrus McCormick and a mighty prelate among those who had made Chicago the Presbyterian Rome. As the leading benefactor of his church, McCormick had subsidized the Chicago seminary which later bore his name, where he installed Dr. Patton as Professor of Didactic and Polemical Theology. Patton thought he heard unsound doctrine preached by David Swing at the Fourth Presbyterian Church, and brought charges before Chicago Presbytery. The resulting heresy trial went against Swing, but the decision was reversed in his favor by the Synod. After this vindication, David Swing left Fourth Presbyterian and established a nondenominational protestant Central Church downtown, where he labored for some years as Chicago's most influential clergyman, carrying even more weight than Philip Armour's personal preacher, the great Dr. Frances Wakely Gunsaulus, because in addition to speaking before large crowds, Swing wrote regularly for the newspapers. Having failed to destroy Swing or run him out of town, Patton and McCormick prayed and took counsel together; and in 1881, Patton went to Princeton Seminary as Stuart Professor of the Relations of

Philosophy and Science to the Christian Religion, later became president of Princeton College, and lived to be ninety-one years old. Meanwhile David Swing recommended to his hearers and readers such books as Demarest Lloyd's *Wealth Against Commonwealth*. He also spoke highly of Lyman Gage for the series of meetings the banker organized to examine all points of view on matters concerning capital and labor. This Lyman Judson Gage was so open-minded that he welcomed socialists and anarchists to his forum. It tells much of Gage's character that in 1891, after he had fought to save the Haymarket defendants, and furnished a platform for socialists, the directors of the First National Bank elected him president. But it also tells something of Chicago: a city in which a man whom his enemies called a parlor liberal could become head of a big bank was not a city entirely in the grip of Philistines. William McKinley made Gage his Secretary of the Treasury a few years later; the dignified, frock-coated McKinley was the lackey of a hard-boiled Cleveland industrialist named Mark Hanna, and both master and man would have spat on the Grand Old Flag before they would put a bleeding-heart in office. So it can be seen that Lyman Gage was not only enlightened in viewpoint, but tactful in manner. His background had been typical; born in New York State, he had left school at fourteen, and served his time keeping books in a store for a dollar a week and sleeping on the woolen-goods shelf; he reached Chicago in the 1870s, and achieved the First National presidency at the age of forty-five. He had suffered hardships like Field and Pullman, but money and power had not turned him mean. Though not a wide reader, he came upon the same idea of the social contract that haunted John S. Wright. And in his notebooks, Gage set down that the Haymarket affair "led me and others of like mind to consider whether repression by force might not be supplemented by moral methods. It was evident the social fabric was being torn by mental misunderstanding which might be healed by a better comprehension of the ideas and motives which actuate men in their relations with each other in the social state." Once a month the group of lawyers, ministers, trade unionists, businessmen, and agitators met at Gage's house, all agreeing to some extent with the banker's belief that social welfare could be advanced by orderly discussion.

At this time Gage, the banker, appeared to be the chief guardian of Chicago's conscience, for Clarence Darrow had not yet started to champion the underprivileged. On the contrary, Darrow held an important post in Philistine ranks as staff lawyer for the North Western railroad. But he had met a practical idealist for whom he had deep respect: she was Jane Addams, returned from abroad and starting her first decade of achievement as the last ten years of the nineteenth century came on.

During her travels Jane had visited London and there, on a series of trips to the East End slums, had encountered the idea that dominated the rest of her life. It was a doctrine of social amelioration that was called settlement work, because its fundamental rule required that privileged and educated people, seeking to cure evils in the slums, must themselves move into blighted neighborhoods and settle there as residents. Young men from the universitives, led by Arnold Toynbee, had pioneered the movement, and the first London settlement house was named for him. Looking through Toynbee Hall, Jane saw that the reformers intended not only to help the "poorer classes" become less poor by improvement of earning power in the future, but also proposed to brighten their lives here and now, with music, literature, theatricals, drawing classes, visits to art galleries, pursuit of hobbies, and the simple comfort and pleasure of friendly conversation in attractive rooms. All this was easier said than done, and the reformer Toynbee died of exhaustion in his thirty-second year. But Toynbee Hall lived on to give Jane Addams the central idea that she developed in Chicago.

Jane Addams returned to the United States in June 1888, accompanied by Ellen Gates Starr, who also had visited Toynbee Hall. At some point during their conversations as the train carried them from New York to Chicago, Jane said, "I have at last finished with the everlasting preparation for life." All that Jane lacked was a place to begin, and she found it at 335 South Halsted Street, one mile west of State Street and one mile east of Ashland Avenue, where the mansion of Charles J. Hull was waiting for the wreckers. Charles Hull had been born in 1820 at Manchester, Connecticut, and he resembled many a Chicagoan in the harshness of his early life. He managed to acquire a rudimentary education during the few hours of leisure available on his grandparents' farm, and eventually found his way to the Harvard Law School, where he lived mostly on oatmeal until he obtained a degree. Hull then went to Chicago and gave up law in favor of real estate speculation. The stampede from Chicago lots in the 1857 panic trampled him into bankruptcy, but like John S. Wright, he hung on somehow, and made another fortune. The Halsted Street house had been a suburban villa when Hull built it, but by the time he died in the winter of 1889, the neighborhood had changed. Poor foreigners lived all around in squalid tenements, factories filled the air with greasy smoke, and the iron tires of drays battered the cobblestones, while the drivers added their cursing and cracking of whips to the horrible din. This was in contrast to Jane's childhood, and to Rockford Female Seminary with its quiet lawns. Yet it fitted well with what Jane referred to as her "very simple plan to rent a house in a part of Chicago where many primitive and actual needs are found, in which young women, who had been given over too exclusively to study, might learn from life itself."

Charles Hull's plan when making his will also had been simple: he left his entire estate, since his wife and children were dead, to Miss Helen Culver, who had been his confidential secretary for many years. Miss Culver found herself in control of land and securities worth $4,000,000. She distributed one fourth of his estate among Charles Hull's other relatives, and then began to look for ways to put the remaining money to work for the benefit of Chicago. Some years later she gave $1,000,000 to President Harper to finance biological studies at the university; but at the time Jane Addams went house-hunting, Helen Culver acted only as landlord, renting the old Halsted Street mansion as she would have to anyone who offered enough to justify keeping it from destruction. And so on September 14, 1889, Jane Addams moved into Hull House, the "place of work and residence" which remained her home, although she traveled far on occasion, until her death forty-six years later. For one year, Miss Culver watched her tenant; at the end of that year, she came to Jane and placed in her hands the deed to the house and lot, and other Chicago property. "It is what Mr. Hull would have done," said Helen Culver.

Ellen Gates Starr and the housekeeper Mary Keyser moved in with Jane at the founding of Hull House settlement. They knew what they planned to do, for Miss Addams had defined their purpose in practical terms. She proposed "to provide a center for a higher civic and social life; to institute and maintain educational and philanthropic enterprises and to investigate and improve conditions in the center's neighborhood." But from the beginning, Miss Addams said that she and Ellen Starr were not merely reformers, looking down from heights and improving the minds of people below. There would be benefits for those who came to live and work at Hull House equal to the benefits they might be able to confer: at college and on their travels and at the fashionable school where Ellen had been teaching in Chicago, Jane and her partner had seen that "young people felt a fatal want of harmony between their theory and their lives." In offering an answer to that question, the two pioneer settlement workers "wanted to make a place, if they could, in and around which a fuller life might grow, for themselves and for others."

In 1889, there was no such thing as a social worker. A minister, priest, or ward boss might give practical help to the distressed poor; men like Philip Armour would sometimes meet appeals to stall off the landlord, pay hospital charges for a superannuated worker, or arrange the fix for an old employee's son in trouble with the police; and Victor Lawson might sign a check to send a broken-down reporter to a home for alcoholics. The poor themselves did all they could to prevent starvation when neighbors lost a breadwinner, or a breadwinner lost his job. But the idea of educated people devoting their entire time to the problems of the foreign-born, poverty-ridden, slum-dwelling lower classes was as dazzling in its novelty as it was unsettling in its implications. Jane Addams's nephew wrote that she learned her trade by the case method, and cases were available from the start. The day Jane set up shop, a few neighbor women came in out of curiosity. They found there genuine courtesy rising from goodness of heart. One of these first visitors later recorded that "If you went to the House you were welcome; if you called, you were called upon. If you let the young women know there was anything they could do for you, they did it if they could." And that was the first work performed by Jane Addams and Ellen Starr: what any good neighbor would do. In the first week of Hull House they washed the newborn and the dead, looked after children, and sat with the ill and old. Before very long Jane got accustomed to being called at three o'clock in the morning, just as though she were a doctor.

Paying their own expenses and sharing the work by night and day, a number of young women now enlisted with Jane Addams, to pass the rest of their lives either as residents, or as servants of the Hull House idea in other places. Among the first came Julia Lathrop, who had gone to Rockford Female Seminary from a wealthy home in Chicago, and later graduated at Vassar. Julia went out with Jane as an amateur midwife, remarking while they were delivering a baby, "This doing things we don't know how to do is going too far. Why did we allow ourselves to be rushed into midwifery?" The handsome black-haired Julia Lathrop became one of the Chicago sociologists, for it was she who inspired the studies known as *Hull House Maps and Papers,* a survey such as had never been attempted, giving the facts about conditions of daily life among twenty-one nationalities crowded into the Nineteenth Ward. Another recruit was Dr. Florence Kelley, a graduate of Cornell, who came to the House, as James Linn recorded, with three children by a divorced husband and "a fixed fierce resolution that she would make the salvation of women and children from blind industrial greed the work of her life." Governor Altgeld was to make Dr. Kelley Chief Factory Inspector of Illinois in 1895. Meanwhile, Mary Rozet Smith came to Halsted Street from Walton Place, not far from Mrs. Palmer's house. A graduate of the Kirkland School, where Ellen Starr had taught, and barely twenty years old, Mary was "tall, fair, and eager" when she entered Hull House. In the founding days when cash sometimes ran short, Mary Smith obtained help from her sympathetic father. Lacking the rigorous education of the other pioneer associates, Mary has been credited by Linn with devoting her time to the children at Hull House, whom she treated "with manners and respect," and to "making life easier for Jane Addams and keeping her courage up."

Jane Addams saw courage of a kind that could hardly be dreamed of at Rockford Seminary in the streets around Hull House. She recognized its quality by instinct rather than by ever having experienced anything like the tribulations which called that courage up. Absolute financial helplessness, for example, was something inconceivable to a woman of Jane's background, yet she immediately perceived it as the continuing fear of all working people. In her memoirs Jane wrote that early in the life of Hull House, she got a call "to come quickly to the house of an old German woman, whom two men from the county agent's office were attempting to remove to the County Infirmary. The poor old creature had thrown herself bodily upon a small and battered chest of drawers and clung there, clutching it so firmly that it would have been impossible to remove her without also taking a piece of furniture. She did not weep or moan or make any human sound, but between her broken gasps for breath she squealed shrilly like a frightened animal caught in a trap. The little group of women and children gathered at her door stood aghast at this realization of the black dread which always clouds the lives of the very poor when work is slack, but which constantly grows more imminent and threatening as old age approaches."

Miss Addams ended the distressing scene by getting rid of the county men. But the widespread fear of the poorhouse had ample justification, and Jane Addams carried perpetual distress in her mind because of the unnecessary idleness and forlornness of the old women in the County Infirmary. There were very few old men—they seemed to die off, while the elderly indigent women lived on, though often longing for death. Jane wrote, "To take away from an old woman whose life has been spent in household cares all the foolish little belongings to which her affections cling and to which her very fingers have become accustomed, is to take away her last incentive to activity, almost to life itself. To give an old woman only a chair and a bed, to leave her no cupboard in which her treasures may be stowed, not only that she may take them out when she desires occupation, but that her mind may dwell upon them in moments of revery, is to reduce living almost beyond the bounds of human endurance." The best that Jane could do for old ladies committed to the County Infirmary was to get them out for two-week vacations at Hull House; in entertaining these guests, Jane characteristically maintained that she received as much as she gave: "The reminiscences of these old women, their shrewd comments upon life, their sense of having reached a point where they may at last speak freely with nothing to lose because of their frankness, make them often the most delightful of companions."

An even more rewarding companion to Jane Addams was her lifelong friend Mrs. Joseph T. Bowen. Born Louise deKoven, she came to Hull House in the first group of Chicago girls who had found in Jane Addams an understanding of "that search for the heroic and the perfect that so persistently haunts the young." Later on as the wife of Joseph Bowen, and a woman of position, Louise frequently helped Jane by making her own house available when all the guest bedrooms at Hull House had been filled. Mrs. Bowen also served for years as president of the Hull House Women's Club, the parent organization of some fifty other neighborhood clubs pursuing as many different lines of interest. Serving often as Jane's traveling companion, Louise Bowen sometimes took over the burden of delivering the lecture at a speaking engagement, since she knew what Jane would say on any topic. And like the other close friends, Mrs. Bowen laughed at Jane's mild eccentricities. For one thing, the principal founder of Hull House was an inveterate picture-straightener; she also could recall the location and subject of any picture hung in the entire Hull House establishment, which expanded in a few years into several new or remodeled buildings around it. Miss Addams would pause on her way downstairs and say, "What became of that picture?" if cleaners had removed one. She also remembered the position of each table and chair—but laughed at herself for being so fussy. One day Miss Addams inspected the walls and pictures on the stair so closely that she didn't look where she was going, and rolled to the bottom after tripping over an unexpected step. Jane took no harm, but the tumble caused a sensation, and Mary Smith arriving after the excitement said reproachfully, "Oh, Jane, why didn't you wait till I could get here? Didn't you know that severe shocks are good for my asthma?" Miss Addams apologized for falling at the wrong time.

After almost half a century of friendship, Mrs. Bowen wrote, "It was fun going around with Jane Addams." But Louise Bowen never got over her amazement at her friend's invariable custom, when they shared a hotel room, of dressing completely in a closet, even to the perfect arrangement of her hair. And Jane Addams's impulses toward generosity were so strong, Mrs. Bowen said, that it was almost impossible to make her keep anything given her at Christmas. When they had become old women, and the bad back troubled Jane again, Mrs. Bowen installed an elevator in her house for Jane's use. After Jane died, a friend said to Louise Bowen, "I'm glad to see you still have the elevator—the one thing Jane wasn't able to give away." Jane even habitually gave right of precedence in going through doorways, standing aside to everyone, and this was something Mrs. Bowen did not like. At last she said, "Next time you refuse to go ahead of me, I'll pinch your arm." The time came, Jane automatically stood aside, and Mrs. Bowen pinched; after that Miss Addams went ahead, as her friends thought proper.

In spite of Mrs. Bowen's pinch, Jane's humility and courtesy set the tone at Hull House for residents and visitors alike. To the latter, it could be an experience of almost indescribable importance; a Greek American, later a prosperous merchant, who first entered the place as a boy, recalled of Miss Addams' house that "we walked into it as though we walked into our own house, and in that nurturing warmth that animated everything and all, there sounded in our ears the soft words and sentences of the young women of the House, the only soft and kind words we immigrant boys heard in those days." Yet strangely enough, in the early days there seemed to be one woman in Hull House whom no one could account for.

This mysterious figure was an occasional occupant of the bedchamber on the second floor which turned out to be a haunted room. Distinguished visitors used the room from time to time, and reported difficulty in sleeping; Canon Barnett and his wife had a particularly restless night during which they felt an indefinable anxiety. Jane Addams and Mary Smith then passed a night in the room, hoping to locate the trouble; they waked suddenly and saw what appeared to be a woman in white. Miss Addams called out, "Who is it, please?" The figure glided away, seeming to pass through a locked door. Jane assigned no more guests to this chamber, converting it to a store room and then to a dressing room for the Hull House theater. Some girls preparing for a Christmas play reported that they saw a lady in white sitting on a box looking at them. That was the phantom's last appearance, but Mrs. Bowen recorded that on three subsequent occasions she put out fires that had started in the room with no discoverable explanation of their origin. Jane never investigated the history of Hull House to find what old sorrow the ghost might have embodied, for there was too much palpable grief and suffering around her to warrant the time for psychical research. Much of the tragedy that so frequently overwhelmed Jane's poverty-stricken friends simply could not occur in comfortable surroundings; for example, Jane never forgot the request of a factory woman after her four-year-old boy had died because of falling from a roof when she left him unattended in order to work. The woman had another child, a baby whose crib she left in a neighbor's kitchen during factory hours. After the funeral, Jane said, "Is there anything we can do?" The mother answered, "If you could give me my wages for tomorrow, I would like to stay at home all day and hold the baby. The boy was always asking me to take him and I never had any time."

Frances Willard also was fighting for the women of Chicago, using general and political methods, in contrast to Jane's direct help in particular cases. But as time passed, Jane Addams with her colleagues accomplished more actual legislated reform than Frances Willard. However, Miss Willard made her presence felt on the Chicago skyline in the early 1890s, with the building at La Salle and Monroe streets that was called the Woman's Temple, headquarters of the International Woman's Christian Temperance Union. And it was appropriate that so competent a woman as Miss Willard should entrust the design of the Union headquarters to one of Chicago's ablest architects, John Wellborn Root.

When his family fled from his native town in Georgia at the approach of Sherman's army, the fourteen-year-old John Root had been taken to England, where he studied music and architecture. By 1869, young Root was back in the United States and taking his degree in civil engineering at New York University. He then put in a year as draftsman with James Renwick, designer of St. Patrick's Cathedral, and came to Chicago in 1871 to help rebuild the city after the fire. Taken on in the office of Carter, Drake, and Wight, John Root met Daniel Hudson Burnham, with whom he formed the most important architectural partnership, except perhaps for that of Dankmar Adler and Louis Sullivan, in the history of Chicago building. The young partners started their business against the depression of 1873, and in the beginning their optimism was as great as their combined talents, for the founding architects of Chicago, men like John M. van Osdel and William W. Boyington, were still in practice, with the advantage of past performances which had earned respect and confidence among the city's businessmen.

As the depression deepened into 1874, Root was able to devote time away from the office to the musical and theatrical activities of Chicago. The tradition of home entertainment, traceable to the fiddles of Kinzie and Beaubien, continued to grow in Root's lifetime, and even after his firm became busy he put in many an evening playing the piano for amateur opera, and in producing plays and concerts. His interest in music was so great that for a time he acted as critic for the *Tribune* in addition to his architectural work; and with his kindly good-humored air, unfailing courtesy, and evident creative gifts, John Wellborn Root was one of the most admired men in Chicago. Daniel Burnham also cut a figure, having found the work he was born to do in combining the functions of architect, engineer, promoter, and civic planner. He revered the concept of bigness, constantly reminding his partner that big jobs made big architects. To show what he meant, Dan Burnham was laying seige to the meat packer John B. Sherman, before the depression had run its course, with suggestions that he build a large new house. Burnham not only built the mansion, but in two years married Sherman's daughter Margaret. Not long afterward, John Root married a daughter of the prominent lawyer Henry Stanton Monroe. The young lady had been "finished" at Miss Porter's School, in Farmington, Connecticut, which had begun to draw Chicago patronage away from the high schools and private day schools where a generation of Chicago's privileged young women had usually completed their educations. John Root acquired a brilliant sister-in-law by this marriage: Harriet Monroe had literary skill, and competence as a critic of art and architecture. Her biography of Root was to be an influential account not only of his career, but of the collective work achieved by Chicago builders in the later nineteenth century. Root himself had much to say about his calling, and maintained that "The object of all this study of architectural styles must be to acquire from former times the spirit in which our predecessors worked; not to copy what they did. . . . Where architects faithfully follow out the logic of a predetermined theory of their building they have purity of style."*

"Whatever is to be spoken in a commercial building" Root maintained, "must be strongly and directly said." A client who encouraged John Root in this doctrine was Owen F. Aldis, a promoter who became acquainted with Burnham and Root in 1882 when they designed his Montauk Block at the southeast corner of Dearborn and Monroe streets. Here the architects and client contended with a problem whose solution made possible the herd of mighty buildings that rose in the business district of Chicago. With an aggregate weight amounting to incalculable millions of tons, the stone towers rose from the marshland that had impeded the progress of Father Marquette; and to an engineer's eye their presence seemed as a great a wonder as if the buildings had risen from Lake Michigan itself. In 1873, an architect named Frederick Baumann had summed up his twenty years' experience in a monograph, *The Art of Preparing Foundations for all kinds of Buildings with particular Illustrations of the "Method of Isolated Piers," as followed in Chicago.* Burnham and Root had followed Baumann's methods until Aldis came to them as agent for the Boston shipping men Peter and Shepard Brooks, who wanted to make some money through ownership of a building in Chicago. Aldis had told them that the steeply rising prices of land in the downtown district meant that buildings must also rise high; to ensure future profits, the Montauk must have at least ten stories. Root and Burnham estimated that the weight of brick and stone walls plus cast-iron beams would put dangerous

*Quoted by Carl W. Condit, *The Chicago School of Architecture.*

pressures on isolated piers; and Root suggested that the stone masonry of the Montauk's base should rest on what he called a "floating raft"—a 20-inch slab of concrete reinforced with steel rails. Thus the building distributed weight over its whole area instead of bearing directly on the narrow strips beneath the footings of the walls. "Unit pressures were thus materially reduced," Mr. Condit says, "and reasonable uniformity of settlement assured." Root and Owen Aldis thought of the raft as "a steel foundation with a concrete envelope to prevent rusting." The Montauk was the first building to carry the name of "skyscraper" and the Brookses found it such a good investment, after its opening in 1882, that they came back three years later and started negotiations to put up another large Chicago building under the same auspices, with Owen Aldis controlling the investment, and the firm of Burnham and Root in charge of design and construction. These Brooks brothers evidently did not believe in meddling with success. And they had their reward. The new Monadnock Block turned out to be a hit, both as a commercial project and an example of commercial art. At first, many Chicagoans doubted that the Brookses had another winner on their hands, and thought the promoters and builders had invited bankruptcy by locating on Jackson Street, which did not deserve the title of boulevard at the time. In fact, the south side of Jackson from State Street to the river presented nothing but an array of sheds and shanties.

Harriet Monroe recorded that Aldis "kept urging upon his architects extreme simplicity, rejecting one or two of Root's sketches as too ornate." Before long, John Root was saying he thought he would "throw the thing up without a single ornament," and the result was the building we have today. Montgomery Schuyler, the country's leading architectural critic, approved of its walls that "are real walls that carry themselves, and that may be properly thickened at the base," thus enabling Root to give an inward curve of the exterior at the top of the first story, which he answered with an outward curve at the parapet 215 feet above. The president of the Boston Architectural Club addressed his colleagues on the subject of the Monadnock Building: "It took prodigious courage to do this thing. It is an achievement unsurpassed in the architectural history of our country. . . ." European and American critics have continued to praise Root and his building to the present day, and Carl W. Condit writes in *The Rise of the Skyscraper* that the Monadnock "presents in its relentless exactitude the formal beauty latent in the commercial style" and that it "remains today the last great building in the ancient tradition of masonry construction."

Burnham and Root turned to a newer tradition in dealing with Frances Willard and her commission for the WCTU world headquarters building.

The novelty they offered was the steel frame construction that William Le Baron Jenney had demonstrated when he completed the Chicago office of the Home Insurance Company in 1885. That building stood until its demolition in 1931 at the corner of La Salle and Adams streets as an object of interest to historians of architecture, who have called it the first truly modern commercial structure in the world—a skeleton of iron and steel beams bolted together, like the members of a suspension bridge, with the walls applied as a curtain supported throughout by the interior framing. On this principle, the curtain walls could be made of any material including glass.* Over the steel frame of the Woman's Temple Root placed an outer dress that failed to harmonize with the modernity of the engineering. But it was not surprising that a pupil of James Renwick should turn to the French Gothic and the Romanesque when the sketches for this building took form on his drawing board. The Temple stood from 1891 to 1926 at the corner of La Salle and Monroe streets, a picturesque H-shaped structure of thirteen stories, its stone base anchored to a raft of concrete and steel, with arches over deeply revealed windows at the ninth floor, and dormers and pinnacles climbing above to a steeply pitched roof at each end of the H. Frankly romantic, the Woman's Temple came off well, and many a Chicagoan recalls it with pleasure to this day. But though the Temple soon filled to capacity with first-class tenants, it caused financial problems that gave men the chance to say that women did not have the ability to put through a big deal. The idea of building the temple had originated with a member of the WCTU, Mrs. Matilda Carse, who suggested that a Temperance Building Association be formed with a capital stock of 500,000 shares to sell at $1.00 each, plus $300,000 worth of bonds paying five percent to investors. The Association sold its bonds to Chicago capitalists, who considered them a prime investment, given the building's location and the reputations of the architects. It thus came about that on completion in 1892, the underwriters rather than the Association owned the building, except for an equity of $76,618.05 that the women had

*In his authoritative and fascinatingly detailed *History of the Development of Building Construction in Chicago,* the structural engineer and university lecturer Frank A. Randall gives full credit for pioneering the complete metal-framed skyscraper to Jenney and his Home Insurance Company Building, but also points out that Jenney himself regarded skeleton construction as an evolution from older building practices. Randall noted that European builders used cast-iron beams as early as 1775. Louis Sullivan wrote that rolling mill salesmen added promotional encouragement to the steel frame building idea in order to make an additional market for "structural shapes that had long been in use in bridge work." Carl Condit salutes Jenney for "his great technical innovation" in the Home Insurance Building which had "no wall in the usual sense of the word but only a succession of vertical and horizontal bands of masonry or weatherproof metal covering the outermost columns and beams."

subscribed. Members opposed to Miss Willard brought this up at the fourth biennial convention of the World WCTU in 1897: Miss Willard's enemies said that the Temple's net income was $100,000 a year, and that all they needed, to retire the bonds and take full possession of this fine property, was to raise $300,000 in cash, surely no impossibility for an organization with 200,000 loyal members. Frances Willard was ill—a dying woman with only a year to live—but she made a stout reply, assuring the critics that she had already raised $100,000 in pledges, including a promise of $50,000 from Marshall Field. The debate in convention reached no satisfactory end, but gave a *Times-Herald* reporter the chance to write that "The hold which the Temple idea has taken upon the women is something extraordinary. They sobbed when reference was made to giving the building up, and prayed whenever the officers jealous of Frances Willard seemed to have the best of the situation." This picture of sobbing, quarreling women fell far short of justice to Miss Willard and her colleagues, for although they responded to emotion at times, the WCTU delegates never produced anything near the amount of nonsense that a national political convention could generate. And when Frances Willard died in the following year, the nation recognized this indomitable woman's victory in channeling the protective instincts of women into a political force. Thousands of people filed past her small body as it lay on view in Willard Hall, the lofty meeting room that Root had designed at the Temple; and later on, mourners deposited the ashes of Frances Willard at Graceland Cemetery on North Clark Street.

During the time that Frances Willard rose to her position of importance in the world, Bertha Palmer had become without question the most influential woman in Chicago. And it was natural that the men who ruled the city should turn to Bertha when it became necessary to organize their women in support of a project that concerned every Chicagoan—the World's Columbian Exposition of 1893. The idea had been born some time before that date; Lyman Gage recorded that he first heard of the proposed Exposition in 1889, when Edward F. Cragin came in with "a pad of paper in his hand and a pencil behind his ear." Mr. Gage recalled that Cragin asked a detailed question: "Can I put you down as in favor of holding a great world exposition in Chicago, four years from now, to celebrate the four-hundredth anniversary of the discovery of America?" Lyman Gage replied that Chicago was comparatively new, "with the most heterogeneous population of any city of its size on earth." And in the years that the city had been going through its struggles for wealth, "the esthetic sense of the people had been comparatively dormant." Cragin disagreed, but Gage said, "We are just not up to it. And it would cost millions that we cannot secure." But Lyman Gage was willing to be proved wrong, and within a year accepted the presidency of the Board of Directors of the Chicago World's Fair, as the original promoters called themselves. They went to Washington, where Chicago's Senator Charles B. Farwell helped get a resolution through both houses of Congress that called for a world exposition to mark the four-hundredth anniversary of the voyage by Columbus to the New World. Committeemen and Congressmen alike were pleased to overlook Leif Ericsson, the first known European discoverer of North America, whose explorations antedated those of Columbus by nearly five hundred years. The Chicagoans had a more immediate problem in the wording of the resolution, which failed to specify where the show should take place. This was due to activities in New York City, where politicians and boosters had waked up to the possibilities of a Columbian Exposition, and had taken measures to see that it should be held in their town. New York money passed in bribes and entertainment, and the pressures shifted as Lyman Gage groped in the stink of Washington to find his hidden opponents, and probably wished that Senator Farwell, a routine political wheelhorse, possessed brains and enterprise comparable to his own. Gage faced defeat on the day he received a report from trusted spies that fresh money had arrived in town for the purpose of attaching a rider to the resolution stating that New York should have the show. The New Yorkers started a whispering campaign that the list of Chicago pledges was a fake; they also got to the chairman of the Joint Congressional Committee and persuaded him to issue a statement that the Chicagoans might as well return to their prairie, for "New York is too strong, and offers not only the most eligible site, but ten million dollars." Even more diabolical was a cartoon in which the artist showed the principal cities as women standing around Uncle Sam, who holds a bouquet labeled "World's Fair." All the women are pretty except Chicago, a scrawny half-grown girl in an evening gown with a pattern of little pigs. Her mouth is wide open as she demands the prize, large diamonds blaze at her bosom, her thin arms are bare, and on the hands she stretches toward Uncle Sam are white kid gloves that end at her wrists. New York, a beautiful society girl, gazes at this creature with well-bred scorn.

Gage and his friends got the bad news in one of the Capitol committee chambers, asked for a short recess, and retired to an anteroom, where they decided their only hope was to commit the credit of Chicago as a municipality; returning to the larger room, Gage told the Congressmen that he stood ready to pledge that his people would raise a kitty of money to exceed any other offer, that it would be hard cash, and that he "would place the declaration on a business basis within twenty-four hours." This smelled good to the Congressmen, and they recognized that the men in Gage's crowd were bankers and industrialists, who would be good for more in the long run than a gang of publicity men from New York. Then somebody pulled back—according to rumor, it was Pierpont Morgan—the New York lobbyists' bankroll vanished, and Chicago won the day. The Illinois Legislature hurled an enabling act through its mill with the speed of a projectile, big money immediately appeared in Chicago as Gage had promised, and the city had the privilege of inviting the whole world to the shores of Lake Michigan, with a little more than two years in which to get ready.

8

The World's Fair

NOW THAT THE HOLDING OF THE WORLD'S COLUMBIAN EXPOSITION IN Chicago had become a city-wide commitment, the men who brought this responsibility home were quick to share it with their women. And everyone took it for granted that Bertha Palmer should preside over the Board of Lady Managers. This board had 115 members, including doctors, lawyers, authors, artists, teachers, community leaders, temperance workers, and agitators to secure women the privilege of voting who were known as suffragettes. In those days, not a woman could vote at a municipal, county, state, or federal election, although any derelict male who slept on the floor of a saloon could be turned out to vote on call—staggering, booze-sick, hands trembling so that a political henchman had to guide his fingers on the ballot.

In addition to the noted women on the board, there were some who had no other listing than "wives of prominent men." As such, their influence over their husbands measured their influence in the community. But whatever powers she might or might not wield in the world of practical affairs, each member of the Lady Managers' Board saw in the fair an opportunity to improve the lot of women all over the world. Already the great planned event was taking on different meanings for different people. The hotel owners, for example, foresaw a period of solid bookings. The storekeepers took their cue from Marshall Field: they would do business, he said, such as had never been done before. The artists, architects, authors and journalists of Chicago also felt the excitement of a great opportunity drawing near: as professionals, they had the assignment to design, build, advertise and record the fair; and as Chicagoans, they shared with businessmen a general emotion that rose above satisfaction in achievement or gain—a pride in what Jane Addams called "our dear city." Chicago would now demonstrate to the world that it had sufficient resources of taste and talent, as well as financial means, to put on a show that would equal or even surpass the Paris Exposition of 1889.

The bawds, thieves, confidence men, and politicians of the city shared in the excitement as Gage's people announced plans from day to day and the size of the project came into public consciousness. Visitors would come to Chicago not in thousands but millions, and of these a large part would be suitable material for the operations of swindlers, sneak thieves, and various other looters and exploiters. Arrangements must be made for the fleecing of these victims in an expeditious manner, decently and in order, and without scandal. On that point, orders came from high up: there must be no scandal. The politicians threatened to doom any thief who harmed the city's reputation while the fair was on. All classes, indeed, felt the warmth of civic pride, and the criminal classes turned to Mike McDonald as their Lyman Gage. Meanwhile, Carter Harrison began campaigning for his fifth term as mayor, promising an open town for citizens and visitors alike during the fair, which was to begin in the spring of 1893. Harrison and McDonald went well together; they both deplored any invasion of Chicago by out-of-town hoodlums, sharpers, and pickpockets. The authorities took pains to see that no pickpockets be allowed to work the entrances of the fairgrounds, where people would crowd together going through the gates. The managers did not like the idea of visitors being robbed of their wallets at this point and left with no money to spend inside. Eddie Jackson, dean of Chicago pickpockets and the most respected member of his craft, acted as negotiator with the politicians. The resulting agreement stipulated that any pickpocket arrested at the gates would have to return the loot if the victim could be found, otherwise it would go to the police; and *in addition,* no matter what became of the booty, the thief would have to pay $10 to the arresting officer for his release. To ameliorate this harsh measure and to encourage thieves to work elsewhere, it was also agreed that all pickpockets arrested in the downtown district between eight A.M. and four P.M. would be released on arrival at the Central Station House.

Gambling house proprietors met at the summons of Mike McDonald and drew up a charter to govern their activities during the months of May to October in 1893 when the fair would be open. Confidence workers also appeared at this meeting, their delegation taking seats under direction of their chief Tom O'Brien, King of the Bunko Men. It was thought that World's Fair business would be so good that each swindler and gambling man could operate at a profit while paying taxes according to a scale of forty to sixty-five percent on net income, deductions being allowed for expenses. This boodle went to politicians and police; McDonald charged the recipients a cut of the money for his work as collector, while exacting a consultant's fee from the payers for his services in seeing that their money went to the right places.

It was estimated that the Tom O'Brien mob took in $1,250,000 from the confidence game during the fair's six-month run, leaving a profit of half a million after deducting the McDonald payoff plus operating expenses. Though expensive and complicated in operation, the confidence swindle rested upon simple basic tenets: A and B are confederates, unknown to the victim C, who is invited by A to join in cheating B. Thus it follows that the victim or "mark" must have larceny in him, as McDonald put it, in addition to gullibility and greed. When O'Brien or Red Jimmy Fitzgerald operated, they presented the game as a drama that required scores of confederates playing parts against a prepared setting that the victim would believe to be a bank, brokerage office, horse-betting room, or gentlemen's club, according to whatever variation of the basic situation the swindlers selected as most likely to deceive that particular mark.

Anticipating the fair, Chicago landlords demanded a 300 percent rise in the rents paid by keepers of disorderly houses. A man named Christopher Columbus Crabb was the city's ablest pander, constantly lecturing his fellow bawds on the need for efficiency and modern business methods. This accountant of vice had worked as a salesman at Marshall Field's, leaving in 1887 to act as consultant for Lizzie Allen, one of the foremost brothel-keepers in the city. Crabb also had dealings with Minna Everleigh, to whom he sold the mansion at 2131 South Dearborn Street where Minna and her sister Ada claimed to operate the world's most sumptuous house of prostitution. These two viragos were objects of jealousy because they got more publicity than Lizzie Allen, Carrie Watson, and Victoria Shaw, their nearest rivals in the vice trade, but the names of all five appeared in the regular newspapers, as well as in gutter publications such as the *Chicago Street Gazette*, which was edited by Shang Andrews, who had written a sensational novel called *Wicked Nell*. In the *Gazette*, he reported the doings of jockeys, actors, politicians, pugilists, whores, and criminals in a brisk and readable manner. Andrews published lists of recommended resorts as a readers' service, but also warned of diseased or drunken prostitutes, identifying the offenders by name and address. Shang Andrews served a useful function as trade editor to Mike McDonald's domain, and all these things—the smooth-working industries of vice, booze, gambling, and stealing—were part of Chicago's reputation, as well known to the country at large as its industrial achievement and financial power. There was something sinister about Chicago. It could be a dangerous town. And the hint of danger was dramatic when it came into the national mind along with promises of grandeur and excitement such as the world had never seen.

A million people in Chicago was the last count when the planners of the fair got down to work. And though Chicago's million included some capable men and women, it was obvious that outside artists, experts, and celebrities must join in the planning, and promise to attend when the fair began. Away to Europe went Bertha Palmer, carrying the seals and authority of the mayor, the governor, and the presidents of the fair and the United States. Mrs. Palmer stopped in England, where it became known that Queen Victoria looked with favor on the Chicago project; and Princess Alexandra with her husband Albert Edward, Prince of Wales, looked with favor on Mrs. Palmer. Wales never dissembled his liking for the handsome, rich American woman. The Prince promised to see that a glittering British delegation made the trip to the fair. With this assurance of royal patronage, Bertha Palmer went to Paris, where she received an equally warm welcome in high places.

Back home in Illinois, Lyman Gage handed on the presidency of the fair to Harlow Niles Higinbotham, who was a partner of Marshall Field, and a typical Chicago magnate of the second rank. He differed from the norm only in having been born on a farm near Joliet rather than in New England. The prairie winters of his boyhood had so tempered Higinbotham that he did not mind the feeling of working in a refrigerator that sometimes paralyzed Field's associates; on the contrary he prospered mightily, and had achieved millionaire's rank by 1890, at the age of fifty-two, when he agreed to head the councils of the fair that Lyman Gage had launched and financed.

Time came rushing at them now, fast Chicago time which expended itself so rapidly that the planners agreed there could be no hope of starting the fair in the proper anniversary year of 1892. The best they could hope for would be to dedicate the grounds and some half-finished buildings toward the end of that year, opening for business in the following spring; meanwhile the directors must choose a site, so that their supervising architects might proceed to draw up the master plan and enlist the eminent colleagues who would carry it out. These planners were Daniel Burnham and John Root, working with Frederick Law Olmsted, who was to be responsible for landscaping the grounds. It might be said that Olmsted and

Root also designed the waters of the Columbian Exposition, for they selected a site that included the lakeshore and lagoons of Jackson Park, a
semi-wild area of dunes and brambled paths and winding roads that extended to the water in what was then a remote reach of the South Side.
On this site they marked off 686 acres for landscaping by Olmsted, to be
the setting for a grand design by Root, as consulting architect, which
would be built under Burnham's orders as chief of construction. Root had
to fight hard for this location all through the autumn of 1890; for many
Chicagoans failed to appreciate the wildness of Jackson Park, thought it
an unsightly wasteland of marshes, and carried on propaganda to place the
festival a mile and half inland, in Washington Park, which was already laid
out with formal terraces and pavillions. With intense conviction and un-
shakable courtesy, Root argued his case for Jackson Park, emphasizing the
opportunity that the marshland would afford for "a Venetian effect of
palaces and lagoons against the lake's beautiful open spaces." At last he
carried his point, and made a ground plan for the fair, showing a Court
of Honor around a basin, a Wooded Island, and sites for the buildings of
states, nations, and industries fronting on lagoons and reached by boats
and bridges, or along wide avenues from which one viewed the lake. The
plan passed the board of architects which Root and Burnham had assembled without a suggestion of change except in a few minor details.

This board of architects included such famous Easterners as Richard
Morris Hunt, designer of Marshall Field's Prairie Avenue house, and the
fabulous Vanderbilt chateau at Asheville, North Carolina; and the influential partnership of Charles Follen McKim, William Rutherford Mead, and
Stanford White, whose office had turned out a series of romantic shingled
seaside villas that were now overshadowed by their stone mansions, clubs,
and libraries in what might be called an American metropolitan style, a
derivation from Colonial classic with additional richness and elegance
inspired by the Italian Renaissance. Also from the East came George
Browne Post, like Root an engineering graduate of New York University;
in a few years Post would leave as his Middle Western monument the
Wisconsin State Capitol. At Chicago, it pleased him to learn that the
Columbia Exposition would not be a mere "cattle show" and he was glad
to receive the Hall of Manufactures as his part of it. Other architects came
from Boston and Kansas City, and the Chicagoans who agreed to work
with Burnham and Root included Henry Ives Cobb and the firm of Adler
and Sullivan, designers of the Auditorium, the vast structure that still
dominates a part of Chicago at Congress Street and Michigan Avenue. The
junior member of this firm was a son of the Mr. Sullivan from Boston who
had come to Chicago as a dancing master when the small new city took

its first steps toward social grace; after studying architecture in Boston and Paris, young Louis Henri Sullivan had returned to Chicago, where his brother had become a railroad executive. The skies of Lake Michigan, as Louis envisioned them, were waiting for new shapes to rise, in a new architecture, unfettered by tradition. In this approach to the art of building, Sullivan did not disavow his personal traditions, which came in part from Richardson, and from his contacts in Paris with the Art Nouveau. A small man, but with presence so commanding that people remembered him as tall, Sullivan occupied a high place in the city at the time of the fair, and like John Root and Henry Ives Cobb, had been elected to the Chicago Club. Everything about him suggested elegance, creativity, and controlled force, so that the failures of his closing years were to seem all the more tragic when they came. Dankmar Adler, his engineering partner, had served in the Civil War, and impressed those who dealt with him as a man of rock-like integrity. The young Wisconsin architect Frank Lloyd Wright, for a time Sullivan's assistant and disciple, said that Dankmar Adler stood on his foundations solidly, like an old Byzantine church.

There existed a possibility that churches of that kind might have more influence on the outward aspect of the fair than Greek temples if Sullivan's ideas should be followed in the plans. John Root had sketched a variety of free and inventive ornaments for the buildings that made one recall the Woman's Temple rather than the Monadnock Tower. On the other hand, the Easterners wished to follow McKim, Mead, and White in a uniform style based on classic orders. The beauty of Root's master plan lay in its provision for a classic Court of Honor around a formal and symmetrical basin, which could contrast with picturesque and non-traditional architecture around the irregularly bordered lagoon, where the principle buildings were assigned to Cobb and Sullivan. And now the people of the city, only half convinced the project would be ready on time, began to understand what Root was trying to achieve in persuading the architects to work together. Miss Monroe put it that the members of the public for whom Root had been working "were beginning to recognize in this man a leader; one aware of beauty, persuasive to make them long for it, strong to make it real for them. Though scarcely conscious of their allegiance, they were bearing him on their shoulders during those weeks of civic exertion, and he felt behind his creative force that mighty force of public sympathy which alone can nerve great souls to put forth their utmost power."

On the blustery Sunday evening of January 11, 1891, Root invited friends to his narrow Astor Street house to meet the visiting architects. "That night," Harriet recorded, "he escorted some of his guests to their carriage and was stabbed by the sharp winter wind." Next day Root came down with pneumonia, and in four days he was dead. His life ended in the afternoon, and they laid the body out for a watch night that the family shared with Daniel Burnham. For Miss Monroe, "Death had made its power known at last." Harriet was better prepared for that revelation than Frances Willard had been, a small child held over a coffin, or Jane Addams, a young girl at the house in the snowstorm. Harriet wrote that through the night "my Aunt Nettie, the wife of my best-beloved Uncle Lewis Mitchell, sat on the dark upper curve of the stairway. . . . Afterwards she told a strange story of Dan Burnham's pacing out the hours and talking to himself at times under the room where his partner lay dead. He seemed to be rebuking supernatural powers: 'I have worked, I have schemed and dreamed to make us the greatest architects in the world—I have made him see it and kept him at it—and now he dies—damn!—damn!—damn!' His snatches of soliloquy through that night of despair, before he emerged to new dreams, took the form of wrath, and he shook his fist and cursed the murderous fates as he paced back and forth between intervals of comfortless sleep on the living-room couch."

Daniel Burnham's cry of distress was echoed throughout Chicago, and Harriet said that never before had so many strong men wept for the loss of one among them. An architectural designer said, "We'll get together and do the best we can, but the mind is gone." Burnham appointed Charles B. Atwood chief consulting architect to the Columbian Exposition, and also head designer for the firm which was to continue as D. H. Burnham and Company. And the piles of blueprints grew on the floors beside the drawing tables, while Burnham seemed to go on without sleep or rest in hurrying his cast of architectural stars toward the dedication date that was now only a few months more than a year away.

Other arts and artists had their place in the preparations, and Harriet Monroe learned of painters and sculptors who were receiving large commissions. Also her friend Theodore Thomas, condutor of a classical orchestra in Chicago since 1871, had accepted responsibility for a program of music to last all through the Columbian Exposition summer. Harriet saw that the authorities had found patrons to support every art but one, for poetry was omitted from the plans. She became convinced that the dedication would be incomplete without a poem, and to make sure the thing was done properly, decided to write it herself. This was far from an absurd idea, for Miss Monroe was a published poet, and had written an appropriate dedicatory ode for Adler and Sullivan's Auditorium, an occasion on which the President and Vice-President of the United States had been present. Now a woman of thirty, Harriet had received her "finishing" at the same convent in Georgetown, D.C., where Bertha Palmer had gone; in more recent years, Henry S. Monroe's law practice had dwindled, and Harriet had gone out in the world to earn her living. Why this attractive woman never married is a mystery and will probably remain so; at any rate she would have been involved, one way or another, in the writing trade, for she possessed an organized talent of the kind that satisfies itself only in professionalism. She got along by working as art critic for the *Tribune,* writing articles, giving literary lectures, and selling an occasional magazine poem, though rates for poetry were deplorably low. However, Miss Monroe was now about to earn one of the highest fees paid to an American poet up to that time, and in addition, to appear as successful plaintiff in a landmark suit for copyright infringement.

In her opening move for the dedicatory ode, Harriet approached two members of the Committee on Ceremonies whom she had met as art collectors through her work on the *Tribune.* They were the industrialist James W. Ellsworth, and Charles Tyson Yerkes, a financier who had derived riches from manipulating street railway ownerships and franchises. Ellsworth was a conventional wealthy patron of the arts; Yerkes was entirely different, a bird of exotic plumage among the sober citizens on the Board of Trade. In his native Philadelphia Yerkes had drawn a sentence to the penitentiary for criminal mishandling of municipal securities. Released after seven months, he came to Chicago, where he made himself a master of bribery and corruption, putting the city's transportation into a tangle that took years to straighten out. Yerkes contributed another Chicago phrase to the language, when he dismissed suffering riders' pleas for enough cars to give them breathing room during rush hours with the comment, "The strap-hangers pay the dividends." There was something about Yerkes that fascinated literary people and Theodore Dreiser made him the central character of *The Titan.* Charles Yerkes earned Miss Monroe's regard when she came to his office in March 1891 with her question: Would the Committee on Ceremonies recognize the art of poetry by decreeing a poem for the Dedication, and would they ask her to write it? Yerkes answered: "I don't know what the other members of the committee may think about it, but I hope we can give you the commission, because we shall want a poem that will live." Harriet recorded, "I was thrilled, and at that moment only a grand response to his faith in me seemed possible. I left the office as if on wings."

After the next committee meeting Harriet received her commission to write a "Columbian Ode" for the ceremonies now scheduled to be held on October 21, 1892, the "new calendar" date of the four-hundredth anniversary of Columbus's arrival in America. The Committee suggested that in the course of the poem Harriet should provide two or three songs, which would be sung by a chorus of 5,000 voices under direction of William Lawrence Tomlins, conductor of the Apollo Club, to music by the Boston composer George Whitefield Chadwick. She immediately started to block out the work, with an opening salutation to Columbia, then "a procession of nations to the festival, led, of course, by Spain; second, back to the past—the coming of Columbus and the choral song of his sailors; third, the awakening of America—the wilderness, the pioneers battling with harsh nature and savage man, and conquering with a song of triumph; fourth, the procession of the great dead—the founders led by Washington, the fighters led by Lincoln, the artists led by our own architect who had just died; fifth, an invocation to the Columbia of the future—her search into nature's secrets, the march of science; and finally, her leadership of nations to a warless world of liberty and love. Throughout I was determined to use no classic images—Columbia was crowned not with laurel, but with

> . . . dewy flowers
> Plucked from wide prairies and from mighty hills,

and she moved through vast virgin spaces toward the splendors and triumphs of modern civilization and an era of universal peace."

After making her outline and writing the songs and some key passages, Harriet suffered a nervous breakdown. Miss Monroe put the blame on getting up too soon after minor surgery. The symptoms, however, were mental: using her writer's eye even while suffering, Harriet noted of one seizure that "A little feather fluttered against my forehead, light as the silver wing of a dragon-fly, and blew me down—down—to the slippery darkness of the underworld. The solid earth yawned away—I walked on a bottomless abyss." After a summer of recuperation, Harriet got back to the ode, and she finished the first version in the early months of 1892. Harriet did not know that James Ellsworth had turned against her, and now was trying to withdraw the commission and ask John Greenleaf Whittier, then in his eighty-sixth year, to write the poem. Ellsworth told the committee that there had been disquieting reports about Miss Monroe's health, and asked what guarantees existed that the young lady would deliver a usable poem as agreed. And if Harriet did produce a manuscript, he urged that they submit it for judgment by an expert. In the spring of 1892 Harriet delivered the first draft of the ode. Ellsworth sent the manuscript to William Morton Payne, poetry editor of *The Dial,* a recently founded Chicago literary magazine. The only part of his report that the committee passed on to Harriet was a suggestion that she omit three and a half lines referring to John Root. This she refused to do, and all through the summer of 1892, Ellsworth continued to press for rejection of the poem. Harriet spent the summer with the widowed Mrs. Root and her children at Deerfield, on the Connecticut River, where she worked at the final version of the ode, rewriting and improving it in a number of places. Returning to Chicago in early September, Harriet laid this final copy before the committee, and then astounded both friend and enemy by asking one thousand dollars as payment for the poem—or, to be precise, for the license to make use of it, by performance and printing, for one time in connection with their ceremony. Mr. Bumble himself was not more appalled by Oliver's request for seconds than the committemen at this demand for money by a *writer*—furthermore, a female writer, and a scribbler of verses at that. Harriet refused to be bullied, and pointed out that the least of the architects, sculptors, and painters were getting more money for their services to the fair than she was asking. "The bill was paid," Miss Monroe recorded, "but the opposition now attempted the final insult of complete cancellation of the poem, no part of it to be read or sung on the great Dedication Day, then only a few weeks away. The Committee on Ceremonies finally voted to turn the decision over to the Council of Administration, the supreme governing body of the Fair." The committeemen summoned her before the council on the evening of Friday, September 23, to defend her poem and her unprecedented action of insisting on payment for the work. Mr. Ellsworth was represented by his attorney, who spoke first, erroneously stating that the poem ran to twenty thousand words, which was ten times the actual length, and increasing the mention of Root from three and a half lines to sixty-four. The lawyer had taken the tone of a prosecutor, but while he spoke Miss Monroe had been studying faces, and she saw that Harlow Higinbotham, who sat in the chief seat, had the face of a decent man. When called on, she spoke directly to Higinbotham and reviewed her commissioning by unanimous vote of the Committee on Ceremonies, spoke of the time and work she had expended, corrected the errors of her prosecutor, pointed out that Mr. Chadwick had already written music for the songs, which were at that moment in rehearsal by Mr. Tomlins and his army of choristers, and closed by asking, "Would it not be an unjust discrimination to oust the high art of poetry from your inspiring program?"

Harlow Higinbotham said, "Miss Monroe, will you read the lines referring to Mr. Root?"

Harriet read,

Back with the old glad smile comes one we knew,
We bade him rear our house of joy today;
But beauty opened wide her upward way
And he passed on. . . .

Higinbotham said, "It is entirely fitting that Mr. Root should be remembered in this way." They asked Harriet to read a few more passages, then excused her from the room while the council came to a decision. It was a victory for Miss Monroe: all her songs were to be sung by the chorus; the first seventy-five lines, and the lines about Root were to be read, along with as much of the rest of the poem, selected by the author, as could be read in ten minutes. A few days later, Mr. Higinbotham recommended that Harriet herself should be the reader; after thinking it over she suggested, with thanks, that it might be better to engage an actress to read before such a large crowd, and it was so ordered.

An Exposition Ball took place on the night of October 20, and Mrs. Palmer led the grand march, to the music of Sousa's band, wearing crimson velvet with crystal and gold embroidery, and a diamond tiara. October is a grand month in Chicago, and the next day, Friday the twenty-first, turned out an especially fine example of what a day could be under the benign sky of Indian summer. Cavalrymen in dress uniforms trotted through the city, with General Nelson A. Miles at their head; flags flew, bands played, and dignitaries rolled by in carriages of state. At the Exposition Grounds, the invited crowd entered a tremendous hall in the partially completed Manufactures Building, and Theodore Thomas experienced the first of many vexations when a guard tried to stop him on his way to discuss matters with Mr. Tomlins. At last a fanfare crashed out: it had been written as the entrance music of the President of the United States, and but for tragic circumstances that kept him at the bedside of his dying wife, William Henry Harrison would have now marched on the scene. In his place came Vice-President Levi P. Morton, under escort of Harlow Higinbotham, Potter Palmer, and other officials. Governors of states and foreign ambassadors followed, all dressed in Prince Albert coats, shuffling up the long aisle to the "Columbian March" by Professor John Knowles Paine of the music department at Harvard. As they filed past, the notables came under scrutiny by Miss Monroe from her seat in the section reserved for the five hundred artists of the fair. When all were seated, there came a welcome by the mayor, and it was time for the "Columbian Ode." The reader was the New York actress Sarah Cowell Lemoyne, a tall, handsome woman with a fine voice; and the chorus, three blocks from Theodore Thomas and the orchestra, came in nobly on cue. And at the end, as the enthusiastic applause subsided, ushers ran up with laurel wreaths for reader and author "from the ladies of Chicago." Then Daniel Burnham tendered the buildings, including some not yet started, to Mr. Higinbotham, and introduced his architects as "the artists of construction." Higinbotham handed out medals and appreciative words to all the "sons of art" employed on the exposition. Then Mrs. Palmer was speaking, about the contributions of women to the fair, and the interesting things that would be shown next summer in the Woman's Building, which was to be prominant on the grounds. Bertha Palmer concluded, "Even more important than the discovery of Columbus, which we are gathered together to celebrate, is the fact the general government has discovered women."

Again Mr. Higinbotham came forward, and accepted the buildings from the builders, as Harriet observed, "and tendering them to the National Commission; President Palmer, of that body, accepting the much-tendered buildings and tendering them in turn to the United States Government" in whose name the Vice-President tendered them to Humanity.

So far, the proceedings had been both interesting and inspiring; but experienced participants in public ceremonies knew this was too good to last. On the sidelines, two orators had been warming up, and now it was their turn. First came the gray-moustached Colonel Henry ("Marse Henry") Watterson of Kentucky, whose act was dated even in 1892. He gave them thirty-five minutes of arm-waving that had gone out with Stephen A. Douglas. Then the sufferers came to their feet at the first chord of "The Star-Spangled Banner" and many made their escape on the assumption that the national anthem signaled a close to the proceedings, although they could see Cardinal Gibbons in his red robe on the dais still waiting to give the go-home prayer. Those who sat down again paid a stiff price, for Chauncey M. Depew of New York now took the rostrum. He could be delightful in a small group, but today he put his hearers in mind of vaudeville's dreaded bore, the Chinese juggler On Too Long. The audience whispered and rustled until at last the bald, gaunt Depew ended his oration, and Cardinal Gibbons stretched his hands in mercy as he intoned the concluding prayer. Five thousand voices sang a postlude, the Ninth Symphony chorale, while the people broke for the exits.

One might suppose that even though Harriet was conscientious, like any good Chicagoan, she might now take a few days off and relieve the strain on her nervous system, worn as it was by more than a year of preparation for her day at the Fair. But nothing of the sort could be arranged, for she now had on her hands the prospect of litigation against one of the country's most powerful newspapers, the *New York World*. A *World* reporter had obtained an advance copy of Harriet's ode, and had sent the poem to

New York in one of the longest press telegrams ever filed from Chicago. It had appeared in full, except for one lost line, on the front page of the *World* for Sunday, October 23. The editors knew that the author had reserved copyright and forbidden publication. Nevertheless, they had ordered their Chicago man to get a copy, telling him they would take their chances with Miss Monroe and her copyright. It made them angry when Harriet's lawyers announced suit for theft of literary property, since Joseph Pulitzer, publisher of the *World*, detested writers who had lawyers. Therefore the *World* men refused to settle out of court, and forced a trial at which a jury awarded Harriet five thousand dollars. Harriet's case set precedent for all subsequent litigation in support of authors' rights to their work. In the end, after losing two appeals, someone had to go into Pulitzer's soundproof study with news that the *World* must not only pay damages to Harriet, but also lawyers' fees, and the court costs. And it may have made Pulitzer even more unhappy to reflect that Harriet would have been glad to sell the New York rights for two hundred dollars.

Dedicated in high style and tendered to all mankind, the fair that its directors saw in actual existence, after the fog of oratory blew away, stood far short of completion. Daniel Burnham found himself faced by a combination of circumstances which he was especially well fitted to deal with, and made his contribution as expediter on all fronts. In pushing the 10,000 workers toward their goals, he showed the qualities that had made him such a useful partner to John Root.

Burnham radiated a feeling of confidence to his associates, yet was no mere booster, but a singular and complex character, not altogether understood by many who thought they knew him. He fascinated Miss Monroe, who recorded that the only novel she ever longed to write would have presented Burnham as hero. But she felt that the story "could never have done justice to the utter sincerity of the various phases of his egoism; to his magnanimity, for he generously granted everything—almost—to his family, his numerous dependent relatives, his friends and clients, even his detractors and enemies, or to the deep-hearted affection expressed in words, tone of voice, manner of touch and handclasp, which he made himself feel for the big businessman whom he won over and served. To himself, and to most of the world in general, he was always right; and by knowing this so securely he built up the sheer power of personality which accomplished big things. As Director of Works he carried the Columbian Exposition through countless constructional and artistic crises. . . ."

Burnham had little to fear from any artistic emergency, for he numbered among his troops such men as the sculptors Augustus St. Gaudens, Daniel Chester French, Karl Bitter, and Frederick MacMonnies. The group so impressed St. Gaudens that he said, "This is the greatest gathering of artists since the fifteenth century." That might be true enough, but there were omissions from the gathering: for example, Emile Antoine Bourdelle, Auguste Rodin, and Claude Monet were not there, and one could head a roster of absent Americans with Thomas Eakins, Winslow Homer, and Albert Pinkham Ryder. The fair was all the poorer for taking shape without help from such artists, and they in turn missed the comradeship about which St. Gaudens made his enthusiastic remark. There was so much to do—French must complete a colossal statue of Columbia to dominate the formal basin, an enclosed sheet of water 1,200 yards long; Hunt must bring to reality his Administration Building, with its dome the highest point of construction in the fair; Post had to face the problem of designing for his Hall of Manufactures the three-arched hinged trusses that allowed the breath-taking span of 345 feet; George Atwood and his draftsmen must bend for hours over the boards to finish plans for the Palace of Art, while the Chicagoans Henry Ives Cobb and Louis Sullivan pressed on with the only large buildings at the fair that did not conform to the "classic" or Beaux Arts style followed by William Hunt, Charles McKim, and the other architects from the East. Conform they did in one respect, which was to observe the uniform roofline on which all had agreed, domes and towers to be added at discretion. The felicity of Root's ground plan was such that the basin of the Great Court could be lined with classical structures, while the irregularly bordered Lagoon provided advantageous sites for Cobb's Romanesque Fisheries Building, with ornaments such as Root had suggested, and Sullivan's Hall of Transportation, which was to be an entirely original design. It would also differ from the others in its use of color, something that Sullivan and Root had hoped to see in every building at the fair. The exposition's colors would derive mostly from lights rather than from the walls of buildings which were made of a material called staff, plaster of Paris mixed with hemp fibre, cast in molds and nailed or wired in place. Leaving this material in its natural white would not only be appropriate for Hunt's classic facades, but would save money and time. It also gave the publicity men an idea, and before they were done, the name White City meant Columbian Exposition anywhere in the world.

One might estimate the cost of the White City by differing systems of bookkeeping, as the unusually harsh winter of 1892–93 began. Some estimates were that twenty million dollars lay out there in Jackson Park, under a sky like cold iron beside a lake that showed gray-green where the ice broke up along the shore. The figure of forty million dollars appeared on the worksheets with which other financiers were figuring, but either way, or split down the middle, it came to a prodigious sum, perhaps not translatable into the dollars of the 1970s, for this was hard money, packed with energy and work, explosive with buying power. The land was rich and money sound; nevertheless another financial panic now came in sight. Once again, the combination of greed and mismanagement, under the inscrutable astrology of economics, was on the point of causing little men to go broke, and big men to scuttle for shelter like cockroaches in a beam of light. The papers told the familiar story: confusion in Washington, gamblers in Paris and London dumping American securities and demanding gold. The approach of panic tried the nerve of Chicago magnates who had backed the Columbian Exposition; and Marshall Field looked more austere than usual in his daily appearances at the club. But the city's rulers were irrevocably committed to the fair, even though no man could calculate the final price. One way of reckoning the price might be in human lives, for eighteen workmen died in accidents during the winter.

Throughout the winter, Burnham spent the daytime hours at the grounds, and frequently stayed overnight in a log-house camp on the Wooded Island. Here he would entertain colleagues at supper, offering good whiskey, sherry, and claret, and a North Woods stew heated in an iron pot at the fire that roared up the throat of a stone chimney. When they went to their bunks and dropped off to sleep, tired from carrying out Burnham's orders, and replete with his wine and food, a quiet descended on camp and island as deep as that of the Wisconsin or Michigan wilderness. They were a little over four miles from the place of the Fort Dearborn massacre.

Panic hit the country one month ahead of the fair's opening on the first of May 1893. After four years out of office, President Steven Grover Cleveland had been inaugurated for a second term on March 4; many who voted for him thought they had elected a great man who would save the country, but others were not so sure, and times grew hard. Today one looks for something to say about Cleveland, and finds about all one can do is record that he was the fattest man to occupy the White House until the accession of William Howard Taft in 1908. At any rate, Cleveland came to the opening exercises of the World's Columbian Exposition, indicating the importance and significance of the day.

May 1 turned out bleak and chilly, and Cleveland looked unhappy as he entered the fairgrounds in the first of a long line of open carriages, accompanied by young Cyrus McCormick and Harlow Higinbotham. Nineteen carriages back came Bertha Palmer, still in good position with two hundred in line, and at her side was the Spanish Duchess of Veragua, whose husband was the only living descendant of Columbus. The Duke was up ahead, escorted by its owner in one of Potter Palmer's carriages. Attend-ing the Duchess and Mrs. Palmer were Lyman Gage and the Auditorium promoter Ferdinand W. Peck, recognizable by his trademark, a white top hat. When the column of carriages arrived at the fairgrounds, bugles blew, troopers drew sabers, the dignitaries left the vehicles and approached a platform near the basin, and Grover Cleveland took a shot of whiskey against the chill. Then he advanced to the platform's edge, and uttered formal words: ". . . splendid edifices . . . American enterprise . . . exalted mission . . . human enlightenment . . . Brotherhood of nations. . . ." When the wind had blown his words away, the President pressed a button and the fair came to life. Down from the colossal statue of the Republic fell the canvas cover, the waters of the fountains rose, and up snapped the flags of forty-seven nations around the Peristyle. Motor launches darted out, sailboats and gondolas followed them, steam whistles began blowing and bells ringing in every part of the grounds, guns boomed from warships on the lake, General Miles yelled "Fire!" and cannon roared in answer, while seagulls whirled up crying in a shaft of sunlight that burst through thin gray clouds. The guests then sat down to a lunch of consommé, soft-shell crabs, julienne potatoes, cucumbers, filet mignon, French peas, broiled snipe, celery, tomato salad, strawberries with cream, biscuits and cheese, Roman punch, coffee, brandy, and freshets of champagne.

In the afternoon Mrs. Palmer led a delegation through the Women's Building, a triumph for the lady managers, designed by a woman ar-chitect, Sophia Hayden of Boston. Standing in the center of the Great Hall, Mrs. Palmer charmed all beholders with her silvery blonde hair, her dark eyes and clear skin, all set off by an elegant costume; indeed, Bertha cut a queenly figure, and that aspect of her personality is what the Swedish artist Anders Zorn had caught, in one of the most delightful portraits of an American woman ever painted. In this work Zorn showed his under-standing that Chicagoans and Americans longed for a queen to love and take pride in, a gracious queen who lived in a palace, helped poor girls, tried to make things better for everyone, and put on a show with jewelry, clothes, carriages, and state occasions. In fulfilling this role, Mrs. Palmer had become the leading public lady of her time. Now Bertha spoke briefly, mentioning the social injustices suffered by women in general, the abuses that she and Frances Willard and Jane Addams had long opposed from their Chicago strongholds. Away with exploitation, forced dependence and helplessness, said Mrs. Palmer; it was neither unfeminine nor unwise for women to compete with men in lucrative industries, if the work was such that women could do.

Many things bearing out Mrs. Palmer's words lay all about them in the

[183]

building, where creations of women in glass, china, wood, metal, thread and fabric could be seen. Women from the ends of the earth had given of their skill and scholarship in needlework, domestic science, the growing of flowers and plants, drawing, painting, cooking, and every kind of delicate and accurate handwork. Murals by Mary Cassatt adorned the walls and Mary Fairchild MacMonnies, the sculptor's wife, had contributed the figure of "Primitive Woman," while nearby St. Gaudens' "Diana" stood in classic grace, a statue that Mrs. Palmer had rescued from officials wishing to eject it from the Fair because of its nudity. "We now dedicate our Woman's Building to an elevated womanhood," said Mrs. Palmer, "and we know that by so doing we shall best serve the cause of humanity."

Mrs. Palmer had welcomed the Columbian Exposition as the greatest opportunity in her time to advance the cause of women's rights, and committed all her resources, including the castle on Lake Shore Drive, to its success. The mansion became a travelers' aid headquarters, and at times as many as half a dozen babies would be lying asleep on Mrs. Palmer's bed while she took their mothers to the fair. All day Bertha's carriage ran back and forth in the service of elderly persons, which was the kind of practical generosity she also showed in providing lunches of beefsteak and strawberries with cream, at the restaurant on the roof of the Woman's Building, for the girls who worked on the fair grounds as guides and messengers.

Bertha Palmer also served the Exposition by acting as chief hostess to distinguished guests, and accepted responsibility for looking after the comfort of Eulalia, Infanta of Spain, highest-ranking royal personage to attend the fair. Eulalia had gained a reputation of being hard to handle, had scandalized older people by smoking cigarettes in public, and was known to be fond of brandy and champagne. Used to getting her own way as daughter of King Alfonso, the Infanta was an early model of what we would now call a member of the fast international set, and the State Department warned Bertha to use extreme care in dealing with her, as though Eulalia were a shipment of nerve gas coming west on a rough roadbed. Mrs. Palmer remained calm, and assigned Hobart Chatfield Taylor, who fortunately happened to be Spanish consul in Chicago, as Eulalia's chief escort. This was a sound move, for Chatfield-Taylor would not trip over his feet at the sight of royalty. Then Bertha set aside a grand suite at her husband's hotel for Eulalia, and installed special furniture that included all the fittings of an Egyptian parlor, and a huge bed inlaid with mother-of-pearl. In the dining room Mrs. Palmer put her own china, glass, silver and gold plate, suitable for anything from toast and tea to a formal banquet. Bertha found time to recruit and instruct a staff of waiters, maids and footmen from among the most experienced and trustworthy employees at the hotel, whose sole duty would be to wait on the Infanta. Mayor Harrison also felt obliged to show extra courtesies to Eulalia, and when he went to greet her at the railroad station, he left his horse at home, put on a long-tailed coat, and substituted a gleaming, cylindrical silk topper for his familiar black slouch cavalry hat. But Eulalia, like certain wines of her country, failed to travel well. She arrived in Chicago tired, cross, and possibly suffering from a hangover. Later that day Chatfield-Taylor reported that when she inspected the Spanish Building at the exposition, the Infanta gave the impression that she couldn't care less. There was worse to come. Mrs. Palmer had scheduled an evening reception for the Infanta at the castle on Lake Shore Drive, with a guest list that included Vice-President Adlai Stevenson, General Miles, Robert Lincoln, the novelist F. Hopkinson Smith, Anders Zorn, the governors of New York and Kentucky, several Russian princes, distinguished delegates from every country represented at the fair, and Julia Ward Howe, author of "The Battle Hymn of the Republic." This was the most impressive gathering yet held in connection with the fair, and Chatfield-Taylor checked every detail of transport from royal suite to Palmer mansion. When he called for the Infanta, she asked a surprising question: "Your Mrs. Palmer—is she the innkeeper's wife?" Yes, one could put it that way, for the hostess of the evening was indeed married to the owner of the hotel where Eulalia occupied a royal suite. The Infanta said she could not possibly go to the house of such a person. It is easy to imagine Chatfield-Taylor's annoyance; the Chicagoans were only playing a game with all the visiting royalty, trying to add a little ceremony, a little public fun to the summer of the fair; and even the richest of the hospitable townspeople had cause to worry about the future. He politely indicated to Eulalia that begging off from the reception at the last moment was something that couldn't be done. The royal lady arrived at Bertha's house more than permissibly late, and in a vile temper. On a dais stood a thronelike chair, to which Mrs. Palmer led her guest, giving no sign that there might be anything unusual in the Infanta's manner. But those unfortunate enough to be brought up for presentation thought it extremely unusual, for all they got from Eulalia was a hostile glare. The fascinated guests saw the Infanta of Spain complaining, with gesticulations, to their beloved hostess. There was no question that Eulalia was putting on a performance of open rudeness, which she climaxed by flouncing out. Mrs. Palmer rose above it, giving not the tiniest sign of vexation; disregarding the vacated throne as though it had vanished along with Eulalia, she turned to the two hundred other guests and urged them to eat, drink, and enjoy themselves, which they proceeded to do. Next day, accounts of the party made a sensation in Chicago, but Bertha said nothing, then or later, about the Infanta's conduct. The Infanta may have concluded that she had gained nothing by offering rudeness to the innkeeper's wife. At any rate, she indulged in no further public tantrums, and proved to be a good tipper on departure from the hotel, distributing $400 in ten-dollar gold pieces among the employees who had served her. And when Carter Harrison stood again in the La Salle Street Station, silk hat in hand, to see the Infanta off, she told him "Chicago is a great and beautiful city now. But in thirty years it will be the grandest place on earth."

The charm of the World's Columbian Exposition lay in its being so different from home, for it was evident from that first evening, when the electric lights came on, that even the rich people did not live in surroundings such as this. It was the first spectacular use of electricity, and when the fountains sprang up under the changing colors, and each building outlined itself in rows of brilliant lights, a new sight was presented, like nothing that anyone had ever seen before. In a way, the chains of incandescent bulbs made a finer and grander effect than we obtain with neon tubes, for there were millions of separate lights in the display, giving an effect of jewelled richness. Nobody minded the chill of spring evenings, and when parties ended at the fair, men and women would drive home in open carriages, singing the popular song of that year, "After the Ball."

During the first weeks, attendance at the fair did not come up to expectations, but the show itself exceeded anything the visitors had imagined. For nearly everyone, it came as a new conception of life, a combining of uplift, entertainment, and education such as the speakers and performers on the Chautauqua stage had so far only sketched and suggested. But here was the hyperbole of the pulpit and lecture platform, spread in the reality of more than two hundred buildings on winding drives, broad avenues, and waterways, set between lake and city. If the World's Columbian Exposition could be rebuilt today exactly as it was, we all would gladly go; but it would not hit our tired sensory systems one one-thousandth as hard as it did those of our fathers, to whom it came without precedent, a thing of genuine wonder. Among those who sensed the quality of the fair as an experience was Joseph Kirkland, who studied the crowds to see how the vision of the exposition affected people like those in his realistic novels of the back country. Kirkland reported that one old farm woman said, "I'm mighty near the other side as 't is, and I hope to goodness, that when I get thar, it will have a similarity to what I'm seeing now before me—and I think most likely that it will." Another literary man at the Fair was the novelist Hamlin Garland, an important figure in Chicago after the success of the frontier stories in *Main-Travelled Roads*. Garland had used his parents in the book, which revealed the bareness of their lives. Now he was proud to bring them to the fair, even though Mr. and Mrs. Garland found it overwhelming, and Hamlin recorded "The wonder and the beauty of it all moved these dwellers of the level plains to tears of joy which was almost as poignant as pain."

To protect the wondrous spectacle from foreign invasion, General Miles took charge of the military department at the fair. A distinguished warrior, he had directed the slaughter of Nez Percé and Apache Indians from 1877 to 1886. Now he busied himself in assigning guards of honor for dignitaries, galloping up and down on a black horse like a Civil War equestrian statue come to life. He put on a number of parades and reviews, and did his best to provide such edifying military spectacles as Joseph Kirkland recommended. That able novelist and historian had reflected the spirit of the times when he suggested that "There might be (what is so fine a feature of foreign reviews) a sham battle; an attack and defense of a fortified post; or the meeting of two armed forces of which one (the weaker) intrenches itself under cover of its skirmishers, who, when driven in by overwhelming number, retire only to unmask the 'deadly earthwork,' pierced for artillery and backed by a solid line of musketry. The entire paraphernalia of war should be there; the intrenching tools, the military telegraph, the balloon service, the ammunition hurried up from the rear, the stretchers picking up the wounded, the field hospitals with their terrible appliances, and all. These, with the roar of artillery, the rattle of musketry, the bugle calls and shouts of command, would make a splendid spectacle. Thousands of veterans would feel their hearts thrill anew at the long-remembered sights and sounds. Patriotism would revive, in hearts long given over to the pursuit of gain, at the sight of a living picture of the late deadly struggle by which their prosperity was made possible. As to visitors from foreign nations, we should be proud to show them, not how great is our military strength, but, on the contrary, how little is needed in a nation of self-governed freemen. They well know that, strong or weak in a show of arms, we are invincible in the defense of our home." The note he struck was full, round, and flawless, as though from a tuning fork. In perfect harmony, a Georgia woman told fellow members on the Board of Lady Managers that she "knew no North, no South, no East, no West," and this Mrs. William Felton added, "We are all dear sisters engaged in a work full of patriotism and loyalty under the Grand Old Flag in the home of our Fathers."

While it was gratifying to see Old Glory waving so proudly, anxiety countinued to gnaw the hearts of the Chicago men who had backed the fair, when the Western state banks began to fall apart and the nation's prosperity went down in economic wreckage. During the period of the fair, from May to October, more than 8,000 business houses failed throughout the country, 156 railroads went bankrupt, suffering grew. It was therefore all the more astonishing that when warmer weather arrived, attendance at the fair increased to such an extent that the total of visitors came to 27,000,000 before closing day. This meant that nearly one half the country's population, three out of every seven men, women, and children in the United States, had visited the Chicago fair. And they did it at a time when money had become scarce, jobs few, and wages low. Without question the people had seen a vision out there on the prairies and the lake, a better way of doing things, that could make men and women better human beings if only they could get the hang of it, and take it home. The vision did not confine itself to intellect and high art—there was a rousing side-show colony along the Midway Plaisance, the green that ran between 59th and 60th Streets to Washington Park. Starting with Old Vienna and its red-coated band, the Midway offered Streets of Cairo with camels to ride, a Dahomey Village, a German Village, Javanese dancers, Eskimos, Wild West marksmen, a Pompeian House, a Chamber of Horrors, a captive balloon from Paris, a Turkish mosque and Algerian café, a Persian harem, a full-scale Venus de Milo molded in chocolate, and all manner of freaks, jugglers, tumblers, and variety performers, along with many kinds of refreshment booths and small restaurants, serving exotic or Middle Western snacks for those who preferred to sit and watch the crowds go by to the shouts of hawkers, the thumping of tom-toms, and the whine of Oriental pipes. A dancer called Little Egypt shone as the Midway's brightest star, although some observers called her performance indecent. It seemed so to Anthony Comstock, the New York vice crusader, and even Mrs. Palmer worried, fearing that Little Egypt might attract rowdies to the Midway entrance near the Woman's Building. Bertha may have been relieved to hear from one of her colleagues, the feminist and short-hand expert Ida C. Craddock, that Egypt's dance was "a religious memorial of a worship that has existed for thousands of years all over the world." That may be dubious anthropology but the Midway as a whole turned out to be the most substantial hit in the history of American show business, and flourished all summer long, while over it there loomed by night and day the passenger-carrying wheel that took its name from the Illinois engineer George Washington Gale Ferris. Seated in this device, one rose to a height of 250 feet and got a splendid view of the grounds. At night the Ferris wheel itself made a fiery circle with its necklace of lights, and from it one saw rockets in the sky and lights across water and heard the singing of gondoliers, and the music of distant bands.

Everyone enjoyed a visit to the Midway, but it was an especial delight to children, among whom none was more enthusiastic than Franklin Delano Roosevelt, eleven years old at the time his parents took him to the fair. Eleven is not a bad age for a trip of that kind, which Franklin made in the private railroad car belonging to his father, James Roosevelt of Hyde Park, New York. As he strolled along the Midway, young Franklin Roosevelt had no way of knowing that a man who was making a reputation before a scholarly council in another part of the fair would be among the instructors later on during his time at Harvard College. The learned man was Frederick Jackson Turner, a professor of American history from the University of Wisconsin. The American Historical Association held its convention as part of the fair, and at one of the meetings, on July 12, Turner read a paper entitled "The Significance of the Frontier in American History." It proved to be one of the most influential essays ever presented to scholars in this country; its central idea, that a unique American culture derived from the existence of a frontier on which a new kind of energy generated itself, captured the minds of historians and sociologists as nothing since Spencer's slogan out of Darwin's book had captured them. Turner also said, "And we have now exhausted the last American frontier."

Frederick Turner may well have been right, but the dangers of the frontier had not abated for people who came to Chicago in 1893. Mike MacDonald had used his abilities in deploying thieves, politicians, and police against the visitors. It would seem that Darwin's muskellunge had crawled from the Chicago River and found lurking places in the town; for the police themselves admitted that at least two hundred persons who came to the fair that summer were never heard of again. Some, no doubt, simply kept going West, broken by the financial panic and leaving insoluble problems behind them, unaware that Turner had said the last frontier was closed. But fifteen of them, having answered an advertisement for lodgings, had disappeared forever into a strange house on Sixty-Third Street. Others got the overdose of knockout powders, or the knife in the ribs, and then the drop in the lake, or a prairie grave. But not all those who preyed on the visitors did so with murderous intent; the confidence men, aristocrats of crime, left their victims alive and in good health. And the confidence game itself, as practiced in Chicago during this period, was an authentic expression of American genius, based as it was on business procedures, and carried on with the ritual of high finance. It deserves study. Most of its chief practitioners came to Chicago for the fair, and they were men of talent, superior in some ways to their victims, though it must never be forgotten that dupes and operators alike were greedy and dishonest. Without that basic premise the con men would have had to find other work.

The opening scene of the Chicago confidence drama seldom varied. after selecting a victim or mark, a member of the gang, known as the roper, planted a pocketbook where the mark would find it, in a maneuver called dropping the poke. By careful timing, the roper would always manage to share in discovering the poke; the two would then examine the contents, which turned out to be a bundle of certified checks for large amounts, letters signed John D. Rockefeller and J. P. Morgan, lists of figures apparently in code, and the owner's address, usually a suite at the hotel in whose lobby the poke had been planted. Returning the wallet then to its owner, the mark would find himself overwhelmed with the gratitude of a dignified, well-dressed gentleman, apparently a person of importance, but actually a master criminal known as the inside man.

"Thank God, gentlemen," says the inside man, after looking through the poke, "I wouldn't mind losing these letters, and the checks are a mere bagatelle. But had I lost this list of code figures, it would have cost my syndicate a million dollars." Next the inside man tells the mark that he represents a syndicate that has managed to tap the telegraph wires of the New York Stock Exchange, and so, using a code for secrecy, he can place buying or selling orders for stocks in other cities ahead of quotations already made but not yet reported. With this advance information he always can come out ahead at someone else's expense, placing a sure-thing bet that would be patently dishonest if the story were true. But it is a hoax, even though the inside man insists on rewarding the mark by making a few hundred dollars for him on the next turn of the market. For this step in the game, known as the convincer, the crooks take the mark to a suite of rooms equipped as a brokerage office and crowded with men who appear to be customers or employees. If the swindle is connected with racing, the same premises are presented as a private betting club. In either case, the mark sees a bustling crowd of clerks, bulletin board markers, and speculators, impersonated by actors, broken-down newspapermen, and disfrocked clergymen who have fallen in the world because of women or drink. The rascals play their parts with convincing realism, some even impersonating Rockefeller, Morgan, and before his death in 1885, ex-President Grant, a convincer indeed because of his known connection with a shady brokerage house. By the time of the world's fair, many a visitor to Chicago felt that with business as bad as it was, he could use a sure thing. But in the end, something always went suddenly wrong, and the mark came out poorer though almost never wiser, sometimes hunting up the inside man and thrusting more money on him. And the result would be the same.

Except for being used as hunting grounds for ropers in search of marks, the precincts of the fair were reasonably safe. Nobody felt like making trouble, for example, when listening to Theodore Thomas's orchestra, although its leader had much to contend with. One vexation came from the problem of a certain piano about which one would suppose there could be no difficulty whatsoever. The matter involved Jan Paderewski, the Polish composer and pianist, who had made his first American appearance two years before, at the age of thirty-one; and now, at the height of his youthful energy and genius, he was the finest interpretive artist to appear at the fair. The virtuoso carried with him his own Steinway piano, and Theodore Thomas found it impossible to tell Paderewski that Steinway pianos could not be used in public performance at the World's Columbian Exposition, for the directors had granted a monopoly to another brand. When the date for Paderewski's appearance drew near, orders came down to bar any contraband piano from the grounds. Nevertheless, Paderewski played on his Steinway in every concert he gave at the Chicago fair. Thomas had simply brought the piano through the gates, defying anyone to stop him as he did so; and nobody cared to go that far with one of the city's most distinguished men. It was a rare instance of Art carrying the day against Bureaucracy, and common sense slashing through red tape. All the same, the exposition brought disappointment to Theodore Thomas when the directors told him they could not find money to make it possible for the Chicago Symphony Orchestra to play out its schedule of concerts. Thomas had first conducted serious music in Chicago twenty-two years before, immediately after the great fire, and had founded the colony of trained musicians that had grown large enough and sufficiently experienced to organize itself as the Chicago Symphony in 1891. He had planned to deploy his men in both popular and classical performances at the fair; and he felt distress when the Department of Liberal Arts canceled the programs. Thomas resigned as Director of Music; and Burnham seized his pen to dash off a characteristic note in his bold handwriting, to inform Thomas that the park was desolate without him, and one of the four great arts had been dethroned.

Burnham wrote in the same letter that the architects, sculptors, and painters had been lucky to make their deals when backers had first raised funds and laid plans; money had been plentiful and panic not yet a problem. And it is obvious that whereas orchestra men must have paydays, statues and paintings require no money once they have been bought or borrowed. Many of the artists who might have contributed to St. Gaudens brotherhood now had representation at the Fair: pictures by the Americans Homer, Inness, Whistler, Hassam, and Sargent drew crowds; the French government loaned 690 art works, the paintings among them mostly by the likes of Rosa Bonheur, Bouguereau, and Carolus-Duran. The private collectors of America made it possible for visitors to see the work of Manet, Monet, Renoir, and Degas.

For all the painting and sculpture on display, the impact of the fair was architectural, and to Louis Sullivan, an architectural disaster. He took it as a crime that people should come to the fair, hungry for esthetic standards, and be exposed to a display of derived architectural forms in classic shells untrue to the frameworks inside them. His Transportation Building was a different thing, frankly constructed of plaster, with its entrance surmounted by five arches set one within another, and reminiscent of the treatment Adler and Sullivan had given the main hall of the Auditorium. Decorated in Sullivan's personal style of ornament in gold leaf, and orange, red, and yellow stucco, the arches contrasted to flat spreading eaves that carried the eye in horizontal lines. Sullivan had something to complain of in the critical treatment of this structure, for some of his colleagues denounced it, and Montgomery Schuyler wrote a review that contained more censure than praise. Other critics gave Sullivan good marks for producing a building that had the merit of recalling no European structure, which could not be said about the plaster palaces of Hunt and Atwood. And Claude Bragdon congratulated Sullivan for designing "The only building at the Fair which *looked like what it was*—an enclosure for exhibits." The fame of Louis Sullivan and his building reached Eliel Saarinen, then a nineteen-year-old student in Finland, who placed a photograph of the Golden Doorway over his drawing board, and called it a guiding star. When Sullivan charged that the Chicago fair would corrupt American taste for at least fifty years, he was refusing to accept the classic as the grand ceremonial style of the Republic, and also the style of American historical imagination, as Thomas Cole had demonstrated sixty years before in the series of allegorical paintings called "Course of Empire." The classic was, indeed, a style of painters' fantasied architecture, as Piranesi, Benjamin Haydon, and "Mad" John Martin had shown in many haunting pictures of vast imaginary buildings. Montgomery Schuyler settled the question from the public's point of view when he wrote that the buildings of the Columbian Exposition should be taken as stage settings, their purpose "temporary and spectacular"; as such, they had achieved success, and were "admired by all the world." The plaster palaces earned admiration, and understanding too, from country and small-town visitors who looked down the basin to the mighty dome of the Administration Building, and saw that Richard Hunt had sited the structure on a grand version of the courthouse square that centered every American city and county seat of the period.

A visitor who admired the fair, but in his own manner, was the historian Henry Adams, who came that summer to stand under Hunt's dome and try to determine what the fair was saying to him. Adams was a grandson and great-grandson of American presidents, and he had spent ten years on the nine volumes of his *History of the United States During the Administrations of Jefferson and Madison*, had traveled throughout the world developing historical theories, and was a tired man of fifty-five, worn but not broken by his labors and a personal tragedy, when he came to the fair early in its opening month. Adams had made the trip in the party of Senator James D. Cameron, old Simon Cameron's son. After seeing the sights during the first week of the fair, Adams went to Boston, where his bankers told him he was insolvent because of the money panic. And Adams decided in September, like many another American, that if he was to be reduced to poverty, he might as well have one more look at the Chicago fair. He returned in good late summer weather, and found that his first impression had been right—the World's Columbian Exposition was a finer show than the Paris Exposition he had visited in 1889. He knew most of the men who had created the fair, and was a close friend to John La Farge and to St. Gaudens, who had designed the hooded figure called *The Peace of God* at Rock Creek Park in Washington as a memorial to Adams's wife, a suicide. Of all Americans living at the time, Henry Adams was the man to look at buildings, and become part of them, and tell how it felt; in this field he was soon to write an interpretation of the French Gothic, *Mont-Saint-Michel and Chartres*, that brought him additional fame, although he originally intended it only for his circle of friends. Along with sensitivity to buildings, Adams had a certain clairvoyance by which he saw energy as the material of history. He and his brother Brooks had made studies of coal production, steam engines, and dynamos, on the trail of something they were unable to define; but the brothers knew it had to exist. Chicago would release it, not far from Adams's post of meditation under Hunt's dome, in another fifty years.

Adams moved with the times. He had learned to ride a bicycle, "solemnly and painfully" as he put it, not long before his second visit to the Fair, and he also had accepted the telephone and the electric trolley car. It was September now, and the fair had shaken itself together as a spectacle that Adams suspected of containing important facts. Approaching the sixth decade of his life, the historian thought of himself as a man still in search of instruction and enlightenment, a quest that he later described in *The Education of Henry Adams*. There he wrote that "As a starting point for a new education at fifty-five years old, the shock of finding one' self suspended for several months, over the edge of bankruptcy, without knowing how one got there, or how to get away, is to be strongly recom mended . . . at Chicago, educational game started like rabbits at every building, and ran out of sight among thousands of its kind before one could mark its burrow."

In scenic display the Columbian outdid the Paris Exposition; but an even more astonishing thing about the Chicago Fair was that it existed at all—"more surprising, as it was, than anything else on the continent Niagara Falls, the Yellowstone Geysers and the whole railway system thrown in, since these were all natural products, in their place. . . . " Astonishing as it might be, the Columbian Exposition stood in undeniable reality on the shore of Lake Michigan, but Adams asked, was it at home there, and could the average American be made to feel at home when he visited the place? In answer to this question Adams wrote that the Ameri can visitor "had the air of enjoying it as though it were all his own; he felt it was good; he was proud of it; for the most part, he acted as though he had passed his life in landscape gardening and architectural decoration If he had not done it himself, he had known how to get it done to suit him . . . he seemed to have leaped directly from Corinth and Syracuse and Venice, over the heads of London and New York to impose classical stand ards on plastic Chicago. . . . One sat down to ponder on the steps beneath Richard Hunt's dome. . . . Here was a breach of continuity—a rupture of historical sequence! Was it real or only apparent? One's personal universe hung on the answer, for, if the rupture was real and the new American world could take this sharp and conscious twist towards ideals, one's per sonal friends would come in, at last, as winners in the great American chariot race for fame. If the people of the Northwest actually knew what was good when they saw it, they would some day talk about Hunt and Richardson, La Farge and St. Gaudens, Burnham and McKim, and Stan ford White when their politicians and millionaires were otherwise forgot ten."

In two weeks Adams found material for study to fill a hundred years. He concluded that the industrial exhibits tried to "teach so much and so quickly that the instruction ran to waste." But he found time to study the models of Cunard steamships, and to calculate on several sheets of paper that according to the given increase of power, tonnage, and speed, the growth of the ocean steamer would reach its limits in the year 1927

"Another generation to spare," Adams wrote, "before force, space, and time should meet." An uneasy feeling about electrical power haunted Adams: "One lingered long among the dynamos, for they were new, and they gave history a new phase. Men of science could never understand the ignorance and naiveté of the historian, who, when he came suddenly on a new power, asked naturally what it was; did it pull or did it push? Was it a screw or a thrust? Did it flow or vibrate? Was it a wire or a mathematical line? And a score of such questions to which he expected answers and was astonished to get none." That was what might prove to be frightening about this Chicago fair; for "probably this was the first time since historians existed, that any of them had sat down helpless before a mechanical sequence." As Adams saw and felt it, "Chicago asked in 1893 for the first time the question whether the American people knew where they were driving." Adams answered that he for one did not know, but would try to find out, and recorded that "On reflecting sufficiently deeply, under the shadow of Richard Hunt's architecture, he decided that the American people probably knew more than he did; but that they might still be driving or drifting unconsciously to some point in thought, as their solar system was said to be drifting to some point in space; and that, possibly, if relations enough could be observed, this point might be fixed. Chicago was the first expression of American thought as a unity; one must start there."

Many Chicago magnates thought they had ended there, as the money panic roared louder and the country's economic structure collapsed; few of them had Adam's inner resources against demoralization at the prospect of insolvency; words were his medium, and when he got them right, the value did not fluctuate. But there were grim days at the Board of Trade, and only the fat, sleek rats who infested its cavernous building appeared to be content; these creatures lived on spillage from the bags of grain laid out on sampling tables, and lived so well that they were acknowledged to be the finest rats in Chicago. But their human patrons had much to endure that summer, and one of the greatest burdens was an infestation of arrogant parasitical Englishmen at the Chicago Club. Upholding the tradition of Chicago hospitality, the members had been quick to extend privileges to British visitors, in some cases admitting persons as guests who could scarcely have obtained membership in a comparable English club. Their pockets stuffed with cigars, these men would lounge all day, propping feet on tables, sofas, and windowsills, ordering employees upstairs and down, and behaving like occupying troops. Their habit of wearing hats indoors might be excused as the custom in certain London clubs, though not in Chicago; but their indignant rejection of all bills for meat and drink wore out welcomes in an embarrassing manner, and it became necessary to ease the spongers out, bitterly indignant though they were on being told to take themselves off.

Another troublesome visitor was the Duke of Veragua, who had a good place on opening day, and received scores of invitations to lunches, dinners, suppers, parties, and balls. To everybody's alarm, it became obvious that the rich food and cataracts of drink were too much for Veragua. Shortly it became known that he was no grandee, but only the proprietor of a debt-ridden hacienda in what amounted to Arkansas or Mississippi in Spain. The people running the fair were much perplexed as to how to get this fellow out of town. They sent Veragua hints that the time had arrived when friends must part, but he still hung on; comments appeared in the papers, the *Times* editorializing that "It would not be dignified for a guest of the United States Government to be in a hurry about taking his departure." At last the fair's managers persuaded the Duke to accept a suitable gratuity and go home. Most unfortunate; but on the whole, good-class foreigners and Englishmen of the superior type gave little trouble, and Chicagoans enjoyed entertaining them. Some of the younger men at the Chicago Club managed to forget the business depression, and furnished themselves and their guests a delightful resort, in setting up a temporary club which they called The Argonauts. They built their house in the shape of a Spanish galleon at the end of a downtown pier, with two decks and a bridge looking over the lake. It was always cooler out there, a pleasant place to lunch or dine before using the club gangplank in boarding one's yacht, yawl, or launch for the trip to the fair. At night the clubmen posted a mandolin orchestra on a barge moored fifty yards away, reckoning this, after experiments, the perfect distance from which to hear the music of stringed instruments across water. Women prized invitations to dine with the Argonauts before an evening at the fair, knowing that they looked well by ship's lights, or in the glow of Japanese lanterns on the decks, making effective entrances to the cabins and dining saloon, which were banked with flowers, while their hosts stood attentive in crisp white linen suits, and messboys deftly served the productions of a French chef on silver and china bearing the Argonaut insigne, a full-rigged ship. "After the Ball," indeed; Mrs. Astor's supercilious chamberlain Ward McAllister knew nothing of The Argonauts, and almost nothing about Chicago, when he expressed doubts that visiting the fair was *quite* the thing. He suspected that it wouldn't do, remarking that "In a social way Columbus was an ordinary man," though any schoolchild could point out that he must have known the Queen of Spain. McAllister fretted about the fair, and it disturbed him that Chicagoans had ballrooms at the tops of their houses, which he proounced wrong. Only the ground floor was correct, though one can't understand why; most likely McAllister felt that Midwesterners forgot their place when they had ballrooms on *any* floor of their houses. But here was hope: for McAllister told Chicagoans "The fact that a man has been brought up in the West does not mean that he is incapable of becoming a society man." Next he offered instructions on the icing of champagne, but at last gave Chicago up when he read a statement by Mayor Harrison, promising hospitality to one and all. Talking of this to reporters in New York, McAllister said, "It is not quantity but quality that society people here want. Hospitality which includes the whole human race is not desirable."

The fair reached perfect flavor as the end of summer came on. By this time various sets of Chicagoans, who could go there as often as they pleased, had marked out favorite places on the grounds. Harriet Monroe's group liked to organize parties at the restaurant on the roof of the New York Building, watch the sun go down over the city, stay overnight at the Japanese Inn, and see the sun rise out of Lake Michigan, through the columns of the Peristyle. Others could never get enough of the moving sidewalk that carried you on a slender pier over the lake itself; and always there were the water rides, in canoes, gondolas, launches, and even in sailboats that helpers on the banks drew through the canals. At last the days of early Indian summer arrived with the month of October, and a series of unforgettable pictures followed each other in the soft air. It was a treasure of indestructible delight to Miss Monroe, for example, that one autumn day she saw a procession of horses, "from tiny Shetland ponies to heavy Percherons and the shining temperamental stallions of the Czar." And fifty thousand October roses bloomed on the Wooded Island, a sight that a Chicago woman called "the refreshment of a lifetime."

The fair was to end on October 31; and an American Cities Day on October 28 presented Chicago's mayor as principal speaker. Carter Harrison cried, "I intend to live for more than half a century still, and at the end of that time London will be trembling lest Chicago shall surpass her and New York shall say: 'Let us go to the metropolis of America!'" The old man bowed to the kind of applause that comes when an audience loves a speaker, and then went home. He arrived ahead of family and servants, entering an empty house to relax in his favorite chair. Though vigorous at sixty-eight, Carter Harrison had gone through an exhausting day. As he was resting, someone rang the bell, and wearing house coat and slippers, the mayor went to the door. There he confronted a disappointed office-seeker who shot him dead. The man, Prendergast by name, was one of those dreary egotists whose personal grudge and misfortune had blotted

out all feeling that anyone else had a right to exist; it was before the day
of effective psychiatric defense for a crime of that kind, and the murderer
himself ceased to exist when he went to the gallows a few months later.
His act brought genuine sorrow to the city, which forgot the mayor's
failings in ceremonies commensurate to the public grief. Miss Monroe
observed that the still available resources of the fair made possible "a
funeral pageant in which the troops and bands of all nations joined for an
effect of mournful beauty." Following the hearse they led Carter Harrison's thoroughbred mare, riderless and sidestepping nervously at the
sound of drums. The family kept the mare at their farm after that, and
nobody ever rode her again.

9

Hard Times

IF CHICAGO HAD BEEN GUILTY OF SINS, IT MIGHT BE SAID THAT A PERIOD of expiation began as the winter of 1893 clamped down, and in the countingrooms, men spoke of a mysterious entity called "business": it was bad, very bad. The newly formed Chicago Association of Commerce tried to put a good face on hard times when its founders said they had organized as an expression of a "broader conception of metropolitan life" that the world's fair had helped to bring into being, and that they were a "virile body of nearly five thousand men who are proclaiming the doctrine that to make a fetish of trade and to worship at an office shrine is to stunt the soul and to shut out the joy that comes of giving a helping hand where society needs it." Opportunities for the joy of helping were numerous: one could see the unemployed sleeping by thousands on the floors and stairways of City Hall, and in parks and police stations. An army of beggars, and pitiful persons who tried to give themselves a semblance of usefulness by sweeping sidewalks and fighting to open carriage doors crowded the business streets. When the police drove them from one block, they would invade another, or join the lines outside soup kitchens and storefront missions that dispensed food along with the gospel. Only the highest Divinity knew where these men's wives and children holed up; abandoned children filled the orphanages beyond capacity, and every day the police gathered babies left in the streets, some of them dead. The newspapers did not fail to report these things, but the sharpest pair of eyes inspecting the miseries of Chicago were those of an Englishman, the famous London reformer and editor William Thomas Stead.

The son of a Congregational parson, Stead was a zealous crusading journalist and a sociological reporter of the first rank, working in the tradition of Henry Mayhew in organizing statistics, taking down reports of witnesses, and making as many direct observations of his own as the hours of working days and nights would allow. He was a good man, who instinctively admired Chicago even before he saw it. As founder and proprietor of the British *Review of Reviews,* Stead could not deny that his descriptions of matters in need of reform often made sensational reading. The *Review* had a large audience, and Chicagoans rejoiced when Stead printed an enthusiastic article, "From the Old World to the New, or, a Christmas Story of the World's Fair" in December 1892. It was the finest kind of publicity, the sort money can't buy, and the directors invited Stead to visit the fair at any time that suited him. The editor had long been interested in Chicago, and had heard rumors that some sort of people's movement was stirring in the American West. Accordingly he asked his brother, the Rev. Herbert Stead, to go over to the States ahead of him and spy out the land. Thinking about Frances Willard's efforts to destroy the international liquor traffic, Stead wrote to Herbert that Chicago "might become the center of the English-speaking race, so far as moral reform is concerned." Herbert replied with a warning that the Americans appeared to be just as much committed to the pursuit of wealth as any Englishman, and advised against coming to the United States. Nevertheless, W. T. Stead came to Chicago; he arrived in late October, caught a glimpse of the fair as it closed, and suggested that the buildings be preserved as a center of enlightenment and social service. Stead learned the extent of economic depression in Chicago, and asked how the city planned to attack the problems of unemployment in the coming winter with corrupt municipal government and ineffective welfare agencies. The future looked black, except for the reform movement that he perceived struggling to shape itself among enlightened businessmen and church people who had before them the example of unselfish citizens like Jane Addams, William D. Lloyd, and Dr. Sarah Hackett Stevenson, president of the Woman's Club. People of that sort, including Mrs. Palmer, urged Stead to remain in Chicago and benefit the city by reporting it as an outsider peculiarly fitted by talent and experience for the task. Stead replied, "It is impossible to describe Chicago as a whole." However, he decided to look into certain aspects of the city's life and within a week was holding press conferences on his findings. On November 12 Stead hired the Central Music Hall for two mass meetings, "to consider whether, if Christ visited Chicago, he would find anything he would wish to have altered." Large crowds attended both meetings, and Stead caused a violent reaction when he addressed the audience at the afternoon session with a list of Chicago shortcomings which included political corruption, toleration of vice, and the greed of employers who took advantage of bad times by exacting more hours of work for lower wages. He finished his speech by saying that people who made no effort to relieve the sorrows of the poor were the real crucifiers of Christ. A leading socialist jumped to his feet and cried, "If the pleadings of Editor Stead in the name of Christ and for justice cannot shake you, may somebody use dynamite to blow you out!" At this point the meeting got out of hand, and a man rushed from the hall yelling, "No dynamite! Christ is enough for me!" At the meeting that night, it was proposed and carried that a five-member committee be appointed, representing business, labor, education, the churches, and the women's movement, to plan the structure of an organized and permanent effort to cure the social abuses of Chicago. Having made this contribution, Stead left next day for Canada, while the *Tribune* editorialized that he had evolved nothing less than a civic federation for Chicago, something that might prove to be of tremendous significance and value. But some people thought Stead a crank, fundamentally unsound in spite of the interest he had roused. As if to answer this criticism, Stead returned on December 1, announcing that he planned to spend the winter putting together a book which would take its title from the mass meetings, *If Christ Came to Chicago.*

Shortly after his return, Stead had trouble with those of his allies who were temperance workers, for he had praised the generosity of saloonkeepers in saving thousands from starvation by setting out their customary free lunch even for men who could no longer buy the traditional five-cent glass of beer. Stead estimated that the publicans fed sixty thousand men per day; he talked to Hank North, a Clark Street saloonkeeper who was ladling out 36 gallons of soup and slicing 72 loaves of free bread every day, along with enough meat and cheese to put strength into hundreds of men, including skilled workers who had exhausted the money they raised by pawning their tools. Stead gave credit to North and other saloonmen for directly meeting a need; and he also assigned blame to those who seemed to deserve it, and after his first survey of the city, chose a powerful foe.

"If a stranger's first impression of Chicago is that of the barbarous gridironed streets," Stead announced, "his second is that of the multitude of mutilated people whom he meets on crutches. Excepting immediately after a great war, I have never seen so many mutilated fragments of humanity as one finds in Chicago. Dealers in artificial limbs and crutches ought to be able to do a better business in Chicago than in any other city I have ever visited. On inquiry I find that the second salient feature of Chicago was the direct result of the first. The railroads which cross the city at the street level in every direction, although limited by statute and ordinance as to speed, constantly mow down unoffending citizens at the crossings, and these legless, armless men and women whom you meet on the streets are merely the mangled remnant of the massacre that is constantly going on, year in and year out. And nothing can be done. With a weird and solemn tolling of their bells, as regularly as the sun rises these great engines slay their man in and upon the streets of Chicago."

Complaints about running over people within city limits were old stories to the railroads; Clarence Darrow in his railroad office had filed notice of six or seven such cases in a routine day. Stead hit a more sensitive target on December 15 when he told a gathering of clubwomen that he had seen a Civil War veteran thrown into the street by a landlord for sixty dollars rent. This had been done in the name of respectable people. "Who then are the disreputable? Those who are dowered by society with all the gifts and opportunities, and who have wealth, leisure, and talent, and live entirely self-indulgently, these are much more disreputable in the eyes of God and man than the worst harlot on Fourth Avenue." Here the audience buzzed indignantly and many of the women walked out. Stead called after them that he was glad to see them bestirring themselves. Then he left the platform. Jane Addams was present but could not save the meeting; word of the unpleasantness reached the newspapers, which had failed to cover the event; city editors now sent reporters to Dr. Stevenson's home, where Stead was a guest. The reporters were such a rough-looking crew that when the Irish maids saw them approaching, they ran upstairs screaming that jobless men were attacking the house. Stead tried to explain: "I merely stated a truism, and those who argue that I was mistaken in assuming that some mere fashionable society ladies were present at the philanthropic meeting must be singularly unaware of the habits of the creatures in question." This failed to satisfy the *Tribune*, whose editors wrote that Stead's speech to the clubwomen had been gratuitous and insulting; whether those adjectives were accurate or not, Stead had managed to found the Chicago Civic Federation, which became the permanent repository of the city's conscience, and the general staff for all who enlisted, from that time on, under the banner of municipal reform.

Stead began collecting material for his book by putting on rough clothes and working for three days in the snow-removal gangs, where the only pay was a meal and a night's lodging. Jane Addams listened to his account of how this had felt, as he stood before the fireplace at Hull House; she was regretting the error in judgment that had caused her to advise a young clerk, sacked from his job, that the best course would be to go on the snow gangs for food and shelter. Some sedentary men could do it and survive, as Stead had done for three days; but this young man lacked the requisite inborn stamina, and to Jane's never-forgotten distress, the hardships killed him. It was not that Jane had withheld anything; hundreds of other people had brought insoluble problems to Hull House. But she told Stead, and wrote in her memoirs, that "one of the first things we learned at Hull House was that private beneficence is totally inadequate to deal with the vast numbers of the city's disinherited." Stead had no trouble in understanding Jane's position, for by now he had fallen in love with Chicago, and he wanted the city to live up to his vision of what it could do. In talking to Philip D. Armour, Stead became so enthusiastic that he said he had long felt that the Vatican should be moved to Chicago, with the Pope living in full panoply beside Lake Michigan. Though no Catholic, Armour expressed hearty agreement, for the establishment of the Pope at Chicago would mean an increase in land values. That wasn't what Stead had in mind; he was groping for a symbol around which he could organize a civic center; and his dream of using the buildings of the fair ended when they burned up in a spectacular fire. The one building that escaped destruction shows what Stead had in mind and the visitor to Jackson Park today can see the Art Palace, rebuilt in permanent materials, as the Museum of Science and Industry. But with or without those buildings on the South Side, Stead had become convinced, as he had told his brother, that "Chicago might serve as the center of the English-speaking race, so far as social reform is concerned."

Stead took only two months to write *If Christ Came to Chicago! A Plea for the Union of All Who Love in the Service of All Who Suffer.* The book was published in the early spring of 1894, and started its career by selling out a first edition of 100,000 copies in one week; two hundred thousand more copies were sold in a short time, the dealers and distributors carrying the books away as fast as they came from the presses, in a perishable binding that makes this work a rare item today. Though he had much to say about commercialized vice, Stead also offered some galvanizing reports on Chicago's tax collections, aldermen, and police. He wrote that "The policeman has many privileges in Chicago, including among other things a discretionary right to kill. In the equipment of a Chicago policeman, one indispensable item of expense is eleven dollars which he must pay for a first-class service revolver, and this revolver is bought for use and not for show. He may fire promiscuously at any citizen who does not choose to obey his summons to halt." Stead then turned to the Chicago daily press, nine newspapers, not counting the foreign-language dailies: readable they were, and yet, he reflected, although James Gordon Bennett could send Henry M. Stanley to the heart of Central Africa to find Dr. Livingstone, "the Chicago papers, either individually or collectively, cannot find out who it is that boodles in the City Hall. It is one of the most wonderful things I ever heard of. . . ." Stead maintained that only two out of sixty-eight aldermen were not for sale, and as much as $25,000 had been paid by railroad interests for a single vote in council. It seemed that some businessmen preferred paying bribes rather than personal property taxes; valuations in many cases looked suspiciously low. Marshall Field had been allowed to value six fine horses at $20 apiece; in his stables stood six carriages valued at $30 each, while his grand piano stood on the tax rolls at $150. George M. Pullman also kept ten $20 horses, to pull six $30 carriages, and his daughter Florence soothed his ears by playing Chopin on a piano worth only $150, according to his tax return. Victor Lawson owned but $300 worth of personal property, a total valuation that had also been accorded to Carter Harrison; only eight aldermen paid anything at all, and these eight averaged $212.50, or enough for three horses and a piano on the Marshall Field scale of valuation.

Stead had discovered that the operators of the vice industry received more realistic personal tax assessments than the reputable folk, though still below true values. He had investigated the wealthy pander Carrie Watson, for example, famous for her red-coated coachmen, elegant carriages, and sleek black horses, and discovered that she paid personal property taxes on a total valuation of $4,000, which would be only a small fraction of her jewelry alone, in any realistic appraisal.

For all Stead's high-minded intentions, the sale of his book was mostly due to his reports on the vices of Chicago. Here he entered Shang Andrews' territory, where he found himself in frequent agreement with that experienced gutter journalist. For example, they both thought Carrie Watson a smart woman, and agreed that unremitting industry and attention to business had been the secret of Lizzie Allen's success in accumulating a fortune of over half a million dollars in association with Christopher Columbus Crabb. They also expressed respect for Vina Fields, a Negress who conducted a brothel in which forty to fifty boarders of her race catered to an all-white clientele. Madame Fields insisted on a certain display of decorum, forbidding solicitation from windows, drunkenness, and the wearing of immodest costumes in the parlors. Stead reported in his book that Vina was "bringing up her daughter who knows nothing of the life of her mother in the virginal seclusion of a convent school, and she contributes of her bounty to maintain her unfortunate sisters whose husbands down south are among the hosts of unemployed. Nor is her bounty confined to her own family. Every day this whole winter she had fed a hungry, ragged regiment of the out-of-works. The day before I called, 201 men had had free dinners of her providing."

Although Stead discerned good in Madame Fields, the managers of vice impressed him on the whole as a bad lot. There was no redeeming grace in Mary Hastings, for example, who earned a place in his pages by conducting a vicious resort at 144 Custom House Place, the narrow lane that ran between and parallel to Clark and Dearborn streets. The Hastings woman boasted that she staffed her place with girls whom other brothel-keepers had thrown out for fighting and stealing, and boasted that no client could suggest an act too disgusting to be performed in her establishment. On certain nights, Madame Hastings produced obscene shows, but in this aspect of the business stood second to Kitty Plant, daughter of the renowned Roger Plant whose Under the Willow had been the most infamous resort of a former generation. The spectacles for which Katy served as producer and director, according to Stead, were "unnatural and worse than bestial." Worse than that was the practice of some procurers who made it their business to lure young girls into their houses for seduction or rape by clients who demanded virgins. Stead had exposed this trade in London, and it also existed in Chicago; the street novelist Shang Andrews used it as one theme of *Wicked Nell*. The heroine of this story specialized in simulating virginity; but in talking to the procuress about a prospective visit from Mr. Brown, a rich merchant, Nell suggested that they lure one of his own daughters to the house. The pander rejected this idea, and sent Nell to a nearby school to scout for a victim. It is interesting to read next in Andrews's novel that Nell gave Mr. Brown a dose of knockout powder, stole his clothes, and got him into trouble with the police. Later on it turned out that Mr. Brown was a widower, Nell married him, went to finishing school, and entered high society. On his part, Stead took no flights into fiction, but documented an industry founded on human degradation, which was "not interfered with by the police, because it is held by large wholesale houses, so the story runs, that it is necessary for them to have certain amusements for the country customers. Entertainers are attached to the large wholesale houses, and when the country customer comes in to make his purchases, the entertainer personally conducts him around the sights of the town. Merchants say that the first night a country customer comes to town he is taken to the theaters; next he is taken around to the questionable resorts, and on the third night he insists upon going to the gambling halls. The questionable resorts are run if not under the patronage of the police at least with their cognizance."

Although he gave vice and corruption thorough coverage, Stead did not limit his book to those subjects; on the contrary, his most eloquent pages dealt with possibilities for an enlightened future in an ideal city. First he would take over the street railways, and run them on hydraulically produced electricity to provide free transportation. Then he would cultivate the lakefront, as in the dreams of J. S. Wright, and make it one long public garden with space for boating clubs, playgrounds, and parks: the fair had shown the way. Next he would build a dozen People's Palaces at intervals throughout the city, where libraries, classrooms, museums, and lecture halls would be open to everybody. To this he would add free medical service, and education at college for all who could qualify, regardless of ability to pay; the eight-hour day would be universal, and many workers would live in tall apartment buildings, tended by cooks and maids who stood on the same social level as office workers. The great height of buildings would make it possible to have plenty of open space around them, and there would be one vast plaza around the finest building of all, the central Municipal Palace, in an enlargement of the traditional American courthouse square like that which R. M. Hunt created for the exposition. The dome would rise to be seen along the radiating avenues from every quarter of the city. There would be many festivals throughout the year, climaxing on Chicago Day, anniversary of the Great Fire. Stead imagined how this might be celebrated during the first mayoralty of Mrs. Potter Palmer. He could hear the bands playing, and see people marching in from each neighborhood, and gathering under their banners, in the blue Chicago October, around the magnificent palace in the central square. Stead closed his book like the evangelist he was, with a direct appeal: "Are you willing to help? If Christ came to your city, would he find you ready? If so you have not long to wait. For the least of these, My Brethren, are a numerous tribe, and an hour will not pass after you close this book before your readiness will be put to the test."

That general political unrest which W. T. Stead had heard of had by now become a powerful factor in the life of the Middle West. Its name was Populism, and it centered on Chicago. Out on the prairies the farmers had been suffering as badly as the people of the cities, but theirs was an old trouble and not the sudden pang of a collapse in the money market. Ever since the Civil War, largely fought by their sons as it was, the farmers had been watching the prices of what they had to sell go down, while prices of the things they needed to buy kept going up. As a result, the farmer's discomfort became extreme, and then turned in many cases to actual suffering, when lawyers and bankers took away the land, and degraded the farmer to day labor and his wife to domestic service, while his sons went to the bad and joined the Navy, or landed in jail, and his daughters sold themselves on city streets or entered houses of ill fame. This was not just the lantern-slide ballad, or the chromolithograph of the villain, and the girl going into the storm, that succeeding generations smiled at; it was the tragedy of human wreckage that accumulated in the wake of falling farm prices and rising prices of manufactured goods. Since neither major political party paid much attention to the countryman's complaints, a Farmers' Alliance took shape to fight the trusts with their rigged prices, the railroads with their discriminatory freight rates, the bankers, the city lawyers, and above all, the thieving, lying politicians who robbed the farmer and kept him poor. Various rural organizations joined the Alliance, and by 1892 the resulting Populist Party nominated a candidate for President of the United States. This new party's platform was horrifying to the speculators on the Chicago Board of Trade: in one of its planks, the Populists were actually demanding the use of government funds for loans to farmers and to facilitate the marketing of produce. It was enough to make the board's grain-fed rats run squeaking to their holes in terror, could they have understood the infamous document. The Populist demand for a graduated income tax was of course nonsense: a man's earnings were his own. But it might be possible to hold debate over the Populist claim that the unlimited use of silver in Federal coinage would benefit the country as a whole, for not everyone regarded the gold standard as sacred and untouchable. Against this background, the Populist Party drew 1,041,600 votes in 1892. But Grover Cleveland ascended to the throne, the nation's commercial structure collapsed, and the possibility of a farmer-labor coalition seizing power gave the big men of Chicago more nightmares than Lobster Newburgh. The two major parties were much alike; from one mile above the earth's surface, there would be no discernible difference between them. In the United States, one should always look at the third parties to see how the land lies, and by the time the fair had opened, the farmers of the Populist Party had stated some aims that were bound to earn the friendship of socialists and union workmen in the cities: the labor movement could heartily approve the Populist demands to restrict immigration, and thus ease the competition for jobs. Union men also agreed in the call for abolition of the Pinkerton Agency and other outfits that supplied private police and strikebreakers; and they stood shoulder to shoulder with the Populists when it came to endorsing the eight-hour day.

This Populist agitation looked good to the militant Chicago working man, for he was beginning to hear, like a tremor in the earth originating on the prairies, the idea of One Big Union. A further encouragement to the members of the Chicago labor movement came during the second month of the fair in 1892, when the Governor of Illinois proved to them that one politician had gained high office without forgetting the working population of his city and state. John Peter Altgeld, a Chicagoan who became Democratic governor of Illinois in 1892, was one of the most intelligent men of his time, but his physical equipment for attaining popular office was poor. He was lame and bent in body, and suffered the facial handicap of a deformed lip; yet his blue eyes could light up the unfortunate face, and he knew how to catch and hold the attention of a crowd. Altgeld had been born in Germany and brought as a child to Chicago, where he became a lawyer, and then a rich owner of business property. He financed the Unity Building on Dearborn Street, with sixteen stories rented to capacity by 800 tenants. A guidebook said of the Unity: "Six elevators carry 6,000 people daily and are usually crowded uncomfortably."

When he came to office, Altgeld caused excitement by sending for the records of the anarchists' trial that had taken place six years before. The governor let it be known that he would hear arguments on the question of pardoning the three men in prison. It was not Altgeld, however, who had revived the case: that had been done by the Chicago police, who started the year 1892 with spectacular raids on socialist hangouts. The Chicago *Herald* observed that this activity had one purpose, which was "to show men who had been putting up money to keep down anarchist movements that the followers of Parsons and Spies were not yet dead." The paper revealed that a Citizens Association had raised nearly half a million dollars, all of it spent by police and special agents supposed to be wiping out the radical movement in Chicago. At last the sponsors had decided they were wasting money, and the business became unprofitable to police and private detectives. Captain Bonfield and two other notable anarchist-takers on the force were discredited and suspended at the time that a committee of businessmen completed the fund for a monument in memory of officers who had lost their lives in the Haymarket blast. They erected a suitably inscribed statue of a helmeted patrolman on guard: after all, policemen *did* run risks for citizens, and still do. But the Chicago Knights of Labor suggested that the inscription should be: *"This monument is erected to commemorate the brutality and unheard of infamy of the Chicago police in 1886."* And Fielden, Schwab, and Neebe remained in prison. There they would stay, most people thought, for although Governor Altgeld might review their cases, it would be committing political suicide to release the men. Altgeld took months to study the matter, and during that time rumors came to be accepted as fact that he had decided not to risk his future by pardoning the three prisoners. Altgeld was writing a long analysis of the trial, stating that he could not accept Judge Gary's ruling that the State did not have to identify the bomb-thrower or even prove that he came under the influence of the accused men. "In all the centuries during which government has been maintained among men and crime has been punished," the governor was writing, "no judge in a civilized country has ever laid down such a rule before." Altgeld noted that it had been charged that Gary conducted the trial with "malicious ferocity" toward the defendants, that he continually spoke against them to the jury, and that his venom and malignity were without parallel in all history. These charges, Altgeld wrote, "seem to be sustained by the record of the trial and the papers before me." Accordingly, the Governor issued full pardons for Fielden, Schwab, and Neebe on the morning of June 26, 1893. Next morning the *Tribune* fired an opening volley with the statement that Altgeld had proved himself "not merely an alien by birth, but an alien by temperament and sympathies. He has apparently not a drop of pure American blood in his veins. He does not reason like an American, nor feel like one." In New York, the *World* ran a cartoon across its front page showing Altgeld as an acolyte worshiping a black-robed figure which held a sputtering bomb over ground labeled "Illinois." The press was not unanimously hostile: the *Chicago Times*, for example, editorialized that the three pardoned men did not belong in jail, and that releasing them had been "no more than right." The governor used almost the same words on the morning of the 27th, when an aide said, "The storm will break now." Altgeld replied, "I was prepared for that. It was merely doing right."

Of all the Chicagoans disposed to argue with the governor on questions of right and wrong, none could have been more violently against him than George M. Pullman. One feels a certain amount of compassion for any historical figure as thoroughly worked over by hostile writers as Mr. Pullman, and yet one is bound to admit that Pullman could have avoided most of the strife and rancor that troubled his last years. Even close associates walked softly rather than provoke his anger, and office employees trembled with fear at his frown. These drudges, perched on stools in the outer room, had occasion to smile only when Pullman's daughter Florence came tripping in; she would enter his sanctum without hesitation, and the office serfs would hear their employer talking in a gentle tone of voice, and even laughing; and after her visits, things went easier for a while. But it was useless to ask Pullman for sympathy with anyone else's point of view; as Harpagon personified avarice, this man was arrogance. One expression of his contempt for others could be found in his handwriting. Where many of his peers among Chicago magnates prided themselves on the clarity of a bookkeeper's script, learned in days of clerkship, Pullman's writing was illegible and his signature looked like a crushed spider. Yet one feels sorry for Pullman, because he believed he had done his employees a favor by building a town for them, and never could understand why they resented him, and detested his model village. Pullman made it hard for observers to believe that his purpose in building the model town for his employees had been benevolent and unselfish; the profit motive entered into his dealings with the employee tenants to such an extent as to make one think either that Pullman's personality had become so saturated with the principle of buy low and sell high that he was unable to recognize his own motives—or, he was simply a mean, overbearing skinflint. The employees favored the latter interpretation when they found out that Pullman bought water from the Chicago system at five cents per thousand gallons, and resold it to the tenants of his model town at ten cents per thousand. He put an even more astonishing mark-up on gas, which he bought for 33 cents per thousand feet, and parceled out to tenants at the rate of $2.25 for the same measurement. Pullman said that ingratitude from "his" working people gave him pain, but he did not care what "outsiders" might think or say. A Presbyterian minister said, "I preached once in the Pullman church and by the help of God, I will never preach there again. The word monopoly seems to be written in black letters over the pulpit and the pews." Obviously this preacher was a radical, and might be insane; but where employees were concerned, Pullman had done more than see that they had a fine place to live—he was proud of them as people. It was true that he had broken their union in 1884, but eight years later, just before the panic exploded, Pullman boasted that a typical group of his employees was "forty percent better in evidence of thrift and refinement and in all outward indications of a wholesome way of life than any comparable group in America."

George Pullman had done as much as any radical for the ultimate strengthening of the labor movement in Chicago when he first fought the unions; in 1893, he stood at the verge of conferring an even greater benefit on organized working men by furnishing the opposition that was to make a national figure of Eugene Victor Debs, secretary to the Brotherhood of Locomotive Firemen, and editor of their magazine. Debs came from Terre Haute, Indiana, and seemed to have inexhaustible energy in his wiry frame; he could make half a dozen speeches, travel three hundred miles on union business, and relax over drinks at the end of the day. But Gene Debs grew unhappy about the policies of the conservative railway craft brotherhoods, and the thought of One Big Union came into his mind. He left the Brotherhood and called a meeting at Chicago in June of 1893 to found an American Railway Union that would include previously unorganized men, such as track walkers, section hands, and engine wipers, who did the hardest work and drew the lowest pay. By November Debs had eighty-seven lodges of his A.R.U. in operation, and in the spring of 1894 he won the first victory by any union over a major railroad when he shut down the Great Northern for two weeks and forced its president, James J. Hill, to grant nearly all his demands.

The battle between Debs and Jim Hill had interest for Pullman, who did not wish to see any weakening of railroad managements that bought and rented his cars. By now the depression had reduced travel and Pullman feared a decline in profits. He fired 2,200 men in the shops and reduced the pay of those remaining; he offered 50 percent less than prevailing wages, take it or leave it. The suffering that fell on Pullman's people, whether fired or still working, did not come near the owner himself, not did it trouble any stockholder, of whom the largest was Marshall Field. Indeed, the Pullman balance sheet for the fiscal year ending in the middle of 1894 showed that dividends had increased from $2,520,000 in the previous year to a record $2,880,000, with no less than $25,000,000 of undistributed profit riding the books. During the same period the company had reduced wages by $2,752,018, an amount so close to the swollen dividends that there was no use trying to convince the rank and file that the boodle had not come directly from their pockets. Although his rates ran as high as twenty-five percent above those for similar quarters in Chicago, Pullman continued collecting full rent, and evicted all delinquents. The old man seemed to wish to play the villain, committing such deeds of malice as the firing of an employee when he saw him throw a piece of paper on a street in the model town. At the office, Pullman inflicted his arrogance not only on the pen-pushers at the outer desks, but on his equals, who came to transact important business. Ernest Poole wrote, "Men waited on his pleasure, and they waited long."

As the Pullman workers saw it, Debs had achieved an almost miraculous victory in the Great Northern struggle when he forced Jim Hill to rescind a wage cut. Therefore Debs might be the one man in the country who could relieve the agony that had begun when Pullman the employer stopped paying wages while Pullman the landlord continued to collect rent. They began applying for membership in the American Railway Union, and Debs did not discourage them: this might be a step toward founding the national workers' commonwealth, the One Big Union he hoped to see in operation before he died. But he knew that he had cut Jim Hill out from the herd of managers and capitalists and dragged him down alone. Pullman with his connections to a hundred railroads was more dangerous; and the railroads themselves were now preparing to fight in a pack, with the organizing at Chicago of a General Managers' Association controlling ninety percent of transport in the United States. After the winter of 1893–94, the Pullman workers had come to such despair that almost all the men who were still in the shops took membership with Debs. He now had more than 3,000 of them, and they were begging him to lead them in a strike that would cause their A.R.U. brothers—now 150,000 strong throughout the country—to refuse to handle trains containing Pullman cars. Debs knew that federal judges hated the thought of a workers' boycott on anything, and they would be especially rough on transport workers in any such activity; the railroads had seen what happened to Hill when he faced Deb's people without allies, and proposed to put Debs himself in that position, through their General Managers' Association. Nevertheless, Debs gained an important ally in Chicago; like Paul approaching Damascus, Clarence Darrow of the North Western Railroad's legal office decided to join ranks with those he had persecuted, and walked off his job to enlist as Debs's personal counsel and attorney for the union.

Darrow was just in time for one of the biggest fights of his career. On May 9, Pullman had raised hopes that he might deal in a reasonable manner, when he agreed to allow a union committee to state the case. But all he would say to them was that he thought himself generous to provide any work at all. Next day, the members of the grievance committee did not have even their underpaid jobs to rely on, for Pullman fired them all, and ordered his agents to kick them out of their houses. Was Mr. Pullman surprised, on the following day, when 3,000 men downed tools and walked out? It is scarcely to be believed that he did not expect it, and it seems likely he welcomed it, for now Gene Debs was committed to fight not only Pullman, but the railway managers' combine, and ultimately, the Federal courts, and the nation's ruler in the White House. Debs proceeded with caution, hoping he would not have to resort to boycott. But on June 20 a Pullman sempstress named Jennie Curtis appeared before a meeting of A.R.U. delegates to tell a story that turned out to be one of those identifiable hinges of history by which the misfortunes of an obscure person cause results of astounding variety and reach. A slender, tired-looking girl, Miss Curtis told the delegates that her father had recently died, after thirteen years of work in the Pullman shops, and on the day of his burial, company agents demanded payment of $60 back rent. They had evicted the girl, and put her on part-time work, withholding most of the wages as installments on the rent for quarters she no longer occupied. After hearing Jennie Curtis, the delegates told Debs what they wanted to do, and on the following day Pullman heard about it. They gave him four days to start negotiations with the union. If he refused, no A.R.U. member would handle a Pullman car anywhere. Pullman replied that he had nothing to discuss with the A.R.U., and on June 28, the twenty largest railroads in the country found themselves unable to roll a Pullman car out of the yards. Nearly 150,000 workers had joined the boycott, and the General Managers' Association welcomed the battle, knowing the hatred of federal judges for Debs, unions, and boycotts, which they could forbid, with technical justification, as combinations or even conspiracies restraining trade. The country couldn't tolerate restraint of trade, for under Cleveland it seemed that business was bad enough without this added interference by the working man. Sharing in these convictions, the managers began to schedule Pullman cars for trains that never had carried them before, and for mail trains. Debs and Darrow saw that this move was intended to put the Pullman strikers and their boycotting friends in the position of hampering the U.S. mail. On June 29, the A.R.U. members on all railroads walked out, taking along the switchmen without whom trains could not safely run over the tracks. At once the managers sent out agents from their Chicago offices to recruit 100,000 toughs to serve as armed guards and strike breakers. Debs telegraphed every lodge in his union: "Use no violence." The question was, should the Pullman cars roll? And men were ready to fight on both sides of this question. But at first there was no violence in Chicago where the heart of the controversy lay; and Debs had moments of hope that he might be able to get the strike into arbitration, for in spite of the mostly hostile press, the A.R.U. had acquired a number of respectable and influential supporters. The mayors of fifty-six American cities, including Hopkins of Chicago, had urged that Pullman come to terms; Jane Addams begged the manufacturer to stop playing King Lear and start to look at things from a reasonable point of view. And in the mellow gloom of the Union Club in Cleveland, the capitalist-politician Mark Hanna choked on his toddy and smashed his cigar to bits against an onyx ashtray as he bellowed, "That damn' fool Pullman! Any man who won't meet employees halfway in these times is an ass!" Mr. Pullman said he would define his position: this amounted to a statement that so far as rents were concerned, his manufacturing company had no connection with his land company, which had to earn its three and one-half percent; and as to wages, "the workers have nothing to do with the amount they receive; that is solely the business of the company." This was no progress, heavily underscored, with worse to come: the managers asked the Attorney General of the United States to appoint their lawyer, Edwin Walker, Assistant Attorney General for Chicago. The White House gave approval, the railroad man took office, and his first act was to request an injunction which would bring Federal troops into Chicago to break the strike. He made his move before

Circuit Court Judges Peter Stenger Grosscup and William Allen Woods, who signed papers that made Walker military ruler of the town. At once Walker called on Washington to send in government soldiers, and bugles blew at Fort Sheridan, conveniently near the city. Out came the enlisted men, losers in civilian life and similar to the roughs who had enlisted as private guards; and the officers, a somewhat better educated set of losers who lived an odd life outside the streams of culture and commerce. They rode in to the North Western Station, formed ranks, and marched to the Battle of Chicago. It was unconstitutional. One did not need to be smart as Clarence Darrow to know that Federal soldiers could not be ordered against citizens unless the State governor asked for them; if he wanted armies, he had his own, the militia. Altgeld had not asked for troops, for there had been no serious trouble at Chicago. The picketing at the Pullman plant had been orderly, with Gene Debs standing by to keep it so, and the police under Chief Brennan had reported no disorders on any Pullman or railroad property within city limits. Nevertheless here came companies A and C, with drummers rattling sticks on the rims of drums, Old Glory flying ahead. Darrow heard the drums and saw the companies wheel onto the lakefront south of Randolph Street when he went for a stroll on the morning of Independence Day. Then he hurried to the South Side where he figured trouble would start. Governor Altgeld sent President Cleveland a telegram: "Waiving all questions of courtesy, I will see that the State of Illinois is able to take care of itself. Our military force is ample. . . . To ignore a local government, when the local government is ready and able to enforce the law, not only insults the people of this state by imputing to them an inability to govern themselves, but is a violation of a basic principle of our institutions. I ask the immediate withdrawal of the Federal troops from active duty in this State." He got no answer.

On July 5 the managers sent a Pullman train into Chicago on the Rock Island line. After a day of struggling to push aside overturned freight cars, Chief Brennan got the train to its downtown station. That night many freight cars burned, set on fire either by strikers, by Federal troops, or by mobs of hoodlums who entered the South Side after dark. Whoever started the fires, violence was what the managers wanted, and if the strikers burned railroad property, they played the employers' game, for the mayor called on the governor, and Altgeld added six companies of State militia to the armed host gathered in Chicago. Next morning a fight broke out in the yards, soldiers fired on a crowd, and three civilians fell dead; other men and women received wounds from bayonets and bullets. Before nightfall, Federal agents working for Edwin Walker arrested Debs and put him in jail. Grosscup and Woods charged Debs with criminal conspiracy and impeding the U.S. mails, and tied up Darrow in red tape when he came to the prison to make bond for his client. The papers blared with headlines about THE DEBS REBELLION. President Cleveland at last acknowledged Altgeld's message; he rebuked the governor by letter and took a bow, although the members of the A.R.U. and plenty of other people made it clear that they were in no mood to join the applause. The vanity of politicians kept Cleveland from realizing this, while he fed his complacency by reading attacks on Altgeld, such as the editorial in *Harper's Weekly* which called the Illinois governor a dangerous ruffian. And doubtless Cleveland obtained gratification by looking at the numerous cartoons portraying Altgeld as a maniacal arsonist flourishing a torch and trampling on Liberty and Justice. But the managers had their violence, and $300,000 worth of railroad property burned in the next few days, a cheap enough price for destroying the union. Thugs and soldiers killed thirteen men and women before the strike collapsed a few days later. The Pullman Company took back the workers one at a time, paying the same wages they had struck against, and confiscating their A.R.U. cards; but those who had been prominent in the strike went on a blacklist and never worked again, unless they established false identities. They would all be dead before the day arrived that put the government by the union member's side and the boss on the blacklist.

No one in the United States doubted that Debs would get a term in jail, and Judge Grosscup himself took the case to make sure he did not escape. In the courtroom, Debs scarcely appeared to be the fire-breathing dragon that some cartoonists had made of him. He looked like a small-town editor with a long, humorous face and a friendly manner. And in this, his first big case, Darrow began to show how his informal, reasonable approach could hold a jury's attention and turn them his way. The reporters thought Darrow was going to win when he subpoenaed George M. Pullman as a witness, but Pullman was tipped off and left town ahead of the process servers. Immediately Darrow put Pullman on trial *in absentia;* he was summoning every member of the Manager's Association, and planned to show them in criminal conspiracy to depress wages and use Federal troops to attack and murder citizens gathered in lawful assemblies. Next morning one juror was missing; the clerk handed up a doctor's note saying the man was sick but could return in three days. Instantly Judge Grosscup cried that he adjourned further testimony, Darrow was up yelling, and Grosscup flailing with his gavel like a comedian in the old burlesque routine called "Irish Justice." It was the end of the conspiracy charge against Debs and the seven union men indicted with him, but the other federal judge who had signed the injunction now sentenced them all to six months in jail for contempt, a charge that did not have to go before a jury. Darrow thought the Supreme Court of the United States would throw this out, but he was wrong; and even though Lyman Trumbull joined him in appealing, the high court endorsed everything the Chicago judges had done. Debs and the others served their sentences. Men in saloons and livery stables said that Grosscup and Woods had licked Debs and Darrow; Pullman had knocked a union into splinters; and Grover Cleveland had put John P. Altgeld down for the count. Most men thought it was all out of their own hands anyhow.

Because of the time that appeals and arguments consumed, Debs and his colleagues did not go to prison until late in 1895. By then a Senate Committee investigating the strike had brought out the figures on profits and wages, and called on Pullman for the testimony that Darrow would have elicited had he been able to get the manufacturer in court. Through it all Mr. Pullman continued to play the villain's role; when leading citizens urged him to help establish a relief fund for the defeated and jobless strikers, he said he saw no need to give these people a present of money.

Pullman had helped to lay additional solid flooring under the labor unions, even though it appeared that he had scored an overwhelming victory for his way of doing things. The death of Debs's union caused hours of talk in beer taverns and meeting halls around Clark Street and North Avenue where German socialists gathered and harangued each other, forefingers waving as they checked off the ailments of society point by point. These men envisioned a close relationship between the Populists in the back country and the factory workers in the big towns, a combination of native born and Swedish farmers with foreign born city proletarians. If you wanted to deal with foreigners, Chicago was the place. By 1895, out of the metropolitan population of around 1,600,000 nearly a million were Poles, Swedes, Norwegians, Danes, Bohemians, and Greeks, more than in any other city in the United States. Chicago had more Bohemians than any other city on earth, except Prague; and was third city in the world for Swedes and Norwegians, fourth for Poles, and fifth for Germans.

The working men in all cities found it harder than ever to get jobs, and wages kept on going down, while debt-ridden farmers went to market and found themselves deeper in debt. They groped by instinct for the answer, Chicago working man and Wisconsin farmer, lumberman up in Michigan, gandy dancer on Jim Hill's main line: among other plagues there was something wrong with money itself, the politicians had become crooked as monte-throwers, and the bosses had cash drawers in place of hearts. Cyrus McCormick had said it: "Nothing promotes efficiency in a plant better than an extra man for every job, waiting in a long line at the hiring gate."

Henry Demarest Lloyd had issued his *Wealth Against Commonwealth* in 1894, beginning his journey into the Socialist Party. His father-in-law, old Deacon Bross of the *Tribune*, had died in 1890. It is obvious that Bross would not have cared for *Wealth Against Commonwealth*, an attack on monopoly capitalism that showed the way for muckraking journalists in the next generation. As we know, the Deacon had channeled his share of the *Tribune* around Demarest Lloyd; by this will one-sixteenth of the paper went to his grandson, who helped to found the Communist Party of America in Chicago, two years after the first World War, but later became a Republican and a vociferous opponent of Franklin D. Roosevelt. Demarest Lloyd stayed on the left until the day he died in 1903. Other progressive Chicagoans with undeniable standing included Jane Addams and the women of Hull House, at that time starting their long fight for laws limiting the hours of work for women and children, and calling for safety measures around machines that chewed up fingers, hands, and arms in Chicago factories. And there was the unassailably rich Lyman Gage, and Dr. David Swing, and Mrs. Potter Palmer.

Bertha Palmer had gone to Europe after the fair, and did not get back to Chicago until the smoke of the Pullman battles had blown out over the lake, and a counting house prosperity had revived. But the city's emotional reserves were depleted, and the people had need of a show to divert them. And when it came in the year 1895, the show turned out to be fascinating though scarcely edifying. It was a fantastic murder trial which revealed what had happened to some of the visitors who disappeared in Chicago after coming to visit the fair. The central figure of the case was Dr. Herman W. Mudgett, a Chicagoan who has been neglected, and denied his place in the history of American crime. For Mudgett was the most heartless and monstrous killer of human beings about whom we have any record. It will be granted that Mudgett cannot be compared as a killer with military men; what we have here is a free-lance murderer, working on his own, but in that line Mudgett stood supreme. Like many another man of achievement in Chicago, Herman W. Mudgett came from New England stock, having been born in a leading family of Gilmanton, New Hampshire. In 1879, Mudgett had entered the University of Michigan medical school under the name of Henry H. Holmes, the alias he maintained for the rest of of his life. He paid his way at Ann Arbor by a $12,500 life insurance swindle based on the theft of a cadaver from the dissecting room. Abandoning his wife and infant son on graduation, Holmes established practice in the Chicago suburbs at Wilmette, and without divorcing his wife, married Myrtle Belknap, daughter of a rich manufacturer. Twice Mr. Belknap nearly died after swallowing medicine the young doctor compounded, but did not suspect poisoning until he found that Holmes had tried to take over his estate by forging a series of property deeds. Belknap called police who came to the doctor's office, arriving just before Holmes left by the back door. After staying out of sight for three years, Holmes returned to Chicago, presented himself as the inventor of a copying machine, and set up offices in the Monon Block on South Dearborn Street. The machine failed, and Holmes moved to the neighborhood around Sixty-Third and Wallace Streets on the South Side, where he got work in a drug store owned by a widow named Holden. Here during the next few years Holmes committed most of his crimes; he was to confess the murders of twenty-seven people, and may have killed twenty-three more.

Mrs. Holden was probably Holmes's first victim, for she disappeared early in 1890 and no one ever saw her again. Holmes announced that he had bought the drugstore at some time before Mrs. Holden moved away, leaving no forwarding address. Prospering at the retail drug trade combined with a business in stolen goods, Holmes started to build a house across the street from the store late in 1892. It was a large building for that part of town, 162 feet long, with three stories over the basement, and piers of bay windows rising to false battlements. The neighbors called the place Holmes's Castle, and noticed something odd about those bay windows. They were covered by sheet iron.

Inside the castle there were ninety rooms. Acting as his own architect, Holmes had watched closely as the workmen followed his designs for a labyrinthine interior of trap doors, concealed stairways, winding passages, windowless chambers with chutes leading to the cellar, airtight closets, and a stairway at the top of the house, like that which David Balfour's uncle invited him to climb, leading to a door that opened on air thirty feet above the back alley. Later investigation showed that one room was a big safe, almost bank-vault size, with an aperture for a gas pipe. Some of the rooms were sound-proofed; and one bed chamber was found to have walls of iron and asbestos, with an opening arranged to allow the flame of a blow-torch to reach every part of the room.

When the castle stood completed in the spring of 1893, Holmes announced that he planned to operate a lodging house for visitors to the fair, and advertised for roomers in the newspapers. From among the hundreds of visitors who disappeared, the police were later to trace about fifty to the castle's doors. However, Holmes's confession included no roomers attracted by advertisements: the persons he confessed to killing had all been friends.

The case of Holmes's Castle and its owner, named the Monster of Sixty-

Third Street by Chicago newspapers, came to light as the result of work by Detective Frank P. Geyer of the Pinkerton Agency, who picked up the trail while investigating what at first appeared to be a case of life insurance fraud. A man named Benjamin F. Pietzel had taken out a $10,000 policy at the Chicago branch of the Fidelity Mutual Life Association in the early autumn of 1894; he thereupon moved to Philadelphia and set up as a manufacturer's agent under the name of B. F. Perry. Shortly afterward a fire broke out in Pietzel-Perry's office, where the police found him dead, apparently as a result of burns. Next, one Jeptha D. Howe appeared, identified Perry as B. F. Pietzel, and collected the insurance, supposedly on behalf of the dead man's daughter. Howe was a confederate of Holmes, who pocketed most of the insurance money. It was a case of murder, for Holmes had killed the insured man before setting the office fire. All this came out when Holmes's confederates started talk that put the investigators on his trail. After much hard work, Geyer and other private and police detectives built a case against Holmes which proved that Chicago had been the background for the career of the greatest civilian murderer of the age.

When the trial began on October 28, 1895, the state charged Holmes only with the murder of B. F. Pietzel, but the preceding investigations in Chicago, and Holmes's confession, showed that after Mrs. Holden, the next persons he butchered in the house on Sixty-Third Street had been Mrs. Julia Conner and her eight-year-old daughter, Pearl. Holmes then killed a young girl from Texas, Minnie Williams, and dissolved her body in acid vats beneath the castle. He next murdered Emily Van Tassel, a Chicago girl whom he had used in experiments connected with his theory that the human body could be drawn out to twice its length; police found the apparatus in his torture chamber. The next to vanish at the monster's castle was Emeline Cigrand, a pretty nineteen-year-old blonde who had just started to earn her living at the new female occupation of stenographer. Miss Cigrand had been engaged to a man named Robert Phelps, who was never seen again after he called for her at Holmes's house. The monster said Phelps also had been torn apart in stretching experiments. Next came Nannie Williams, Minnie's sister; she signed over property to Holmes, and then was seen no more. Holmes had killed her, boiled the flesh from her bones, and stored the skeleton with two others in a chest that detectives later dug up in his cellar. So it had gone as Chicago police searched the Castle, with its cellar graves, its boxes of bones, and its tanks of acid that gave forth dreadful odors. They also found the bodies of two little girls asphyxiated in a trunk; Holmes explained that he had lured the children into a game of hide and seek before he locked them down and

[219]

adjusted his gas pipe. He said he could still recall their innocent looks as he shut the trunk lid. After unsuccessful appeals on his conviction for the Pietzel murder, Holmes went to the gallows on May 7, 1896. The *Chicago Journal* editorialized: "A sigh of relief will go up from the whole country with the knowledge that Herman Mudgett or Henry H. Holmes, man or monster, has been exterminated—much the same as a plague to humanity would be stamped out."

The hangman could dispose of Mudgett-Holmes, but other malefactors remained beyond his reach, and they disturbed the prosperous classes of Chicago as greatly as the monster's execution had comforted them. The men of substance thought there was a general danger in the Populists, forming ranks to invade the city somewhere in the haze that could be seen from high Chicago windows when farmers burned off the prairie, south and west of town. There *was* something out there: the Populists had sent an army of unemployed men under General Jacob Seckler Coxey to demonstrate in Washington for a program of public works. The police arrested Coxey for walking on the Capitol lawn; but the Populists increased their vote by forty percent in the Congressional elections of 1894, and were seeking a national leader in the sullen spring of 1896. As they looked around for a standard bearer, many of the younger people in the party began to take an interest in William Jennings Bryan of Illinois. The Salem high-school debater was now thirty-six years old, a graduate of Chicago's Union College of Law, and a veteran of two terms on the Democratic side in the House of Representatives in Washington, though he had been unsuccessful when running for the Senate in 1894. This young Mr. Bryan had an imposing and authoritative air that would lead you to take him for a Shakespearian actor or big-church preacher if you did not know him. He had perfected the art of oratory during his years of working before juries downstate and in Chicago courts, in political campaigning, and in trouping on the lecture stage. With his black hair brushed back from his high forehead, his piercing eyes, and his long thin flaplike mouth under an acquiline nose, Bryan was accounted a handsome man. He stood over six feet tall and his broad chest made a sounding board for a voice of singular beauty that could soar like a trumpet; he used it with exquisite modulations, throwing it with the belly muscles into his chest where it vibrated and gained sonority, mixing the head tones in the pharynx, letting it rip when the time came, then throttling back to a soft, confidential, contrasting whisper that had them leaning forward to catch every syllable. Most orators of Bryan's class relied on the jug to get them primed and started, but this man was a serious folk artist, and worked his magic by perfect and complete control. And so, like the New England spellbinders Emerson and Phillips Brooks, Bryan never went on with liquor in him. He was, indeed, a teetotaller; however, we can hardly pass over his gluttony at table, so noticeable that people said of him that while trouping the countryside south of Chicago, in one week he would eat enough fried chicken backs to cover a barn. But when the great chance came at the Democratic Convention at Chicago in 1896, Bryan had not yet developed a paunch from those huge cornbelt dinners, and he appeared to be in training like a prizefighter preparing to go for the heavyweight crown; he had in mind the heavyweight title of politics, the Presidency of the United States.

Bryan had tried to talk sense in his Senatorial campaign; he would not make this error again. When he arrived in Chicago for the convention of Democrats, he had decided to deal in emotion rather than reason; and he knew he had come to the right place to deliver an emotional message, for this was the heart of the nation and capital of the prairies, where a defiance of the East and a challenge to the accepted order was struggling to express itself. The men and women making the challenge did not ask for statistics, for logical arguments, nor arrangement of facts in debate—they asked for a voice. And that voice dwelt in William Jennings Bryan, silver tongue of the plain people.

Bryan had an issue when he came to Chicago with the delegates in the first week of July 1896. It was the proposal to allow free coinage of silver as a remedy for the troubles of the agrarian West. After the Civil War the value of gold had increased while that of silver declined; and the Republican Congress ruled that debts contracted with paper money had to be paid in gold. This compelled mortgage-ridden farmers to pay back twice as much as they received, or lose their tools and land to Eastern bankers. President Cleveland, meanwhile, had ordered the Treasury to stock up on gold, while Bryan advocated buying large quantities of silver and making it into coins to increase the money supply. Just how the augmented supply of silver money, or any other money, would get into poor men's pockets, nobody knew for sure. But silver coinage became a symbol of the broad national issue, should bankers control the Treasury, or should it be the other way around? The farmer, the small businessman, and the worker on day wages suffered most from the gold standard, and they were the Democratic rank and file; therefore Bryan planned to make the Democrats the silver party. The word "silver" had an easy sound to it, while the Republicans as the gold party made one think of high prices, bankers' books, and money locked away beyond the reach of ordinary men.

Bryan had a speech, prepared and tested long before the convention at

Chicago. Up and down the Middle Border, he had worked out a talk on silver coinage, trying it on audiences in churches, Grange halls, and school-houses, polishing it through innumerable repetitions, adjusting the rhythms, honing every phrase, synchronizing each gesture and turn of the shoulders and head. Coinage was only the ostensible subject of "The Speech," as Bryan called it to his friends; it was no monetary essay, but a poem, a work of art. And he had rehearsed it so thoroughly that he could tailor it to any audience, soothing them at one place, and rousing them to shouts and rages at another, when he judged them ready.

Bryan had an opportunity, of which he took advantage when asked to arrange a debate on the convention floor. He staged the discussion on July 8, a hot day with the crowd of 15,000 shifting uneasily on resinous plank seats and trying to relieve the humid discomfort with palm leaf fans. Bryan would appear last, and he arranged that a pair of inferior speakers preceded him. First he scheduled Pitchfork Ben Tillman of North Carolina, a cracker with the whining voice and slovenly enunciation of the rural South. Next Bryan put on Senator David B. Hill of New York, who tried without success to explain the technicalities of money and banking. Where Pitchfork Ben had offended the crowd, Hill did worse—he bored them. A reporter scribbled a note to Bryan: "This is a great opportunity." Bryan handed it back with the written reply: "You will not be disappointed." And as the fretful noise following Hill's tedious speech died out, Bryan walked up the wooden stairway to the platform. Standing with an elbow on the lectern, he waited until the hall was quiet, and then started in a conversational tone:

"I would be presumptuous, indeed, to present myself against the distinguished gentlemen to whom you have listened if this were a mere measuring of abilities; but this is not a contest between persons. The humblest citizen in all the land, when clad in the armor of a righteous cause, is stronger than all the hosts of error. I come to speak to you in defense of a cause as holy as the cause of liberty—the cause of humanity."

The audience settled back; they knew they were in good hands as Bryan smoothly carried them on to the question of whether or not believers in free silver coinage should take control of the Democratic Party. He let the voice out a notch as he intoned, "With a zeal approaching the zeal which inspired the crusaders who followed Peter the Hermit, our silver Democrats went forth from victory unto victory until they are now assembled, not to discuss, not to debate, but to enter up the judgment already rendered by the plain people of the country."

There was a stir of approval and a murmur of opposition; Bryan was easy and confident as he modulated to: "I say it was not a question of persons, it was a question of principle, and it is not with gladness, my friends, that we find ourselves brought into conflict with those who are now arrayed on the other side. . . ." Now Bryan turned to the gold delegates from Massachusetts and New York, and startled them with a sudden increase in the power of his voice: "When you come before us and tell us that we are about to disturb your business interests, we reply that you have made the definition of a businessman too limited in its application. The man who is employed for wages is as much a businessman as the corporation counsel in a great metropolis; the merchant at the crossroads store is as much a businessman as the merchant of New York; the farmer who goes forth in the morning and toils all day, who begins in the spring and toils all summer, and who by the application of brain and muscle to the natural resources of the country produces wealth, is as much a businessman as the man who goes upon the Board of Trade and bets upon the price of grain; the miners who go down a thousand feet into the earth, or climb ten thousand feet upon the cliffs, and bring from their hiding places the precious metals to be poured into the channels of trade are as much businessmen as the few financial magnates who, in a back room, corner the money of the world. We come to speak on this broader class of businessmen. . . ."

Now it was running hot and strong, with Bryan lining out the beat as the voice began to fill the hall, yet spoke to each man separately:

> Ah, my friends!—My friends, we say not one word
> against those who live upon the Atlantic coast,
> but the hardy pioneers
> who have braved all the dangers of the wilderness
> who have made the desert to blossom as the rose—
> the pioneers away out there [*Pointing to the West*]
> who rear their children near to nature's heart,
> where they can mingle their voices
> with the voices of the birds—
> Out there where they have created schoolhouses
> for the education of their young
> churches
> where they praise their Creator
> and cemeteries
> where rest the ashes of their dead—
> these people, we say,
> are as deserving of the consideration of our party
> as any people in this country.
> It is for these that we speak.
> We do not come as aggressors. . . .
> We have petitioned,

and our petitions have been scorned;
we have entreated,
and our entreaties have been disregarded;
we have begged,
and they have mocked when our calamity came.
We beg no longer;
we entreat no more;
we petition no more. . . .

And then he let them have it for the first time wide open and with all his force: *"WE DEFY THEM!"*

A roar like the explosion of a depth charge came from the audience; Bryan held up his hands for quiet, dried his forehead with a white handkerchief, took a sip of water, and walked around a little bit, a few steps to the right, to the left, back to the lectern, and started again, easy and slow, neighborly, a man talking this thing over, and ran along through a discussion of tax laws, national banks and currency, what Jefferson thought about paper money—"I stand with Jefferson"—and slowly, easily, began building pressure and raising the beat like the coxswain of an eight-oared shell as he nears the finish. Bryan said that the national temper had changed in the last three months; the probable Republican candidate McKinley, who had been compared to Napoleon, was now thinking grim thoughts about St. Helena. Why was this? It was because "No personal popularity, however great, can protect from the avenging wrath of an indignant people a man who will declare that he is in favor of fastening the gold standard upon this country, or who is willing to surrender the right of self-government and place the legislative control of our affairs in the hands of foreign potentates and powers."

One might wonder where those foreign potentates had been lurking before their sudden entrance, but no matter; Bryan knew what he was doing and he went on into a passage stating that the gold standard fell far short of being the standard of civilization, and:

You come to us
and tell us that the great cities
are in favor of the gold standard;
we reply that the great cities rest
upon our broad and fertile prairies.
Burn down your cities and leave our farms,
and your cities will spring up again
as if by magic; but destroy our farms
and the grass will grow
in the streets of every city in the country.

[224]

He paused, and the deafening yell of the crowd came back. Bryan waited until they could hear him, and went in for the kill:

> If they dare to come out in the open field
> and defend the gold standard as a good thing
> we will fight them to the uttermost.
> Having behind us the producing masses
> of this nation and the world,
> supported by the commercial interests,
> the laboring interests
> and the toilers everywhere,
> we will answer their demand for a gold standard
> by saying to them:
> You shall not press down upon the brow of labor
> this crown of thorns,
> you shall not crucify mankind
> upon a cross of gold.

Bryan stepped back, there was a moment of silence, and the crowd went mad. Screaming, pounding each others' backs, they rushed to lift Bryan to their shoulders and carry him around the hall. Men fought in the aisles, punching and kicking, for a chance to touch him. They kept it up for an hour, and even the gold men joined the emotional debauch. Next day they nominated Bryan for President.

What had happened in Chicago was more than an uproar of rubes and political hacks. Something important had started out there, for in addition to taking over the Democrats, Bryan now convinced a majority of the Populists that he was the man they were looking for. The *Tribune* people, backing McKinley, regarded Bryan as a serious threat, and they had reason to; with inexhaustible energy he stumped the country, presenting his lyric variations on the theme of a class struggle between Eastern Republican bankers and the "toiling masses," who were laborers, little storekeepers, and farmers. This was Bryan at his best: he was nothing like the seedy, paunchy figure that the present generation recalls from his last days, at the trial about teaching biology in Dayton, Tennessee. And at that unfortunate closing scene there was to appear in angry opposition to Bryan another notable figure from Chicago, the railroad workers' champion Clarence Darrow. He, too, was much the worse for wear. It would be distressing to see what life had done to the two old men, now so far below their highest capabilities. But in 1896, Clarence Darrow campaigned with Jennings Bryan, running for Congress on his Democratic ticket; and John P. Altgeld ran for Senator from Illinois. And Bryan was the tireless leader, and his silver voice rang out at every whistle stop, and they heard it on Wall

Street, and stumbled over moneybags in fright. There was poetry in that Democratic-Populist campaign: Vachel Lindsay at sixteen went to a Bryan meeting, and heard him

> Bidding the eagles of the West fly on,
> Bidding the eagles of the West fly on. . . .

Though the magnificent voice urged them on, the eagles flew at last to a place of disappointment and defeat. Darrow and Altgeld did not get elected, and Bryan failed, by only 600,000 votes of 13,600,000 cast, with the electoral college vote 271 to 176 against him. This defeat compelled the progressive forces of Chicago to fall back on direct social service, with their only political effort the pressure at Springfield by the Hull House women. Altgeld came back to Chicago no longer rich, his United Building in other hands; Darrow tried to establish him in practice as an office associate, but the governor was tired; he died after six years of obscurity. He had earned a place in the Chicago story by pardoning the anarchists and fighting Grover Cleveland on the question of troops against the Pullman strikers, but Altgeld's memory was neglected until Lindsay placed on his grave a poem called "The Eagle That Is Forgotten," and mentioned him along with the party leader in another poem on the campaign of 1896:

> Where is that boy, that Heaven-born Bryan,
> That Homer Bryan, who sang from the West?
> Gone to join the shadows with Altgeld the eagle,
> Where the kings and the slaves and the troubadours rest. . . .

Something had ended too, perhaps, at the Chicago convention of 1896; the magnates were happy to think so, though some were more decorous in their rejoicing than the Union League members who got word of Bryan's defeat over the grill room ticker, and took off on a game of follow-my-leader all over the clubhouse, upstairs and down, leapfrogging through the lounge, and scrambling over tables in wild triumphant hilarity.

Randolph Street from the corner of Clark and State Streets, 1865. *(The Bettmann Archive)*

Crosby's Opera House, West Washington Street, 1866. *(The Bettmann Archive)*

Strikers attack police van at time of Haymarket bombing, 1886. *(Brown Brothers)*

Street railway workers clash with police, 1888. *(Brown Brothers)*

The Auditorium in the spring of 1890, showing the row houses on South Michigan Avenue at East Congress Street. *(Brown Brothers)*

Harriet Monroe in 1892. *(Brown Brothers)*

John Peter Altgeld, Governor of Illinois, 1892. *(Brown Brothers)*

Mrs. Potter Palmer (Bertha Honoré), 1892. *(The Bettmann Archive)*

Potter Palmer in 1892. *(The Bettmann Archive)*

The Masonic Temple (originally called the Capitol Building), at State and Randolph Streets. Built in 1892, destroyed in 1939. *(The Bettmann Archive)*

The Woman's Temple on South LaSalle Street, from a German print of 1893. *(The Bettmann Archive)*

Illumination of the Grand Court at the World's Columbian Exposition, 1893. *(The Bettmann Archive)*

Administration Building at the Exposition as Henry Adams saw it. *(The Bettmann Archive)*

Northwest Pavillion of the Palace of Machinery at the Exposition, 1893. *(The Bettmann Archive)*

South Entrance of the Electricity Building at the Exposition, 1893. *(The Bettman Archive)*

Exposition visitors strolling in the amusement area near the Ferris Wheel, 1893. *(The Bettmann Archive)*

Mayor Carter Harrison (in bowler) shortly before his assassination in 1894. *(Brown Brothers)*

National Guard fires on Pullman strikers, at Loomis Avenue and 49th Street, July 4, 1894. *(Brown Brothers)*

Freight engine wrecked near Pullman plant during strike of 1894. *(Brown Brothers)*

National Guard cavalry patrol accompanies train during Pullman strike, 1894. *(Brown Brothers)*

dler and Sullivan's Chicago Stock Exchange, built 1894, destroyed 1971. *(The
ettmann Archive)*

William Jennings Bryan on his first Presidential campaign, 1896. *(Brown Brothers)*

Charred program picked up after the Iroquois Theater fire, December 30, 1903.
(The Bettmann Archive)

Traffic jam at Randolph and Dearborn Streets, 1905. *(The Bettmann Archive)*

Marshall Field in 1906. *(The Bettmann Archive)*

Bathhouse John Coughlin in 1911. *(Brown Brothers)*

Vachel Lindsay in 1912. *(The Bettmann Archive)*

egroes under protection of police leaving their house in the riot zone, July 29, 919, and taking with them their Victor Victrola. *(Brown Brothers)*

Results of the riot, "Back of the Yards," July 30, 1919. *(Brown Brothers)*

Rioters stoning a Negro to death, July 29, 1919. *(Brown Brothers)*

Edgar Lee Masters in 1919. *(The Bettmann Archive)*

On the near North Side in the late 1920s: the Water Tower contrasts with the Palmolive (now Playboy) Building and its Lindbergh Beacon. *(The Bettmann Archive)*

In the relaxed 1930s, middle-class Chicagoans enjoy golf and riding near Belmont Yacht Harbor, Lincoln Park. *(Brown Brothers)*

The Potter Palmer house as it looked in the early 1930s. *(The Bettmann Archive)*

Goddess of Grain, took her place in 1930 on the tower of the Board of Trade.
n Brothers)

Another of the fantastic peaks that rose from the booming 1920s: the Corn Products tower, completed at Wells and Lake Streets in 1930. *(Brown Brothers)*

Towers stand silent on the empty river, summer of 1935. *(Brown Brothers)*

Climax of fantastic and romantic architecture in downtown Chicago: buildings at the northeast corner of the Loop, where the Michigan Avenue Bridge crosses the river, summer of 1950. *(The Bettmann Archive)*

The Marina City apartment towers open a decade of new building in 1962. *(The Bettmann Archive)*

The architecture of threat: John Hancock Center, which destroyed a civilized neighborhood in 1968. *(Courtesy John Hancock Mutual Life Insurance Co., Owner/Developer)*

IO

George Ade and Friends

THE MAGNATES IN THEIR VICTORY AND GLORY SOMETIMES REVEALED shortcomings like those of other men. They did not always remain calm, for example, when subjected to questioning and criticism; even the cool and remote Marshall Field could react to provocation, as he did on the day of a visit to his office by Alzina Parsons Stevens, a member of the Hull House group. Altgeld had appointed Mrs. Stevens an inspector of labor conditions for Chicago, and at the disturbing interview she reported her discovery of several bales of women's coats and jackets in a tenement under quarantine for smallpox. Preparing to burn the merchandise by authority of newly passed laws, Mrs. Stevens had found in each garment the label of Marshall Field and Company. She had removed the labels, and now asked would Mr. Field care to have them disinfected and returned to the store? This enraged Field, and to the dismay of his associates, he began slapping his desk and yelling that Mrs. Stevens was a termagant, no lady, and an unsexed woman. Perhaps Field expected Mrs. Stevens to run out of the office with a handkerchief at her eyes. Much to the contrary, she gave him a reply that eyewitnesses recorded as magnificent and scorching. The meeting ended at that, and Field labels joined Field garments in the fire. This was in the morning; at lunch time not a man dared speak to Marshall Field as he crossed the club dining room to the millionaires' table. Although one might covet his money, it could not be said that Marshall Field in his sixties, at the height of his fame and power, was a happy man.

And he was soon to lose George Pullman, who died in 1897, at the age of sixty-four, his death possibly hastened by the emotional strain of fighting with employees he insisted were ungrateful until the last breath he drew. Chicago city had annexed the feudal model town, and Pullman went into the darkness, having been recognized in life as the world's greatest builder of railroad cars.

Field's experience with Mrs. Stevens showed that the monarchs of Chicago did have to risk an occasional interview with some enthusiast or arraigner, for the humblest citizen in all the land, as Bryan had sung, might clothe himself in the armor of a righteous cause and demand a hearing. But in the main, the big men of the city sat secure during the late nineties, while "business" grew active in the glow of enthusiasm for the new era, the coming twentieth century. The rich men had so much on their side: Darwin and Spencer, and the belief supposedly derived from their writings, that the acquisition of property indicated superior biological heritage. Most of all, they had public opinion, for the opinion-making journalists did not start shooting at them until Stead and Demarest Lloyd came along, and the time of numerous and influential muckraking reporters was still some years away. The merchants, bankers, and manufacturers lived in an atmosphere of approval by others equal to the approval they felt for themselves; it had come down from the Manchester ironmongers and before them from the time of the Rev. John Dyer, the eighteenth-century Englishman who expressed the feelings of an era in a didactic poem, "The Fleece," on the subject of sheep and the wool trade:

> To censure trade
> Or hold her busy people in contempt,
> Let none presume. . . .

But this respect for wealth did not govern the editorial writers, who attacked or defended men of power according to their papers' policies. The street railway manipulator Yerkes, for example, was the subject of scathing editorial comment because of his dealings with aldermen. Yerkes came to the end of the line when he fought the second Carter Harrison, the grand old mayor's son, who was elected to his father's office, broke the traction lobby in Springfield, and roused the people of Chicago to such an extent that a mob gathered at City Hall and threatened to hang the aldermen unless they loosened Yerkes's grip on the traction lines. It was no idle threat, for members of the crowd brought ropes with them. When they heard the mob yelling and saw the ropes, the whey-faced boodlemen dived under their desks, where they cowered until Harrison told the angry citizens that for once the councilmen had voted toward the public good. This second Carter Harrison made his most important contribution to Chicago when he defeated Yerkes and ran him out of town. Many Chicagoans believed that Harrison had Yerkes measured for a prison term. It was said that in the face of this threat, Yerkes called a meeting of financiers and vowed to incriminate them all if anyone brought him to court, whereupon they assured him, in alarm, that the heat would be taken off and that nobody was going to jail. Theodore Dreiser made this a scene in a novel based on Yerkes's career; it was only a small part of the literary material he found in Chicago. He had felt the need to write about the city even before he got his first newspaper job. Up from a wretched home in Indiana, Dreiser had been trudging the back streets as collector for an installment furniture house, and reading Eugene Field's column in the *Chicago Daily News*.

The literary and theatrical world that Field described was closed to Dreiser when he arrived in Chicago, leaving him to get his early impressions from the varied crowds of foreigners, and the streets of new small frame houses in the outskirts from which the big buildings near the lake appeared to be a range of distant mountains. Dreiser found reality in the raw streets and treeless yards, for here was the bleakness of poverty, relieved by Orthodox and Roman churches, bulbed or steepled, rising among tiny cottages and enormous gas tanks, churches with gaudy altars and banks of burning candles giving off the smell of hot wax; and he also found an occasional blaze of color at workingmen's saloons where stacks of red and green glasses reflected themselves in glistening mirrors. When he was older Dreiser said of this period, "Chicago was so young, so blithe, so new." Just to be a part of it made him "crazy with life." He passed his first Christmas with relatives in one of those small houses on the far West Side: on Christmas Eve he saw snowflakes falling into the light of street lamps and coating the cobblestones; he watched his sister Alice run to the neighborhood store; her feet twinkled under her skirts, and she stopped at the corner to do a little dance under the gaslight in the snow.

By now Dreiser had landed a newspaper job, but it was temporary and had nothing to do with writing. The *Herald* had taken him on to hand out gifts in a letter-to-Santa-Claus promotion in the circulation department. During Christmas week he stood behind a counter from half past eight in the morning until eleven at night, and from eight to five-thirty on Christmas Day. The job sickened Dreiser, for the gifts were "the shabbiest mess of cheap things you could imagine." The children clutched the mean toys and went away; Dreiser observed that "they had eyes too sunken and too dry for tears." After another year of drudging at small commercial jobs,

Dreiser again managed to connect with a daily paper. This time he landed in the news department on the *Evening Post*, where his first assignment was to go from door to door selling a novel the city editor had written. His territory was the South Side, and he marveled at the tennis courts and croquet lawns in Hyde Park. Eventually the large earnest young man became a reporter, began to get the feel of downtown Chicago, and looked in at fine restaurants and saloons, taking special notice of the Auditorium, where a large papier-mâché tiger stood on a shelf above the bar. At an appropriate time, the frock-coated manager would raise his finger, a bartender would pull the tiger's tail, and the beast would give a life-like growl, the signal for drinks all round on the house. That manager caught Dreiser's interest, with his fine clothes, Bay Rum, and knowledgeable air; here was the model for Hurstwood in *Sister Carrie*. But Dreiser had not yet reached the point of tackling a novel. He was having trouble developing the facility to write for a daily paper. Unhappy at Dreiser's clumsy handling of routine news, the editor put him on the racetrack beat, and warned that if Dreiser failed here, it would mean the sack. Panic hit Theodore Dreiser when he entered the press box at Washington Park Track, for he had not the remotest idea of what he was supposed to do. He expected no help from other newspapermen; they tended to form cliques, leaving strangers and rivals to look out for themselves. For instance, Finley Peter Dunne of the *Herald* covered the dowtown hotels, and entered into an alliance with the future theatrical producer C. B. Dillingham, then a reporter for the *Chicago Times*, to discourage all opposition. Combining against Frank A. Vanderlip of the *Tribune*, they invented a series of visiting foreign celebrities who always seemed to omit the *Tribune* when granting interviews. Vanderlip abandoned the hotel beat, got himself in the financial department, and later became an associate of Lyman Gage, an Assistant Secretary of the Treasury, and president of the National City Bank. But Theodore Dreiser was not looking nearly so high at Washington Park. All he wanted was not to be fired from his job; and he suffered one of those attacks of hideous empty inadequacy that make the victim feel unworthy of membership in the human race. In contrast, there sat next to Dreiser a reporter who seemed completely at ease. And of this man Dreiser wrote in his Chicago memoirs: "His voice was so soft, his manners and mood so kindly. He was so neat and well-dressed, in no hurry, and indicated that I need not be. He told me to do this and that, and by virtue of this advice my pathetic little job was saved." The well-dressed, generous, kindly man was George Ade, the same who had watched the glow of Chicago's burning as a five-year-old perched on a fence in Indiana, eighty miles away. Son of the Kentland bank cashier, George went to college at Purdue, where he was happy to cheer football players wearing noseguards and round leather helmets, and accept membership in a fraternity, about which he said in later years "If I have a particular fondness for Sigma Chi it is because it helped me when I needed help. It gave me encouragement at a time when I lacked courage. It took me, a long-legged and bewildered country boy, and showed me how to wear a spike-tailed coat and a high collar. It patted me on the back and said, 'Go ahead; keep up your nerve: fool 'em as long as you can.'"

At the commencement exercises for the Class of 1887, George delivered a speech on "The Future of Letters in the West." Years afterward he recalled working on his oration for several weeks, "rubbing out shorter words and putting in longer ones." After this triumph, Ade went to work writing catalogues and advertisements for a patent medicine firm in the college town. One of his most effective creations promoted a cure for nicotine addiction called No-Tobac. Ade's college friend John T. McCutcheon drew the illustration, a Roman soldier slaughtering a dragon labeled "Smoking Habit." Results were guaranteed if the customer followed directions, of which the first was "Immediately discontinue the use of tobacco."

George Ade's motivation was a fascinated interest in his fellow men, and he reasoned, "If you want to keep tab on the human race, you must go where the interesting specimens are assembled." That meant Chicago to an Indianan, and Ade went to the city in 1890 to join McCutcheon in rooms on Peck Street. McCutcheon told Ade he had been living on Wabash Avenue, but there had been police trouble over some women lodging there, and he found it prudent to move. George immediately started looking for work as a reporter, applying first to the morning edition of the *News,* which became the *Record* and then the *Record-Herald.* The city editor said, "If you can prove you're not a college man, you might be able to get into the advertising department and make forty dollars a week." But George accepted twelve dollars a week as a cub reporter on the city staff. His first assignment was the daily weather story, and Ade's biographer Fred C. Kelly says he tackled it with enthusiasm that could not have been greater if he were covering the elopement of an archbishop with a chorus girl. He wrote good stuff from the day he started on the paper. At the Democratic Convention of 1892, Ade was present when a German band played "Marching through Georgia" and the Southern rednecks went wild with rage. He wrote of their "maniacal, furious, and frantic explosion of wrath" as they kicked in the bass drum, and a German cornetist bent his horn over a cracker's skull in the fight that followed. Ade even relished the shabbiness of the lodgings he shared with McCutcheon, who said that he saw from their window "in the foreground a morgue for empty bottles, and old packing-cases; in the middle distance, a row of chimneys; and in the distant prospect, the stately uplift of the Polk Street Station tower outlined against the western sky." Thus the scene in the eye of a graphic artist; George Ade the writer, emerging from the house on the same day saw and heard how "Dripping trolley-cars went by, hissing in disgust, the dirty water lifted by the wheels." He had left the long words in the college halls; and he began to publish stories that linked themselves into novels in which he created the first fictional Chicagoans to move and live. They were people like Artie Blanchard, the young clerk in a large office, on the lowest rank of employment above manual labor. Working on the books at twenty dollars a week, the brash and good-hearted hero of *Artie* confided in the narrator, who was Ade himself, that he wasn't overcome with awe at what he saw above him on the business ladder: "If they wanted me to be president of the whole shootin' match, I'd jump in, grow some side whiskers and put up as tall a con game as the old stiff we've got down there now. . . . Say! I know a lot o' boys that's just got sense enough to put in working hours and then go ridin' a wheel. . . ."

For all his bold talk, Artie had anxieties that were open to a sympathetic eye. His father had been a foundry worker on the South Side; and Artie knew that the way up through the lower middle class would not be easy. And he could be hurt: one day he reported that he had received a snub from an acquaintance named Bancroft Walters, son of a rich roofing manufacturer, who had been shipped home after two years at an Eastern college. Artie had doubled his fist and then said to Walters, "I don't want no explanation. I pass you up." But that had not healed the hurt inside, and Artie poured out the story: he had gone to school with Walters before the old man started making money. But coming in that morning on the train: "This is straight, so help me. He threw me down. He'd never seen me before. All because he was out with the swell push and had this queen with him. . . . I don't trot in her class. But to think of that stiff turnin' on me because I spoke to him. That's what put the hooks into me. I won't forget it—never. I was sore, but it was worse'n that. It made me feel rotten."

Artie's girl had a similar anxiety about status in Chicago. After the first time Mamie Carroll went out with him, Artie reported: "I took her home but not all the way. She stopped on the corner and said that was far enough. I sized up that the house was on the bum and she didn't want me to see it." The truth was that Mamie worked in a printing house at eight dollars a week, but Artie had claimed to be on the Board of Trade, so they both had some owning up to do. Next time he took her out, she laughed at his jokes and "put an added pressure on his arm. The gaslights leaped into balls of flame and Artie felt himself rising into the air. What more ould he ask? 'About Tuesday night, Mame?' 'Yes—or Monday?' 'Good enough.' " And he steered her into a florist's shop to " 'get into line with a bunch o' violets. There's nothin' too rich for the sunshine o' the North Side.' " At last, after misunderstandings and quarrels, Artie and Mamie became engaged. On a summer night they had ridden their bicycles down into Jackson Park, where Mamie accepted his proposal of marriage. They mounted the machines and started northward; there were fireflies all around. Artie watched "the lighted patch of roadway fleeing before his wheel." Mamie swung close beside him, and he suddenly started singing. Their lights glided away, leaving the park empty and quiet. Here George Ade ended the novel without indicating whether or not he thought Artie would ever achieve the power of the old fellows with side-whiskers he said were no smarter than he was. One feels that Artie did not make it, but also that he did not sink to the level of the free-lunch cadgers.

In a few more years, Ade gained a worldwide reputation as a humorist; yet below the surface of his work ran a vein of sadness, like the sadness of Chicago. Ade's stories were usually about losers; if the hero or heroine did not lose, there usually would be a secondary character who met with disappointment because of someone else's success. He wrote of these things in a plain style that let human values show through without the slightest sentimental bid for pity or approval.

Ade had modeled Artie Blanchard on Charlie Williams, a youth who worked in the art department at the paper. The barbershop near the *Record* office furnished Ade with Pink Marsh, the black porter, who impressed Mark Twain as absolutely convincing, the first contemporary Negro in American fiction to be presented as he actually was. Pink Marsh took a disillusioned view of his position in society: he was on the bottom with no hope of rising. George Ade found another loser in an elderly man who lived with various metropolitan types in a cheap hotel, and liked to sit in an all-night restaurant telling harmless lies about his importance and his powerful connections. Ade turned the talkative old fellow into the central figure of *Doc Horne.* In the novel, a malicious person made a false charge against Doc, detectives came for him, and the disgrace of being jailed, dragged to night court, and written up in the paper broke his heart. The Doc was another in Ade's gallery of people from the Chicago hinterland, downstate or up in Michigan or Wisconsin, whose lives took unexpected turns in the city. Ade showed his interest in Chicago's domestic service, which was often performed by natives from the hinterland, rather than by English, Irish, and German immigrants, in "Buck and Gertie." Buck came from Michigan, and Gertie from nearby Wills County, and they left the service of the middling-rich Chamberlains to find more satisfying work preaching on street corners and banging the tambourine and drum with the Salvation Army. The uniformed soldiers of the Lord also made an impression on a young Chicago boy named Edward Sheldon, who was to write *Salvation Nell* for Mrs. Fiske while he was still at Harvard.

George Ade's success as a playwright lay ahead of him at the time he was making his early achievement in fiction, but the stories always contained dramatic scenes, like that in "Effie Whittlesy" which could have made a one-act play. Ade presented a successful businessman, Mr. Wallace, who had come to Chicago from downstate and married a woman of noble blood, a Twombley of Baltimore who had relatives in Virginia. One day Mrs. Wallace greeted her husband on his return from business with the news that she had found an excellent kitchen maid and waitress. This pleased Wallace because good servants were scarce and he liked a well-run house. His wife was astonished when the master looked at the new maid on her entrance to the dining room and said, "This isn't Effie Whittlesy?" The maid exclaimed, "Well if it ain't Ed Wallace!" Mr. Wallace said, "This is Effie Whittlesy from Brainard. I used to go to school with her. She's been at our house often. I haven't seen her for—I didn't know you were in Chicago." Effie said, "Well, Ed Wallace, you could knock me down with a feather." He asked how Effie had been getting on, and she said, "I had a good job with Mr. Sanders the railroad man on the North Side, but I left because they wanted me to serve liquor. I'd about as soon handle a toad as a bottle of beer." Mrs. Wallace now recovered enough to say, "That will be all for the present, Effie." After the girl left the dining room, the lady said, "Effie! And she called you Ed!" Wallace answered, "My dear, there are no misters in Brainard. Why shouldn't she call me 'Ed'? She never heard me called anything else." This idea was unwelcome to a Twombley of Baltimore; and Ade gave his story a simple ending, with Ed making it possible for Effie to go back to Brainard. For once in Ade's early fiction, there was no loser: Wallace had behaved like the gentleman he was, and his wife recognized it.

George Ade was aware that neighborhoods could change with terrifying speed as swift Chicago time went by; in "The Barclay Lawn Party" he wrote of a merchant's house on the West Side, "a red-brick cube with a high and mournful roof" on a once sylvan street, "surrounded and doomed, but not yet surrendering." Ade had observed that "The Barclay girls were ready to move into a new house on the boulevard, but Mr. Barclay preferred to remain at home. The Methodist church was only three blocks to the west." At last the girls decided to give a lawn party, which started well, but the Barclays had not allowed for the change in the neighborhood, and soon a crowd of shirt-sleeved men gathered and made the guests uncomfortable by staring at them over the fence. The crowd grew larger and refused to go away. A policeman came along and told them to disperse. One man stood his ground. The policeman took the man by the neck, then swung his rosewood club. There was an ugly scene, and some of the women had hysteria. Mr. Talbot, the oldest daughter's fiancé, attempted to console her: " 'Let your father stay if he wants to, but you and me can go live wherever you say.' Ungrammatical and undiplomatic, true, but it served the purpose and it had to happen some time."

In one of his early stories called "The Judge's Son," George Ade took material from the squalid Freedom Hotel, whose occupants were "a community of equals, all worsted in the fight." An educated, alcoholic derelict told George that "Money talks here in Chicago, and if you haven't money you're little better than a tramp." Ade's character learned the truth of this remark when a fellow derelict, whom he had befriended and helped, unexpectedly inherited a fortune and refused to recognize him on the street. Another story in that cluster described a ragged man who had educated himself in libraries. Talking to Ade, he dug from his shabby pocket a copy of Henry George's *Progress and Poverty*. Then he reached deeper and brought out " a brass 'knucks' with a blunt head and three staring fingerholds.

" 'I'm savin' that for the coon,' he said."

Ade's fiction appeared first as newspaper feature writing, and he produced a great deal of it, sometimes contributing five stories a week to the morning edition under its various names, and later to the evening *Daily News*, his work appearing on the same page with that of Eugene Field. Ade often had help from his old collaborator of the No-Tobac advertisement; John T. McCutcheon understood what his friend was looking for, and walked the streets beside him, sketching from life with his strong, graceful, confident line. McCutcheon became an author and war correspondent, and he traveled the world, according to Ade, like a Mexican jumping bean, but he was first of all an artist, and one of the most gifted who ever worked as a cartoonist and illustrator; his drawing retains its strength and charm, because of what seems to be an absolutely spontaneous line, unforced but satisfying composition, and delightful humor. McCutcheon disappointed publishers in one thing only, that he was incapable of wounding another human being, and so his political and wartime cartoons conferred some kind of humanity even on such villains as the German Kaiser.

Many able young men worked on Chicago papers at the time George Ade and John T. McCutcheon were beginning to get established. They knew Ray Stannard Baker, later to investigate the oil companies; Brand

Whitlock, future novelist and politican; Will Payne, in later years a standby on the *Saturday Evening Post*; and Carl Emil Schultze, who created the comic strip called "Foxy Grandpa." In Ade's eyes, however, Schultze's greatest feat was persuading a tailor to keep him fashionably dressed for a retainer of $2.50 a week. Such an arrangement had its uses, for in early days Ade's only banking connection was with Heymann, the pawnbroker in the *Inter-Ocean* building, who sympathized with young reporters. Ade soon began to earn a comfortable bachelor living but not much more, until 1896 when the first selection of his newspaper pieces appeared in a book called *Stories of the Streets and the Town. Artie, Pink Marsh,* and the Doc Horne stories followed, and George Ade entered the company of approved and nationally recognized authors when William Dean Howells took notice of his work. Howells burbled, "But our life, our good, kind, droll, ridiculous American life, is really inexhaustible, and Mr. Ade, who knows its breadths and depths as few others have known them, drops his net into it anywhere, and pulls it up full of the queer fish that abound in it." And it was on September 17, 1897, that George Ade took out of his net the first in a series of pieces that would make it a matter of indifference, so far as fame and recognition went, whether or not Howells or any other critic commented on his work. The first of the Fables in Slang came from Ade's pencil as an experiment. He wanted to get complete freedom in diction, tell a very short modern story, suitable in length for a daily newspaper feature, and point it at the end with a sardonic or ironic moral. And so he offered Chicago "The Fable of Sister Mae Who Did as Well as Could Be Expected." There were two sisters, Louella the brainy one "whose features did not know the value of Team Work," and Mae, "short on intelligence but long on Shape." Every Saturday night the boss "crowded three dollars" on Louella, until Mae married a wheat speculator and got her sister a five-dollar job as assistant cook. Moral: "Industry and Perseverance bring a sure Reward." The simplicity, the utter disillusionment in the story of Louella and Mae achieved instant recognition in the minds of readers, a perfect hit. In this first fable, Ade had struck a pattern that did not require the slightest modification: everything he needed was there, including the happy thought of capitalizing in the manner of an old primer. This device served to slow the reader down in the short piece, and invited him to relish common words and idiomatic phrases. It was also to be effective in revealing the emptiness in the big talk of politicians, salesmen, and press agents.

After that George Ade wrote the fables for more than twenty years, although he used a frugal hand with actual slang. He wrote the stories in a simple conversational style, occasionally bringing in a figure of speech hat was fanciful but not fancy. The easy colloquial diction, the use of capital letters, the peppering of genuine slang, and the honesty of approach made the fables as popular a series of writings as any American author ever submitted to his public. The literary quality of this "slang" did not come in for recognition until later on; but this harmed nobody, for George had already earned his varsity sweater as an author. People did not think of his fables as literature, any more than one thinks of water as a chemical compound. But they thirsted for everything that Ade would give them. They told each other about the fable dealing with a wedding and its moral: "If it were not for the Presents, an Elopement would be Preferable." They loved the economical way he related the "Fable of the Day's Work and the Morning After," in which a man gorged on delicatessen and a mixture of strong drinks, waked in agony, called a doctor, and gasped, "Doc, it's my own fault. I ate some grapes last night." Moral: "Avoid Fruit." Although he was a devout Purdue man, Ade saw the absurdity in many of the graduate rites. He described the food at an alumni banquet and the stupefying speeches: "Along about midnight the Cowards and Quitters began crawling out of Side Doors, but most of the Loyal Sons of Old Bohunkus propped themselves up and tried to be Game." The bachelor Ade seemed to know by instinct how things could go in marriage; one of many sketches showing this insight was "The Fable of the Brotherhood of States and the Wife who was Responsible for the Jubilee." The plot ran like a train on rails: a homegoing husband had stopped to pick up "a basket of Gem Melons, because the Grocer did not keep the Kind she liked." He also stopped at a saloon, where he encountered a friend from Tennessee, and drank two mint juleps. Then, "as he looked at the fading Sunlight through the Kaleidoscope of Prismatic Flashes" he forgot about his wife, and "beheld 50,000 star-eyed Sirens in white, all singing 'Dixie.' He felt a great love for the Southland welling up in his Heart." As a result "Hubby arrived home at 2 A.M., carrying the handle of the Basket." When the wife protested, he explained that he would have been there at 6:15 "if she had not asked him to purchase all those supplies." Moral: "Usually the Woman is to Blame."

In his own way, Ade authenticated the reports of W. T. Stead about the entertainment of customers from out of town, by describing the activities of a certain Mr. Knight Byrd, an employee at a commercial house whose debilitating duty it was to take visitors around the city after dark while the boss went home for eight hours' sleep. Ade had a horror of addiction to alcohol, though most readers failed to perceive it, and would accept his pieces on the order of the "Fable of the Periodical Souse, the Never-Again Feeling and the Ride on the Sprinkling Cart" as nothing more than funny writing. Here Ade observed, "It is an historical fact that when a Man falls backward from the Water Wagon he always lands in a Crowd."

Although Ade was aware of the danger in hard drinking, he enjoyed many convivial evenings with the members of Room Number Six, an inner circle of the Chicago Athletic Association. He became generous in providing hospitality and lending money immediately on request. This he could afford after the first book of fables reached its national audience late in 1899, and the question of syndication came up. Shortly before this, the editor had started pressing George to get his fables done in advance so that they could be distributed in syndication, but nobody said anything about more money for the author, whose salary for everything came to $56 a week. Ade wrote to Victor Lawson as publisher that he "had passed his usefulness in the 'Streets' department and would like to be at liberty for an indefinite period." Writhing in anguish at the thought of paying more money to an employee, Lawson replied that as to Ade's having come to his limit of usefulness, "you are probably the sole and exclusive owner of that information." Lawson then suggested that Ade write two stories a week instead of six, the closest he could make himself come to offering a raise. Depressed by Lawson's close-fisted approach to the problem, Ade put his affairs in the hands of R. H. Russell, an experienced syndicate man. This agent offered Lawson one fable a week for thirty dollars. When Lawson turned nasty, Russell walked to the door and said, "It was Ade's suggestion that you get the first chance." Lawson called him back and signed the contract. And in a short time Professor Brander Matthews of Columbia University placed himself at the head of those who were beginning to realize that Ade's "straight" fiction and his fables were all of a piece. "His portrayal of life is almost absolute in its perfection," Matthews wrote. "In reading it you experience something of the bliss of looking at your own photograph." Meanwhile, Russell had succeeded in bringing the author's share of the national syndication fees up to $1,000 a week, and it would appear there was nothing more for Ade to do but keep on turning out fables, which he wrote in a seemingly effortless way. But George also took an interest in the theater. Thirty-two first-class dramatic and vaudeville houses were alight in Chicago at the end of the Nineties; and Ade joined other local writers in setting up a Green Room, a supper club where visiting actors could relax after work. Here Ade met Sir Henry Irving, Ellen Terry, Joseph Jefferson, E. H. Sothern, Julia Marlowe of the glorious voice, Otis Skinner, Lillian Russel, Modjeska, and Mrs. Fiske, all of them finding him good company. Ade was witty, yet he sometimes showed an odd honesty that was country born. He showed the quality when someone at the Green Room ridiculed a line from a Bartley Campbell melodrama, "Rags are royal raiment when worn for virtue's sake." After the chuckles subsided, Ade said, "But it's true, isn't it?" He started his writing for the stage with the comic opera *The Sultan of Sulu*, which opened at Chicago's Studebaker Theater on March 11, 1902, with Frank Moulan as the potentate who asked if he might have "two little wives instead of one big one" and put a phrase in the language when he sang Ade's lyrics about the cold gray dawn of the morning after. *The Sultan* was a hit and Ade followed it with two plays, *The County Chairman* and *The College Widow*, that ran for years; for a while he had four companies working in Chicago and New York, where both plays ran simultaneously, and seven or eight companies touring the United States, Canada, and Europe. The enormous theatrical income, plus syndicate money and earnings from eleven more collections of fables, added up to riches that were acknowledged to be great even in Chicago. Ade's brother invested his money for him and assembled a 2,400-acre estate called Hazelden near Kentland, to which the author retired in 1920. At the time of his initial success at the turn of the century, Ade had been one of the handsomest young men in Chicago, and it was seen that the enchantment of his personality affected women as well as it did his male cronies. He had women friends, some of them actresses; people thought he had special and reciprocated fondness for Elsie Janis, the musical-comedy star; others said that he might have married Ellen Terry, who did find a Chicago husband in James Carew, a handsome actor. There was no question about his liking for Amy Leslie of the *Tribune*, who would have been a fine Mrs. Ade, with a remarkably euphonious married name. But he never married. Why was this? Nobody knows. Ade was very close to the people, the folk—yet separated by his genius, and inside him, perhaps, was something that had to be alone. He lived the last years of a long life at Hazelden like Scott at Abbottsford, although in better financial shape, and he joined another alumnus, David E. Ross, in giving the Ross-Ade football stadium to Purdue. Ade always liked to have Purdue and Sigma Chi people at Hazelden picnics, where hundreds of guests ate the fried chicken which he said guaranteed the success of any party, "provided it is prepared by women over thirty years of age." Ade said, "I receive one thousand paeans of praise for the fried chicken to one compliment for my books." There were plenty of people at Hazelden to wait on the owner, even to serve him breakfast at three or four in the morning, as he sometimes ordered it, but George Ade said, "I have no servants; we all just work here together."

Finley Peter Dunne equaled George Ade in success and fame during the time that each was founding a career in Chicago. Where Ade had expressed the yearnings of people who came up to the city from the outback, Dunne was Chicago born. His father had come to town as an Irish immigrant carpenter, and had prospered as a contractor and dealer in building lots. On the Chicago *Post* in the early Nineties, young Finley Dunne followed the tradition of the barroom that governed nearly all reporters: the convention was so strong that Melville Stone, editor of the *Daily News*, remarked that "every competent journalist was expected to be a drunkard, and my staff lived up to the standard." The favorite *Post* saloon was run by Jim McNarry, who impressed Dunne by the directness of his approach to any question. One day Casey the bartender called to McNarry, "Is Mr. Dunne good for a drink?"

"Has he had it?"

"He has."

"He is."

Dunne liked McNarry's style so much that he began doing pieces about an Irish publican named "McNeery." When Jim McNarry asked Dunne to use another name, the writer created Martin Dooley and put his place of business on Archer Road in the industrial South Side. Dunne also supplied a foil for the saloonkeeper in the person of Hennessy, who shoveled slag for a living, and with his dense ignorance and brutal prejudice stimulated Mr. Dooley in his comments on the topics of the day. Dooley's all-inclusive irreverence delighted the *Post* readers, and his first appearance in book form was one of the publishing successes of 1898. Six more collections followed, establishing Dooley and his creator as famous and influential Americans. People cornered each other to read aloud the conversation of Mr. Dooley, and though he was Roman Catholic and a seller of whiskey, Protestants and Prohibitionists loved him. Dooley made a number of penetrating observations, including the remark that "Th' Supreme Coort follows th' iliction returns." Glancing over the sensational newspapers, Dooley saw that they devoted a good deal of space to the misbehavior of rich people, and almost none to "Th' short and simple scandals of the poor." He was not a great reader, and thought only three books worth study: "Shakespeare, th' Bible, and Mike Ahearn's histhry of Chicago." Dealing with men whose muscle actually built Chicago, Mr. Dooley had an infallible gauge of national production: during a decline of the stock market, he said, "I wanted to rush to th' tillygraft office an' wire me frind J. Pierrepont Morgan: 'Don't be downcast. It's all right. I just see Hinnissy go by with his shovel.' " Those who set themselves above Mr. Dooley did so at some risk: the country never forgot that he greeted Colonel Theodore Roosevelt's account of his service in the Spanish-American War with the comment that T. R. should have called his book *"Alone in Cubia."*

Finley Peter Dunne shared with Ade a feeling for the gradations of class in Chicago, and the struggles of poor and scorned outsiders. Dooley instructed his friend: "Aristocracy, Hinnisy, is like real estate, a matther iv location. I'm aristocracy to th' poor O'Briens back in th' alley, th' brewery agent's aristocracy to me, his boss is aristocracy to him, an' so it goes, up to th' Czar of Rooshia." He maintained that Hennessy would move "to Mitchigan Avnoo" if he got rich, hire a patronizing coachman, and put on airs. His sons would be dudes, he would support his daughters' husbands, and come back to the old neighborhood only to lord it over his former friends. ". . . 'I don't want ye iver to speak to me whin ye get rich, Hinnissy.' 'I won't,' said Mr. Hennessy." In 1900, enriched by Dooley's extraordinary success, Dunne moved to New York, became an editor of *Collier's*, and went into smart society.

Chicago reporters in the Nineties considered themselves a special breed. Talent amounting to genius could appear among them, as Ade, Dunne, and McCutcheon demonstrated. And others such as Frank Vanderlip and Brand Whitlock had the unmistakable air of competence; small salaries and long hours were not entirely discouraging, for hopes ran high in Chicago at that time, with the new century coming nearer every day. Feeling themselves to be different from the men of the counting houses, and in some important ways superior to them, a group of Chicago newspapermen founded and maintained a club, the Whitechapel, that has significance in the history of taste. What these American journalists had done, in their city on the prairie, was to revive the tradition of the eighteenth-century Hellfire Club of Medmenham Abbey, with its crypt, its skulls and bones, and its gruesome humor. Chicago also had a conventional Press Club, but the Whitechapel was different: to begin with, its name referred to the district of London where a mysterious criminal known as Jack the Ripper had horrified the world by killing and mutilating a number of women. The name was engraved in crimson glass over the door of the club's first headquarters on the alley behind the Oriental Building at 122 La Salle Street. One entered a lounge called the Skull Room, opening into the bar, which was known as the Blood Room. On a coffin-shaped table in the lounge were three skulls, said to be those of Negroes hanged in Cook County Jail. Members summoned the bartender by clacking the jaws of the skulls, which were wired to springs. After getting his bearings, the visitor would become aware that every lamp in the room was made from a human skull, with the light coming through red, green, yellow, or purple glass in the eye openings. These skulls were the gift of a non-journalist member, Dr. John G. Spray, a psychiatrist who was himself a startling sight, for he had allowed his blonde hair to grow down to his shoulders while the ends of his moustache brushed his coat lapels. In the Skull Room the lurid glow from Dr. Spray's lamps fell on a collection of ropes that had been used in hangings, knives and hatchets that had been the tools of murder, and a series of photographs taken at a Chinese beheading. If this made one queasy, it was not a good idea to retreat into the Blood Room, for two skeletons sat in armchairs at each end of the bar, and other grisly souvenirs were on display. These included several bloodstained leather shirts in which Indians had died fighting soldiers in the West, presented by a war correspondent of the *Daily News*. The same donor had given the Blood Room an Indian girl's head which he had brought back from a graveyard in the alkali country. The trophy was described by Wallace Rice, lawyer and amateur poet: "The complexion was Indian of course, and there were two long braids of black hair which parted in the middle. Near the parting at the hair line was a bright crimson feather from a red-headed woodpecker that had a startling effect. Our physicians withdrew the brain and eyes, stuffed out the eyelids, and one of our artists painted staring eyes on them."

This object was kept in a box; the fun came when members got a chance to ply a guest with so much drink that he went to sleep in his chair, whereupon they would take out the head and prop it in front of him. They would then wake the sleeper, whose astonishment and disgust would furnish merriment for the jokers. In spite of the ghastly decorations, the members claimed that the club was a center of good conversation. Finley Dunne always said that the talk there had been the best in the world, but unfortunately no one could remember any of it. One would be well advised to bring new stories to the Whitechapel Club, for whenever anyone tried to palm off an old joke, the members would rise from their chairs and burst into the "Chestnut Song" with its chorus:

> Adam told it to the beasts before the fall—
> He told the same thing, he told the same thing!
> When he told it to the creatures
> It possessed some novel features,
> But to tell it now requires a lot of gall.

Without question there were men of wit among the Whitechapel's members. One was Ben King, the writer of humorous verse, who inscribed to an indigent friend the lines:

I say, if I should die tonight
And you should come to me and there and then
Just even hint 'bout paying me that ten,
I might arise the while,
But I'd drop dead again.

The club roster included Hobart Chatfield-Taylor and Captain Bonfield of the Haymarket case, who may have shared an interest in the stories of a frequent visitor, a Canadian Indian named Honoré Joseph Jaxon, who lived in a deer-hide teepee he had erected in the building of the *Chicago Times*. When Coxey's Army marched to Washington in 1894, Jaxon went ahead as chief scout, living off the country and sleeping in the open, wrapped in a tarpaulin. Though not a member, Jaxon was allowed to introduce a man at the Whitechapel who caused the most remarkable episode in its history. This person signed the visitors' book: "Morris A. Collins, president Dallas (Texas) Suicide Club." Some of the members recognized Collins as a man who called himself a poet and social critic in writing letters to the Chicago papers advocating public death chambers for people who wanted to die because they were "outlawed by the ruling class." His message was: "Imagine in all the great cities of the country the death chamber to which I have referred, looming up sad and sombre, with a long train of weary, careworn people trudging thither to find an exit from a world in which they have been denied the poor boon of satisfying their bodily wants with things which the labor of their hands might produce were they not refused the chance to work. Let this thing continue —for it soon would become popular—and it is just possible that the spectacle would touch the hearts of the ruling class and cause the establishment of a better system. . . ." Forty years old and the son of an itinerant preacher, Collins had a sort of tired distinction about him when he visited the Whitechapel; members noticed that he took considerable interest in the collection of skulls. A few days later, Collins killed himself with a revolver in his hotel room; he left a note for Jaxon, asking that his body be given to scientists for dissection. The relatives in Texas refused to permit this, and Jaxon asked the members of the Whitechapel to "help him dispose of his dead friend's remains." Collins had claimed the title of poet, which caused the clubmen to think of Shelley, and to suggest that they cremate Collins on the shores of Lake Michigan as Trelawny and Byron had burned Shelley's body on the Mediterranean shore. Cremation was not nearly so familiar as it is today, and the project seemed fantastic and distasteful to the average Chicagoan of the time. Nevertheless, Finley Dunne and Wallace Rice approached James W. Scott, publisher of the

Chicago Herald, with a request for money to do the thing in style. Scott put up $500 on condition that the story be kept for the *Herald.* The clubmen selected a site thirty miles south of Chicago on the Indiana dunes, planned a program, engaged undertakers, and claimed Collins' body at the city morgue, where it had lain for nearly a month. And in the evening twilight of July 16, 1892, about forty members of the club descended from an Illinois Central train at the lonely whistle stop called Miller's Station. Undertakers lifted the coffin from the baggage car and placed it in a farm wagon which the members followed over a lonely, sandy track to a dune where a pyre of cordwood was waiting. An undertaker opened the box and revealed Collins, enfolded in a white robe. They put a chaplet of oak leaves on the forehead, and hoisted the wrapped body to the top of the pyre. Honoré Jaxon came forward, wearing a black clerical gown, and lifted an axe with which he beat in the head of a tar barrel; then the members marched three times around the pyre, singing a dirge to the music of two harps and a zither. Several speeches followed, Jaxon invoked the Great Manitou, Wallace Rice read a poem, the club president quoted Shelley, and others read from Socrates and Plato. At this point a display of the aurora borealis appeared over the lake, sending long, wavering bands of rose-colored light across the dark sky. These northern lights illuminated the scene as various members stepped forward to speak or read and Rice said, "We mourn not, but are here to render our tribute to one who had the courage to die." At last, all members joined in reciting a poem of farewell, and at eleven o'clock, each man took a torch, dipped it in tar, lighted it, and applied it to the pyre. The cordwood burst into bright flame, which must have been visible for miles out on the lake. As the body twisted in the heat, one arm rose slowly and fell back. The members stood by until dawn, when nothing was left but ashes, which the undertakers put in an urn. They noticed that in some places the heat had vitrified the sands of the dune. And in a few more hours the *Herald* came out with its exclusive story: "MAN'S BODY BURNED TO ASHES!"

The story was less sensational than the headline. In fact, though they received criticism for indulging what some took to be morbid tastes, the clubmen had helped to make cremation an acceptable thing. That was the club's only public achievement, and after moving to a two-story house on Calhoun Street, the Whitechapel ran into money trouble and closed its doors.

II

Work for the Night Is Coming

THE LORDS OF CHICAGO HAD LITTLE TIME FOR FUNERALS IN THE LATE 1890s, busy as they were in consolidating their gains and properties throughout the city that had created itself in half a century of time. A typical consolidator was the respected leader Marshall Field, who had made himself sole commander at the store, as he was in all his other interests; Levi Leiter had attempted to push Field out by lining up everybody in the place against him; spies reported the treachery to Field, who gave commands, so that it was Leiter who had to go at showdown time. However, Leiter went out a wealthy man; he moved to Washington, set up in society, and continued to play the market and deal in real estate. The old man stood behind his son Joseph, who set out in 1897 to buy all the wheat in the United States and Canada, having read in the paper that there was bad growing weather abroad and the European crop due to fail. Young Joe Leiter figured those people over in Europe would pay a good price rather than starve; and he went to work on the proven Chicago principle of buy low, sell high. First the buying: Curtis Jadwin and other operators around the wheat pit at the Board of Trade noticed that somebody was ordering wheat for future delivery in 100,000-bushel lots. In December the buyer had contracts calling for delivery on January 1 of more wheat than all the elevators in Chicago could contain; and the news from Europe was good, people were beginning to starve. It now became known that the man attempting to corner the market was Joe Leiter, and on the morning of December 9, a crowd of visitors gathered in the balcony to watch the trading in the wheat pit, the circular arena into which some three hundred brokers had crowded themselves to wait for the opening bell. The price of wheat at the last quotation of the previous day had been 95 cents per bushel. To meet that price and satisfy Joe Leiter's contracts, many a fortune might be swallowed up; it could mean horses out of stables, dogs out of kennels, daughters going behind counters or typewriter keyboards, sons coming home from Exeter or Yale. George Horace Lorimer, the reporter who became editor of the *Saturday Evening Post,* felt the dramatic tension: "Every eye was on the clock. . . . Only the clacking of the tireless instruments and the shrill cries of the messengers echoed from the lofty ceiling. Then it came with a clang and a mighty roar. The crowd rushed together until the men in the pit were lifted from their feet. The wriggling, writhing, swaying mass bristled with wildly waving arms until it looked like a monster with a thousand tentacles. Men, with faces reddened and distorted, howled and raved, now shaking clenched fists across the pit, now signaling frantically with crossed fingers. To the people in the gallery, the meaning of this madness was not clear. But they knew that men were being made and ruined in those few minutes, and that was enough."

That day Leiter sold off some wheat in order to quiet the market, leaving the price at $1.09. "Settling day was three weeks off," Lorimer explained, "and there were big fish in the net who might break its meshes were they too soon lifted above water." The biggest fish was Philip Danforth Armour, who employed 50,000 people in his pork-packing plant, his Armour Refrigerator Line on the railroads, and his Armour Elevator Company, with warehouses a solid wall along the Chicago river. Armour liked to gamble on the Board of Trade when he thought he had a sure thing; but on this gloomy afternoon, he had to admit that young Joe Leiter had caught him on the wrong side of the market, with a fair chance of taking all his money and driving him out of town. At such disaster, men had turned on the gas without lighting it, or said goodby to themselves in hotel rooms like Morris Collins. Philip Armour, at sixty-five, had no intention of going that way, but he was in trouble. His money had been riding on his notion that the price of wheat would go down, and he had been issuing markers, and Leiter's people had been covering them, to deliver wheat in Chicago on the first day of January 1898. He now owed Leiter millions of bushels, and if he did not deliver, he would have to pay Leiter at the market price on reckoning day. With three weeks to go, the Armour warehouses stood empty, for the old man had not foreseen the panic that had just come to a head in the pit at the Board of Trade. Leiter now considered himself sure of his kill in the United States, and the news from Europe continued good: after a summer of drought, a plague of mildew had destroyed the remaining grain crops over there.

The beauty of Leiter's work lay in the fact that there was plenty of wheat available in the United States and Canada, if one bought at the source and arranged one's own shipping; but Armour had waited too long, and now it would not be possible for the railroads to get enough wheat to Chicago by pay-off day. It was one of the greatest things that ever happened on the Board, and it pleased and excited the people of Chicago, now that the story was out, like the holding of a political convention or a prizefight. All were happy at the thought of old Phil Armour's imminent ruin; not that they had anything against him, but it would be such a remarkable, astounding occurrence. And while Joe Leiter led no popularity contests, the average Chicagoan called it dog eat dog. Then came a heightening of dramatic interest when the news got out that Old Man Armour didn't seem to understand that he was licked. The railroads alone can't bring Leiter his wheat? Send part of it by water through Duluth, said Armour. The harbors are frozen and the Sault locked with ice? Send fleets of tugboats to break the way. The tugboats can't do it all? Use dynamite. For Armour had leaped to last-minute action, and all through Minnesota, Montana, Kansas, Nebraska, North and South Dakota, and Manitoba, the telegrams flew with orders to buy and ship, concluding: DO AT ONCE THIS MUST REPEAT MUST BE DONE.

Armour's agents routed out steamboat men who had thought they were through for the winter, dynamiters smashed ice and cleared channels, and lines of ships came down Lake Michigan from the now navigable straits of Sault Ste. Marie. Meanwhile, the railroads brought wheat in thousands of cars on specially scheduled freight trains: Armour had influence with the railways because of his refrigerator cars. The story of Armour's defiance was featured in the papers, but Joe Leiter talked big and said, "I control the heaviest individual line of wheat in the country." And Armour's ships and cars kept coming to Chicago, unloading, and going back for more in a hurry. The price of wheat eased to 97½; Armour packed his warehouses, and rented all the additional space he could find; still the grain kept coming. Now Armour stored it in railroad cars on acres of tracks in the Chicago yards, and still it kept coming; at the end of December, he moored 134 vessels in the river and harbor, all stored with grain for delivery to Joe Leiter. On December 31, Armour notified Leiter that he was ready, as contracted, with 8,000,000 bushels of wheat for cash. Young Joe hadn't expected it to turn out quite this way; old Levi had to come from the East, leaving his markers in banks to raise $7,500,000 to save his son from financial suffocation under that pile of wheat. And the Europeans, though hungry, were still able to work sums in arithmetic: international wheat failed to go sky-high for Joseph Leiter and in the end, only a few people starved to death. In Chicago, men shook their heads and chuckled, "It doesn't pay to fool around with old Phil Armour."

Old Phil was an addict of work, arriving at his office shortly after sunup, and working till the sun went down. When someone asked him why he put in so many hours on the job, he answered, "What else is there to do?" One sight that gladdened the packer's eyes was other people working, and if they weren't making a great deal of money at it, so much the better. However, P. D. Armour had human juices in him; he would listen to a hard-luck story, and he liked to spread a few gold pieces after visiting the deathbed of an old bookkeeper or stockyards watchman. It is also true that Armour empowered Dr. Gunsaulus to found the technical institute, and that he patronized worthy causes and left money to charities; and it is good that rich men should do this.

Having said that, and contemplating the public benefactions of Chicago millionaries with respect and gratitude, we must admit that the newspapermen in Henry Koster's saloon were right when they invariably greeted the publication of a magnate's will by remarking on the lack of pockets in a shroud. Their point was that neither Armour nor any other wealthy benefactor of Chicago ever denied himself a single comfort to provide a public institution after his death. But one should not denigrate Philip Armour, for he had solid achievements to his credit; and many people benefited from the rational methods of slaughtering and dressing the meat crop that Armour developed, along with other packers such as the German-born Nelson Morris, and Gustavus Swift, who came from New England. These men shared Armour's enthusiasm for the refrigerator car, and his belief that no part of any animal in their pens should go to waste. They compiled an amazing list of by-products, for in addition to meat, Chicago packers could fill your order if you needed any glue, gelatin, isinglass, hair, felt, bristles, soap, glycerine, ammonia, dried blood, bones, bone meal, poultry food, albumin, neat's-foot oil, pepsin, knife or toothbrush handles, buttons, chessmen, mouthpieces for pipes, backs for brushes, or extracts from thymus, thyroid, pancreatic or salivary glands. When the packers developed a canning process in the 1880s, Armour took the lead. He would never admit that his company sold any tainted meat to the Army during the Spanish-American War in 1898; nevertheless, an enormous quantity of rotten meat got into the cans the soldiers opened in camp and field. The blame fell on jobbers, sutlers, and officers in the Quartermaster Corps. Nobody cared to admit having started the train of corruption where the bad meat originated. One has the feeling that Phil Armour would not knowingly have sent out meat that was absolutely inedible; nevertheless he shared in the disgrace the tainted-meat scandal brought Chicago.

When he bet the short side of the wheat market against Joe Leiter, the old man followed a principal that had worked well for him in a previous adventure. All through the Civil War, the packers had been getting rich, but Armour realized good things must end. Though only thirty when the call came to save the Union, Armour had not taken to the field, and so had been able to view the progress of events with an objective eye. By early 1865, profiteers had forced the price of pork to an astounding level; since the government was paying, everyone continued happy in Washington and Chicago, and Armour was one of the few who looked ahead and realized that the grafters' market in pork would collapse when the soldiers came home. He made his play in February, remarking: "I'm a bull on Abe Lincoln and a bear on the hog." He took a million dollars from short sales of pork, brought the money down from Milwaukee, where he had been active in the hide and tallow line, and set up in Chicago. By the last decade of the century Armour was doing a business of $100,000,000 a year in untaxed money. He worked in a La Salle Street office where he kept a battery of telegraph instruments clacking throughout the day; Armour also had a telegraph instrument at his house, with the "bug" hammering against the traditional empty Prince Albert tin, and a tobacco-chewing operator on duty all night long at overtime wages. Armour became one of the first big users of the telephone; one regrets that he could not have lived to the time of the limousine telephone, which he would have delighted in. Whether or not he knew about the bad meat in those cans in 1898, Philip Armour had behaved like a useful citizen five years before, when the panic struck and people ran to get their money out of the Illinois Trust and Savings Bank. Six feet tall, with his heavy shoulders not yet bent, he strode down the two-block line of waiting depositors and said, "My name is Philip Armour. Bring your checks to me at my office." He had stacks of paper money and bags of coins up there, and his clerks cashed more than a thousand checks in three hours, halting the run. Armour considered himself to be a man with a good eye for business talent, and he encouraged young fellows at his office. However, he made his favorites come to the office on Christmas and New Year's day, even though there was nothing to do. The thought of granting time off gave him pain, and he spoke sarcastically to the young dancing men on his staff if they betrayed signs of fatigue the morning after a ball. He liked to hear the preaching of good, hard-twist religion, and believed that Gunsaulus and

[271]

other clergymen could pray him into Heaven when the time came. Whether or not he was right in his plans for the next world, Armour showed undeniable wisdom in this one when he summed up his philosophy of life: "Always keep at it. Don't let up. I always had a great respect for facts. Facts can be discounted at any bank, but a theory is rarely worth par. Stick to facts!"

Before the century reached its end, Chicago had become the greatest slaughtering and packing city in the United States. The business had developed organically along with the railways that took its product to consumers. Since early times, seven stockyards had grown according to natural needs: the first having been the Matthew Laflin Bull's Head Yards of 1848, with the nearby Bull's Head Hotel for cattlemen. Next came a smaller yard, established in 1853 a mile and a half west of town by J. H. Dole for the new Chicago, Burlington and Quincy Railroad; the following year the Michigan Southern Railway built yards on the Ulrich family property at the corner of Twenty-Second and State streets. In 1855, the Fort Wayne and Chicago line established yards at Stewart Avenue and Mitchell Street. Each of these shipped on one railroad only, and the Bull's Head continued to serve the city as a whole until all four were replaced by the Sherman Stock Yards, in 1856, on property owned by Willard Franklin Myrick, at the lakefront between Twenty-Sixth and Thirty-First streets. At this point the old Bull's Head Hotel became the Washingtonian Home for Inebriates, an institution that lived on for some years after developers tore the building down in 1890. During the Civil War, C. F. Loomis operated the Cottage Grove Yards. Immediately after the war, Long John Wentworth sold 320 acres on Halsted Street below Thirty-Ninth Street to a syndicate that formed the Union Stock Yards, with the lines of nine railroads running in, their names a majestic roll: Illinois Central; Michigan Central; Chicago, Burlington and Quincy; Michigan Southern; Fort Wayne and Chicago; Chicago and Alton; Chicago and Danville; Chicago and North Western; Rock Island, Chicago and Pacific. In 1875 a tenth road came in with the spur of the Baltimore and Ohio, originally called the Baltimore, Pittsburgh and Chicago, and later the Baltimore & Ohio and Chicago Railway. In 1886, the three-year old Chicago Real Estate Board held its annual banquet at the Palmer House, and the three main floral decorations on the tables were noteworthy both as artifacts and historical symbols. They represented Fort Dearborn, the Bull's Head Hotel, and a vacant lot with the sign: For Sale.

Though the majority of Chicagoans drew their living from other industries, the packing business held a sort of emotional dominance over the town as the century turned. The extinguishing of life that went on at the stockyards always lay in Chicago's consciousness. Day after day, the killers would turn an incalculable tonnage of live flesh into dead meat. But the energy of the prairie and the corn lived on, in carnivorous men, women, and children throughout Christendom who fed on the product of Chicago slaughterhouses. In addition, one thought of all those toothbrush handles and other useful objects; but as a general thing, it didn't bear thinking of. As intelligent animals with well-developed nervous systems the pigs invariably started screaming after the Judas pig had led them into execution pens, and they saw what was happening, and felt themselves jerked into the air by one leg, and swung toward the knives. Until one got used to it, the screams were appalling. Steers and heifers bawled like foghorns when they smelled blood, making a sound of brute terror that could be heard far away. Even farther off one was aware of the stockyards by the smell of blood and dung; the wind would blow it into any part of Chicago, a dark smell that disturbed the mind. Chicagoans could learn to live with the thought and presence of the stockyards; but to a visitor the experience of a first inspection could be overwhelming. So it was with Rudyard Kipling, when he saw hogs slaughtered and heard the shrieks suddenly cease as knifemen "jauntily" killed each animal, then a sound "as of heavy tropical rain." Kipling detested the "huge wilderness" of Chicago and its "grotesque ferocity." But he was willing to write, "I have found a city—a real city—and they call it Chicago."

It appears probable that Rudyard Kipling would have felt less distaste for Chicago had he settled there for a while, and come to know the great men of the town. Though a lord of language, Kipling suffered from an obsessive desire to fawn on generals, emperors, and men of power; he wrote a groveling memorial poem on the death of Edward VII. Such a writer might be expected to see imposing virtures in Pullman, Armour, Field, and the others; but one hesitates to guess how they would have reacted to the author, small, swarthy, spectacled, moustached, and nervous in manner as he was. Perhaps it is just as well that Kipling merely visited the stockyards, cursed Chicago, and went on his way. In his brief visit he overlooked scholars and scientists whose achievements were more valuable to the city and the world than the feats of organization that had made the business barons famous. Among the scientists, one of the most important was Dr. Greene Vardiman Black of Evanston, who has probably done more for the health and comfort of his fellow human beings than any other man in the Chicago story. Today, Dr. Black can be seen in bronze, seated in a thronelike chair at the southern edge of Lincoln Park, where he can look across the lawn of Curtis Jadwin's mansion, now the palace of a prince in the Roman Church, and over to the walls of the country's handsomest apartment house, No. 1550 North State Parkway. The doctor is the only man born in Illinois to have the honor of a monument in the park, and he well deserves it, for before he died in 1915 at the age of seventy-nine, he had laid the foundation of modern dentistry in more than five hundred books, papers in scientific journals, and published discussions and reports. Dean of the Dental College in Northwestern University from 1897 until his death, Dr. Black had started his career as a self-taught, empirical investigator after a frontier childhood at his birthplace on a farm near Winchester, 240 miles southwest of Chicago. Eventually he became a professor of dental pathology and bacteriology, and gave the scientific world a classic essay on *The Formation of Poisons by Microorganisms,* which he followed with his *Study of the Histological Character of the Peristeum and Peridental Membranes.* In 1908, Dr. Black published *Operative Dentistry* in two volumes; *Pathology of the Hard Tissues of the Teeth,* and *Technical Procedures in Filling Teeth.* Greene V. Black saw dentistry as an art as well as a science, and designed 104 different cutting instruments for the proper excavation of cavaties. This remarkable man was one of the Chicagoans who upheld the doctrine of work with energies comparable to those that Dan Burnham and Phil Armour used in driving themselves along. He was tall and sturdy, with a dark beard that grayed as he got older, and at last matched the cigar ash with which he sprinkled his waistcoat, morning, noon, and night. Not since Senator Seward at the Lincoln convention in 1860 had Chicago seen so prodigious a smoker of cigars as Dr. Black; he chainsmoked his Havanas, lighting one from another, to the astonishment of three grandchildren, as he sat in his leather armchair relaxing in elastic-sided slippers after a day of writing, teaching, working in the laboratories, and designing instruments at his drawing board. Then he would retire to his study where a huge desk held a mass of manuscripts, proofsheets, and books, through which he would plow his way so far into the evening that the children wondered if he ever slept. He sometimes spent a morning in the study, and on those days the children often waited outside on the stairway with some question for their grandfather to settle. When he emerged, Dr. Black would be concerned that they had been kept waiting, and would invite them in, and take from his desk drawer the tin box that contained dried venison, a much appreciated treat. With good luck the children could divert the professor's attention from his work long enough to persuade him to play them a few cylindrical wax records on the phonograph, which he referred to as "Mr. Edison's machine." Dr. Black rigged some sort of recording device, and in 1914 played records of forty family voices on Mr. Edison's machine, a tribute both to his ingenuity and to his interest in family conclaves. This benefactor of mankind gave to science his discoveries in the making of dental alloys, as well as the designs of instruments, along with his teaching to generations of dentists at Northwestern. When his wife could persuade him to take a vacation, Dr. Black would make it a long trip, as Chicagoans usually do, once they have left the lakeshore. Caught in a blizzard on a mountain in Alaska, the doctor froze one hand; he proceeded to cut off part of a finger to stop the gangrene. Greene Black's son, Arthur Davenport Black, followed him as dean at Northwestern, and was a noted dentist and oral surgeon, famed among other things for his cleft palate operation. The old doctor's grandson Gilmer Vardiman Black was one of the city's most gifted architectural designers, both son and grandson showing that contrary to popular belief, Chicago talent tends to stay in Chicago.

They were sons of Martha, those Chicagoans of electrifying and incessant energies; among them the scientists like Dr. Greene V. Black worked as hard as the tight-fisted men in the countingrooms. The literary scholars also drove themselves to interminable labors, and though the labor never ended, from time to time along the way there blossomed remarkable results. In this company one of the most diligent was William Rainey Harper, who headed the new University of Chicago that visitors to the Fair could see in process of construction beyond the Midway. Henry Ives Cobb had designed the quadrangles in the adapted Collegiate Gothic that had begun to come off so well at Yale and Princeton; journalists wrote approvingly of the university's gray city that would remain beside the lake after the White City had disappeared. Medieval towers and courtyards might surround William Harper, but his goals were modern and he drove toward them with the energy of a dynamo. The splendid closing passage of Harper's life began on a day in early October 1892 when he led a procession of students, professors, trustees, and visiting dignitaries into an uncompleted lecture hall, and faced the convocation amid ladders, buckets of plaster, and workmen hurrying to finish their jobs. Dr. Harper was a short sturdy man inclined to stoutness; the eyes behind his spectacles were keen. He said, "We shall now sing 'Praise God, from Whom All Blessings Flow.' " The path that had led William Rainey Harper at thirty-six to the presidency of a brand-new university had been plain from the beginning. He had come out of Muskingum County in the heart of Ohio, another of the Scotch-Irish breed like the McCormicks, Pattersons, and Medills. He graduated from Muskingum College at the age of fourteen, delivering the salutatory oration in Hebrew. After graduation the prodigy continued to study languages, working in his father's drygoods store and playing the cornet in the town band for pocket money. He next entered Yale as a graduate student, arriving at New Haven in September 1873, younger than many a freshman entering the undergraduate college at the same time. The Yale commencement of 1875 saw the eighteen-year-old William Rainey Harper assume the gown, title, and privileges of a Doctor of Philosophy. His doctoral dissertation was "A Comparative Study of the Prepositions in Latin, Greek, Sanskrit, and Gothic." That summer the new Yale Ph.D. became head of a small college in Tennessee, and got married; after one year he moved to another of those numerous Ohio colleges, Denison at Granville. Dr. Harper kept on studying Semitic languages, then a rare specialty outside theological seminaries, and not a leading study even there. In 1879, the young scholar came to Chicago where the Baptist Union Seminary had need of his services as a Hebraist and student of the Old Testament. The Baptists did not wish to see the Episcopalians, Methodists, and Presbyterians outstrip them in the production of a learned clergy, and Dr. Harper was the best man they could possibly have brought to town. He labored for them as though he heard continually echoing in his head the gospel hymn "Work, for the Night Is Coming," and in addition to teaching, published a series of essays that evolved in *The American Journal of Semitic Languages and Literature,* which in turn became parent to about thirty other learned journals that circulated throughout the United States in the interests of a scholarly ministry for all churches.

In 1886, he accepted the call of Yale to its Chair of Semitic Languages. His decision to leave was the primal cause of the University of Chicago: the Baptists disliked seeing their star performer go, and began discussing the possibility of reviving a secterian college, called Chicago University, which had starved to death on the South Side after the fire of 1871. At Yale, Harper gave the impression of having learned to live without sleep, putting in eighteen-hour days editing, organizing, lecturing, and writing, moving from one activity to another with the air of a man who had all the time in the world, and without the slightest lessening of his amiability toward anyone who asked for advice or help. It seems that Dr. Harper must have been a master of efficiency before the days of time and motion studies, and that he antedated William James of Harvard in the discovery that second, third, and even fourth layers of energy and endurance could be uncovered and used if one would only "work through the hard place." Dr. Harper's performance on these principles was so good that he became a nationally known professor, somewhat in the manner of Woodrow Wilson at a later time; and in addition to his teaching and study at Yale, he functioned as president of the Chautauqua Summer Arts College. The high-class entertainments and lectures staged at Lake Chautauqua had attained great prestige; and now it could be said that everybody knew Dr.

Harper. He was the nation's headmaster, and people who had never met him respected and trusted him. At New Haven, it was known that more mail came in at Yale Station for William R. Harper than for all the rest of the university, students and faculty together. It became evident to all who took an interest in such things that New Haven could not hold Dr. Harper, any more than the Baptists had been able to, and scouts from other places were after him with offers of presidencies. The situation was that although he had a graduate degree, Dr. Harper was not socially a Yale man, since he lacked membership in a four-year class. This prevented Harper from attaining enough clout in the Yale Corporation to knock old Timothy Dwight loose from his job as president of the university. And Harper now was obviously too big a man to sit in a small chair, so the only question was, which outside offer would he accept?

Few realized that Dr. Harper had an amazing idea in mind, which was to start a new university, and to start it at the top: first-rate in its faculty, libraries, and laboratories, and offering graduate studies. Furthermore, he would have a university press; a four-quarter academic year; equal emphasis on teaching and research; and absolute freedom to theorize on any topic, including religion. Dr. Harper believed that when he got his university tuned up and running smoothly, it would compete only with Harvard; this was not arrogance, but the sober conviction that anything was possible, if one made the right plans, worked hard enough, and got the proper backing. He found a patron in John D. Rockefeller, who was beginning to turn from the management of his oil empire to considerations of philanthropy. Rockefeller had heard of the dead Baptist college out in Chicago, and so all things worked together for good. Among his talents Dr. Harper had the gift of writing plain, orderly, precise and forceful English, and he put this gift to use in the prospectus for a university, dividing his manifesto into sections which he called "bulletins," and placing them, one at a time, before Rockefeller and some of the rich men in Chicago. In 1890, a board of trustees was formed to revive the old Chicago University; Rockefeller promised money, and Harper raised matching gifts in Chicago and agreed to be president, providing the trustees accepted his bulletins as ruling documents for the new institution. Dr. Harper wanted no misunderstandings about freedom to investigate and teach; he also warned that the Biblical studies would be scholarly rather than secular, an endorsement of the "higher criticism" which the hellfire preachers of the Middle West had identified as Satan's propaganda. John D. Rockefeller and the trustees approved Dr. Harper's plans to the last detail. Thereupon, Harper and Rockefeller mounted bicycles and led a procession of ministers and businessmen, also on bicycles, out Drexel Boulevard and around on the Midway to inspect the site of the new campus. Partially completed buildings sheltered the first classes in 1892; and while the lecture halls might not be finished, Harper had made a working library available, and a big one for that time, by purchasing in Berlin a second-hand collection of more than 200,000 usable books and pamphlets. He made good on his promise to recruit a first-rate faculty: among the first arrivals were the novelist Robert Herrick who came from the Massachusetts Institute of Technology to the English Department on the Midway; the poet-dramatist William Vaughn Moody; James Henry Breasted, who left the University of Berlin to become the first teacher of Egyptology in the United States and the founder of Chicago's Oriental Institute; and the president's brother, Robert Francis Harper, a distinguished Assyriologist. The list of gifted recruits was long; it included Jacques Loeb, the physiologist who served as model for Max Gotlieb, the dedicated researcher of Sinclair Lewis's *Arrowsmith;* and his colleague Abraham Michelson, co-author of the Michelson-Morley experiment with light rays which helped prepare the way for theories of relativity, and the first nuclear chain reaction, at Chicago University in 1942. Among its rapidly developing strengths, the university organized a department of sociology that engaged in direct observation of the city around it; from this came a series of studies in metropolitan life, some in collaboration with workers at Hull House and other social agencies, that were free from the jargon that sociology departments in other universities inflicted on those who tried to read their findings. The Chicago studies have produced in recent times such classic surveys as *The Professional Thief, The Saleslady, Domestic Discord, The Gang, The Ghetto,* and *The Gold Coast and the Slum.* Reading the titles makes one want to read the books, and they are readable. Dr. Harper's honesty and thoroughness had inspired his first battalions of investigating sociologists, as they fanned out over Chicago, making the city both a source of theory and a laboratory of fact; and the tradition lived on.

Looking after every detail from morning till night, Dr. Harper had his university functioning, and granting earned degrees from A.B. to Ph.D., within two years of that first convocation in Cobb Hall. He continued to carry on scholarly research that was good enough to pass muster with colleagues at other universities, as in the case of his *Critical and Exegitical Commentary on Amos and Hosea,* which he worked on in fragments of spare time until he had it ready to publish in 1905. Meanwhile, the University of Chicago had held a decennial celebration in 1902, complete with a tent, bands playing in the quadrangles, lawn parties, lunches, teas, receptions, and processions of robed academicians, just like the bicentennial at Yale. The accomplishments of ten years had been amazing, but Dr.

Harper refused to take credit, giving it to his faculty instead. He said that every faculty member had to do something more than teach classes; he might devote himself also to research, or he might write books, and it was perfectly acceptable if they were popular books; or he might help to man the university's administrative committees. But each faculty member must make his own choice as to what he did, aside from teaching; he was not to expect detailed instructions from above. "It is enough that he should do something and be somebody," said Harper, "for more than one type of man is needed to make a university."

A type of man who caused a sensation in Chicago came to the new university from Cornell and took a post in the Department of Economics. His name was Thorstein Bunde Veblen, and he was an indigent scholar, very shabby and ferocious, when Harper took him on at the recommendation of a star economist, James Laurence Laughlin, who had studied under Henry Adams at Harvard before going on to Cornell and Chicago. The doctor was pleased to accept Laughlin's protégé, and soon discovered that Veblen was a formidable fellow in his own right. Born on a farm in a part of Wisconsin inhabited solely by Norwegian immigrants, Veblen had managed to support himself while taking graduate courses at Johns Hopkins, and he later qualified for a doctorate of philosophy at Yale. Veblen was unable to get even an usher's post in a New England preparatory school, and he had gone back to the farm, where he spent seven miserable years until Laughlin came to the rescue in 1891. At first it seemed that the University of Chicago was an ideal place for Veblen. Like the sociologists of the new institution, he observed the city and drew material from it. Like Robert Herrick, he disliked much of what he saw; and where Herrick put his reaction to commercial Chicago into the notes from which he wrote *Waste, Memoirs of an American Citizen, The Common Lot,* and *Chimes,* the first work of fiction to use the university as background, Veblen treated the city as a source of data from which he proposed to draw scientific conclusions. The result was a book, *The Theory of the Leisure Class,* in which Veblen gave another Chicago phrase to the language by writing of "conspicuous consumption." In a work that was not always easy to understand, for Veblen did not write with Harper's clarity, the sage appeared to be arguing that rich people indulged in fine houses, clothes, carriages, games and time-wasting social activities not because they enjoyed these things, but to demonstrate that they owned and controlled the power of wealth. There was something in it. William Dean Howells wrote with enthusiasm on *The Theory,* and Veblen became a celebrity. He was the first wild-man professor of a now familiar type who speaks in tongues, and gives the impression that he has come to grips with an essential and central idea, against which he grapples as Jacob wrestled the angel. One should read Veblen's book not as a reasoned work of social theory, but as an expression of his unhappiness in a predatory society, and his distrust of it. There is a glimpse of Dr. Harper in the passage where Veblen identifies among contemporary villains the "captain of education" who is nothing more than a captain of industry in disguise. Veblen did not fake his pictures of the leisure class, for he went into it as the husband of Ellen Rolfe, whose family held shares in the Santa Fe Railroad. His life with Ellen was not ideal, and he sometimes showed interest in other women; he took European vacations without his wife, and Chicago tabbies had plenty to say about it. There was a scandal, Ellen left him, and the trustees said Veblen must go. Dr. Harper could not save Veblen's job, or perhaps did not think it worth a big fight. The captain of education was also superintendent of the Hyde Park Baptist Sunday School; one wishes to think he would have resigned as president of the university before allowing Veblen to go over a matter of academic freedom. Be that as it may, the doctor's lack of action in the professor's defense served to confirm Thorstein Veblen's opinion of him. Veblen moved on to Stanford, left there after similar troubles, found haven at the New School for Social Research in New York City, and died in 1929.

Until his death in 1906, Dr. Harper dominated the university, but not by the direct force of personality. It seems that when controversy threatened, Harper had a way of presenting his case so tactfully that others would take it up as their own. A friend remarked that "It was not strange that a man who could set the whole country to studying Hebrew could secure a majority following in a board of trustees and a faculty." Whatever his method was, he built a genuine university, with graduate schools to which young men and women eagerly came from all over the country, but most especially from the central valley, which had long needed a recognized center for advanced studies. These young people would have been justified in thinking that of all the stimulating sights spread before them in Chicago and its new university,the most amazing was Dr. Harper himself. The president would tutor students, but to obtain his help they had to observe farm hours. Getting up before five A.M., the doctor would make coffee for himself and the first of the three secretaries who served him in shifts throughout the day, and be ready to tutor or counsel a student at 5:30. This was the quietest part of his day until his late evening reading period, during which he kept up his studies in several fields. Dr. Harper also continued as president of the Chautauqua's higher education department, editor of learned journals, and superintendent at the Sunday School. He discovered a way to replenish his energies when attending a public meeting, of which there might be two or three a day. The method of regeneration was to take a nap when anyone stood up to deliver a speech, sleeping upright in his chair, leaning on his hand. Observers took him to be in an attitude of respectful attention, merely shading his eyes; the patter of hands at the end of a speech would bring him to, refreshed and joining in the applause. Dr. Harper recognized that his one weakness was excessive anxiety over details. He revealed this in his book, *Religion and the Higher Life:* "To the unthinking mind the man who occupies a high position is an object of envy. If the real facts were known, in almost every case it would be found that such a man is being crushed—literally crushed —by the weight of the burdens he is compelled to carry." But he was carrying his burdens with no outward evidence of strain throughout the closing years of the century, when Chicagoans began to measure the world.

Everyone in Chicago and the rest of the country reckoned the beginning of the new century from January 1, 1900; there was no use pointing out that the year belonged with the last decade of the nineteeth century. Nor did it matter, for the changes that resulted in modern Chicago had already taken place, causing the emergence of three orders or estates of people in the city. The men of power with their families and retainers made up the first order; then came the working people in the offices and plants, and likes of Hennessy, Artie Blanchard, and Jurgis Rudkus, a strongbacked greenhorn immigrant, fresh from Lithuania, who lived back of the yards and put in twelve hours a day sweeping out a slaughterhouse; and the third estate was that of the seekers—students who had made their way to the city because of teachers like Black and Harper, other young men and women who wanted instruction in singing, acting, dancing or painting, or literary people like the heroine of Hamlin Garland's *Rose of Dutcher's Cooley*, the Wisconsin girl who had come to town to observe life and write about it, or Ade and Dreiser, or Vachel Lindsay up from Springfield to study at the Art Institute, but knowing well the city itself would be his academy, hungry as he was for pictures, music, theater, and friends.

The seekers loved Chicago, which enchanted them wherever they turned their eyes. James A. M. Whistler, the grandson of an early military Chicagoan, had been teaching that mean streets could be beautiful, especially when clothed in mist, and this the lake supplied often enough, in fogs that sometimes towered over the highest skyscrapers. And at evening, the lights on the masts and gleaming from the cabins of ships at piers along the river, or riding in harbor, added the feeling of Oriental lanterns to the fascinating mysery of Chicago. In the daytime, on a brisk spring morning, a member of any of those three estates might feel that the monuments of the new age were already completed, as he walked in the Loop, the downtown business district. This area had received its name when the elevated railway looped around it in 1892, and presented many fine sights to Curtis Jadwin, Artie Blanchard, and the twenty-two-year-old Vachel Lindsay as they went about their business early in the new century. All three would recognize the Board of Trade at La Salle and Jackson streets as the commanding structure of the city. Never mind what Montgomery Schuyler said, this was a building. It had taken three years to put up, with its 322-foot tower containing a clock striking a bell that weighed two and a quarter tons, the tower finished off by a copper weathervane in the form of a ship nine feet long and eight feet high. The main hall was eighty feet high, with a stained-glass skylight that cast a green, purple and crimson glow on the wheat pit and the other trading posts. Something had happened to this building: about nine years after its opening, engineers observed that it was settling too much. Far below street level, the swamp was sucking the vast structure down. To stop the sinking, the engineer said they would have to decapitate the building, reducing its weight several thousand tons by cutting off the tower. In 1895 the weather-vane came down, along with the huge bell, and four stories of tower in the eclectic American Gothic style. The Board of Trade building leveled out now at a system of mansard roofs, turrets, and finials, and seemed to have become broader and heavier after losing its crest, appearing to squat across La Salle Street, an angry building, surly and watchful. A Chicagoan beginning a lunch-time stroll in front of the Board would most likely start east on Jackson Street toward Michigan Avenue, where he could look out on the new Lake Front Park: for years, lines of wagons had crossed the city with the earth from excavations, and the trash and garbage of industries, to build out the land on which this park stood. Beyond it ran the Illinois Central tracks, and beyond them the lake lapped at the railroad breakwater. The trains made a nuisance of noise and dirt, but it was a miracle that this park existed; powerful men thought it foolishness, and failed to see the necessity for it. Victor Lawson wrote from Egypt ordering his employees to do everything they could to destroy the park. Reaching from the Nile to the Chicago River, he reminded Managing Editor Charles Dennis, "As you know I have never believed in a lake front park. There is no need of one because there are no people in that section of the city to go to it. The only people who need it are my friends Ferd Peck, Montg. Ward (who strikes me as being the only 'all hog' competitor the Illinois Central has) and the other property owners along Michigan Avenue facing the Park. The lake front should be used to produce revenues for the city."

When ordinary citizens walked toward Michigan Avenue and saw the park ahead, they were glad it was there. And as he strolled east on Jackson Street with the Board of Trade behind him, the Chicagoan out to admire the town in 1901 would pass the excellent Hotel Grace at Clark Street, the Union League a little farther on, and then the brick wall of the Monadnock Building at Dearborn Street. On the northeast corner of the same intersection the Great Northern Hotel rose fourteen stories, one of the last designs that John Root had done with Daniel Burnham. The Great Northern delighted the eye with its rows of bay windows, making a generous proportion of glass against its plain brick walls. Inside were eight dining rooms and a café, in addition to 500 guest rooms. There were several good hotels in this neighborhood; when he reached Michigan Avenue the walker could turn in at the Leland Hotel, and warm himself at a cheerful fire in the lobby on cold days. But only persons of assurance would make casual use of the Leland, or its neighbor to the south, the Richelieu, for these were houses of the highest tone. Walking north on Michigan Avenue from the Leland, one passed the new Art Institute across the way at the foot of East Adams Street. The impressive structure had grown from an academy of Fine Arts established in 1879; by 1901, when Vachel Lindsay began to haunt its corridors, the Institute had acquired many treasures under the stewardship of Martin Ryerson and Charles Hutchinson, businessmen who had made themselves collectors of art. On the landward side of the Avenue, one now passed the Pullman Building at Adams Street; corbelled and turreted, the romantic skyscraper showed that Mr. Pullman had not stinted his architect, Solon Spencer Beaman, when the plans lay on his drawing tables. The building had 125 office suites, and on the upper floors were 75 residential apartments with views of the lake. Two blocks farther north, between Monroe and Madison Streets, the pedestrian would pass one of the finest clubhouses in town, the Chicago Athletic Association, and perhaps glimpse such members as George Ade or Robert R. McCormick on their way through its revolving doors to use the baths and gymnasiums. Henry Ives Cobb of World's Fair and Chicago University renown had been the architect. And then at Randolph Street the new Public Library came into view, the wide windows of its Reference Room overlooking the lake. A greater wonder lay ahead, for after turning west on Randolph Street, one saw the Masonic Temple looming at the corner of State Street, its mansard roof at the top of twenty-two stories, 302 feet in the air. The work of Burnham and Root, this building was a town in itself with its 53 miles of electrical wiring, ten retail stores, and 543 office suites. Some people said they got a swooning sensation when they looked from the rotunda on the ground floor straight up to the skylight in the roof. Recovering from this spell of vertigo, one might continue west on Randolph Street and pass

Adler and Sullivan's Schiller Tower, which housed a theater resembling that in their enormous Auditorium farther south on the lakefront. One then might go along on Randolph to La Salle Street, drawn as though by a force of gravity emanating from the colossal city and county buildings on southeast corner. Collectively known as the "Court House," these vast structures of granite and limestone occupied the city's first municipal square; on an upper floor was the richly decorated Council Chamber where the aldermen held their conclaves. John Van Osdel, James J. Egan, and Alexander Kirkland had designed the buildings; concrete mats and wooden pillars distributed the incredible weight beneath. The engineering was a triumph, but when it came to outward appearance, there were visible signs that the architects had not always been able to agree. The result was hard to describe. On coming in sight of the double structure, a newly arrived Irishman remarked, "That never was built in this country."

Starting on the five blocks down La Salle Street back to the Board of Trade, the stroller had good things ahead; at the northeast corner of La Salle and Madison streets, for example, he would pass the Tacoma Building, the work of William Holabird and Martin Roche, architects who put their mark on Chicago. As young men they had worked in Major Jenney's office with Louis Sullivan, Daniel Burnham, and John Root, and later as their own masters had developed a vigorous commercial style, still living in Chicago architecture. The Tacoma was good to look at with its large surfaces of glass in projecting bay windows; it stood on floating concrete rafts, and under its skin the architects had stretched a skeleton of cast iron, wrought iron, and Bessemer steel. Holabird and Roche designed a pair of elegant buildings on Dearborn Street in the Old Colony which had a round tower at each corner, and the Marquette, still one of the finest office structures ever built, with its "Chicago windows," the long pane of glass flanked at either side by a narrow sliding sash. The design as a whole gave an impression of dignity and power. Similar virtues displayed themselves on La Salle Street as one proceeded southward past the Woman's Temple at Monroe Street and walked on to Adler and Sullivan's Stock Exchange Building. Here until recently the passer-by stopped to enjoy Sullivan's ornamentation of the first three stories, a trustworthy work of art to which one could return in any mood and obtain refreshment. Across the street stands the Rookery, a granite fortress that was comparatively new when Lindsay first saw it, the result of another combined operation by Burnham, Root, Owen Aldis, and the Brookses of Boston. The bold and strong building more than held its own with the nearby Board of Trade, as it does today with another Board of Trade on the site of the previous one. In this

[284]

walk, one would have seen only a few of the new buildings that had begun bringing architectural students and critics from all over the world to Chicago. It would have taken months to examine the Loop in detail, and years to inspect all of Chicago with its architectural follies and grandeurs, failures and successes.

And yet for all the fascination that Chicago architecture might exert on the spectator, a still more interesting show walked the streets, in the varied crowds of people. Here were the native types of New England and the Middle West, the adults usually with a characteristic guarded expression, the children looking around them as though they owned the city. But a youth just up from Springfield, as Lindsay was, expected such people; it was the parade of the foreign born that astounded him, the multitudes brought hither, as the Prayer Book put it, out of many kindreds and tongues. Their presence was a strange thing, and young Lindsay did not try to settle in his mind immediately what it all signified. He made a plan, and wrote to his parents, "Now for five years I must master Chicago, as typical America to the *nth* power, and make a name that will make my living. I must in Chicago learn the art of selection in all matters."

Having arrived in town on the second day of the new century—January 2, 1901—Lindsay joined with another student to rent an apartment on South Paulina Street, two blocks west of Ashland Avenue, for which they paid $14 a month. Next day he registered at the Art Institute, lunched on lemons and crackers, and in the evening saw E. H. Sothern play Hamlet. A few nights later, he saw Bernhardt and Coquelin in *Cyrano de Bergerac*. He managed to buy tickets to these and other plays on his slender allowance from Springfield by living mostly on milk and stale pastry marked down in bakers' shops. He found his way to the Public Library like an iron filing to a magnet, and began to read Shakespeare, Rossetti, Blake, Emerson, and Marlowe's *Faustus* which sent him reeling like a drunken man. After three weeks on Paulina Street he moved to lodgings down on Kenwood Avenue near the university, added apples and Uneeda Biscuits to his diet, and got a job in the toy department at Field's. All the while, Lindsay kept writing poems; he sent one to William Dean Howells, who returned it with a letter calling it obscure and bad. For ten months Lindsay sorted boxes at Field's from 8:30 to 5:30 for $12.00 a week. After the ten months, he gave it up because there was no way to earn this money and also do the reading, writing, and studying for which he had come to Chicago. Looking at Lindsay's career after it was over, Edgar Lee Masters concluded that the parents in Springfield should have sent more money, which they could have afforded, or r.one at all. As it was, Lindsay managed to hang on in Chicago for four years, absorbing much of what the city had to give, but deprived by poverty of many things that would have been good for him. Lindsay had powerful longings for a perfect city, and Chicago gave him some notion of what such a place ought to be. He wrote in his diary, "We need new pioneers who will hew down the stairways of horrible shame, and likewise the marble halls of ugliness . . . . Chicago University needs an informal underground leader in matters of art, to whom all will go who feel the desire for beauty rising up within them."

Vachel Lindsay had lived in Chicago for a few days less than three years when the city experienced another of those sudden catastrophes that reminded one of the primal energies concentrated there. On December 30, 1903, a matinee crowd had filled the Iroquois Theater in the Loop. During the performance a fire broke out backstage and a flame shot out, then receded. Without panic the people rose and filed toward the doors; the curtain jammed coming down and the fire roared into the auditorium again. Now the people began to push, and they discovered, but too late, that in violation of all rules for theater design, the front doors swung inward and could not be opened, because of the crush against them. And the side doors were locked to prevent anyone from sneaking in without a ticket. Within five minutes 602 people died, most of them from suffocation at the immovable doors. About half the dead were children. On January 1, 1904, the *Tribune* ran a front page cartoon that needed no title, showing a door marked "Exit" locked with an enormous lock that had a spider web growing over it.

Other primal energies burst out in Chicago during the next two years; and their power, which exploded with city-shaking force, came from the demand of workers for a better life. Grinding struggles took place in the stockyards, for example, and when the employees walked out on strike, the managements took it as an act of war, and brought up thousands of Negroes from the rural South to keep the slaughterhouses working. The Negroes lived under siege in barracks on the packers' property; the striking Irish and Bohemians never forgave these black men for coming in, nor the employers for recruiting them. The bitterness lasted through decades, and is with us yet; and another unforeseen result of the labor war came from a visit by Upton Sinclair, a young reporter seeking material to put into articles for a Socialist magazine, *The Appeal to Reason*. Sinclair was a superb story-teller, and during the two months in 1904 when he lived among stockyards workers and felt the melancholy poetry of the West Side, he decided to put his material into a novel to be called *The Jungle*. Appearing as a serial in *The Appeal*, the story told how a Lithuanian immigrant named Jurgis Rudkus worked in the jungle of Chicago under conditions that robbed him of humanity, and turned him into a hoodlum and strikebreaker. In the closing pages, Sinclair the propagandist took over and subjected Jurgis Rudkus to a sudden conversion at a Socialist lecture that caused an abrupt change in the tone of the book, but up to that point the story had been so real, so thrilling, and so moving that few readers resented the closing sermon. The magazine serial made such a sensation that Doubleday, Page and Company offered to publish it as a book. But first the Doubleday people would send their own man to Chicago to make certain that the story had a libel-proof factual basis. Editor Isaac F. Marcosson went out and satisfied himself that the book's disclosures of horrors in Chicago and the packing industry were true. Doubleday then successfully published the novel, but with a different result from what the author had intended.

In the passages of the story describing Jurgis's work on the slaughter-house floor, Sinclair had given a nauseating picture of the conditions that the packers permitted. They not only accepted the meat of diseased animals, but the process of dressing and packing even the sound meat was filthy beyond belief. This was what Doubleday had questioned, and now that the reputable firm issued Sinclair's book, and it seemed that everyone in the country read it, there came an outburst of indignation that went clear up to the White House, and caused President Teddy Roosevelt to turn his flashing glasses in the direction of Chicago. Mr. Dooley had it that "Tiddy was toying with a light breakfast an' idly turnin' over th' pages iv th' new book with both hands. Suddenly he rose from th' table, an cryin': 'I'm pizened,' begun throwin' sausages out iv th' window. . . ." The result of Roosevelt's disgust was the sending of a commission from the Department of Argiculture to Chicago; but these men accepted the packers' assurances that all was well and Upton Sinclair an irresponsible Socialist troublemaker. An unconvinced T.R. then sent out his own people, who reported that *The Jungle* could be read as fact all the way through. After that, President and Congress were of one mind, and within six months a Pure Food and Drug Act and a Beef Inspection Act had passed into law. Sinclair said, "I aimed at the public's heart and hit it in the stomach."

One can imagine what Philip Armour would have said about *The Jungle* and its author; but he had died in 1901, and his rival Gustavus Swift had died in 1903, a year after Potter Palmer's death. It seemed that a race of giants was beginning to disappear; this was hard to realize, for the founders of modern commercial Chicago had given an impression of permanence like that of the huge and solid buildings in the Loop. It was reassuring to see Marshall Field proceeding on his accustomed way in 1905, apparently indestructible although past his seventy-first birthday. In 1904, Mr. Field had shown the same mettle he exhibited when Leiter left him;

this time he faced his general manager Gordon Selfridge, who said that he wished to go into business for himself, but would of course delay departure until his replacement was ready. Field looked at Selfridge without emotion and said, "You may leave right now." Selfridge went to London where he became England's greatest retail merchant. In Chicago, Field continued without this right-hand man who had been so valuable that he received ten percent of the profits. The great store, in its way a work of art, filled as it was with wonderful things that Field's buyers brought back from all over the world, was also, according to some observers, a monument to democracy. For any woman, in theory at least, might enter the place, eat in the restaurants, use the retiring rooms, try on the clothes, order goods delivered, and later return any merchandise that failed to suit. But there were limitations. Poor foreign women without money or command of English were seldom seen in the aisles at Marshall Field's; the trade was entirely middle- and upper-middle class. These women did receive courtesies and privileges of a gratifying kind, and Mr. Field himself would sometimes lurk in corners to see that all went well. As for Selfridge, he often patrolled the aisles, wearing a white carnation and bowing before the rich and great. One could estimate one's rating with the Field management by the warmth of Selfridge's greeting; but some felt that the ultimate accolade was conferred or withheld by Charles Pritzlaf, the former coachman who opened doors at the carriage entrance. If he touched the brim of his hat, one would have to be satisfied, and gracious: "Good morning, Charles." If Pritzlaf lifted the hat from his head, it meant that he was acknowledging the presence of high quality. Suppose Mrs. Palmer's carriage drove up: Pritzlaf would bow like a Prussian general before the Kaiser, his hat a good ten inches above his head, while he snapped a clicker in his left hand to signal his assistants forward. But when Mrs. Arthur Caton came to the store, the doorman indulged in no flourishes; everyone now knew Delia Caton was Mr. Field's good friend; and everyone in his employment also knew that the lady did not wish to draw attention to that fact.

Marshall Field had a heavy trial to endure in 1905 when the teamsters called a strike. They enraged Field, and the heat of his rage burned through the coolness of his manner. A Boston Irishman named Cornelius Shea had organized the teamsters, and Field considered him to be in open rebellion against the government. Five thousand men had climbed from their wagons to follow "Con" Shea on the picket lines, and there was bloody fighting on the streets. Field said, "All I ask is my right to use the public highways." To maintain this right he spent thousands of dollars on strikebreakers, put his wagons at the service of the police, and vowed that he would never allow a striker to return to work at the store. During this trouble, Field might have taken comfort from reading about the birth of an uplifters' organization in Chicago, the International Rotary Club of business and professional men, which was destined to help many worthy causes in future years, and to be widely imitated. Chicago could give you a Rotary Club of beamish businessmen; and in the same year of 1905, the city also gave birth to an organization, the International Workers of the World, which appeared to be at last the One Big Union that had long been awaited by the radical members of the laboring class. Guns at Fort Sheridan, warships at the Naval Station: Mr. Field and his friends might take comfort in their presence when the Pinkertons reported what had taken place in the Labor Hall on Lake Street. For there stood Big Bill Haywood, blind in one eye from a mine accident, calling for an aggressive union to represent anybody who worked for a living, whether or not he had a valued skill. Haywood said, "I don't give a damn whether the skilled workers join us or not. We're going down into the gutter to get at the mass of workers and bring them up to a decent plane of living." Father Hagerty, a priest disfrocked for urging Colorado miners to revolt, brought in the I.W.W. Preamble with its opening sentence that struck like a bullet: "The working class and the employing class have nothing in common." The date was June 27, 1905, and to make the call to class warfare unmistakable, Haywood cried, "Fellow workers, this is the Continental Congress of the working class. We are here to confederate the workers of this country into a working-class movement in possession of the economic powers, the means of life, in control of the machinery of production and distribution without regard to capitalist masters." Among the 200 delegates from thirty-four radical organizations who heard his words were Eugene Debs, "Mother" Mary Jones, veteran of fifty years as an agitator, and Daniel De Leon, scholarly leader of the Socialist Labor Party. They made Chicago capital city of the migratory worker, the lumberman, the seasonal farmhand, the traveling printer, all the grades of vagabonds down to the men who claim no occupation other than that of tramp or hobo. Along West Madison Street, the homeless wandering laborers found lodgings, cheap food, drink, entertainment, and education, although the courses of instruction might be no more than the lectures of quacks in storefronts, or sermons preached by officers of the Salvation Army. Nevertheless, West Madison was a tribal gathering place, and though the dirt and disease of the city's underside were all too evident there, the men had friends along the street to whom they looked for encouragement whenever they managed a Chicago layover. They had, for example, the counsel of Nina Van Zandt Spies when trouble came; for after marrying an Italian and living in Rome, Nina had returned to Chicago and her own version of social service. A Vassar graduate, she might have found a place at Hull House, but preferred to go her own way. Many a radical organizer owed a debt to Nina for bail money and lawyers' fees, and all through the West, where the migratory workers gathered in trackside jungles, men would be studying pamphlets that Nina had provided, and the word would pass that Chicago would never be an entirely hostile place so long as August Spies's widow lived.

It is not possible to pronounce whole-hearted condemnation on Marshall Field for his abhorrence of Bill Haywood, Nina Spies, and the I.W.W., for they advocated Populism along with their other doctrines, and thus filed claim that any American fortune was a theft from common property due for immediate redistribution. That was not a good thought for an elderly man, and may have had something to to with Field's custom of descending from his carriage each morning a few blocks from his place of business, and unostentatiously walking the rest of the way. His personal happiness, as we know, could not have been overpowering; his son Marshall Field II had entered Harvard in 1889, traveled with a sporty crowd, and left college the following year to marry Albertina Huck, a brewer's daughter. The younger Marshall Field now lived within a block of his father on Prairie Avenue, and there were four grandchildren, two boys and two girls. In the late winter of 1905, Field gave a *"Mikado"* ball for the two older grandchildren, transforming the ground floor of his house into the town of Titipu, scene of the comic opera by Gilbert and Sullivan. Mrs. Caton was present, her husband remaining at home because of illness. It was a serious illness, and Arthur Caton died that summer. Mrs. Field had been dead since 1896, and Marshall's friends approved when he married Delia at St. Margaret's, London, on September 5, eighteen days after his seventy-first birthday. The party went to Claridge's for a wedding breakfast, and Ambassador Whitelaw Reid proposed the toasts. This was a long way from the hard rock of Conway, Massachusetts, and Mr. Field was to have only two months of undisturbed happiness. On November 22, 1905, as the Fields paused on their way home for a New York visit, they received bad news from Chicago: Marshall Field II had been seriously hurt by the accidental discharge of a gun in his house at 1919 Prairie Avenue. Stepping from a chartered train in Chicago the following morning, Field scolded the reporters who pressed around him; and another crowd of newsmen angered him at the hospital. Marshall Field II had become a Roman Catholic when he married; he died after taking the last rites on November 27. Many wild rumors followed young Field's death, including a tale that he had been shot elsewhere and brought home to die. People were willing to believe the newspapers had suppressed the true story because the elder Field was a big advertiser. But in fact, the papers investigated every rumor; their reporters, and Field's private detectives, proved beyond question that the young man had accidentally shot himself, and that the accident had taken place at his home. Five weeks after the son's death, the father caught cold; pneumonia developed and the elder Marshall Field died on January 16, 1906. Connoisseurs of Boston and Chicago wills agreed that Field's was the best yet, the longest and most complicated. It disposed of an estate amounting to $120,000,000, a sum that would excite no more than passing interest today. It is therefore necessary to risk annoying the reader by asking him to bear in mind that Field's millions lay in old-fashioned armor-piercing high-explosive dollars, mostly protected from the tax men. Marshall Field's money had come from rising land values; bank stock; the Pullman Company; the International Harvester Company; railroad and street railway bonds, some of these tainted by political corruption; and from low wages and high prices at the store. But one thing should be accorded to him, and remembered, and put to his everlasting credit: where retail sales were concerned he believed in value for the money and courtesy to the customer. The young man in the dark suit carefully laying out goods and watching the customer's eyes lived on in the frosty merchant prince until the day he died.

The year 1906 took from Chicago a greater benefactor than Marshall Field when Theodore Thomas also demonstrated the danger of colds to elderly gentlemen. He fell victim to pneumonia brought on by rehearsing in a drafty auditorium for the opening program at the new Orchestra Hall that Daniel Burnham had designed. Christian Friedrich Theodore Thomas had given Chicago an orchestra ten years before the Boston Symphony began. Year in and out, he had provided a fifty-week season, telling his audiences Chicago was the only town outside New York that would support such a schedule of concerts.

Orchestra Hall on Michigan Avenue, handsome and spacious as it was, could take its place as one in a number of improvements Thomas's old friend Daniel Burnham envisioned for the city. For ten years Burnham and his associates had been working on a plan that was to combine buildings, streets, parks, beaches, streams and Cook County wooded areas into one grand design of a harmonious whole. In a sense the city itself would be one building, the separate units joined by lines in perspective and pathways of use, like Swedenborg's Heaven, for which the exact measurements were written in a book, or the White City of the fair, or the splendid human city of Vachel Lindsay's dreams. In January 1904, Burnham had moved the workroom for this project to the top floor of the seventeen-story Railway Exchange that his firm had completed on Michigan Avenue at Jackson Street. From this vantage point he looked out over the city north, south, and west, and had the lake at his feet. With the help of his associate Edward H. Bennett, and members of the staff, Burnham placed on paper the ideas of John S. Wright and other visionaries in a form that could be translated into actuality. It needed only substantial financing, and the help of citizens who had sufficient influence to hold off the greedy men who wanted the lakefront for their own purposes. Burnham too proposed to exploit the lakefront, but for esthetic rather than commercial uses. Here they had at the center of town the small park that Victor Lawson tried to destroy; north lay Lincoln Park; to the south was Jackson Park with the Midway and Dr. Harper's university gray and stately on the green; and at the city's back, there grew many acres of unspoiled woodlands in the Skokie Marsh, and the basins of the Des Plaines and Chicago rivers. Closer in there was a virgin forest known as the Peterson Woods, south of Peterson Avenue, and there were untouched glades in the Gibbs Woods north of Gibbs Street, and another lovely spot could be found on the Chicago River south of Central Avenue. Prudent action could save all this from the tree killers and land butchers who destroyed cities with their steady enmity toward beauty and their love of ugliness. For Chicago this need not be. The wildwood and the city park could be preserved, and new linking boulevards added to those already in existence, all this in the first comprehensive metropolitan plan set down for a city in the United States. The automobile was still under control; in general the horseless carriages were piloted by ex-coachmen; and the begoggled young men who took to the roads in racing cars did little harm. Most Chicagoans traveled by their own legs, or by boat, train, or street car, or pedaled in health and comfort on bicycles, like Artie Blanchard and his girl, or Dr. Harper. Fortunate in being able to plan for people rather than machines, Burnham produced a masterpiece of city design, most of which was realized, and much of which proved indestructible, even when the automobile got out of hand, years after Burnham's death.

Burnham completed his scheme under the patronage of the Commercial Club, a businessmen's organization, founded in 1877, which had absorbed a similar group called the Merchant's Club in 1907 to become a forum of discussion about the future of Chicago. In 1909 the Commercial Club sponsored one of the most beautiful examples of book-making the world has seen in *The Plan of Chicago* by Daniel Burnham and Edward H. Bennett, with pictures by Jules Guerin. The tints in Guerin's watercolors were accurately reproduced, including those of the frontispiece, a bird's-eye view of the ideal city reaching from Indiana to Wisconsin, with a blue-green lake, and the bluish tan prairie stretching to its flat horizon. Striking as it was, this opening work by Guerin scarcely prepared the reader for the center spread, wide pages of the heavy book opening to show Burnham's vision of two causeways built out into the lake from Chicago Avenue on the north, and Twenty-Second Street on the south, to join at an arched breakwater off Jackson Street opposite the Loop. In the west, Guerin had caught the lemon-golden glow of a Chicago summer sunset, and against it showed the inland plaza that Burnham had planned for the intersection of Halsted and Congress streets, with the fabulous domed central structure that was to be a colossal enlargement of Hunt's Administration Building at the fair. This was the vision of W.T. Stead, a palace of the people so grand and huge that nothing petty or dishonest could take place beneath its dome. Burnham's Middle Western instincts had told him that no city would be properly planned without a courthouse square; but he recognized the essential nature of Chicago by proposing a union station at Twelfth and Canal streets, which would have released many acres below Jackson Street for commercial development. This real union station has not been built, but the plan as a whole took shape, and became a reality, much as Burnham and his associates had laid it out. His opening statement in the book had been: "The time has come to bring order out of chaos." To achieve this end, Chicago must put to use its two dominant natural features, "the expanse of Lake Michigan, which stretches, unbroken by islands or peninsulas to the horizon; and a corresponding area of land, extending north, west, and south without hills or any marked elevation." From these materials he proposed to evolve "the city as an organism in which all the functions are related to each other." Burnham went on, "Now, while it happens that the planning of a new city imposes straightness as a duty, and diagonals as a necessity, it is equally true that a virtue should be made of these hard and fast conditions." Therefore Burnham welcomed the long streets already in existence, descendants of the early plank roads. He liked Archer Avenue (Mr. Dooley's "Archey Road"), Clybourne Avenue to the northwest, Blue Island and Cottage Grove Avenues running through the far South Side. "There is a true glory in mere length, in vistas longer than the eye can reach, in roads of arrow-like purpose that speed unswerving in their flight; and when the opportunity of level ground permits, the glory should be sought after." On roads straight or curving one would go from formal parklands in the central city to the woods, where in spring the bloom of thorn, the crab apple, and wild plum were features of the landscape, and overhead the forests of elm, oak, ash, willow, and cottonwood still grew as they had grown for Kinzie and du Sable. Burnham was a lover of trees, but what he saw most clearly was the lakefront. Here he wanted a boulevard to follow the shore, and knowing his patrons, Burnham pointed out economic possibilities in addition to the esthetic gains: "Imagine this supremely beautiful parkway, with its frequent stretches of fields, playgrounds, avenues, and groves, extending along the shore in closest touch with life of the city throughout the whole waterfront. What will it not do for us in health and happiness? After it is finished will the people of means be so ready to run away and spend their money in other cities? Where else can they find such delightful conditions as at home? We should no longer lose so much of the cream of our earnings, now spent in other lands. . . ."

The Commercial Club showed the original paintings and drawings by Guerin and Bennett at the Art Institute, holding a private viewing before opening the exhibition to the public. Guests at the preview were enthusiastic; the *Tribune* reported one woman saying to her husband, "Oh look, John, even the tugboats will be smokeless." A Frenchman was quoted as saying, "Ah, Paree, eet has nothing so fine." The reporter saw art students pleading for admittance; there was no room for these young people that day, but "tomorrow the barriers will be down and they may gorge themselves with the glories of the Chicago that is to be."

As a boy Burnham had been a poor student; the son of a prosperous drug wholesaler, he had failed the entrance examinations at both Harvard and Yale after barely managing to graduate from Central High School. Now he was the teacher of a city; indeed, he taught the country, for he headed the government commission that completed and enlarged L'Enfant's original plans for Washington, D.C., and he also laid out the metropolitan planning of Cleveland, San Francisco, and Manila. Harriet Monroe had not been sympathetic, but she was seldom present on the Sunday afternoons at Burnham's house in Evanston during the early years of the new century, when he would walk after lunch on a terrace beside the lake, expounding his ideas to a train of people—family, friends, associates, students, employers, and visitors from foreign countries. At times he would halt, and the train would halt, moving again when he moved on, until he had led them across the entire estate. All stayed for supper, which Burnham cooked in a battery of chafing dishes, after running down the cellar stairs and returning with bottles of claret in his arms. It was Burnham's unfaltering enthusiasm that swept the masters of Chicago to agreement on his plan. But he could not have brought it to reality without two indispensable helpers, Aaron Montgomery Ward and Charles Frederick Wacker.

Sixty-six years old when the Burnham book came out, Montgomery Ward was typical of his kind in having risen to wealth and power from a humble position in the world. After grade school in rural Wisconsin, Ward labored in a barrel factory, then in a brickyard, and behind the counter of a general store. He came to town in 1865, clerked two years for Field and Leiter, then took to the road as a drummer in the early 1770s. Swarming through the hinterland, these traveling salesmen took orders for Chicago reapers, plows, wagons, stoves, tools, soap, candles, whiskey, musical instruments, printing presses and type, cameras, clothes, shoes, and innumerable other items of commerce. Ward observed that the customers in country stores sometimes failed to obtain satisfaction. He decided to set up a company to handle retail selling from a catalogue by mail, with satisfaction guaranteed. By the late 1880s, Montgomery Ward and Company has become a large concern with thousands of employees, and the house of Sears, Roebuck had risen on a similar plan. There was business enough for both, and their catalogues, listing and describing an incredible variety of merchandise, were fascinating to read. In 1900, Ward built an imposing tower on the northwest corner of Michigan Avenue and Madison Street, with a 24½-foot weathervane, "Progress Lighting the Way for Commerce," modeled by J. Massey Rhine. Leaving daily management to associates, Ward had turned his attention to city planning and the protection of Burnham's ideas. The heart of the scheme for central Chicago depended on keeping the ground clear, except for the Art Institute, from Twelfth Street north to Randolph Street east of Michigan Avenue to the lake. Long before Burnham's book appeared, real estate operators had tried to break into the parkland by every means from attempted establishment of squatters' rights to lawsuits against the city. To frustrate these people, Mr. Ward maintained such constant surveillance that he became known as the watchdog of the lakefront. Whenever he saw suspicious-looking carts moving onto the terrain, or men setting up surveyor's instruments, Ward sent lawyers hurrying to the spot, and from these challenges grew a number of prolonged and costly legal battles in the Illinois courts. Montgomery Ward bore the expense, stood fast under the abuse, and saved the lakefront from the land hogs for the people of Chicago and their visitors. It was due to his faithful watch that the tract now called Grant Park was available when the City Planning Commission came into existence after the publishing of the Burnham book in 1909. Daniel Burnham died on a trip to Europe in 1911, and the guardian of Grant Park died the following year. Fortunately for the plan, Charles Wacker had accepted appointment as head of the Commission in 1909, and was able to give full attention to its problems. A Chicago-born brewer and trader, Mr. Wacker was an enlightened businessman of the same breed as Montgomery Ward. A vigorous fifty-three when he took charge, Wacker put in the next seventeen years on the plan. He gave himself to the work: some days he would make four or five speeches, show lantern slides at schools, and go out in the evening to give one more talk. It was he who persuaded the people to vote the bonds and taxes to purchase thousands of woodland acres and build broad thoroughfares and recreation piers along the lake. He died before the completion of the Outer Drive, but saw his name memorialized in Wacker Drive beside the river.

During the years that Wacker, Ward, Burnham, and the members of the Commercial Club were working to increase the general assets of Chicago, a large class of persons had been busy at activities yielding no social benefits whatever. These were the bawds and thieves, inheritors from the army of rogues who descended on the city during and after the Civil War. There was a fourth order to be reckoned with in addition to the owners, the workers, and the seekers. This fourth estate comprised the criminal classes, together with the politicians, judges, officials, and crooked police-men who drew sustenance from them. One might call this order of Chica-goans the takers; they stood alert to seize any unguarded thing of value, starting with the crumbs that fell from the rich men's tables and going on to the virtue and good repute of this city, establishing for Chicago an inerradicable reputation for wickedness and crime.

Any survey of criminality in the Chicago of the early 1900s should center on the fact that Mike McDonald was by then no longer in full practice as impartial arbiter of the crime industries. He had placed the administration of confidence games, for example, in the lands of Johnny Rafferty, who maintained offices in Whiskey Row, the west side of State Street between Harrison and Van Buren. Rafferty enjoyed the business, and got much satisfaction from the roping and playing of a mark. He chuckled with glee when the inside man did his work so well that the swindlers were able to take all the money the man had with him, and dispatch him to his bank at Terre Haute or Galena for additional funds. This procedure was known as putting him on the send. Rafferty used to say, "I love a good thief." He was in ecstacies when Snapper Johnny Malloy and his gang ran through a classic confidence game at blinding speed, dropping the poke in the Congress Hotel lobby, playing the mark, putting him on the send to Peoria and stealing the nine thousand dollars he brought back, all within ninety-six hours. Thereupon they cooled out the mark, that is, frightened him out of investigating his loss, with a fake police raid on their headquarters, which they had presented as a racetrack bet-ting room. Rafferty's people were good thieves, the best in the business, and it made no difference to them that their booty might be someone's life savings, or money for education, medical expenses, or meeting whole-salers' bills. According to these scoundrels, every mark had larceny in him, or he wouldn't go on the send. This was true enough, and made the success of the game a significant comment on the spirit of the times.

The aristocratic confidence men paid operating taxes only to the judges, politicians, and high police officials. But many of the lower police took tribute from pickpockets, lottery-ticket salesmen, street gamblers, hold-up men, saloon keepers, prostitutes, and brothel-keepers. There were honest officers of every rank, like Captain Max Nootbar of the First Ward, which included Whiskey Row and the near South Side. But police salaries were so low, and corruption so generally accepted, that good cops faced continual discouragement of every kind, including punishment from crooked superiors when they disturbed vested interests. The citizens have not been indifferent to this state of affairs: throughout its history, Chicago has continually appointed commissions to point out its faults and recommend measures of correction. In 1903, for example, an investigator hired by a group of businessmen brought in his findings. Working at the head of a force of private detectives from out of town, the investigator revealed that the Chicago police force was in disgracefully bad condition. The situation was such that any honest cop lived in frustration trying to work with some colleagues who should have been retired for decrepitude, and some others no better than uniformed hoodlums, and addicted to morphine and cocaine. The police force failed in such primary duties as controlling traffic and protecting citizens in the streets, and many officers shared in thieves' loot, sent in false duty reports, and loafed in saloons when supposedly on patrol. The report recommended that after cleaning out the bad cops and the deadwood at the station houses, the authorities should recruit two thousand intelligent young men to the Chicago force within the next two years. Nothing was done, and during the winter of 1905–06, residential streets became so dangerous that the people in North Side neighborhoods hired private watchmen to patrol after dark. In other parts of the city, one risked meeting hold-up men of such inhuman brutality that they not only robbed the victims, but tied them to posts, tortured them with knives, and sometimes left them dead.

12

Politics and Crime

THE FEROCITY THAT EXPRESSED ITSELF BY THE TORTURE OF ROBBERY victims was a form of energy that even Chicago found no way to harness for useful purposes. Those who studied the matter reported that the most appallingly violent impulses originated in two areas, the Twenty-second Precinct on the West Side, and the Thirty-eighth Precinct on the North Side. South of Division Street, east and north of the river, the Thirty-eighth had many disreputable saloons, seedy hotels and boarding houses, dance halls, and brothels of the lowest sort. Rapes and murders were common in the precinct, with conditions especially discouraging to lovers of law and order in the Italian district known as Little Hell, that reached from La Salle Street to the river. The stereotype of the lazy, wine-soaked Italian immigrant was erroneous: Chicago's Italians had a sense of personality and a driving instinct for achievement, so that when a large section of them turned to crime, the results were prodigious. Another community of Italians, along with Irish and Bohemians, could be found in the second high crime area, the Twenty-second Precinct southwest of the Loop, where Maxwell Street was the principal thoroughfare, with a concentration of low drinking dens, pawnshops, thieves' hangouts, and disorderly houses. The precinct was known as "Bloody Maxwell" and its inhabitants proclaimed it the world's toughest and most dangerous district. Bloody Maxwell drew continuous criticism in the press: the *Tribune* called it "a festering evil."

Little Hell and Bloody Maxwell were Alsatias, and their savagery made them hazardous for the ordinary citizen or convention visitor out for a good time. The police would turn away well-dressed men and direct them to an area where the brothels, dance-halls, and saloons gave the visitor a reasonable chance to pass an evening without being beaten and robbed. In the 1890s, these less dangerous establishments had collected, for the most part, on South Clark Street. But when the trolley cars came through in 1895, the street started to become respectable, and within two years the brothel-keepers had moved out and colonized the neighborhood around South Dearborn and Twenty-second streets. This area, bounded by Clark Street, Wabash Avenue, and Eighteenth and Twenty-second streets, became the most widely known as well as the largest vice district in Chicago. Extending also for some distance along Archer and Armour avenues, the district was called the Levee, apparently from a tradition that an embankment had once existed along the river a few blocks west. Now that such districts have been gone from American cities for many years, it is hard to imagine what the Levee was like when flourishing at its high point around 1910. From time to time a commission would investigate the Levee, the other vice districts of Chicago, and the state of prostitution in general, collectively referred to as the social evil. Accurate census was impossible, but the newspapers accepted the figure of five thousand for the total number of women engaging in prostitution as inmates of houses in Chicago. The worst aspect of the social evil was the putting of young girls to the trade by force. It had been known since the time of Roger Plant at Under the Willow that procurers sometimes kidnaped and assaulted women. Herbert Asbury's studies led him to conclude that gangs of procurers did business between large cities, shipping consignments of girls under guard, and holding them against their wills until addiction to alcohol and cocaine made them accept the life.

How many of Chicago's five thousand came to prostitution involuntarily could not be calculated; but the greater part of them, most probably, had taken to it because of the low wages paid in the respectable occupations that were open to uneducated girls. But it was not to be expected that big employers would accept blame for the existence of organized commercial vice. Julius Rosenwald of Sears, Roebuck, for example, told the Illinois Vice Commission there was no connection between vice and small wages paid by large firms. He said it was not true that Sears, Roebuck paid its women employees less than eight dollars a week. The facts were that the company had a number of beginners or apprentices at from five to eight dollars a week; these were girls of seventeen or under. There were 119 fifteen- and sixteen-year-old apprentices earing five dollars a week. But more than one thousand women employees had savings accounts; and there were 3,267 women earning an average of $10.20 per week. Among these women the minimum wage was eight dollars a week. To Mr. Rosenwald's way of thinking it was therefore deplorable for the Commission to talk of Rosenwald paying less than eight dollars a week. However, he admitted having a total of 4,700 women employees, and the onlookers could not help making a mental calculation which showed Rosenwald was conceding that he paid some fourteen hundred women less than eight dollars a week. On thing was clear: Julius Rosenwald had offered no competition to vice lords for the services of women and girls.

Whatever their reasons for entering the life, the women found it a miserable existence, and most of them tried to dull the edge of reality by constant use of alcohol, opium, morphine, and cocaine. But there were a few high-class houses where the managers put a fairly good face on the business, both from the harlot's and customer's point of view.

Among the best of the first-class resorts were those operated by Victoria Shaw, Georgie Spencer, and Zoe Millard, three madames of long experience who headed a trade association that met regularly to discuss matters of common concern. But the managers of the most famous parlor-house in Chicago remained aloof from this guild, causing bitter resentment and enmity among the other panders in the Levee district. Holding themselves above the rest were the sisters Minna and Ada Lester, who had taken the name of Everleigh, and opened an establishment in the double house at 2131–33 South Dearborn Street on February 1, 1900, after studying a survey of possibilities prepared by Christopher Columbus Crabb. During their subsequent career, these two harridans obtained much publicity, and were overrated as personalities, but the evidence is that they gave good value in their pretentiously decorated Everleigh Club, where the only drink was champagne, and a client could order a banquet in one of several ornate dining rooms, with food prepared by a chef as good as any in town, and music by a string ensemble. The banquets cost the givers fifty dollars a plate, with the fees for each girl at least that much in addition. Once more the reader is respectfully asked to bear in mind that this was real money: at the time there were instructors at the university, for example, earning less than fifty dollars a week, and yet living reasonably well. It was said that a man who did not spend at least fifty dollars on his first visit was not again admitted by Minna, who inspected would-be customers at the door.

These high-priced transactions started a picturesque passage of Chicago legendry, the myth of luxurious bagnios with valuable art works on the walls, and an air of depraved elegance in the parlors. Other legends sprang from the circumstance that even in the Levee district there still existed the possibility of violence and scandal. Thus originated a story that has been told to the present day, which might be called the story of the corpse in the cab. The tale goes that a prominent man dies in a brothel; at all costs the disgrace must be concealed; two friends put him upright in a cab, and drive to the Chicago Club; they carry him in as though unconscious from drink, and next day announce his death because of heart failure. Another version has it that the prominent man does not die a natural death, but is killed in a quarrel, and taken to his house: nothing is done about the killer; and the police and newspapers are influenced to stand mute.

The variations are numerous; and there is a kernel of truth at the heart of the tale, for a young man of rich family did die at a house in the Levee. His name is no longer of interest, but was published at the time, when the newspapers gave detailed reports of the affair. So much for suppresion: today the case is fascinating not because anyone covered it up, but because it was revealed as drama of the sort that might have occurred at the establishment in Eastcheap operated by Mistress Quickly. The young man's last debauch was under way on the night of January 8, 1910, when he appeared on South Dearborn Street at the Everleigh Club roaring drunk and demanding champagne and morphine, which Minna refused to sell him. This brought on a quarrel with the staff girl, who became enraged at losing her commission on the wine, and flounced out, running up the street in her evening gown to the house kept by Madame Shaw at No. 2104. Shortly afterward, at one o'clock in the morning of January 9, Minna got the young man loaded into a taxicab which was to deliver him to his home on Lake Shore Drive. Of course there was nothing about drunks that Minna did not know, and she was aware that this troublesome patron might countermand her instructions to the driver, but at least he was off her hands.

Next day, the hellion who had deserted the Everleighs ran into trouble at Victoria Shaw's place when she started a fight with another girl, and received a beating from Madame Shaw and the two thugs she employed as bouncers. The girl stayed at the house, sulking and looking for a chance to get even. About this time news came that the rich man Minna Everleigh had ejected was still in the district throwing money around. The Shaw woman immediately dispatched runners who brought him in, drunk as a lord, and some time on that night of January 9 she had the satisfaction of sending this free-spending customer up to her best bedroom. All was quiet then until just before dawn, when the girl who had accompanied the rich youth suddenly began screaming, and rushed downstairs shrieking that her client had died in bed. Madam Shaw at once ascertained they did indeed have a dead man on their hands, and then her cunning brain was inspired to concoct a scheme that could have sent the Everleigh sisters to jail or even to the gallows. Victoria Shaw proposed with the aid of her thugs to carry the dead man down the alley that ran behind the Everleigh Club, break in the cellar door, push the corpse into the furnace, and tip off the police. It was a simple and practical plan which should have worked, except that the bruised and resentful girl from the Everleigh Club overheard it, went to the telephone booth, called Minna, and warned her of the plot. Accompanied by a Negro gunman, Minna hurried to the Shaw establishment, pounded on the door, and insisted on coming in. There followed a great shouting argument with much threatening and cursing, but finally Minna carried her point that the police must be called while the man still lay where he had died; anything else would lead to unfixable trouble for everybody. Madame Shaw gave up, and in the early morning the police came; shortly afterward a private ambulance took the body home. Minna always said that someone had given the young man an overdose of morphine, but the autopsy showed no trace of drugs, and the coroner attributed death to heart disease. How those other madames hated the Everleighs is what this episode reveals, the hatred stark and palpable as we read of it even today; and how they would have rejoiced to see the sisters carried to jail, "for the man is dead that you and Pistol beat amongst you." Thus began the legend of a corpse secretly removed from a bordello; as the story grew, the dead man went all over Chicago, sometimes in a private automobile but usually in a cab. The most curious aspect of the story is its retroaction on the death of young Marshall Field, for now that so many years have passed, people think they recall hearing of a Field scandal suppressed; and yet it was in the papers; and the Everleighs were mixed up in it; and millions of dollars were paid to keep the two viragos from the gallows; and still today in cold gray dimness the taxicab goes chugging up Michigan Avenue, three passengers sitting in the back, two of them alive.

An additional reason for hatred of the Everleighs among other panders was the sisters' refusal to accept the authority of Big Jim Colosimo, who now had charge of prostitution in the same way that Jimmy Rafferty ruled over the confidence men. Colosimo's eminence was a matter of pride to Italians, and showed how they were replacing the Irish in the higher ranks of vice and crime. It was true that Rafferty dealt with the best class of thieves, but Colosimo's empire brought in more money. He levied tribute on bawds and panders according to their ability to pay, took out his fees as handler of the money, and passed on the politicians' take. But the

Everleighs refused to pay Big Jim's collectors: they made their own arrangements, and their relations with the police were so cordial that Colosimo could not bring them into line. It was irregular, it caused talk, and he did not like it; but there was nothing he could do. Aside from the Everleighs, however, all persons connected with commercialized vice in the Levee district bowed before Colosimo. A corpulent and illiterate hoodlum, Jim had been a Democratic precinct captain in the First Ward, which included the Levee, and had married Victoria Moresco, who kept a brothel in Armour Avenue; with her husband's help, she established other bordellos, and Big Jim brought in a gunman from New York named Johnny Torrio as director of security. Alderman Mike (Hinky Dink) Kenna of the First Ward observed that the Colosimos were trying to make something of themselves, and that Italians in general were beginning to be heard from. Kenna also took note that the Italian bombing terror known as the Black Hand was getting good results throughout the city. Mike Kenna appointed Colosimo his official working criminal, the associate that his sort of politican had to have, operating over the line outside the law. By 1910 Colosimo had established a restaurant and cabaret on Wabash Avenue at the Levee district's eastern frontier. He wore fine clothes, with a display of diamond pins and rings, and in moments of relaxation often took a buckskin bag of diamonds from his pocket, and scattered the stones on a black cloth to admire their brilliance. Colosimo's place was one of the first resorts of ill repute that catered to slumming groups from respectable parts of town. The fat man with his diamonds became one of the sights of Chicago, and he made certain that no hoodlums bothered his swell customers. In addition to his managerial talents, Big Jim was a judge of spaghetti: Enrico Caruso and other opera stars visited his place to eat it, prepared just right, and heaped on a large, clean, hot dish with a sauce selected from a list of three dozen kinds. As the steaming platters went by, Colosimo would rub his hands and say, "It may be tea time in Boston, but it's spaghetti time in Chicago."

Aside from Johnny Torrio, who stood at his right hand, Big Jim had several lieutenants, of whom the most important were Ed Weiss, Blubber Bob Gray, Dago Frank Lewis, and Ike Bloom, a squat, swarthy person, constantly smoking cigars, who handled many of the payoffs, besides conducting a notorious dance hall. For some time Bloom's framed portrait hung in a position of honor on the wall of the squadroom at the Twenty-second Street police station. The portrait hit the ash can in the alley on the day honest Captain Nootbar took over. Later on, Bloom came to call and began talking in an insolent tone of voice, whereupon Nootbar kicked him so hard that the cigar shot from his mouth like a torpedo, and he rolled down the station house steps. This incident was the talk of the Levee, whose denizens expected Nootbar's transfer any day. But nothing happened, for Hinky Dink Mike Kenna and his colleague Bathhouse John Coughlin thought Bloom had been talking too much for some time, and had a swift kick coming. Since the Bath and Hinky Dink were absolute monarchs of the First Ward, the handing down of their opinion closed the matter.

Bathhouse John and his partner flourished for more than forty years, openly bartering votes, and never failing to deliver their ward at election time. They accomplished this by intimidation that included mayhem and murder, and by parading armies of alcoholic derelicts to vote at the polls. Kenna had discovered the scientific fact that a professional alcoholic can live for long periods with no food at all, and he kept the wretched men going on beer slops and the leavings in liquor glasses from the saloons under his control. The distinguished Senator William Mason of Illinois had given Mike and Bathhouse John the secret of staying out of jail: at all costs avoid a Federal rap, leaving Washington graft for Congressmen and appointees who understood the workings of it. "Keep away from the big stuff," Mason had said, "and stick to the small stuff." The formula worked so well that miserly Hinky Dink salted down a fortune, and the Bath had money for a stable of thoroughbreds, a Colorado castle, a private zoo, and the most expensive male wardrobe in North America.

Coughlin's mania for clothes made the fortune of his tailor, Meyer Newfield, who constructed suits and overcoats that his star customer never got around to wearing even though he changed costume several times a day. The obsession began to grow on Bathhouse John in the 1890s when he heard talk of the fashions set by the Prince of Wales. Coughlin said to a reporter, "I think the Prince is a lobster in his tastes. When it comes to mapping out style for well-dressed Americans, he's simply a faded two-spot in the deck of fashion. I'm out now for first place and you'll see his percentage drop." Coughlin's vanity expressed itself in another way when he published a song called "Dear Midnight of Love." He claimed to have written both words and music, although the tune had been supplied by an orchestra leader named Max Hoffmann. But the lyrics, which conveyed a sense of numbing imbecility, were Coughlin's own; and he not only had this material printed in sheet music, but gave it public presentation, as an addition to the vaudeville program at the Chicago Opera House. Emma Calvé declined the honor of singing this number, and Bathhouse John enlisted May de Sousa, the thirteen-year-old daughter of a First Ward detective. A packed house sat fascinated as ushers brought out the placard:

May de Sousa and a Chorus of 50
Singing Ald. Coughlin's
DEAR MIDNIGHT OF LOVE

The curtain rose, revealing the Cook County Democratic Marching Band and the fifty choristers, men and women, in evening dress. May de Sousa made her entrance, they played and sang the song, and a storm of cheers and catcalls broke out. Coughlin came on for a bow, happy and unaware that the noisy audience was jeering at him. The ushers came running with baskets of flowers, and Mayor Carter Harrison II stood in his box and bowed to the people, while Bathhouse John shook hands with the soloist and conductor. Next morning the newspapers commented that little Miss de Sousa had done surprisingly well, considering that the lines of the song most nearly approximating sense were "Now I must bid adieu. So cruel, why did we meet? List! love, what shall we do? Good bye, when shall we greet?" The girl did have talent, and later became a star of musical comedy in Paris and London. A Chicago newspaperman named John Kelley amused readers for some time afterward with doggerel that he attributed to Bathhouse John, who complacently accepted credit for "Why Did They Build the Lake So Near the Shore?," "She Sleeps by the Drainage Canal," and "They're Tearing Up Clark Street Again." But Kelley never succeeded in duplicating the utter banality that Coughlin achieved in "Dear Midnight of Love."

Mike Kenna and Bathhouse John had a special touch in public spectacles. When they loaded a chartered train bound for political conventions, they covered the cars with bunting in the national colors, and had a band ready to serenade the passengers coming aboard. But their swarm of hoodlums, political serfs, and camp followers did not simply drift into the railroad station two or three at a time: they marched after another band, from the First Ward through the Loop in a well-drilled phalanx, like West Point cadets, every man in silk hat, frock coat, and white spats, his chest covered with sashes and badges, keeping time, a tightly-rolled umbrella carried like a rifle on the shoulder. Their precision march was a thing of beauty as they wheeled into the train shed and turned by the right flank to mount the cars. Then, as the combined bands crashed into "There'll Be a Hot Time in the Old Town Tonight," Bathhouse John and Kenna would emerge from the stationmaster's office, escorted by railroad police, and climb aboard. There was no risk of going dry on these trips; for example, Kenna and Coughlin stocked their special train to the Democratic convention at Denver in 1908 with 1,000 quarts of champagne, 200 quarts of whiskey, 80 quarts of gin, and 12 crates of lemons.

Everything on the convention train was free, but Coughlin and his partner also liked to sponsor celebrations where the guests paid admission charges and bought their refreshments. They had observed the benefit dance that took place every year for a man known as Lame Jimmy, a fiddler who was one of the best-liked parlor-house musicians on the Levee. Moving in on this affair and making it their own as the First Ward Ball, the aldermen inflated it to such size that it had to be held in the Coliseum. And by 1908, the ball had become notorious for drunkenness, disorder, and displays by exhibitionists. Some people in the Democratic organization began to question the wisdom of flaunting their party's underworld connections, but the Bath refused to listen, and Mike Kenna saw no reason to pass up the $50,000 profit in the ball. Accordingly the greatest First Ward Ball of all time was advertised for December 15, 1908, and Coughlin spent the afternoon with Meyer Newfield for the final fitting of a dress suit made in conventional black except for lavender lapels, with a wide crimson sash to be worn across the shirt front. Completing his costume that evening with pink kid gloves, a red scarf, and a yellow overcoat, Coughlin set off to the ball; on arrival he saw 15,000 people fighting to get in, doors smashed, tables overturned, and chairs broken. With flailing clubs and blackjacks the police detail and 200 bouncers managed to restore order, and at eleven P.M., the aristocrats of the Levee made their entrance. Glittering with diamonds, Minna and Ada Everleigh went to their box; the Colosimos entered to great applause; then came Maurice van Bever, the white slaver, and his wife Julia of the Sans Souci parlor-house; Victoria Shaw, Georgie Spencer, and Zoe Millard walked in, each madame accompanied by a bevy of girls under escort of white-gloved policemen. Crowds gathered around the boxes to stare at the famed panders and their harlots; but if any drunk tried to invade the boxes, bouncers and waiters hurled him down a gauntlet of detectives who hammered his skull with blackjacks as he stumbled by. At midnight, the Bath presented himself before the Everleigh box and bowed to the sisters; they rose, and one took his left arm, the other his right. After the Grand March, Coughlin signaled to bandmaster Henry Erlinger, and thousands of voices burst out singing "Hail, Hail, the Gang's All Here." This ended the march, a general unmasking followed, and "the revelry was ready to begin in earnest."

The uproar continued until dawn, with a great deal of drunken fighting, and bawling of obscene songs, while men dressed as women indulged in gross improprieties. Had the beldames, politicians, and crooked officials present but known it, there was handwriting on the Coliseum wall. For among the crowd were investigators working for a committee that had secretly declared war on the Levee, with the intention of putting the entire district out of business. Next day, Bathhouse John informed the newspapers that the ball had been a great success. But as the year went on, Coughlin reached the conclusion that although no political reforms could touch him, he had best give careful attention to a growing new movement for moral reform; and so the First Ward Ball was never held again.

Instead of a drunken ball, the most significant public event in the First Ward in 1909 was the invasion of the Levee by the English evangelist Gipsy Smith, who led five thousand church people through the district on the balmy night of October 12. The area was absolutely quiet, without even a light showing except for an occasional gleam behind a curtained window. Precise orders had come from high police: while "the reverend" was in the district, there was to be no loud talk or music, no drinking, no jeering, no looking or gesturing from windows, and no admittance of customers. The Bath and Colosimo had endorsed these instructions, the denizens of the Levee obeyed, and Gipsy Smith with his followers, their band softly playing "Where He leads Me I Will Follow," came through deserted blocks to the heart of the area at Twenty-first and Dearborn streets, where they knelt as the evangelist prayed for the redemption of sinners. Then they marched north, the sound of their drums faded away, and the district returned to life. Lights came on, windows went up, and one could hear the jangle of professors pawing ragtime. On the following day some of the papers questioned the wisdom of Smith's march, pointing out that it might have brought young men and boys to the Levee who would otherwise not have gone there.

Some boys who resembled the homeless urchins of Dwight Moody's Sunday School inhabited the Levee and knew no other environment. These were the choreboys and messengers who hung about the brothels, saloons, and dance halls, living on handouts and the tips they earned for odd jobs and running errands. They slept in sheds or under stairways. One of these waifs, a boy known only as Red Top, drew more attention in his death than he had while living. Red Top was not sure of his age, but thought he was about fifteen years old in 1908, when he hanged himself in a woodshed and left a note on a piece of wrapping paper: "They ain't no fun living this way and I'd sooner be dead. I never had no mother or no father or no home. I don't owe nobody nothing and I don't want nobody to cry over me. So Good-bye." A number of landladies and saloonkeepers made up a purse for Red Top's funeral. At the services a Salvationist said a few words about the lost boy, and led a quartet that sang "In the Sweet Bye and Bye." A Negro musician known as Banjo accompanied a woman who sang "Au Revoir"; another Levee musician named Hank North, who had once been in a circus band, played "Nearer My God to Thee" on a muted trumpet, and then Lame Jimmy stood up and sang "The Palms." After this, undertakers carried the coffin to a white hearse, and several carriages of mourners followed Red Top to Oakwoods Cemetery on the South Side.

There is no question that this matter of permitting recognized vice districts fascinated the respectable elements of the city during the twenty years from the fair in 1893 to 1913. In these two decades Chicago doubled its population to more than two million, passed Philadelphia to become the country's second largest city, expanded its area beyond two hundred square miles, and took an undeniable place among the world's great towns. But the citizens could not be unaware of the ugly side, because the newspapers presented it to them every day in some of the frankest accounts of vice and crime ever to appear in print. During that period, Chicago had four strong locally owned papers: the *Daily News*, the *Times-Herald* (later *Record-Herald*), the *Inter Ocean*, and the *Tribune*. In competition were two papers controlled from out of town by William Randolph Hearst, whose evening *American* started in 1900, to be followed in two years by the *Examiner*, a direct challenge to the morning *Tribune*.

These six big papers, and the afternoon edition of the *Times-Herald*, which was called the *Post*, gave work to a number of star news writers who founded a tradition of expert journalism in Chicago which has survived to the present day. And in the early years of the twentieth century, these reporters played an important part in convincing the average Chicagoan that the tolerated "social evil" would have to go. For stories out of the red-light neighborhoods were not only pathetic, like the account of Red Top's death and funeral: often they were angering and shocking, as when the papers reported in March 1907 that a gang of procurers had kidnapped and assaulted an eighteen-year-old girl, and sold her for fifty dollars. Reports of this sort were disturbing, and the citizens' groups continued to probe the evil, bringing out some remarkable statistics, such as an estimate that the landladies sold 27,000,000 bottles of beer in one twelve-month period. Whether or not that finding had value, the commissions and committees in the reform wave, aided by the newspapers, began to be successful in turning public opinion against public vice. In the fall of 1911, Mayor Carter Harrison II decreed that disreputable activities must cease on South Michigan Avenue, which had become tainted with corruption from the Levee a few blocks west. And on October 24 the Mayor caused a sensation by ordering the closing of the Everleigh Club. The sisters' belief in advertising had finally carried them too far when they published a brochure describing the luxuries of their resort. There was no

[308]

offensive language in the pamphlet, which would seem to be merely promotional matter for a small hotel to anyone who did not know what business the sisters were in. Nevertheless, Mayor Harrison decided this was too much, and although the chief of police ignored the closing order for twelve hours, the Everleighs locked their doors for the last time at 2:45 in the morning of October 25, 1911. In the early autumn of the following year, State's Attorney John E. W. Wayman invaded the district with warrants against 135 persons. Many people fled before the arrival of Wayman's police, thieves entered their deserted houses, disorderly crowds of hoodlums got out of hand, and the riot call went in. Six weeks later, on November 20, 1912, Mayor Harrison ordered the police to close all resorts still operating in the Levee, and his orders were carried out. Like his father, this second Carter Harrison had done good things for Chicago, and when he shut down the Levee, he put a stop to all openly tolerated vice districts in the city. But his political career ended when the Democrats turned against him in the next mayoral primaries. Carter Harrison II got the message, with his last three months in office still ahead of him, when he attended a West Side Saloonkeepers' Ball and received cold and rude treatment from the committee. He went home and said to his wife, "The game's up." Today he looks like one of the best mayors Chicago ever had.

13

Golden Age

ANOTHER SIGNIFICANT CHICAGO EVENT IN THE YEAR OF THE LEVEE'S closing, with a slightly more respectable cast of characters, was the Republican National Convention which met to nominate William Howard Taft for a second term in the White House. Theodore Roosevelt had backed Taft for the Presidency in 1908, having himself entered on that office in 1901, succeeding William McKinley, who had been killed like the first Mayor Harrison by a crank with a grievance and a gun. Citing the tradition of no third term, T.R. had refused to run in 1908, and there had been smiles all round when Taft got in; Roosevelt put his arm across Taft's shoulders and cried, "You big, generous, lovable, high-minded fellow!" Then T.R. set out for Africa to hunt big game, all the while keeping up publicity in newspapers and magazines at home. Returning in 1910, Roosevelt found himself troubled by an irresistible longing to get back into the White House; and his old friend Taft began to look less admirable. By the autumn of 1911, Roosevelt had quarreled with Taft and worked himself into a rage. Taft tried to placate the belligerent T.R., but it was no good; the spectacle was far from edifying, although the public enjoyed the show, for it appealed to the cruel child inside every adult that dances with glee when a powerful little bully attacks a lumbering fat boy in the school yard.

Taft found protectors in Chicago, where the party managers announced that they would not tolerate revolt, and began to take measures to keep

Roosevelt delegates from voting. To protect his interests, Roosevelt sent on a man from Pittsburgh named Bill Flinn, keeping in touch twenty-four hours a day by specially installed long-distance telephone connections between Chicago and his long Island house. It was obvious that there was going to be a fight on the convention floor, and the New York and Chicago papers played it up. Mr. Dooley looked things over with his cold Irish eyes, and remarked that a pass to the visitors' gallery at the Coliseum was "a free ticket f'r a combynation iv th' Chicago fire, Saint Bartholomew's massacree, th' battle iv th' Boyne, th' life iv Jessie James, and th' night iv th' big wind. . . ."

The big wind blew into town when Theodore Roosevelt stepped off a chartered train at the La Salle Street Station on Sunday, June 16. Here the crowd greeting T.R. became so unruly that police formed a ring around him and trampled through, hurling men and women to the ground amid screams and curses while Roosevelt grinned, waved a big white hat, and shouted, "I feel like a bull moose!" The convention was to open on Tuesday, June 18, and Roosevelt called a meeting at the Auditorium the night before. Five thousand people filled the place, and fifteen thousand more were milling in the street outside when Roosevelt stood up to speak. It happened that this man was a master of oratory, perhaps the last of the breed in the United States worthy of being compared to Douglas, Lincoln, Bryan, and Fighting Bob Ingersoll. He got his effects by sheer will power, for he lacked imposing stature, waved his short arms like windmills, and had a squeaky voice. Nevertheless, students of oratory ranked Roosevelt high for his ability to arouse audiences and to emphasize and reiterate his points without seeming to fall into repetition. At the Auditorium, T.R. first allowed the people to settle down, as he knew was necessary, but soon got to such an emotional pitch that the reporters wondered what he would have left for the finish. Roosevelt knew what he was doing, for he had villains to condemn in the members of the Republican National Committee who were working to bar his people from the convention floor. They made a splendid collective target, and like the Cardinal in *The Jackdaw of Rheims,* Roosevelt cursed them sitting and cursed them standing, and soon he had the crowd yelling in ecstasy on cue, handling them like a matador with a mob of Mexicans howling *Olé!* at every twitch of the cape. With glasses shining, white teeth grinning, and arms semaphoring, T.R. cried, "Disaster is ahead of us if we trust to the leadership of men whose souls are seared and whose eyes are blinded, men of cold heart and narrow mind, who believe we can find safety in dull timidity and dull inaction." This was a call to arms and Roosevelt next brought them along with consummate skill to a passage of dramatic humility in which he said,

[311]

"What happens to me is not of the slightest consequence. I am to be used, as in a doubtful battle any man is to be used, so long as he is useful, and then is cast aside—or left to die. I wish you to feel this and I shall need no sympathy when you are through with me, for this fight is far too great to permit us to concern ourselves about any one man's welfare." He paused, and then began to line it out in cadence, and they knew that now he planned to blow them out of their seats, as the arms waved faster, the voice rose higher, and the gold-rimmed glasses seemed to shoot flashes of reflected light into every part of the hall. "We fight in honorable fashion for the good of mankind," cried Roosevelt. "We are fearless of the future—unheeding of our individual fates—with unflinching hearts and undimmed eyes—WE STAND AT ARMAGEDDON—AND WE BATTLE FOR THE LORD!" Roosevelt's closing yells blended with the high-pitched braying and shrieking of his auditors: like Bryan sixteen years before he had succeeded in giving his campaign a religious flavor, and most of those present thought the emotional pressure of the Auditorium meeting would carry the Roosevelt people to victory in the Coliseum, where the convention opened next day.

Roosevelt had indeed put fear in the managers' hearts: it was observed they had 600 policemen stationed in the hall, and there was barbed wire under the bunting on the railings of the podium. The chief of police personally shadowed Bill Flinn, who threatened convention chairman Elihu Root with violence; too frail at sixty-seven to fight with his fists, Root had been Roosevelt's friend and Secretary of State, but knew this would not save him if he ran into bruisers on the floor. The anxiety about violence was such that ticket holders had to show credentials at three check points, and some couldn't get in at all. After much yelling and fighting, the convention nominated Taft in bitterness and disorder. Roosevelt then left the Republican Party to run on his own Bull Moose Progressive ticket, opening the way for Woodrow Wilson to enter the White House.

For the owners of Chicago, the year 1913 was not only a placemark in time since the fair, but also the starting point of a new era of progress and prosperity beyond the imaginations of men. War was an impossibility, for thanks to the sounding board Chicago had afforded Theodore Roosevelt, Woodrow Wilson occupied the White House, and all knew him to be a professor of political science and not a man of the sword. Indeed, the big nations could no longer go to war against each other, because of the destructive power of the modern high-speed aeroplane. This left Chicago with no outside danger to fear as it continued on the way toward becoming the largest as well as the most important city in the United States. It was already the most patriotic: a few years before, the *Inter Ocean* had editorialized: "We Americans have some things to regret, but how infinitely more we have to praise and rejoice in. We go forward by looking up, not looking down. Let us look up and go forward. Let the Eagle scream!"

That voice of strident self-congratulation sounded a note on which Chicago would bring the country close to terrible disasters in time to come. But those twenty years following the fair, in contrast to the gilded age that had preceded them, were a golden age for the cultivated people of Chicago. At the height of this brief and glowing Arcadian period in 1910, the Chicago house of A. C. McClurg brought out a pleasingly printed and illustrated book called *In Town, and Other Conversations* by Janet Ayer Fairbank, a literary woman who like her sister, the novelist Margaret Ayer Barnes, had been born to the city's mercantile aristocracy. The book was a collection of pieces that had appeared in the *Record-Herald,* and what Mrs. Fairbank had offered newspaper readers, in a city that had not been in existence sixty-five years before, showed how civilized, in the drawing-room sense of the term, the city had become. The reader is introduced to Mrs. Fletcher, a youngish widow of the bluestocking sort, seated near the open fire in her town house on the near North Side, "pursuing her vocation of tea-making" as she may be found "on any late afternoon during the winter season." We see Georgian silver, antique lace, "one or two charming contemporary French pictures," a Florentine mirror, two pieces of really good Chinese porcelain, but no other ornaments in the uncluttered room, which is saved from stiffness by books and papers lying about. Mrs. Fairbank doesn't say so, but there is without doubt a Healy portrait on the wall. In these surroundings Mrs. Fletcher awaits her guests; the first one is her mother, Mrs. Vane, a part that could have been played by Billie Burke at a later period. We learn that Mrs. Vane's hats "are as modern as her point of view is archaic," and are not surprised when she says, "I think the opera is a good thing in many ways. It makes the papers so interesting." Now Mrs. Fletcher's two admirers make their entrances: one is Mr. Webber, a writer, and the other is Mr. Alexander, a stockbroker who "symbolizes the normal man." Alexander says, "All the husbands at my club are looking as if the market had dropped, now that the dances are coming on. It's a discouraging sight for a bachelor." Mrs. Vane says, "I always think it is very, very inconsiderate of husbands to allow themselves to look tired." Now we hear from Mr. Webber: "Is it worth while, this dashing about for four months of the year, and reducing our nerves to powder—for nothing. Why will we do it?" Alexander answers, "A man must do what's being done." Mrs. Vane tells them that "There is one's position to consider, and what is owing it." At any rate, Mr. Webber thinks, we have afternoon tea, "one of the most rewarding things

[313]

civilization has given us." To this Mr. Alexander agrees, adding, "I am just a plain man, and I like to be comfortable." Outside the curtained windows, "a few indecisive snowflakes drift through the clear gray of a November afternoon."

A summer scene at Mrs. Fletcher's Lake Forest villa opens with the tea things on a broad verandah overlooking the lake from a wooded bluff. The only guest present is Mr. Webber. He asks for lemons, but Hilda the maid reports there are no lemons in the house. Mrs. Fletcher tells her to send the motor to the village for a fresh supply, and it turns out the motor has gone to the station to pick up Mrs. Vane. Then James the coachman must go in the runabout; but James has already gone to the village to get cream for Cook, for it seems the cows on the estate have not given enough milk for the weekend: the dairyman says they're in dry season. Mrs. Fletcher now orders Hilda to try and catch James by telephone at the creamery, and ask him to stop at the grocery for lemons, and then at the express office to see if the hot-house fruit for dinner has arrived from the city. In a few minutes Hilda is back: "I beg your pardon, Madame, but Mrs. Vane has just telephoned from the station to say that her trunk did not come on the same train with her, and what shall she do about it?" Mrs. Fletcher deals with this, and orders the estate express wagon to meet the next train at 6:10. Next comes Jenkins the gardener with a problem about lettuce; then the laundress reports the pumping system has gone wrong; by now the chauffeur is bringing Mrs. Vane, the coachman is running errands, the choreboy is off on his bicycle getting lettuce, and Jenkins has to ride Mrs. Fletcher's horse to the village to bring help for the pumping system, or else they must bathe in brown water. Mr. Webber says, "I prefer it that way." He knows that coming out on an early train, he arrived "before the curtain was up." By dinnertime everything is in order, and Mrs. Fletcher has been smiling and gracious through it all.

Janet Ayer had married Kellog ("Ked") Fairbank, son of the merchant and soapmaker who had been a pillar of the Chicago Club and other institutions for many years. On the first of January, "everybody in Chicago" came to the Kellogg Fairbanks' house at 1244 North State Parkway; by all accounts, the host and hostess were two of the world's most charming and agreeable people. In addition to the town house, they owned a "cottage" at Lake Geneva, something that had begun in the Eastlake style of the 1870s, and grown to a large, airy, balconied structure with an octagonal main hall full of softly faded chintz and comfortable wicker furniture. This was "The Butternuts," which the Chicago novelist

Arthur Meeker called the pleasantest house in America for a visit. Years after Ked Fairbank had died, his widow would look around the dining hall and say, "How we've laughed in this room!"

There was no question that Mrs. Vane and her daughter, as evolved types recognizable to newspaper readers, had placed a considerable distance between themselves and the hosts of the Barclay lawn party, described by George Ade. Mrs. Fletcher had made a reference to *The Golden Bowl* which was not far-fetched; Henry James' first publishers in the United States had been the Chicago house of Stone and Kimball. This firm also gave first or early publication in this country to George Moore, Ibsen, Yeats, H. G. Wells, Thomas Hardy, George Santayana, Max Beerbohm, Paul Verlaine, and George Bernard Shaw. The Stone and Kimball list of native authors included the new realists Hamlin Garland, Harold Frederic, and Robert Herrick, and they also published an influential "little magazine" called *The Chap-Book*, in which they serialized James's *What Maisie Knew*. Henry James said that certain publishers had subjected him to indignities that did not bear thinking of; but he always spoke highly about Stone and Kimball in Chicago, who treated him right.*

The son of Melville Stone who founded the *Daily News*, Herbert Stewart Stone met Hannibal Ingalls Kimball at Harvard; the two young men started *The Chap-Book* at college, and moved it to Chicago in 1894, where it received a new dress from the typographers Frederick Goudy and Bruce Rogers. In 1900 the partners brought out the first book of Ade's *Fables*, and they had a best seller in 1901 with *Graustark*, by George Barr McCutcheon, the cartoonist's brother. In 1902 came *The Story of Mary Maclane*, stark autobiographical writing by a woman from Butte, Montana, who had originally called her book *I Await the Devil's Coming*. As they continued in Chicago, Stone and Kimball did many fine things: they supplied, for example, a badly needed collected edition of Poe; they took over the North American publishing of Kenneth Grahame's *Golden Age*; they brought out *The Ebb Tide*, by Robert Louis Stevenson and Lloyd Osbourne. Each of these books was an example of high quality in design, printing, and binding; and they stand today on collectors' shelves for craftsmanship and beauty. Hamlin Garland recalled the two young publishers and their editor, Harrison Garfield Rhodes, as notable figures on the Chicago scene, "three missionaries of culture, each in a long frock coat tightly buttoned, with cane, gloves, and shining silk hats, pacing side by

---

*Another Chicago firm of this period, the Open Court Publishing Company, brought out Bertrand Russell's *Scientific Method in Philosophy*, Ernst Mach's *Science of Mechanics*, and Hugo de Vries's *Mutation Theory*.

side down the Lake Shore Drive. Their crowning audacity was a printed circular announcing that tea would be served in their office on Saturday afternoons."

Literary and artistic topics could provoke discussion in several parts of town during Chicago's golden age. One of the liveliest centers for news of the creative arts was the Saints and Sinners corner of McClurg's bookstore on Wabash Avenue. This corner was the rare book department conducted by George W. Millard, an expert on bibliography and scarce editions who advised dealers and collectors throughout the world. Against the mellow background of his wares, a group would gather every afternoon for early intelligence on such matters as the fate of Theodore Dreiser's *Sister Carrie*, a novel that divided its action between Chicago and New York, or to hear the latest report of Isadora Duncan, the dancer who had come to Chicago from San Francisco with her mother, sister, and brother like a gipsy troupe. Here in the Middle Western metropolis the public had first recognized Isadora's art when she appeared under the management of local impresarios.

Similar topics would arouse interest at the Little Room, which was actually a big room, the two-story studio of Ralph Clarkson in the Fine Arts building on Michigan Avenue. Much would be said here about the next play scheduled by pupils of the Anglo-American dramatic teacher Donald Robertson, or by those who studied with Anna Morgan, the producer and coach who had given Chicago the first American performances of Shaw's *Candida* and *Caesar and Cleopatra*; and there would be news about the productions of Ibsen, Pinero, Sudermann, Strindberg, and Maeterlinck, subsidized by Arthur Aldis and Hobart Chatfield-Taylor. When people talked of the stage, one would undoubtedly hear about the success achieved by Edward Sheldon, the young Chicagoan who had seen possibilities in uniformed gospel missioners and their street corner bands, using this material to write *Salvation Nell* for Mrs. Fiske. It was said the actress read the play after lunch, and was trying on Army bonnets that same afternoon. In 1906 there would be talk of William Vaughan Moody's challenging social drama, *The Great Divide*. He had written it, along with some lines of enduring poetry, while teaching at the university. After her husband's death in 1910, Mrs. Moody started a catering business which was successful for a time, enabling her to maintain the hospitality of her house on South Wabash Avenue, where artists could always find shelter and help.

The private theaters of Chicago's golden age gave birth to the little theater movement in this country, out of which have come the regional, professional dramatic organizations, playing to educated audiences, that are such valuable features of life in many cities today. A typical private playhouse in the grand Chicago tradition of providing one's own entertainment belonged to Arthur Aldis, whose wife remodeled an old cottage on their Lake Forest place into a small practical theater seating one hundred persons. Mary Reynolds Aldis made actors out of some neighbors whom she drilled as the permanent company of what she called "a progressive little theater," using that term for the first time. They gave an impressive performance of a fantasy in verse by Frances Shaw, wife of the Lake Forest architect Howard Van Doren Shaw. They did well with a similar work, *The Pierrot of the Minute,* by the English poet Ernest Dowson. Mary Aldis's players also worked with scripts from the Irish theater, when Lady Gregory licensed them to present her plays, Yeats authorized a performance of *Cathleen ni Houlihan,* and Synge granted rights for *Riders to the Sea.* The company became well known, and accepted an invitation to appear in Boston. The *Transcript* said that "they act with an ease, freedom and variety rare among amateurs; with simplicity, directness and sincerity not too frequent among any players. . . . As with the acting, so with the plays. There is much that is unworthy and hackneyed in the regular theater; these clever amateurs show how to do it better, both in choice of material and in its presentation."

Many of the same group had taken part in the activities of an open air theater called the Ragdale Ring on North Green Bay Road. Here the producer-dramatist was Frances Shaw, who was happy to work for small but exacting audiences. In landscaping and laying out this open air theater, the producer had help from her brother-in-law, John T. McCutcheon, and from her husband, who also designed the buildings around the central square of Lake Forest. In 1909 Mrs. Shaw had put on a peripatetic play which the audience followed through woods and across ravines, an extraordinary theatrical experience. The Lake Forest scholar and author L. Ellsworth Laflin, Jr., has pointed out that peripatetic drama is descended in part from the Eleusinian mysteries of Greece, and that Maeterlinck used a similar method with *Pélleas and Mélisande.* Mrs. Shaw's play, a burlesque on stock company melodrama called *The Heir of Manville Grange,* had a successful revival in 1922.

In 1911 Arthur and Mary Aldis gave shelter to an Englishman named Maurice Browne by permitting him to occupy the coachman's rooms over their Lake Forest stable. The Aldises wished to help Browne because he was a man of the theater with magnificent plans in mind. He had come to town as suitor of Ellen Van Volkenberg, a talented Chicago girl whom he had met in Florence and followed home to the States. By the summer of 1912 Maurice and "Nellie" were engaged, and he was at work trying to organize a production of *The Trojan Women* by Euripides. Nellie helped by giving recitations and character impressions for paying audiences, an activity in which she got encouragement from Mrs. J. Ogden Armour, who was alert for talent to entertain guests at her estate on the Waukegan Road. Maurice Browne found a young woman of striking beauty to play Andromache in Elaine Hyman, who had fascinated Theodore Dreiser and a literary man of rising reputation named Floyd Dell. At the end of the year, Browne was able to announce that the Chicago Little Theater would open for a season on the fourth floor of the Fine Arts building, where he had created an intimate auditorium with 91 seats. Everything possible for comfort and elegance was there, including programs printed on soft Japanese rice paper to prevent rustling, and a tea room under the direction of Mrs. Moody. After getting his theater ready, Browne postponed the *Trojan Women* and started with plays by Yeats and Schnitzler. When he finally got the Greek tragic drama to suit him, Browne put it on to critical acclaim, and received credit for the best production of Euripides in modern times.

While Elaine Hyman was giving her thrilling performance as heroine of an old tragedy, the so-called new women of Ibsen and H. G. Wells were part of her audience, living in Chicago, and working in its studios and offices. Garland's Rose Dutcher was sister to Ibsen's Rebecca West and Wells's Ann Veronica; actual in life as those in imagination, there had come to Chicago a host of young women whose aim it was to be emancipated, to be somehow connected with the arts, and above all, to resist the conventional pressures that had made life sterile and without promise back in the Indiana and Wisconsin towns. They did not head for New York, a foreign city; they did not need New York, for Chicago had everything that any city could give a seeker for the higher life, and in addition there was the sea-souled lake, as the English painter John Lavery called it, that stayed continually in mind, feeding their hearts and deepening their emotions.

One of the typical seekers, a new woman named Tennessee Mitchell, had come from a small Michigan town where her father was a postal clerk. Tennessee hoped to study with the sculptor Lorado Taft in his barnlike studio on the South Side; meanwhile she supported herself and an invalid sister by working as a piano tuner. When not at this work, Tennessee put in time as a settlement house volunteer; she read Shaw and Wells, and the Chicago realists, saw the plays, heard the concerts, learned every picture at the Art Institute, and after a visit there would take tea with girl companions at the Congress Hotel on the other side of Michigan Avenue. Soon enough Tennessee had no need of girls to keep her from being conspicuously alone, for her vitality and intelligence attracted journalists and literary men in Chicago's upper Bohemia; she met Sherwood Anderson, who had a square face which he wore like a mask, with only his eyes betraying expression. It was said that Anderson had owned a prosperous business, and one day walked out of it, coming to town where he had achieved success in the new trade of writing advertising copy, which could almost be called the invention of two Chicagoans, Albert Lasker and Claude Hopkins. But now Anderson was finding it impossible to stick at his desk, and had begun to spend most of his time wandering along the endless streets of the West Side and running the possibilities of stories and novels through his mind. Tennessee liked Anderson, who had an air of distinction even though Vincent Starrett of the *Daily News* said that Sherwood's suits always seemed one size too big, and his hats one size too small. But the man who interested her most was Edgar Lee Masters, the lawyer who wrote poetry on the side. They became friends, and walked by the lake, talking and watching the gulls, stopping at the North Avenue breakwater to see and hear the surf come in on days when the lake was gray and white, and quoting poetry; and strolling on for dinner at some Italian or German restaurant on North Clark Street. The friendship was to be of importance to American literature, even though it ended in sadness for Masters, and for Tennessee.

Another of the new women who came up to Chicago from a prairie town was a remarkably vital and beautiful girl named Margaret Anderson. Though no relation to Sherwood, Margaret was an admirer of his efforts to find some method of honest writing, as she admired all who tried to achieve high quality in literature and art. Margaret had hurried from the railroad station to Orchestra Hall and a balcony seat for the Chicago Symphony, with Thomas's successor Frederick Stock conducting. By 1913, she was preparing to publish a magazine called *The Little Review*, which came out in the following year as a champion of advanced ideas, with the support of artists, writers, and influential Chicagoans whom the publisher met at Mrs. Moody's house. When she first settled in town, Margaret supported herself with an editorial job on a church paper, one of the hundreds of religious and trade publications in Chicago. These magazines and papers, aimed at special audiences, performed a service for the Chicago Bohemia by supplying jobs for newcomers in search of literary work. A paper called *The Lyceumite* took Carl Sandburg on in 1908, making possible his marriage to the sister of Edward Steichen, the photographer. Lillian Steichen Sandburg was grateful to this paper, house organ for the Lyceum lecture system; Carl might have landed on any of the special-audience publications in town, perhaps on *To-Morrow*, "a monthly handbook of the changing order," issued by the People's Industrial College on Calumet Avenue, to promote "the new values dominating our social, industrial, and intellectual progress." And it is possible that Sandburg might have enjoyed working for *The Papyrus*, even though its publisher seemed to have George Ade in mind when he wrote that the magazine aimed itself at people who wanted to "get away from the Eternal Trite—who are sick and tired of Canned Literature—who demand Thinking that is born of the Red Corpuscle." Sandburg might even have taken a berth on *MIXED DRINKS, The Saloonkeeper's Journal*, but would probably not have cared to do field work for that paper; at the age of thirty he was abstemious and frugal, having had a harder youth than most people, as the child of a Swedish laborer in the Galesburg shops of the "Q" line, the famous Chicago, Burlington, and Quincy railroad, about which the students of Knox College at Galesburg had a song: "Oh the Lord made me and the Lord made you, and the Lord he made the C, B, and Q; This must be true for the Scripture sings, The Lord he made all creeping things."

After a time on *The Lyceumite*, Sandburg went to the *Daily News*, which was prospering because of Victor Lawson's skill as an advertising salesman. Lawson could get the paper so tight that on one occasion an old layout man remarked that aside from advertising they had only room to print "A great many things happened in Chicago today." But Carl Sandburg's copy usually made the paper.

Chicago's literary and artistic community sheltered every kind of talent in the golden age, including the sort that is capable of self-analysis. Of this the leading exemplar was a brilliant, odd, and retiring man named Henry Blake Fuller. A member of an established family, Fuller had traveled much in Europe, but in Chicago he preferred modest lodgings, and took many of his bachelor meals at obscure, unfashionable restaurants. He had written books in the grand literary style, based on his travels abroad, which received praise; but an even greater achievement, from our point of view, was his realistic treatment of the Middle West, in two of the best of all Chicago novels, *The Cliff-Dwellers* and *With the Procession*, and in a book of sketches on the city's Bohemia, *Under the Skylights*. In the novels, Fuller gently satirized the world of pioneer descendants, the owners of Chicago; in the stories, he submitted the artists to the same scrutiny, detecting a certain amount of cant in a kind of attitudinizing that had been inspired, for the most part, by George du Maurier's *Trilby*. His friend Hamlin Garland did not escape, turning up in the sketches as Abner Joyce, author of *The Weary World*, whose work derived directly from the soil. Nor did Fuller spare himself: he appeared as Adrian Bond, full of European travels, finicky about literary style, and almost nonproductive when compared to the prolific Abner Joyce.

14

The Conscience of Chicago

HARRIET MONROE SAID THAT HENRY FULLER'S WIT PLAYED LIKE COL-
ored lights on the topics of conversation at the Little Room. But he was
mostly a listener, like George Ade, and Harriet herself, who had been
living through the first decade of the twentieth century on the little she
earned from art criticism in the papers, and occasional assignments to
teach special classes in English at a school for young ladies. Hard as the
going had been for Harriet, she had maintained her position, which was
partly in the world of Henry Fuller's family. In 1910 Harriet was fifty, still
dedicated to the cause of poetry and determined to serve it in a practical
way. Observing the numerous magazines of Chicago, Miss Monroe envisioned one more, which would give poets the recognition she had demanded for them at the World's Fair. Early in 1911, Harriet laid her plans
before a number of leading Chicagoans to whom she had social access,
including Mrs. Palmer, who promised support; Dr. Gunsaulus approved,
as did Albert M. Loeb of Sears, Roebuck; grumpy Samuel Insull listened
to Miss Monroe; and encouragement came from Arthur Aldis, Hobart
Chatfield-Taylor, and the Evanston banker Charles Gates Dawes. Harriet's request was reasonable: she wanted 100 citizens to pledge $50 a year
for five years to start a magazine of poetry that somehow, by zealous
promotion and frugal management, would be able to give every contributor a least a token payment, and award more substantial prizes from time
to time. Setting up temporary headquarters in the Little Room, Harriet

took as her art adviser the etcher and publisher of fine books Ralph Seymour. As editorial assistants, Henry Fuller and the poet and novelist Edith Wyatt gave the project help. Working from abroad, two of the most important figures in literature joined Harriet's staff, W. B. Yeats as European Editor and Ezra Pound as Foreign Correspondent. From the beginning she agreed with Pound that all kinds of work must be welcomed in the publication that she planned to call *Poetry: A Magazine of Verse.* By early 1912 Harriet was asking for manuscripts from every literary person she knew, or had heard of, including such celebrities as Amy Lowell and Edwin Arlington Robinson, who replied, "I hope to be able to write some poetry—or verse, if you insist. Will you pardon me if I presume to ask why you have concentrated so much deadly emphasis into the sub-title of your magazine?" Miss Monroe also wrote in the summer of 1912 to Vachel Lindsay, who was tramping over the country, sleeping in barns and distributing broadsheets of his own printing that he called "Rhymes to be Traded for Bread." Lindsay answered that he would send several new poems as soon as he could get them ready.

Volume One, Number One, of *Poetry: A Magazine of Verse* carried the date September 23, 1912. The cover showed Pegasus in black and red on deckle-edged handmade light gray paper. Subscribers and purchasers in the bookstores rapidly absorbed two printings of the new magazine, totaling 2,000 copies. These people read Harriet's statement of editorial aim, some critical notes, and thirty-two pages of verse, including work by Pound, Arthur Davison Ficke, Grace Hazard Conkling, and the late William Vaughan Moody, whose widow had released an unpublished poem of considerable length, perhaps the most important writing in this opening number. The magazine was an immediate recognized success; it felt and looked right. Hungry for more, subscribers and buyers in the New York, Boston, and Chicago bookstores reached eagerly for the second number, which proved to be as interesting as the first; Number Three presented a poem by John Reed, two years out of Harvard and attacking the evils of society as a journalistic follower of Lincoln Steffens and Ida Tarbell, who were drawing an unflattering picture of Mr. Rockefeller and his oil company. This showed that Harriet would accept no pressure from conservatives among her hundred backers; for independence and progressive views, she equaled Margaret Anderson, Clarence Darrow, Demarest Lloyd, and the other Chicago intellectuals who by now had a constant fire of criticism pounding the heads of the city's owners. The same issue carried a contribution from Yeats, causing the California poet George Sterling to write Harriet about some verses of his own that "when I saw them next to Yeats I regretted more than ever that they were not my best work. Don't you think you were a bit cruel? Well, next time I hope to do better—and please put me in with someone my size." Meanwhile a giant had arrived, as promised, with material for *Poetry*; in October Vachel Lindsay sent some short pieces, and a longer poem called "General William Booth Enters Into Heaven."

Like George Ade and Ned Sheldon, Lindsay had observed the uniformed men and women of the Salvation Army, and recognized the honesty and sincerity of gospel missioners who worked with paupers, criminals, and social outcasts in the slums of England, Australia, Canada, and the United States. General William Booth, the Army's founder and commander, had died in his eighty-fourth year on August 21, 1912, fighting blindness and old age as he had always fought cruelty, greed, and vice. The drama of Booth's life had impressed the world, and it struck Lindsay, tramping the country as he was that summer, with special force. Indeed, the literary historian Dale Kramer did not exaggerate when he said that "few were in as good a position as Lindsay to recognize the indomitable courage and energy and power of the blind leader." And as Lindsay walked the Santa Fe trail, thinking of Booth, marching lines took form in his brain, to the cadence of a gospel hymn. The completed poem reached Harriet by the middle of October 1912, and she immediately scheduled it for the magazine's fourth issue, due to appear in January 1913. Lindsay added a preliminary note, *To be sung to the tune of "The Blood of the Lamb" with indicated instrument*, and a gloss for each stanza setting forth a Salvationist orchestration of banjos, flutes, and tambourines. Miss Monroe feared these touches might arouse ridicule, but decided to trust Lindsay and include them. By publishing "General William Booth Enters Into Heaven" Chicago's daughter gave her city one of the most important days in its history, and since that day generations of men, women, and children have felt a response of the heart when reading for the first time Lindsay's opening:

(Bass drum beaten loudly,)

Booth led boldly with his big bass drum—
(Are you washed in the blood of the Lamb?)
The Saints smiled gravely and they said: "He's come."
(Are you washed in the blood of the Lamb?)

Blind though he was Booth led with confidence, but his followers were a sorry lot. There were drabs from alleyways, drug fiends, and convicts in that limping procession, damaged and abandoned, ugly, dirty, and sick.

Nevertheless, Booth conducted them straight into Heaven, and it was a Heaven imagined by Lindsay as an American town laid out by W. T. Stead or Daniel Burnham, so that the General

> led his queer ones there
> Round and round the mighty court-house square. . . .

And although as Booth strode along he could not see it, Jesus stood in the courthouse door and stretched his hands above the misfits and losers, transforming them into sages, sybils, and clean-limbed athletes who marched on spotless in glorious new garments. And Booth's sight returned when he knelt at the curb in prayer, looked up, and saw Jesus come through the rejoicing saints and newly created angels to bestow the soldier's robe and crown.

William Dean Howells made up for his early discouraging of Lindsay by writing about "this fine brave poem that makes the heart leap." And the *Review of Reviews* praised "General Booth" as "a glorious and touching work." Not long after this William Butler Yeats came from Ireland to Chicago to address a banquet in honor of Harriet's magazine at the Cliff Dwellers, a club of writers and artists that occupied a superb location at the top of Orchestra Hall.* Miss Monroe saw to it that the number of *Poetry* carrying "General Booth" lay on Yeats's night table. And when Yeats rose to speak at the Cliff Dwellers, he began: "I address my remarks especially to a fellow craftsman. For since coming to Chicago I have read several times a poem by Mr. Lindsay, one which will be in the anthologies, 'General Booth Enters Into Heaven.' This poem is stripped bare of ornament, it has an earnest simplicity, a strange beauty. . . ."

Carl Sandburg was there, along with Lennox Robinson of the Irish Players, Maurice Browne, Ann Morgan, and many patrons of the arts, all happy to hear the good things that Yeats said about Vachel Lindsay and Miss Monroe. Lindsay then read a new poem, "The Congo," with tremendous effect. Recollecting her emotions later, Harriet wrote that this encouragement by the speaker and guests "enabled her to draw a long breath of renewed power." She felt again "that divine excitement" that had come over her at the fair "when called to the front of the stage after the reading of the Columbian Ode, to receive a laurel wreath. This also

---

*The name of this distinguished club refers to the lofty location of its rooms, and not to the title of Henry Fuller's novel. Hamlin Garland had a leading voice in the early management of the Cliff Dwellers, causing discomfort by his austere views on serving cocktails and wine. When more liberal governors got control, someone posted a sign in the lounge: THIS PLACE UNDER NEW MANAGEMENT.

was one of my great days, those days that come to most of us as atonements for long periods of drab disappointment or dark despair."

When Miss Monroe said goodby to Mr. Yeats a few days later, the city seemed to lie under benign skies, the center of a civilized world at peace. Amy Lowell had contributed to the magazine, and wrote to Harriet about her feelings for *"Poetry* my mother, Chicago my adopted city, the city of my heart. . . ." And the visiting English painter Sir John Lavery, who had come to inspect the home town of his beautiful Chicago wife, looked out of his hotel window and praised the lake, the hurrying in the streets, the energy, the "great Olympian buildings" that had "beauty of a high order." He said this was something to paint, a new way of doing things that must be looked at in a new way. The Blackstone Hotel, where Lavery was staying, had been built in 1909 on the site of John B. Drake's house at Michigan Avenue and Seventh Street (now Balbo Avenue). This handsome building came from the architectural partnership of Benjamin Howard Marshall and Charles Eli Fox, anchoring Michigan Avenue on the south. Marshall and Fox were to put another placemark on the avenue two miles north in 1920, when they built the Drake Hotel overlooking Oak Street beach.

In the year that Harriet Monroe published "General Booth" the newspapers had much to say about a craze for tea-dancing that brought many Chicagoans into hotel ballrooms as early as four o'clock in the afternoon. Bournique had been teaching dances called the Imperial Three-Step, the Netherlands, the Rosalle, the Gavotte Pompadour, the Vernona Minuet, and the Cuban Waltz. But nowadays the formality suggested by those titles had disappeared in lively steps called the Turkey Trot and the Bunny Hug, danced to ragtime, and the tango, which required the rhythms of Latin America. In addition, some fashionable girls and men performed the One-Step, the Fox Trot, and a dance with the lovely name of Hesitation Waltz. Wherever these dancers stepped out on the smooth floors, musicians were ready to play for them; but Johnny Hand, the greatest of society orchestra leaders, had grown old and poor before the dancing mania reached its peak. In 1907, the County Tax Board had summoned Johnny for a ruling on his request for a reduction in his personal assessment. Hand was seventy-six, and indignant because the officials had eased the taxes of Montgomery Ward and Company by a quarter of a million dollars. "Why, my dear fellow," he said to the chairman, "I played hornpipes on the fiddle and cello for the grandfathers of all the tax dodgers in the County of Cook, and today all I have to show for it is a fiddle or two, a horn, a cello and one or two other things. Yet I am told to come in here and pay to the County what I do not possess in the way of real money." Chairman Roy

O. West said, "That's nonsense, sheer nonsense. You have money and stocks and bonds buried in your back yard, and we know it." Hand replied, "Why, Mister Man, I have nothing in the world buried but relatives and fond recollections. Of the last named there are some left. Tax me and you take away from Johnny Hand his beloved fiddle and cello, and his musical library." The Board let Johnny go, and the spectators applauded the old musician as he walked out. Later that year, a committee held a subscription ball for Johnny's benefit. The organizers were Hobart C. Chatfield-Taylor, Watson Blair, Henry W. Bishop, James M. Adsit, Jr., Adrian Honoré, and Ferdinand W. Peck. The dance program included an old-fashioned Prairie Queen, and ended with a rousing Virginia Reel. When Johnny Hand died in 1910, the papers recalled that he had played at the weddings of Phil Sheridan, Potter Palmer, Hobart C. Chatfield-Taylor, Frederick Dent Grant, Arthur Meeker, Sr., and Levi Z. Leiter. Hand had also played at the wedding of Delia Spencer to Arthur Caton, before she became the second Mrs. Marshall Field. Along with the Bourniques, Johnny had seen the carriage folk of early Chicago develop a recognizable high society by no means altogether lacking in taste and style.

The Chicagoans who moved in those privileged circles felt a slight jar, like the iceberg's nudge at the side of the *Titanic*, when European war broke out in August 1914. By the fourth day of the month, all the big nations over there were going at it, which showed that the comfortable and widely held belief in the impossibility of another big war had been wrong. Still, it was a fight among foreigners whose generals wore rooster feathers in their hats; and the power of the British Navy would soon put everything right. The immediate problem was to get American tourists out of war zones; many Chicagoans were hurrying back, among them Mrs. Samuel Insull and her son. The patriotic Arthur Meeker, Sr., announced that he would fit out a yacht to bring Chicagoans home if those fellows in Washington bungled the job; and the papers published lists of travelers stranded abroad, and assured their relatives there was no cause for alarm. It all seemed rather jolly; and yet on August 2 the leading *Tribune* editorial pointed out that kings and kaisers were commending their subjects to God, while dragging them from fields that were readied for harvest, to be "given to the scythe themselves." The sombre editorial concluded: "This is, we think, the last call of monarchy upon divinity. It is the twilight of the kings. The republic marches east in Europe."

To Harriet Monroe and her circle, the outbreak of war was the beginning of tragedy which they knew would run a cruel and destructive course without control. Harriet considered suspending *Poetry* during "this sordid interruption of man's finer activities and aspirations"; Ezra Pound wrote to her that "the War is eating up everybody's subconscious energy." It was true; but soon Miss Monroe forced herself to summon up energy and continue the magazine. In her first wartime editorial, Harriet wrote that she would do her best in "trying to uphold ever so little the battered and wind-worn spirit of man, blown hither and yon in the hurricane that was destroying nations." Continuing *Poetry* with that responsibility on her mind, Harriet gave Chicago another signpost in literary history by bringing out in the number for June 1915 the first published verse of Thomas Sterns Eliot, a young man who had sent her a poem that spoke in a new and different tone with disquieting effect. At the beginning of the poem's ninety lines, the reader heard one J. Alfred Prufrock inviting his girl on a walk to observe the evening sky stretched out like a surgical patient waiting for the scalpel. It was a long way from Longfellow, but the "Love Song of J. Alfred Prufrock" conveyed the feeling of emptiness that had begun to anesthetize the hearts of civilized people throughout the world. Edgar Lee Masters and Tennessee Mitchell had felt it, the year before, when their friendship ended. Tennessee then married Sherwood Anderson, who was at last getting on paper the stories that had haunted him through hours of tramping Chicago streets. Masters tried to attain peace of mind by going back to an idea for a novel that he had planned about the inhabitants of a village on Spoon River in downstate Sangamon County. Instead of a novel, he now wrote a collection of brief stories told as elegies in free verse. Published in April 1915, *The Spoon River Anthology** brought Masters worldwide renown. The Chicago poet captured every kind of reader with the simplicity of his central idea: here were the pioneers and their children, most of whom had lived hard and even shameful lives of small achievement and little joy. Masters asked the reader, where are they now?—and answered, *All, all are sleeping on the hill.*

Akin to George Ade in his feeling for losers, Masters touched the vein of dark Midwestern pessimism in his silvery verse. A child of the prairie, he knew that explosive energies poured from the flat ground; and he knew the exhausted sadness that came after the energy had gone. But to educated Chicagoans, this hint of melancholy beyond the city's power and grandeur was itself a sort of poetry. And so in 1915 they could read the

*The title refers to The Greek Anthology of some six thousand short elegiac poems and inscriptions by more than three hundred writers, which grew by successive additions from the seventeenth century B.C. to the tenth century A.D.

Anthology with keen esthetic pleasure, and feel its truth underlined by the European war, while they enjoyed the lovely last days of the best period in Chicago's life.

As it had always been, the lake continued to be Chicago's greatest asset. With the developing of anchorages under the Burnham Plan, thousands of amateur sailors now had harbors from which to put out over blue water except on days of gale wind or freezing weather. But the forest of masts that once appeared to be growing from the water at the ends of downtown streets had vanished; even the famous Wisconsin Christmas tree schooner that came to Clark Street dock each December had sailed away for the last time in 1912. Freight and ore now came down the lake by the power of steam, often in "whalebacks" that looked like surfaced submarines. Resort travelers went overnight in style to Charlevoix and Mackinac Island on the *Manitou* and *Missouri,* grand liners of the Michigan Transit Corporation. One could go to Detroit, Cleveland, or Buffalo in equally fine vessels, but of all the graceful steamers that gathered passengers at Chicago, none was more beautiful than the *Eastland,* a popular ship for excursions along the Wisconsin and Indiana shore.

Launched at Port Huron in 1904, the *Eastland* became subject to rumors that she had achieved her slender lines at the expense of sound engineering, and might have trouble in a sudden squall. The owners knew better: the *Eastland* was the safest ship afloat. But her Chicago bookings decreased over the years, and at last the operators took the *Eastland* away, making her home port Cleveland, where they bought a half-page in the *Plain Dealer* of August 9, 1910 for the following advertisement:

FIVE THOUSAND DOLLARS REWARD

The steamer *Eastland* was built in 1903. She is built of steel and is of ocean-type construction. Her water compartments when filled carry eight hundred tons of ballast. She is 269 feet long, beam thirty-six feet, and draws fourteen feet of water. She has twin screws driven by two powerful triple expansion engines supplied with steam from four Scotch boilers.

The material she is built of, the type of her construction, together with the power in her hold, makes her the staunchest, fastest, and safest boat devoted to pleasure on the Great Lakes.

All this is well known to people acquainted with marine matters. But there are thousands of people who know absolutely nothing about boats, the rules and regulations for their running, and the inspecting and licensing of the same by the United States Government. In the hope of influencing this class of people, there have been put into circulation stories to the effect that the steamer *Eastland* is not safe.

Unfortunately we do not know who the persons are that have caused to be put into circulation these scandalous stories. Their motives, however, are easily guessed. Therefore, in justice to ourselves and in fairness to the 400,-000 people that have enjoyed themselves during the past four years in this palatial craft (and that without a single mishap), we offer the above reward to any person that will bring forth a naval engineer, a marine architect, a ship builder, or anyone qualified to pass judgment on the merits of a ship, who will say that the steamer *Eastland* is not a seaworthy ship or that she would not ride out any storm or weather any condition that can arise on either lake or ocean.

The five thousand dollars went unclaimed, and the *Eastland's* owners proceeded to enjoy four seasons of capacity business on the Speed Queen of the Lakes, as they called their ship in further publicity and promotion. Then, one day early in the summer of 1915, men on Chicago docks looked at each other as they heard the sound of a steam calliope across the water, although no ship could be seen. Only the *Eastland* carried such pipes, and in a few minutes they saw her coming in beyond the breakwater, returning to Chicago and the Lake Michigan run.

One of the first Chicago bookings for the *Eastland* was an excursion arranged by the employees' association at the Western Electric plant in Hawthorne on the South Side. Seven thousand men, women, and children turned out for the holiday on July 24, 1915, paying seventy-five cents for each adult, transportation free for boys and girls of fourteen or under. The committeemen had chartered four ships to carry this crowd, with the *Eastland* scheduled to load from a dock on the south side of the river near the Clark Street Bridge. The morning came gray and drizzling, but the excursionists knew the changeable Chicago summer weather, and expected to see clear skies when their excursion fleet got out from land and headed for Michigan City. At a few minutes past seven, the *Eastland's* complement of 2,500 passengers had trooped aboard, and Captain Paul Pederson gave orders to haul in the gangplank and cast off the stern lines. The ship lay pointed toward the lake, with a steam tug at her bow to help her down the river.

Crossing Clark Street Bridge on his way to work as librarian at the *Chicago Daily News*, John Macausland looked from the trolley-car window and saw the people on the *Eastland's* three decks, laughing and happy in holiday clothes despite the dampness of the morning. He observed that the *Eastland* stood tall and thin at the bows like a racing yacht. Then Macausland gasped, and felt his heart shrink as though he had dropped ten stories in an express elevator at the Masonic Temple—the

Eastland had tilted sharply to the landward side. And then she righted again. On the bridge, Captain Pederson had felt the vessel's sudden leaning and return; and he said to Chief Engineer J. M. Ericson, "Open sea cocks and let in water for ballast."

Then Captain Pederson realized that the ship was listing to the other side, and he heard wood crashing against metal as the icebox in the bar slid across the tilting deck and collided with a bulkhead. The slant grew greater, people began to scream, and leaning rapidly the *Eastland* went on her port side in twenty-one feet of water. During the ten or twelve seconds since the leaning began, hundreds of people had piled at the port rails as though they had come down a toboggan slide; these drowned beneath the ship. Others died below decks, but about fifteen hundred managed to climb out on the starboard flank of the *Eastland,* which protruded from the water, where they tried to keep a grip on the slippery steel plates. Mr. Macausland saw that some of these people were hanging on, and others slipping off into the river. He jumped from the car and ran the rest of the way to the *Daily News* building on Wells Street.

About thirty policemen and volunteers leaped from the dock to the exposed side of the *Eastland* and formed a human chain that helped some passengers into the four tugboats that had come alongside. The total of dead came to 835, including twenty-two entire families, and the cause of the disaster was never determined, nor was any responsibility fixed. Twenty years later, the judges in the Circuit Court of Appeals threw out the last *Eastland* damage suit, ruling the owners not liable for any of the 835 deaths, or losses arising from them. Aside from its legal and engineering aspects, the sinking of the *Eastland* was a typical great Chicago disaster in its suddenness of occurence. It brought to mind the crack of doom when the killer ship struck *Lady Elgin,* and the red tongue licked the audience at the Iroquois.

The destruction of life in the *Eastland* disaster made Chicagoans even more anxious about the European war. And in 1916, Woodrow Wilson returned to the White House with the understanding that the country was counting on him to keep the United States out of foreign conflicts. It was true that Wilson had ordered the killing of a few Mexicans, but they had brought it on themselves by disrespect to Our Flag. At this point, some of the younger business and professional men in Chicago sized Mr. Wilson up, figured where he was taking us, and went away to semi-official training camps in preparation for reserve commissions. Robert R. McCormick, in charge at the *Tribune* since 1911, rode with General Black Jack Pershing in pursuit of Pancho Villa, a Mexican warlord. And by April 1917 Mr. Wilson had worked himself into a rage against the German kaiser, who wore a funny hat with a spike on top of it instead of a silk hat like Wilson and his friend, the high-strung little British ambassador. On the rainy evening after All Fools' Day, Wilson went before Congress and asked for a declaration of war in a pious, flag-waving oration that recalled the screaming furies of Henry Clay. They were all on their feet at the end, howling along with Wilson for a righteous war. One old Supreme Court justice did a cakewalk in the aisle; Wilson went back emotionally exhausted to the White House and enjoyed a good cry with Joe Tumulty, his sympathetic Irish secretary. He said it was a fearful thing to lead a nation into war. Yes, indeed; one sympathizes with Wilson, and knows just how he felt. And at Chicago, the last great hustle of unquestioning patriotism began. Then it seemed that perhaps the patriotism wasn't quite so unquestioning as our leaders had thought: for it turned out that to have a satisfactory war, we would need conscript armies. The point was emphasized by a visitor, the sixty-nine-year-old Marshal Joseph Jacques Césaire Joffre of France, who told Black Jack Pershing and Woodrow Wilson to put through an American conscript law without delay. Black Jack didn't like to hear a foreigner talk that way, and the sawed-off Marshal looked funny alongside iron-faced handsome Pershing. But Congress moved fast and got the Draft Act through on May 18. Within a few months the conscripts were marching down Michigan Avenue in baggy breeches and canvas leggings, on their way overseas to stamp out Kaiserism and make the world safe for democracy. The home front patriots agreed that a man who did not want to fight in the war to end war must be a very bad man.

It shocked the nation to learn that there were many such men; and they made their headquarters in Chicago. Since organizing on the West Side twelve years before, the International Workers of the World had met with some success, and now carried 100,000 members on the roster. They were decent working men, still dedicated to the idea of One Big Union. Their interest in the German kaiser was slight; and their officers had uttered the appalling sentiment that "of all the idiotic and perverted ideas accepted by the workers from that class who live upon their misery, patriotism is the worst." However, the I.W.W. leaders knew that any large industrial strike in wartime would arouse the country's enmity, for it would be labeled treachery to our boys in France. Bill Haywood advised the men in the ranks to proceed with caution until the war was over; but strikes broke out against the copper and timber industries in Arizona and Montana. Woodrow Wilson appointed lawyers to prosecute the I.W.W., and sent police against forty-eight of their halls in September 1917; three weeks later, 101 I.W.W. leaders faced trial in Chicago, after a Grand Jury had worked out conspiracy charges against them. The government had a biased judge on the bench in the person of a bad-tempered, half-educated little man who carried the resounding name of Kenesaw Mountain Landis. Even an admiring biographer of Landis, Mr. J. G. Taylor Spink, has recorded that he bullied lawyers and witnesses, and shamefully abused his powers, especially when he had poor or ignorant people facing his bench. As publisher of *The Sporting News,* Spink was interested in Landis because the judge became commissioner of professional baseball in 1920, the soft job and big pay a reward for his services to the franchise owners in a suit before his court that had challenged their monopoly. Up to the time he obtained this berth, Landis had made a national reputation by clowning as a homespun character in the press; by a decision subjecting the Standard Oil Company to a large fine, which was reversed by the Supreme Court; by the savagery of the jail sentences he handed out; and by his obvious hatred of the defendants at the I.W.W. trial. In the Chicago judicial tradition of Gary, Grosscup, and Woods, Landis made an unfavorable impression on John Reed, who wrote in one of his reports of the trial: "Small on the huge bench sits a wasted man with untidy white hair, an emaciated face in which two burning eyes are set like jewels, parchment-like skin split by a crack for a mouth; the face of Andrew Jackson three years dead."

Everyone in the United States knew the Wobblies, as I.W.W. members were called, would land in the penitentiary when the trial was over. Some thought they should be hanged, for how could there be a worse crime than disloyalty to the Flag, especially at a time of national danger when one might wake up any morning to see a squadron of Uhlans trotting in over Blue Island Avenue, U-boats on Lake Michigan, and Zeppelins overhead. That fear worked powerfully against the defendants, and there was added to it the raving fear of anarchy, which has never left Chicago. Speedy as light would be the trial convicting the Wobblies on a simple charge of treachery to the Allied cause, for their equal indifference to the other side would never count in their favor. But in order to give the thing some color of legality, the government had to bring conspiracy charges, its favorite weapon against citizens who get out of line. These charges were so complicated that the trial lasted five months. During that time, the 101 defendants were crowded into the verminous Cook County jail when not in court. Locked up among drunks and criminals, the Wobblies maintained group discipline and held on to their sanity, with the exception of a young wheatfield worker and artist named Henry Meyers. His hands had fashioned the death masks of six fellow workers killed by lynch mobs, vigilantes, and sheriffs. Now in Cook County jail he went mad, and they took him to an insane asylum.

In court Judge Landis raged on the bench, excluded evidence favorable to the defendants, and snarled at Haywood when he said he believed that the flags and symbols of patriotism had been so monopolized by the employing classes that they had little meaning for working men. At the end of August 1918 the jury took less than an hour to find the defendants guilty. Landis then released the tension within him by sentencing Haywood and fourteen others to twenty years each in prison. He sentenced the next thirty-three men on the list to ten years each, the next thirty-five to five years each, and the rest received sentences of one to three years. In addition Landis imposed fines of $30,000 each on Haywood and the other fourteen twenty-year men; the fines of the other defendants, and the I.W.W. as an organization, totaled more than $2,500,000. When Landis was done, Federal cops and soldiers chained the convicted men in a coffle and marched them through jeering crowds to take them to Leavenworth from the Dearborn Street station. As they marched, the prisoners sang "Solidarity Forever, for the Union Makes Us Strong."

Chicago as a whole applauded its venomous little judge. But the belligerent K. M. Landis, and the sanctimonious Woodrow Wilson, were not for Jane Addams or Harriet Monroe. Jane had already ended her friendship with that mighty man of valor, Theodore Roosevelt, by expressing opposition to war no matter who participated. The taking of this stand caused T.R. to call Miss Addams a foolish and dangerous woman. Some people in Chicago called Jane worse names than this, but she continued to do what she thought right. And Miss Monroe lost her chance for listing among the patriots in March 1918 when she asked "What right have we to send youth into battle while we keep our safe places by the fire? What right has the thinker to his problem, the artist to his vision, the poet to his song, while fresh lives are giving up their hope of thought and art and song?" And so, struggling against the paralysis of ethics that a virulent attack of patriotism had brought on, the conscience of Chicago managed to stay alive. But Edgar Masters wrote to Harriet that the war had filled him with such grief that all he could do was live one day at a time. As for poetry, "Can't write now—have nothing to offer you. . . ."

15

After the Silver Decade

NOVEMBER 11, 1918. WILLIAM LONIGAN, AGED FIFTEEN, CAME UP FROM the South Side with his gang to celebrate the victorious conclusion of America's war to make the world safe for democracy. The elevated train was packed with people, all delirious with joy, for Chicago had been the country's most patriotic city and the Irish district on the South Side the city's most patriotic neighborhood. On the train, a drunk sang "The Star-Spangled Banner," while another drunk on the back platform kept a cowbell ringing as he yelled, "To hell with the Kaiser." The motorman had the whistle howling when the rocked into Fifty-first Street station, and the conductor kept the doors closed, for the train already had taken on more passengers than it could safely carry; but they got to the Loop without accident, and Lonigan's gang rushed downstairs shouting, "To hell with Kaiser Bill!"

It was a great day all over Chicago but most especially in the Loop, where patriotic fervor generated an emotional pressure that had not been felt since the Civil War and the days of the mighty bullshooters, the silver-voiced tenors, the drums and uniforms and screaming eagles. Today was an occasion for even greater joyful excitement, for our boys had gone all the way to France to win the war and stamp out militarism. Young William Lonigan—Studs Lonigan to his friends—had never seen anything to equal the frenzied behavior of the crowds: he told Red Haggerty it was like a nuthouse on fire. Office workers were throwing tons of paper out the windows, auto horns were honking, drunks were fighting and yelling, and women were embracing any man in uniform, while musicians tried to form bands and lead improvised parades through streets so crowded that automobiles could not get through, to say nothing of people trying to march and carry flags. And then, as Studs' creator James T. Farrell recorded,* "He suddenly looked up through the noise and falling paper, and there was Old Glory on a flag pole, furled in the breeze, glinting in the November sunlight—Old Glory that had never kissed the dust in defeat, and he could see it floating, flying over the trenches, ruins, corpses of the fields of France, again Victorious! Old Glory! His Flag! Proudly he told himself: 'I'm an American.' "

The furious joy of Armistice Day in Chicago revived a few weeks later when a detachment of the Black Hawk Division came through on its way to demobilize at Camp Grant. Arriving at La Salle Street station early in the morning of January 13, 1919, the soldiers went to the Coliseum, then marched back up Michigan Avenue and into the Loop just before lunchtime. Their appearance sent a wave of emotion over the city, and at 11:30 A.M. they fell out at State Street and Jackson Boulevard to start on a program of hospitality that continued for twelve hours. As the last train pulled out for camp early next morning, Colonel Philip R. Ward told reporters: "These men can't say much, as they are too deeply stirred for words. But they will never forget it as long as time lasts. It's the greatest thing I have ever seen or heard of. Old Chicago is showing her heart, which is as big as the world."

Another enthusiastic welcome greeted 1,278 Negro soldiers of the 370th U.S. Infantry, on their return a month later. But the social part of the 370th's homecoming was in the hands of Negroes, who arranged banquets, receptions, and dances for the men at various halls and churches in the black section of the South Side. White Chicago's formal welcome was expressed in the voice of Mayor William Hale Thompson, who did indeed have some sympathy for Negroes in addition to a desire for their votes. Big Bill Thompson said, "There may be other battles yet to fight for our country, and if there should be it is safe to predict that the Negro citizen and soldier of the future, like his ancestors of the past and present generations, may be relied upon to stand steadfast in support of the principles of our great republic."

Thompson's words had the hollow sound that typified official utterance in his time. Bloated today with the wisdom that arrives after events, a student may trace the rising use of meaningless verbiage as an index of

*In his great realistic novel *Young Lonigan.*

sickness in old Chicago's heart, that the rest of the country was soon enough to share. For it has turned out that when things go wrong in the United States, the warning signs and preliminary troubles occur in Chicago, though not always receiving immediate recognition as symptoms of disease. At the time of the Negro soldiers' return, for example, Populism came to the surface at a socialist mass meeting in the Coliseum; speakers expressed sympathy for the Russian Bolshevist revolutionaries, and called for a dictatorship of the proletariat in the United States. In rebuttal, the *Daily News* editorialized that any speaker or journalist who advocated such a thing "writes himself down a poor citizen and poor thinker. Such doctrines should be repudiated by the wage earner, as they are sure to be repudiated by every other truly American element of our population that has grasped the meaning of our institutions and our national ideas and principles." The fact was that the truly American elements of the population looked on socialist orators and editorial writers with equal indifference throughout the first years after the war, with a time of thrilling prosperity in sight; and today one has no license to blame them. The country had its problems; but for the average man with a job and family, the main problem then as now was to take care of his own.

There was one problem in the northern cities, however, that lingered on the edge of most people's minds; and it caused a continuing uneasiness, like the shadow of a detached retina, refusing to disappear. The question was, how to find work and housing for the Negroes back from war who would not return to the rural South. In Chicago, the main black belt of the city, sometimes called Bronzeville, held 100,000 Negroes who had settled in what had once been residential neighborhoods of the white middle class. The area extended across Washington Park from the university, and south of the former Levee district from Twenty-first to Sixty-third streets. Old Man Lonigan, Studs's father, was a moderately successful contractor who saw no prospects of building for these Negroes. He resented their presence in Chicago and asked what the world was coming to. Throughout the South Side, Polish and Bohemian businessmen and factory foremen were now the possessors of comfortable houses. They enjoyed their neighborhood life, wanted no changes, and agreed with Mr. Lonigan when he called it outrageous that colored people should settle nearby. The newspapers did not try to hide this problem of racial distrust, and the reporters often made a more valuable contribution to the discussion than their editorializing colleagues. One reporter who dug for the facts was Carl Sandburg, now on the *Daily News*. Wearing a flat cap on the middle of his head, Sandburg went into the South Side on July 13, 1919, to work up a series of stories on life in Bronzeville. Sandburg had published his

Chicago Poems in 1916, and knowing the city as he did, recognized a new type of metropolitan entrepreneur in the real estate brokers who were beginning to formulate procedures that led them to adopt the professional title of realtor.* Sandburg found a white realtor on Wentworth Avenue, at that time a boundary between white and black, and asked the man if he cared to say anything about the bomb explosions that frequently occurred on the porches of the houses rented to Negroes in the white neighborhood east of Wentworth Avenue. The broker told Sandburg, "Not one cent has been appropriated by our real estate board for bombing or anything like that. But I would say to the Negroes, 'We might as well be frank about it. You people are not admitted to our society.' " Then as the towheaded unsmiling reporter took down his words, the realtor continued, "Oh, I've done business with them and they've paid. I've never had to foreclose. But, you know, improvements are coming along the lakeshore, the Illinois Central and all that. We can't have these people coming over here. They injure our investments. They hurt our values. I can't say how many have moved in, but there's at least a hundred blocks that are tainted. We are not making any threats, but we do say that something must be done. Of course, if they come in as tenants, we can handle that situation fairly easily. But when they get a deed, that's another matter. Be sure to get us straight on that. We want to be fair and do what's right." Continuing his search for material, Sandburg talked to a Negro Y.M.C.A. secretary, who told him "The colored people see that if they can't make it in Chicago, it's no use for them to go back South. But there has always been fighting between the Black Belt and the Wentworth Avenue crowd." Sandburg saw that conflicting social forces were about to cause an explosion, and so informed his readers in the *Daily News*. The racial situation reminded some men in Chicago of the week preceding the fire in 1871 when the city had been full of combustible material waiting for a spark.

The conflagration exploded at the end of July and lasted for five days in a race riot that served as a model for such disturbances in years to come. The pattern that Chicago furnished the country began in a mixed crowd, and crowding was partly responsible for all that followed. The black and white people who used the Thirty-first Street beach on the South Side had informally divided the bathing area; a Negro boy intruded in white waters, a fight broke out, and the boy drowned. Some said a white youth had thrown a rock and knocked him under; at any rate, the child was dead. The weather was oppressive, the city nervous because of a trolley car-

*Sinclair Lewis made Chicago the Paris and London of the realtors' great patron George F. Babbitt.

[337]

men's strike; word of race trouble flashed through the South Side like fire from the O'Leary barn, and fighting gangs went into the streets. Studs Lonigan left his usual haunts around Fifty-eighth Street and Indiana Avenue to join a group led by the three toughs Red Kelly, Paulie Haggerty, and Tommy Doyle. They caught a small colored boy on Wabash Avenue, burned his legs with cigarettes, urinated on him, and sent him home naked. That was the greatest feat by members of Studs's gang, but other youths of the same sort killed and were killed in the fighting. After two days of this, on Wednesday July 30, Mayor Thompson sent militia companies into the South Side. The troops entered the riot zone in trucks and taxicabs; according to the papers, they had more trouble with white people than black. One militiaman killed a white man with his bayonet for refusing to move on. In all, fourteen whites and twenty-two blacks ended on slabs in the Cook County morgue as a result of this civil war. They had died in various ways, some shot, some knifed, some trampled with their spines stamped to bits and their chests and faces kicked in. On August 4, the *Daily News* front page displayed an eight-column headline: DEATH TO RIOTERS, JUDGE ASKS. The jurist was Robert R. Crowe, calling for a special grand jury to hang ruffians who participated in mob violence. Crowe said that anarchists had started the trouble, and the time had come to teach them "the lesson that was taught a lot of similar hoodlums through the execution of the Haymarket Square anarchists."

As usual after a disaster, commissions and committees sprang up to study what had happened and make reports. Official findings on the Chicago riots filled thousands of pages, emphasizing the obvious: Negroes and working class whites lived at best in a state of temporary truce where the exigencies of metropolitan housing crowded them together. The white proletariat knew nothing and cared less about the Negroes who formed an upper class in Bronzeville: these were doctors and lawyers, along with some businessmen and bankers, who could live well, travel, and send their children to college. It was lonely at the top of the Bronzeville social pyramid, for there were not many black elite, and their counterparts in white Chicago refused to honor their credentials as cultivated people who might be worth meeting in a social way. The lonely upper-class citizens of Bronzeville were themselves practitioners of color snobbery. Sociologists have recorded, for example, that Robert Sengstacke Abbott, publisher of the *Chicago Defender,* the leading Negro newspaper, though said to be the first black millionaire, suffered a social handicap because he was so *intensely* black; and it could not be denied that the leading families of Bronzeville preferred light-skinned suitors for their daughters, and light-skinned maidens as objects of admiration by their sons. One of the greatest of all Chicagoans was a Negro, Dr. Daniel Hale Williams, and he had such light pigmentation that he could have passed out of Bronzeville and into the white world. But he chose to be a Negro.

Born in a small Pennsylvania town, Daniel Hale Williams had gone to Wisconsin as a youth, and studied zoology, Latin, and mathematics at an academy in Janesville.* Williams later enrolled as a doctor's assistant, went on to the Chicago Medical College, graduated there in 1883, and opened an office at Michigan Avenue and Thirty-first Street in a mixed black and white neighborhood. It was then that Dr. Williams made his choice, identified himself with Negroes, and started a surgical practice among black patients. Because of these people's poverty, Daniel Williams had to perform many of his operations on kitchen tables, but he proved so brilliant a surgeon that he received hospital appointments, a post as clinical instructor at the Medical College, and a seat on the Illinois State Board of Health. In 1891, Dr. Williams organized the biracial Provident Hospital in order to set up the first Negro nurses' training school in the United States. Dr. Williams took contributions from Philip Armour, Marshall Field, George Pullman, and Herman Henry Kohlsaat, the wealthy baker who bought the *Chicago Inter-Ocean,* raising enough money to open Provident Hospital in May 1891, on Fifty-first Street opposite Washington Park, amid much enthusiasm from the neighborhood it was to serve. Professor Redding has recorded that on opening day Negroes came bringing gifts of sheets, beds, old linen, sugar, soap, black current jelly, and loaves of bread. And some contributed eggs, butter, and vegetables on a regular basis thereafter. Money continued hard to come by, and at the end of its first year, in which one third of the patients had been white, Provident showed a deficit. The hospital survived, although Dr. Williams roused resentment by insisting on standards for doctors and nurses that excluded some Negroes; and it turned out that those colored people obtaining staff appointments and nurses' training were nearly always of the ghetto's lighter-skinned class. Dr. Williams never found a satisfactory answer to this question of discrimination among those who were themselves objects of discrimination. But his professional achievements were remarkable, including as they did the first performance of surgery on the human heart. Dr. Williams gave Chicago this outstanding event in scientific history when the police brought a street fighter to Provident in July 1893. The man had a knife wound in his chest to the left of the breastbone, and when Dr. Williams bent above him, he went into a frenzy of coughing and collapsed from

*An extended account of Dr. Daniel Hale Williams may be found in Saunders Redding's *Lonesome Road.*

shock. The book said to treat heart wounds with ice packs, opium, and rest. The opium was to deaden pain, and the rest soon became eternal, for the patient always died. Dr. Williams decided to venture into the unknown, and challenge death, as Saunders Redding put it, with the weapons at his command, which did not include x-ray photographs or sulfa drugs. Assisted by four white surgeons, Daniel Williams opened the patient's chest, and for the first time sewed up a living heart. Fifty-one days later, the man walked out of Provident, to live for twenty years. When news of the operation got around, Dr. Williams gave only one interview, using it to publicize the interracial policies at Provident Hospital. In the following year, Daniel Williams went to Washington and took charge of the Freedmen's Hospital, the government institution for Negroes, founded after the Civil War, now little better than a medieval pesthouse because of graft. Dr. Williams cleaned the place up, put in a competent interracial staff, and operated before audiences of surgeons and students from Johns Hopkins and the University of Pennsylvania. The politics of color castes within the race began to hamper Dr. Williams, and it was all the more painful to him because he sympathized with his opponents. The trouble was that many influential Negroes wanted successful institutions and notable achievements that might be called entirely black; yet Daniel Williams could see no way for Negroes to achieve social and economic equality except by cooperating with white people, as he did. Although his biracial methods accomplished good things at Freedmen's, so much opposition developed that Dr. Williams decided he could no longer be useful there, and he returned to Chicago and Provident Hospital, where he worked through the early 1900s as one of the world's most famous and trusted surgeons, a resident of the ghetto, and a representative of its people. His constant objective was to get Negro doctors into staff appointments at hospitals and postgraduate studies at universities. But few Negro doctors, as Professor Redding recorded, had either time or money for postgraduate work: "Their associations with advantaged white men in the profession were one-sided and tenuous. They were admitted to the Chicago Medical Society and could attend its discussions, but listening to papers was an entirely different thing from studying problems in the morgue and the laboratory, and from watching men at work on them in surgery. And this was what Dr. Dan wanted. He resumed the associations with white men that had been cut off by four years of absence." In 1908, Dr. Williams accepted an appointment as associate attending surgeon at St. Luke's, and his critics seized it as an opportunity to force his resignation from Provident. In 1913, when the American Academy of Surgeons came into existence, Daniel Hale Williams was a charter member. Saddened as he was in his last years by the arguments about where his loyalties lay, this great Chicagoan had the satisfaction of knowing that on the nights of rioting in 1919, Provident Hospital cared for the wounded whether they were white or black.

The ugliness of hatred and fear that caused social tensions did not reflect itself in Chicago's outer aspect before and after the war. When the Blackstone Hotel went up in 1909, central Chicago began to alter its appearance, and much new construction came on the scene, succeeding the Richardsonian Romanesque. Counting from January 1, 1909, to December 31, 1916, after which the pace of building slackened for the two years of U.S. participation in the war, the value of new Chicago buildings reached a total of $775,000,000 hard money. Many splendid designs took shape from the prints as Chicago architects looked for a metropolitan style to suit the grandeur of a city that numbered more than two million inhabitants at the end of 1909, an increase of half a million through the previous decade. In this year the firm of Holabird and Roche saw completion of their La Salle Hotel at the northwest corner of La Salle and West Madison streets, with one of the world's handsomest ballrooms on the twenty-second floor. These architects added a landmark to the lakefront in the same year with the University Club on the northwest corner of Monroe Street and Michigan Avenue. They put Gothic dress on their fourteen-story building, and again designed a great room for the top, which served as the dining area known as Cathedral Hall. The room had stained glass windows, and paneled walls decorated with college arms, the work of German woodcarvers. Clockwise from the upper left-hand corner of the Michigan Avenue wall one saw the heraldry of Brown, Northwestern, Illinois, Wisconsin, Harvard, Dartmouth, Amherst, Beloit, the Massachusetts Institute of Technology, Williams, Princeton, Yale, the University of Chicago, Columbia, Michigan, Wesleyan, and Cornell. Some of the escutcheons carried mottoes, such as Virtue Rejoices in Trial (Dartmouth), True Science with Pure Faith (Beloit), For Christ and the Church (Harvard), and The Word . . . Full of Grace and Truth (Northwestern). An example of the picturesque with a lighter touch than Richardson's, the University Club has worn well through the years on the Michigan Avenue skyline, although architectural historians ignore it, and Frank Lloyd Wright denounced the building as "an effete gray ghost." But there was nothing effete about the Blackstone Theater that Marshall and Fox installed behind the hotel in 1911, and no one thought of bringing such a charge against the Chicago and North Western railway station, completed that same year at North Canal, West Madison, and North Clinton streets, on the west side of the Chicago River. This tremendous station was designed by Charles S. Frost and Alfred Hoyt Granger to show the possibilities of monumental construction outside the Loop. Two years later, D. H. Burnham and Company completed the Butler Brothers warehouses, a pair of titanic buildings on Canal Street just north of the station. One of these huge structures was to be demolished in 1920 to make way for additional tracks into the Union Station, and would be replaced two years later by another building, exactly like it, on Canal Street across Randolph to the north. Meanwhile in the time between the completion of the North Western station and the Butler warehouses, Holabird and Roche had continued to put their mark on commercial Chicago with new buildings identified as Ryerson, Otis, Rand McNally, Illinois Bell Telephone, North American Insurance, and the Monroe, which stood across the street from the University Club on Michigan Avenue. By 1912 the Field Museum of Natural History was completed, after prodigious feats of land filling by the engineer Joachim Giaver, who had also put down the underpinning of the Railway Exchange and Orchestra Hall. Built in five years from designs by the D. H. Burnham office, the museum took its commanding place on elevated ground in the southern end of Grand Park at Twelfth Street (now Roosevelt Road); in accordance with the Chicago Plan, South Lake Shore Drive parted to left and right around it. In 1913, further commercial development outside the Loop took place when the office and storage building of Reid, Murdoch and Company went up on the north side of the river east of the forks and La Salle Street. George Croll Nimmons designed this building to occupy a water frontage of 320 feet, and it survives to the present day as a successful attempt to add commercial and esthetic values to the riverbank opposite Wacker Drive.

During these years, living in apartments came to have wide appeal, and there was no limit to the luxury and elegance that architects provided for those who could pay the rents in new buildings along Lake Shore Drive and the nearby streets of the Gold Coast. Benjamin Marshall had entered the field as early as 1900, with his Raymond Apartments at 920 North Michigan Avenue, remodeled into shops and studios twenty-six years later. In 1906, Marshall presented 1100 Lake Shore Drive to the nobility and gentry. This building is still to be admired at the northwest corner of East Cedar Street, and it offered one apartment per floor in its eight stories, each equaling a town house in convenience and space. On its floor plan, which the real estate firm of Baird and Warner showed only to "individuals and families of unquestioned standing," No. 1100 offered not an elevator nor even a lift, but an *ascenseur* by which the tenant rose to his floor, entering the Salle De Réception, from which he could proceed to the Grand Salon with its bow windows overlooking the Oak Street Beach and the seascape of the lake; or he could enter a sun room called the Orang-erie; or he could step into his Salle de Billard, in each room walking on a floor of honey-colored oak, selected for its grain, and laid by sons of the Italian craftsmen who had worked on Palmer Castle. The tenant dined in a Salle à Manger, slept in a Grande Chambre à Coucher that had a fire-place for chilly mornings. And in hot weather he could ring for refresh-ments prepared in a room especially designed for the cooling of fruit and summer punches. The rent was high at five thousand dollars a year.

Howard Van Doren Shaw drew the plans for the handsomest apartment house erected in 1910, still to be seen in the 1970s at 1130 Lake Shore Drive on the northwest corner of East Elm Street, making the gargantuan towers of more recent construction look cheap and pretentious. Two years later and one block north, Benjamin Marshall again supplied the drive with a fine building, at No. 1200 on the northwest corner of East Division Street. The elegant tan tower, twelve stories high, was listed in Baird and Warner's *Portfolio of Fine Apartment Homes* as one of the new places of residence that met "the changed conditions of modern metropolitan life." At No. 1200 tenants found a *chambre pour malles* (trunkroom) in each apartment, and plenty of extra space available elsewhere in the building, since only ten families were to accommodate themselves in the thirteen stories. The first two floors provided quarters for butlers, chauffeurs, housemaids, and laundresses, while the top floor contained a children's playroom, a gymnasium, and additional rooms for servants.

William Ernest Walker was another architect who had mastered apart-ment design, and he contributed No. 936 Lake Shore Drive on the north-west corner of East Walton Street, which began the wall of beautifully kept houses that was to reach one block north, curve east with the drive at the Oak Street Beach, and finish in 1920 with the Drake Hotel at Michigan Avenue. The block that began at Walton Street showed the visual effectiveness of uniform height, and also gave some idea of the splendid effects that a metropolitan residential lakefront could achieve. Walker's ten-story building at No. 936 opened fully rented in 1913, and by 1917 had one sub-lease available for a carefully selected tenant. Making ingenious use of an irregular lot, Walker presented what may have been Chicago's first duplex apartments, at 942 Lake Shore Drive, in 1915. That was the year in which Benjamin Marshall crowned this line of lakefront buildings with No. 199 on East Lake Shore Drive, the jog in the boulevard that set off Oak Street Beach on the south. Marshall named this building the Breakers because in windy weather the tenants could see and hear the surf coming in over the beach no more than 150 feet from their windows. On a stormy night, the apartments at No. 199 might give the feeling of being aboard on ocean liner: starting from the library fireplace, one could walk seventy feet through the dining and sun rooms to the drawing room; and one could hold a dance in the space provided by opening the sun room into the oval entrance hall.

In 1916 the 200 East Pearson Street Apartments were built on the corner of Seneca Street from designs by Robert S. De Golyer, who later planned the handsome Pearson Hotel on the other side of Seneca Street,* and the elegant apartment houses at 1242 and 1430 Lake Shore Drive. Howard Shaw added a building to Seneca Street at East Walton Place in 1916, increasing the general charm of this neighborhood which was two short blocks west of the lake. On spring evenings, men and women in evening clothes walked to dinner parties in the area, or to dances at the Casino, whose clubhouse on Delaware Place had been decorated by Mrs. John Alden Carpenter, the composer's wife. Also a moving spirit in the Chicago Arts Club, and a member of the Fairbank set, Rue Carpenter was one of the taste-making decorators in this country during the first three decades of the twentieth century.

Because of the war, new Chicago building fell off sharply in 1917 to a total value of $65,000,000, half that of the previous year, and in 1918 it declined to $35,000,000. However, the apartment house at 1550 North State Parkway (continuation of State Street), at North Avenue, had been previously financed, and this masterpiece by Benjamin Marshall came to completion in 1918. The twelve stories looked out over the southern reach of Lincoln Park with Dr. Greene V. Black benign on his monument, and offered the finest apartments, one to a floor above the entrance level, that Chicago had yet seen. The specifications and drawings in the Baird and Warner portfolio showed that the kitchen and pantry sinks were made of German silver, although the floor plans were marked in French. It seemed no more than right that this building should have the most prominent listing in that volume, as well as in Pardridge and Bradley's *Directory to Apartments of the Better Class on the North Side of Chicago.* Servants were handy at No. 1550 in five *chambres de domestique* for each apartment; in addition to the elevators, two stairways rose in the central well, an *escalier de service* and an *escalier principal,* but one would expect everything to be first class at a rental of $8,400 a year. For this one got a grand salon and a petit salon, along with the orangerie and the circular rooms at the north and south ends of the building where round towers engaged the corners. The main bedroom had two dressing rooms "so that a valet can enter the gentleman's dressing room without passing through

*Destroyed in 1971.

the bedchamber." Other refinements included a *caveau de vin* from which the butler could bring selected bottles, a garbage chute in each kitchen direct to basement incinerators, and a range with three broilers, two gas and one charcoal, "so that steaks and fish need never be prepared on the same broiler."

Another previously financed project went to completion in the war years when the State-Lake Theater was completed in the Loop at the southwest corner of the streets indicated by its name. One of the first great baroque movie palaces, the State-Lake flourished during the years in which a visit to the Loop after dark was a family treat, or a pleasing attention by a young man to his girl. And by the time the 1920s got under way, the age of movies had come, providing a mirror in which Chicago was to see an unreal melodramatic picture of itself that it came to imitate and so at last make partly true; for along with that of moving pictures, the era of prohibition also began, on January 17, 1920, when an act to enforce the constitutional amendment forbidding the sale or manufacture of liquor took effect.

The work of Frances Willard and her colleagues had at last brought the nation this law regulating private conduct on a scale never attempted before, attached and bolted down presumably for all the ages to the Constitution, a sacred document powerful in its magic as the Flag itself. Miss Willard had known quite well whose commercial interest in Chicago she had consistently threatened; and Hinky Dink Kenna, saturating his forlorn alcoholics in the First Ward, had recognized his enemies in Evanston. He had sent Miss Willard one of the huge beer glasses used in his saloon; Miss Willard returned a note of thanks, and made the goblet a flowerpot in WCTU headquarters. When Prohibition finally arrived, Frances Willard had been dead for twenty-two years, but Kenna and Bathhouse John Coughlin were still healthy, and in control of the First Ward. The question before them was, how to make money from illegal liquor.

Big Jim Colosimo had continued as executive officer for Hinky Dink and the Bath, but there was trouble here, for Colosimo had grown tired of his hard-working wife, Victoria Moresco. His indifference to Victoria had grown rapidly in the winter of 1919–20, after he engaged a girl named Dale Winter to sing at the Wabash Avenue cafe. This young woman, a respectable musical-comedy actress, had been embarrassed when the manager of a roadshow walked out leaving the artistes with salaries unpaid. Dale had taken the Wabash Avenue job as a temporary expedient, but Big Jim saw she was real class and fell in love with her. It is more remarkable that Dale Winter returned Colosimo's affection; Asbury writes that "perhaps she glimpsed a spark of decency in his black soul." At any rate, Colosimo got fast service in the courts on his divorce action, ridding himself of Victoria in March 1920. Within three weeks he had married Dale Winter, and they returned from the wedding trip early in May. Less than a week later, on the afternoon of May 11, Colosimo went to the café, discussed routine matters with two employees, and walked from the kitchen through the empty restaurant to the lobby. The employees heard shots, and found Colosimo dead from a bullet that had torn off the back of his skull.

The Colosimo funeral took place on May 15, the most extraordinary thing of its kind that Chicago had seen, and its citizens were connoisseurs of such displays, having given that tremendous funeral to Carter Harrison I; and they carried in civic memory the grand ceremonial passage of Abraham Lincoln's body. Cardinal Mundelein barred Colosimo from burial in holy ground, and shut the doors of all Catholic churches against services for him, because of his divorce and remarriage. The mourners found a clergyman, the Rev. Pasquale de Carol, who conducted services at Colosimo's Vernon Avenue mansion. Then a tremendous procession lined up for the march to Oakwoods Cemetery, the place where Red Top lay buried. Leading off were 1,000 members of the First Ward Democratic Club, headed by the Bath and Hinky Dink, every man keeping time to the wailing measures of an augmented brass band, wearing the required silk hat, and carrying the customary rolled umbrella, with broad bands of black ribbon on coat-sleeves. Open carriages crammed with flowers followed; one display took the form of a huge clock with a dial of red and white carnations, the hands pointing to the time when Colosimo fell dead. Three judges rode next, mourning the dead pander; an Assistant State's Attorney bowed to the crowds from an open car; walking because of their inferior social rank, nine aldermen trudged along, shoulder to shoulder with such persons as Ike Bloom, and Johnny Torrio who had very probably ordered the Colosimo kill; and after the judges, officials, politicians, and gunmen, there came large detachments of city employees, courthouse bums, pimps, loafers, and thieves, to the number of about four thousand, bringing up the rear. It was the first but by no means the last great open ceremony in Chicago symbolizing and demonstrating that crime and politics were two aspects of the same thing.

Observers of the South Side underworld theorized that Johnny Torrio had condemned Colosimo in order to get more money for himself by taking control of the lucrative rackets that Big Jim conducted under political license from Kenna and Bathhouse John. The police believed that Torrio had brought in Frankie Uale, the New York head of the Unione

Siciliana, to commit the murder, and they found a witness who saw Uale enter the café shortly before the shooting. But the officers were not overcome with astonishment a few days later when their witness refused to confirm the identification. Considering the entire situation, one is willing to credit Torrio with the executive action that brought about Big Jim's death. But there may have been more to it. Cardinal Mundelein's disapproval of Colosimo's divorce was shared by a conservative, church-going element among bawds and panders that valued family ties as much as anyone, and in addition to this part of the community, one must consider Victoria Moresco Colosimo, the discarded wife. Furthermore, Hinky Dink was a religious man who gave to the church, his wife a paragon of piety. And it seems certain that the Bath would have voted for a rubout, because Colosimo appeared to be neglecting business and losing money. Torrio as chief of security had Iago's reason for bitterness, having borne responsibilities for years without promotion, while Colosimo, as the ascetic Torrio would see it, had done nothing but grow fatter on spaghetti and wine. Taking it all in all, the human probability appears to be that Victoria talked over her injuries with Mr. and Mrs. Torrio, that Hinky Dink's wife had plenty to say about the divorce, that Bathhouse John didn't like the look of things, and that Colosimo died victim of both economics and ethics, a hard combination to beat.

Now that Torrio had stepped up from director of security to chief executive officer, he laid down the pistol, knife, and bomb, to confine himself to formulating policy, leaving field work to his juniors. As deputy he brought to Chicago a hoodlum who was to become the most famous criminal of modern times—Scarface Al Capone. Originating in Brooklyn, Scarface Al was twenty-three years old when he joined the Torrio mob. He had earned a reputation as a slugger who did not hesitate to maim his victims, and the police believed that he had killed at least two men before his arrival in Chicago. Within five years, Capone and Torrio had built up a chain of suburban road-houses, where they supplied the services of prostitutes, and sold illegal beer and whiskey twenty-four hours a day. By bribery and violence, they corrupted Chicago Heights, Blue Island, Burr Oaks, Stickney, Forest View, and other Cook County towns west and southwest of Chicago, transforming them in Asbury's words "from peaceful suburbs into brothel-ridden Babylons."

Most widely known of the corrupted suburbs was Cicero, a municipality southeast of Oak Park, populated mostly by Bohemian workers from the steel mills and stockyards who took pride in their neat yards and houses. When Prohibition came, a West Side gangster known as Klondike O'Donnell appointed himself purveyor of beer and liquor to this town of fifty thousand, distributing the stuff to the existing saloons, and working with his brother Myles and two politicians named Eddie Vogel and Eddie Tancl. All went well for the O'Donnells and the two Eddies until Capone moved into the territory, and took it under his control after a year of violence in the streets. The O'Donnells surrendered and accepted staff appointments with Capone and Torrio; but Tancl refused to knuckle under. In November 1924, Torrio ordered Tancl to leave Cicero; he refused, whereupon Myles O'Donnell picked a fight and shot him dead. During that year, deputized Chicago police entered Cicero, chased Capone down Cicero Avenue with bullets snapping past his ears, and killed his brother Frank in a gun fight. It was said that the flowers for Frank's funeral cost twenty thousand dollars; again Chicago enjoyed the spectacle of politicians and officials in public mourning for a human louse. By 1926, conditions were such that the public was only mystified, and not surprised, when Assistant State's Attorney William H. McSwiggin was found murdered on a Cicero street. He had been an enemy of the South Side O'Donnells, four hoodlum brothers who were enemies of Torrio and Capone, and no relation to Klondike and Myles. As chief of staff heading an army of nearly eight hundred gunmen, Capone might well have ordered McSwiggin's death in an effort to incriminate the South Side O'Donnell clan; at any rate, he drove them out of business, made the Torrio mob supreme on the South Side, and set up headquarters in Cicero, at the Hawthorne Inn on Twenty-second Street. Here the first panoply of hulking, shoulder-holstered sentries at steel-shuttered windows and electrically operated doors was to be observed, later the familiar staging in hundreds of moving picture scenes. When he came out of this fortress and moved through the streets of Cicero, Capone showed no respect for the municipal authorities. He was especially insolent toward the mayor, whose name was Joseph Z. Klenka; on one occasion Al publicly upbraided the mayor, threw him down the City Hall steps, and kicked him when he tried to get up from the sidewalk. Capone also broke up meetings of the town council, and silenced critics and local editors by knocking them unconscious with his blackjack.

As the 1920s rolled along, it was said that the payroll of Johnny Torrio's personal staff came to $1,600,000 a year, plus an incalculably greater amount for politicians. On the industrial side of the ledger, Torrio was reported to have paid one brewer $1,000,000 per month for the product of a Chicago brewery that continued operating despite the Volstead Act; and an estimate by Federal investigators put the gross income of the Torrio-Capone enterprises at seventy million dollars a year. As he got older and richer, Torrio grew conservative, and much desired to remove the element of personal risk from his activities. He had good reason to give this matter serious thought, for his rule extended only over the South Side, Cicero, and the other Babylonized suburbs. But on the North Side, the former choirboy who headed the thugs and hoodlums referred to Torrio and Capone as guinea bastards, and spat whenever anyone mentioned their names. This intrepid gang chieftain was Dion O'Banion, most picturesque of Chicago gunmen, and the last great Irish criminal in the city's history. Said to have been the killer of at least twenty-five men, O'Banion took a hand in labor unions, various forms of extortion and thievery, and with the advent of Prohibition became a liquor distributor on the same scale as Torrio and Capone. He also served the Democratic politicians by delivering the Forty-second and Forty-third Wards at election time; but he gave his allegiance, and the two wards, to the Republicans in the election of 1924 which kept Big Bill Thompson in the mayor's chair.

In line with his policy of reducing violence, Torrio gave O'Banion a part of the Cicero beer business, which kept things quiet for a while. Then O'Banion complained that the five Genna brothers, officers of the Unione Siciliana and vassals of Torrio, had trespassed on the North Side. When Torrio failed to curb his men O'Banion expressed displeasure by giving information to the police regarding the ownership of a brewery, which resulted in a five-thousand-dollar fine and a sentence of nine months in jail for Johnny Torrio. At this insulting betrayal, Al Capone and the Gennas advised Torrio to eliminate O'Banion and his lieutenant Hymie Weiss.

An odd aspect of O'Banion's personality was his interest in flowers, which had led him to buy a half-interest in a shop on North Clark Street opposite the Cathedral, and to practice the trade of floral designer. O'Banion booked a large order for part of the display at the funeral of Mike Merlo, a Torrio lieutenant who died of natural causes on November 8, 1924. This order came from Torrio himself, and Scarface Al sent in an additional request for a gigantic floral bleeding heart. O'Banion may have taken this patronage as evidence that the South Siders were peacefully inclined toward him, and he worked on the orders throughout Sunday, November 9, making everything ready by noon the following day. At that point, three men entered the shop, and a porter working in the back room heard O'Banion greet them familiarly, and ask if they had come about the flowers for the Merlo funeral. It is easy to reconstruct what happened in the next few seconds: O'Banion had a pair of shears in his left hand, one visitor seized his right hand so that he could not draw his pistol, and the other two visitors killed him with six shots through his body and head. The porter looked out and saw O'Banion on the floor among the cuttings, and three men running out of the shop.

Word soon came through underworld sources that the three visitors were Albert Anselmi, John Scalisi, and Mike Genna. They still lived while O'Banion's funeral was taking place, after forty thousand people had viewed his body, the carnation in his buttonhole replaced every hour. A police escort from Stickney, one of the Babylons, accompanied the coffin to Mount Carmel Cemetery, and a procession of ten thousand persons marched with them, stretching for a mile behind twenty-five open automobiles full of flowers; the newspapers said these people encountered ten thousand additional mourners waiting at the grave.

The ferocious Hymie Weiss inherited O'Banion's North Side interest, and evidently felt that business considerations as well as revenge obliged him to hit the South Siders hard. Accompanied by two of his ablest gunmen, Bugs Moran and Schemer Drucci, Weiss fired on Capone's car at State and Fifty-fifth streets, wounding the driver, but Al had left the car just before Weiss pulled alongside. That was on January 12, 1925; twelve days later, two North Side gangsters put five bullets into Johnny Torrio as he was returning to his home near Jackson Park. Torrio survived, and after weeks in the hospital, went to jail to serve the nine months that O'Banion's treachery had brought on him. After that Torrio went back to Italy, supposedly taking along a big fortune; some of the papers estimated that this ratlike man had accumulated thirty million dollars during his infamous career in Chicago.

After Torrio's departure there came a five-year period of wild and sometimes almost senseless gang warfare in which no strategy could be discerned other than the old one of devil take the hindmost. Myles and Klondike O'Donnell deserted Capone to join forces with Hymie Weiss, two of the Gennas died at the hands of North Siders, and Mike Genna met death in a battle with police. In September 1926 a party of North Side gunmen attacked the Capone headquarters at Cicero in daylight, firing machine guns, pistols, and shotguns. Scarface Al lay on the floor during the fusillade and escaped injury. Three weeks later, Hymie Weiss lay dead, cut down by machine gun bullets fired from the ambush of a lodging-house room where the marksman had lurked for three days waiting for Weiss to come by.

The police killed Schemer Drucci, who succeeded Weiss as commander of the North Side mobsters. Next in line came Bugs Moran, who held command when the North Siders sustained the terrific attack in the garage at No. 2122 North Clark Street, a slaughter that took place on St. Valentine's Day. Six gangsters and one noncriminal who had the bad luck to be there at the time were shot to pieces with machine guns on that February day in 1929. Underworld information identified the executioners as John

Scalisi, Joseph Guinta and Albert Anselmi of the Capone gang. These men were found dead in Douglas Park three months later. Presumably Bugs Moran had put them there, but students of Chicago crime theorized that Capone might have betrayed the three gunmen to Moran because he himself was beginning to fear them. Someone had thoroughly smashed the bodies in addition to riddling them with bullets; and police and newspapermen were told by informants that Capone had invited Guinta, Scalisi, and Anselmi to a banquet, after which he knocked their heads in with a baseball bat. There was no question that Capone was capable of such an act, and no doubt at all that Scarface Al had become the head gangster of the entire city not long after the wounding of Johnny Torrio. He held this position, with ferocity and brutality unprecedented even in Chicago, until his downfall in 1931.

During the years that Capone reigned as supreme lord of crime and vice in Chicago, he was also the city's most famous personage, and received much adulation and respect throughout the world. This was due in part to the lively Chicago papers, with their tradition of exploiting local characters and color; and in part to the new talking movies, in which skilled actors such as Paul Muni and Edward G. Robinson gave fascinating performances as Italian gangsters in Chicago.* The star performers and exciting stories made hoodlums appear to be glamorous, while in actuality they were among the dullest human beings who ever lived. If it were not for their supplying of beer and whiskey, two necessary staples for millions of people, the mobsters of the Prohibition era would have remained mostly out of sight, as such rogues had customarily remained in previous years. But the fabulous wealth of the illegal booze industry brought them into the open, to see and be seen in places of public resort. Capone himself often attended the theater, accompanied by eight guards, using nine seats on three rows in this pattern:

. . .

. * .

. . .

Other patrons in the theater would crane to see the famous personage. The flabby, pig-eyed Capone wasn't much to look at, but men told it proudly at the office next day if they caught a glimpse of him. Al was on the public mind, for as Herbert Asbury recorded, "Chicago seemed to be

---

*During the same period James Cagney played the Chicago Irish gangster for all time in *Public Enemy*, which established him as a star.

[351]

filled with gangsters—gangsters slaughtering one another, two hundred and fifteen in four years; gangsters being killed by the police, one hundred and sixty in the same length of time; gangsters shooting up saloons for amusement; gangsters throwing bombs, called 'pineapples'; gangsters improving their markmanship on machine gun ranges in sparsely settled neighborhoods; gangsters speeding in big automobiles, ignoring traffic laws; gangsters strutting in the Loop, holstered pistols scarcely concealed; gangsters giving orders to the police, to judges, to prosecutors, all sworn to uphold the law; gangsters calling on their friends and protectors at City Hall and the County Courthouse; gangsters dining in expensive restaurants and cafés; tuxedoed gangsters at the opera and the theater, their mink-coated, Paris-gowned wives or sweethearts on their arms; gangsters entertaining politicians and city officials at 'Belshazzar feasts,' some of which cost twenty-five thousand dollars; gangsters giving parties at which the guests playfully doused each other with champagne at twenty dollars a bottle, popping a thousand corks in a single evening; and all with huge bankrolls; a gangster with less than five thousand dollars in his pocket was a rarity."

At the top of gangsterdom rose the court of King Alphonse, with its ministers of state, high officers, counselors, and clowns. Scarface Al had advisers on public relations, but of all Chicago journalists who maintained contact with Capone, none stood so close as Jake Lingle, police reporter for the *Tribune*. The relationship appeared to have grown naturally from shared interests, for Al liked his name in print and the journalists who hung around his court, including Lingle, needed authentic background material of the sort that comes out of government offices marked "not for attribution." Therefore the publishers, managing editors, and city editors did not make it a policy to hamper their crime reporters with inquiries as to underworld news sources. The system worked, everybody was happy, and the front office executives at the *Tribune* failed to observe a remarkable quality that Jake Lingle possessed, which might have caused them to put him on the financial page if they had stopped to think about it. For reporter Jake Lingle, friend of Scarface Al, could make a dollar go farther than any man who ever worked for the *Tribune*. On his salary of sixty-five dollars a week, he maintained a suite at the Morrison Hotel in the Loop in addition to his house on the West Side and a summer home in Wisconsin; he wore tailor-made suits and English shoes; he bet big money at the race tracks day after day; and when he was not on the telephone to a bookie, he was talking to his brokers, who maintained for him an active account of $100,000 average value. If they gave these matters any thought, the *Tribune*'s managing editor and its publisher, the starchy

Colonel Robert R. McCormick, may have said to each other, "Perhaps he doesn't eat lunch." But if ever there was a newspaperman carrying around with him an air of dubiety that could be detected about as far as one could see him, it was Jake Lingle. The McCormick managers, along with the Hearst interests, really did know a crook when they saw one: for they employed scores of hoodlums in the circulation wars which they fought on the streets of Chicago. But Colonel McCormick, high in the tower he had built in 1925, and William Randolph Hearst, off in some gloomy castle, or viewing an inane Marion Davies movie in Hollywood, were too important to bother about such things. And so Jake Lingle flourished, widely respected for his obvious dishonesty, and admiringly referred to as "the unofficial police chief of Chicago," for among his friends in addition to Capone he counted Police Commissioner William F. Russell, and enough minor police officials, judges, and politicians to fill a garbage scow.

On the afternoon of June 9, 1930, Lingle got the traditional telephoned dismissal from his city desk shortly after one o'clock, and walked from the Criminal Courts Building over Randolph Street to the Michigan Avenue underpass leading to the Illinois Central suburban station. Lingle was wearing an expensive light gray summer suit, a diamond-studded belt that was a gift from Capone, and a straw hat. He was heading for a train to the race track. Halfway through the underpass, a man stepped up behind Lingle and killed him with a revolver shot in the brain. The murderer ran back up to the east side of Michigan Avenue and disappeared in the crowd. When word of the crime reached the *Tribune* tower, mighty roars of indignation could be heard. The front office assumed that Lingle had fallen in line of duty, and posted a $25,000 reward for the killer. Then a part of the truth about Lingle began to come out. The full story was never told, but it became public knowledge that Lingle supposedly set the price of beer in Chicago, that he controlled the graft from dog racing, and that he took a hand in the closing of gambling houses by the police and their subsequent reopenings when the police were otherwise occupied. Lingle's high police contacts resigned from the force. A *Tribune* lawyer sworn in as special prosecutor spent freely for information, and at length brought a St. Louis hoodlum named Leo Brothers to trial on the charge of killing Lingle. The case was weak, but a jury convicted Brothers after twenty-seven hours of argument, and he went to prison on a fourteen-year sentence, emerging in ten years with time off for good conduct. Brothers had stood mute at his trial, and he vanished into the Midwestern underworld, still not talking. Much mystery remains to this day about Jake Lingle and his death. Analysts of Chicago crime believe that Jack Zuta of the Moran gang arranged for Lingle's murder, perhaps by Brothers in the tradition of using an imported gun for a prominent victim. Zuta died by gunfire on August 1, 1930, at a roadhouse in the Wisconsin woods. He had just started an electrical piano in the bar by dropping coins in the slot, when five gunmen entered and stopped the music with sixteen bullets which also passed through Zuta's body. In Chicago, police opened deposit boxes rented by Zuta and found records of Moran's business activities with notations of payoff money to various officials, and loans on unsecured notes from Judge Joseph Schulman. These records showed that Moran had suffered loss by the closing of a Sheridan Road gambling house, presumably blaming Lingle for the trouble. According to this theory, Moran ordered Zuta to eliminate Lingle, and then had Zuta killed to keep the matter quiet.

Al Capone said that he would find the killer of his friend Lingle, but did nothing about it. The summer of 1930 had not been pleasant for Al, who was beginning to realize that he had been foolish in allowing himself to be made an international celebrity. The uneasy state of Al's nerves was revealed on August 26, when he was playing golf with City Sealer Dan Serritella on a suburban course, and a nearby delivery truck backfired its engine. Scarface Al mistook the noise for the sound of gunfire and dived into a sand trap, while his bodyguards Greasy Thumb Guzick and Hymie Levine pulled weapons from golf bags. The gangsters were beginning to burlesque themselves, and the ridiculous incident drew a three-line one-column heading on the front page of the *Daily News*. There was a feeling now that a day of reckoning might soon be at hand for Alphonse Capone. An honest police captain named John Stege had kept heat on Scarface Al for some time, though more than once transferred to inconvenient posts by political pressure; then as public opinion slowly formed behind Stege, he resumed his desk at the central office and put a tail on Capone that never left him by night or day. There was sound reason for this attention by honest officers, for the Treasury Department at Washington had been building a Federal tax evasion case against Capone, and it was necessary to keep an eye on him. They indicted him in the early autumn of 1931. Capone was convicted, and sentenced to eight years in government penitentiaries. It was said that President Hoover had ordered the Treasury men to 'get' Capone, and the use of income tax prosecutions to imprison men when other crimes are actually under consideration has never appealed to the American public; yet the open indecency and brutality of Capone's career seemed to many people a justification of the means employed to put him in prison. Capone never returned to Chicago; he came out of Alcatraz an old broken man, and died on a secluded Florida estate.

As we take the historical view of Chicago gangsters in the Prohibition period, a curious fact emerges. For we see that odious as these men were, and disgraceful as it was that they should have received admiration, they were not the principle destroyers of civilized life at work in the city. It was now apparent that the greatest enemy to decency in that town was a machine—the internal combustion gasoline engine attached to the driving shaft of the horseless carriage. The manufacturers had released nearly two million cars on the country in 1920; they made and sold 3,800,000 in 1925. Daniel Burnham and the other planners had not foreseen such a stampede, and Chicago began to suffer from the noise, poisoned air, nerve-wracking traffic jams, and danger that the automobile caused as each driver fought for running room and space in which to leave his machine when not using it. Frank Lloyd Wright came through town and gave the matter his usual blunt common-sense reaction. He said to reporters, "The automobile is going to ruin this city. Michigan Avenue isn't a boulevard, it's a race track! This is a dreadful way to live. You'll be strangled by traffic." A reporter asked, "What should we do about it?" Wright answered, "Take a gigantic knife and sweep it over the Loop, cutting off every building at the seventh floor. If you cut down those horrible buildings, you'll have no traffic jams. You'll have trees again. You'll have some joy in the life of this city. After all, that is the job of the architect—to give the world a little joy."

Not everyone saw the danger of the automobile as Wright perceived it in 1925. For in spite of the inconvenience and unpleasantness brought by the motor cars, they did appear to be solving the old problem of finding a way to attach a maritime town to the country around it. This had been a difficulty since early times, and from 1848 to 1854 the city had thrown out 121 miles of plank roads, beginning with the Southwestern Road, which is now partly Ogden Avenue, finally pushed on thirty miles to Naperville and Oswego. Next came the Northwestern Road which is now Milwaukee Avenue. It reached a total length of thirty-five miles in 1854. Then the city built the Western or Saw Mill Road running along what is now Wabansia Avenue, to end in De Kalb County forty-five miles from its beginning. In 1854, Matthew Laflin built the plank road that was named for its destination, the township of Blue Island. And in that year the Lake Shore plank road connected by way of Ogden Avenue to the Southwestern Road and ran up along what is now North Clark Street to Sheridan Road and on to Evanston. A glance at the map shows the organic pattern of the wood-paved roads. These indispensable straight conduits and diagonals across the gridiron plan were the natural main highways in and out of Chicago. Automobiles had begun to choke these arteries long before Frank Lloyd Wright diagnosed the trouble for the Chicago papers.

Even among those who saw trouble ahead, no one who owned a motor car showed any intention of giving it up during the exciting and challenging decade that followed the first world war. The automobile made life especially pleasant in the northern suburbs, although persons lucky enough to be invited for a week end at Lake Geneva would be likely to go up on the train, knowing that their hosts would provide plenty of motor transport after they got there. It was a relaxing trip, for the North Western line offered prompt service, clean cars, and respectful conductors. A splendid place to visit in Lake Geneva was Ceylon Court, the John J. Mitchell estate, where the main house had been the Singhalese pavilion at the World's Fair. Having taken a fancy to this airy palace, the Mitchells had it knocked down after the fair and reassembled seventy miles northwest. The remarkable structure now rose in the center of seventeen landscaped acres at the head of Lake Geneva, with Oriental peaks and gables looking as though they had always existed under Wisconsin sky. In the main hall, guests could examine carvings in teak, satinwood, ebony, mahogany, and cypress. At the center of this octagonal hall stood a circular staircase enclosed within a ring of carved posts supporting inlaid friezes depicting scenes of Eastern mythology. The grounds were equally interesting, for the banking Mitchells had the money and taste to make a visit to their summer home a flawless experience. When they gave a dance, with paper lanterns in the great room downstairs and all through the grounds, the unified effect was sheer delight. Some friends were aware that the Mitchells had a harmless desire not to be outdone in matters of tasteful elegance. With this in mind young Carter Fairbank offered a pleasantry while walking around the grounds after lunch. Admiring the peacocks and other rare birds, he remarked to his hostess that he saw no swans in the pond. That was on Saturday. When he took the Monday morning train for Chicago at the Lake Geneva station, Fairbank noticed several trucks loaded with crates containing large birds. The baggage master explained, "Swans. For the Mitchells."

Ceylon Court at Lake Geneva was undoubtedly a great house, but a number of equally impressive establishments could be found in Lake Forest when the post-war decade of social display, grand parties, and lantern-lit summer nights came on. Indeed, Lake Forest had been the center of estate country for many years. Chicagoans had started building large houses on Deer Path, the Mayflower Road, and other winding streets not long after Presbyterian educators, churchmen, and benefactors planned to make the place an Athens, with schools and colleges of every kind. They did succeed in founding some sturdy institutions: today the Lake Forest Academy for boys, the girls' Ferry Hall, and Lake Forest

College are well into their second centuries. The founders sought a tone of plain living and high thinking, which they took from two admired ministers, one of them the first president at the college, Dr. Robert Wilson Patterson, who took office in 1875, eighteen years after the institution received its charter. Until Dr. Patterson arrived, senior instructors had served also as administrators: now the trustees felt that they had a great man heading the institution. Sprung from Tennessee Scotch-Irish stock, Robert Patterson had come to Illinois by way of Cincinnati, where he had studied at Lane Seminary under Dr. Lyman Beecher, and Professor Calvin Stowe, who married Dr. Beecher's daughter Harriet. For thirty-two years pastor of the imposing Second Presbyterian Church in Chicago, Dr. Patterson resigned that pulpit to take up the work in Lake Forest. His son Robert married Joseph Medill's daughter Katherine, and later became one of the ablest editors in the history of the *Tribune*. The other influential clergyman of early Lake Forest was Dr. James Gore King McClure, installed as the Presbyterian pastor in 1881, and serving the congregation until 1905. The historian Edward Arpee has written that "During the twenty-three years of Dr. McClure's pastorate, he was twice president of the College, and the love and confidence which he inspired caused gifts to flow into the church, the schools, and the city."

The benefactors usually came from among the most prosperous Chicago families, and they saw what the deep glens and high bluffs of Lake Forest offered as sites for summer houses. The next step was to build for residence all year round, and splendid mansions began to take form among landscaped gardens and groves of trees. With successful transplantings from other regions, Lake Forest became an arboreal museum, and today one can drive along roads lined by white and red oak, red maple, hickory, elm, pine, beech, and poplar, with the magnificent indigenous cottonwood towering over all. In deep summer there is an arch of green over some Lake Forest roads, forming tunnels that open on bridges across ravines. No one ever had any trouble understanding why the Presbyterian worthies settled in this place; and it could be seen at the start that the Durands, the Farwells, and certain of the McCormicks, with their connections, and a number of equally substantial "church" families, would be the social and civic leaders in this singularly beautiful suburb.*

With such colonizers coming in, population was sure to increase, a fact that impressed Nellie Durand when her teacher at Ferry Hall asked for

*The Episcopalians established their Church of the Holy Spirit at Lake Forest in 1902. Fifty years later a local man remarked that the Presbyterians were still getting the fashionable funerals, but the Episcopalians were taking over the fashionable weddings. In spite of this Lake Forest remains a Presbyterian stronghold.

an essay on the town in 1880. Nellie wrote that "Yesterday the population of Lake Forest was 1,000, but last night I had a baby brother, so now the population is 1,001." Nellie also showed the Arcadian atmosphere of Lake Forest by owning a pet lamb that followed her to Sunday School over the foot bridge at Deer Path and Sheridan Road. By 1920, the population of Lake Forest had risen to 3,600, and in the following decade, 3,000 more people settled in town. Such a large number of great Lake Forest houses had come into existence by the 1920s that it would take a sizable book merely to list and illustrate them. The trend for creating these handsome estates had begun with Blair Lodge, which Walter Larned built in 1883, and hedged with Japanese quince, as Mr. Arpee records, that made a sensational display of color every spring. Mr. Larned was one of those men of affairs, by no means unusual in Chicago, who took part in literary and artistic life. He found time aside from his law practice to write books, serve as art critic for the *Daily News,* and start the Lake Forest study group that developed into the Durand Art Institute. A man with similar interests, Abram Poole of the Board of Trade, built Elsinore on the lake bluff in 1884. The Pooles were patrons of music, painting, and writing; some years later, the novelist Ernest Poole turned to nonfiction and produced a fascinating book about the founders of Chicago, *Giants Gone.* Ten years after Elsinore, Byron Laflin Smith built Briar Hall on the lake, and imported a number of trees, including arbor vitae, aromatic sumac, European ash, Chinese lilac, cucumber, double-flowering horse chestnut, English elm, European elder, Norway and sweet gum maple, mock orange, red cedar, and slippery elm, many of which were transplanted in slips to other parts of Lake Forest. In 1896, a committee of leading citizens organized the Onwentsia Club and in that year Cyrus McCormick, Jr., built Walden in the southeast corner of Lake Forest. The architect was Stanford White, partner of Charles F. McKim, who had been a leading designer of the World's Fair. A triumph of American romantic landscaping, the grounds of Walden made visitors think of the marvelous terrain that Poe had described in "The Domain of Arnheim." Mr. Arpee recorded that "the house and grounds were charming in a natural way; the pergola was planted with wild flowers. There were attractive vistas in all directions; westward to the ravines lined with oak, maple, and pine, eastward to the shores of the lake and out to the endless horizon; or one could stand on 'the point' from which one could get a sweep of the Lake Michigan shore line northward and south. This 'look-out' over the lake contained a half dozen steel-concrete private bridges crossing ravines, ivy covered. There were thirty miles of private roads, bridle paths, and other paths which Lake Forest residents were permitted to use and enjoy, surrounded with myriads of wild flowers, artfully planted, so that nature received all the credit and human skill and good taste were not immediately apparent." That was a big year for building Lake Forest estates: J. V. Farwell, Jr., settled in his newly completed Ardsleigh just to the north of the McCormick place, and next north Ambrose Cramer built Rothmere, while Edward F. Carry put finishing touches to Broad Lea on the Green Bay Road. Here was one of the Lake Forest private theaters, where two plays by Hermann Sudermann got their first American production.

For twenty years, grand new houses continued to rise on large and suitably landscaped Lake Forest grounds; and perhaps the most remarkable was J. Ogden Armour's Mellody Farm, completed in 1908. As heir to the meat-packing business, Ogden Armour considered himself to have unlimited funds, and he began operations by draining Skokie swamp and laying out five ponds stocked with bass and perch. Next he commanded the construction of a moraine large enough for a tremendous house of steel and concrete, designed after an Italian villa by the fashionable architect Arthur Heun. Armour's engineers then brought in enough black soil to cover two hundred acres around the main house and stables two feet deep in order to facilitate gardening and landscaping. With all in readiness and Mr. and Mrs. Armour at home, the first visitors passed through a formal gateway on Waukegan Road, crossed over the Milwaukee railway on a concrete bridge, and then drove two miles to the main house. On the way they could see a herd of tame deer trotting through woods, and a dozen fine horses running on the meadow. The horses lived in a fireproof stable with their names inscribed over the stalls. Approaching the mansion, Mr. Arpee has recorded that visitors passed "orchards and an orangerie, similar to that of Voltaire at the Potsdam court of Frederick the Great." These supplied fruits, "while greenhouses furnished exotic plants and flowers. Antique vases and statuary from old gardens in Europe, also a beautiful Italian well-head, decorated the formal gardens and the front of the house. Imported marbles were in evidence inside and out. The main building measured 180 by 500 feet, containing a bowling alley in the basement. The first floor contained a dining room with marble walls, a breakfast room, an enclosed porch, a library paneled in Circassian walnut, and off this a little green-paneled Georgian room which Mrs. Armour bought in London. The ground floor also contained an elaborate music room where a pipe organ was concealed in the panelling. The second story contained complete suites for each member of the family of three and for their guests. Mr. Armour's two offices, one above the other, connected by a concealed staircase, were a source of admiration to visitors. The plumbing and hardware were of very special manufacture. Gold and silver were frequently used in door knobs and electric fixtures. There was silk paneling and especially chosen furniture brought over from various countries of Europe. The main building had an elaborate communication system: one direct line to the Stock Yards, and fifteen other direct connections with the outside. There were also fourteen telephones connecting various rooms and buildings on the entire estate."

One might expect to find so much magnificence overpowering, but the total effect was quite cheerful, especially in cold weather when fires in twenty marble fireplaces gave the interior a friendly glow. The Armours continued to make improvements; they built their own power plant, and in 1915 put up a wall just west of the railroad tracks to cut off all sight and sound of passing boxcars.

The owners gave many parties at this enchanting place. Chicagoans recall a special magic in visiting Mellody Farm during Christmas holidays when guests came by train and got out at the private Armour station to be met by top-hatted English grooms who escorted them to sleighs, tucked them under fur robes, and drove with bells jingling up to the grand house whose windows glowed with hospitable light. But the Armour domain may have been at its most attractive in the summer; one night Ruth St. Denis and her troupe danced for the company on a platform built over the reflecting pool in the garden, an unforgettable event. But of all social functions held at Mellody Farm, the greatest was the marriage of the Armours' daughter Lolita to John J. Mitchell, Jr., in the early 1920s. Of this wedding Mr. Arpee wrote, "Arthur Heun, the architect, came to decorate, and he used long-stemmed pink roses everywhere. Lolita came down the rose-embowered staircase dressed in magnificent white velvet, and walked to the floral background, where the ceremony was performed."

Whether or not anybody knew it at the time of this wedding, the luck was turning bad for Mellody Farm. J. Ogden Armour was heading for disaster, and in the next few years he lost his money and his control of the packing plant. And Mellody Farm slipped out of his possession when he sold the place to Samuel Insull and others to raise cash in 1928. The Insull crowd planned to use the property for an Aviation Country Club, an idea they dropped in 1929. A few miles away on a bluff overlooking the water, the Harold McCormicks had abandoned Villa Turricum, which crumbled into the most picturesque ruins ever seen around Chicago—Piranesi on Lake Michigan. This fate did not come to Mellody Farm: in 1947 Lake Forest Academy bought the property, and has occupied it to the present day.

Lolita Armour's wedding had been conventional though elaborate; other Lake Forest weddings of the period sometimes had unusual but pleasingly romantic touches. For example, Claire Childs and Lloyd Laflin departed in a shower of rice over their horsedrawn sleigh one snowy afternoon; and Sarah Brewster Hodges flew away from her father's garden in her new husband's airplane. It makes one think of Scott Fitzgerald's early stories, and this is understandable in view of Fitzgerald's admiration for a Lake Forest debutante, Ginevra King, whom he met when she was visiting St. Paul. Ginevra was one of the celebrated "big four" among the girls of her year; the other three, also Lake Foresters, were Edith Cummings, Courtney Letts, and Peggy Carry, whose family had given Sudermann a private performance. It is interesting to note that the glamor of wealth which supposedly inspired some of Fitzgerald's most effective writing was not the glamor of New York, but of Lake Forest and Chicago. Indeed, Nicole Warren and her father, who caused so much trouble for the hero of *Tender Is the Night*, were rich Chicagoans, analyzed by Fitzgerald in a well-known passage describing how the whole country piped its wealth and energy into the city for the benefit of Nicole and her family. Fitzgerald put down his feeling for the Middle West in a passage of *The Great Gatsby* in which the narrator recalls "the thrilling returning trains" of his youth that took him home from his Eastern college at vacation time: "Those who went farther than Chicago would gather in the old dim Union Station at six o'clock of a December evening" with a few local friends to bid them goodbye, and then board "the murky yellow cars of the Chicago, Milwaukee and St. Paul railroad, looking cheerful as Christmas itself" and pull out into the winter night.

Arthur Meeker, the citizen who proposed to rescue Chicagoans stranded by the European war, was one member of the Armour organization who survived the disasters there, and lived a life of fashionable, cotillion-leading luxury for years. Although he owned a dairy farm and summer home near the Ogden Armour estate, Meeker liked to stay in town and his principal residence was the Chicago house he started to build in 1913, taking possession the following year. Having been loyal South Siders for generations, the Meekers went a long way when they finally made their move, two miles past the Gold Coast to build a stone palace —designed by Charles Platt of the Villa Turricum—at Barry Avenue and the Outer Drive on the upper North Side. Distant though it was from approved territory south of Lincoln Park, No. 3030 Lake Shore Drive must have been worth the trip, and so Arthur Meeker, Jr. recalled the place when he wrote of his Chicago youth after becoming a well-known author, and, in the manner of Henry Blake Fuller, only a part-time resident of his native town. In a novel called *Prairie Avenue*, Meeker presented a rich merchant who disguised his son's murder as suicide. And although it may

[361]

have contributed to the myths surrounding Marshall Field II, *Prairie Avenue* is one of best Chicago novels yet written. The author had equal success in a memoir telling how it was to live at No. 3030, where the servants were so numerous that Haggard, the second man, had nothing to do but clean silver and serve the fourteen-year-old Arthur an occasional snack—"Your bread and milk, sir." The only building for blocks around, No. 3030 looked out on "a vast expanse of sea-gull-haunted sky" and a lonely bridle path where Mr. Meeker rode every morning before breakfast, sometimes as far as the select Saddle and Cycle Club three miles north at Foster Avenue. The outside of the Meeker house stood up to blasts of wind that came down from Mackinac, and the interior was the reverse of cosy. Arthur always recalled a chilly marble entrance hall, and downstairs a men's dressing room like that of a club, with a cocktail bar in the corner, used when the Meekers gave a large party. They could seat sixty for dinner, although for that number Mrs. Meeker did not hesitate to supplement her staff with additional workers from Biggs, the society caterer. The children had a friend in Maude Ginty, Chicago's most popular "company waitress." The ability to greet Maude wherever one encountered her, in the certainty that she would remember one's name, showed an undeniable position among the saved. Another noted outside helper who came to fashionable kitchens was Mrs. Fuge, the extra cook. Young Arthur thought her the stoutest woman he had ever seen, a walking advertisement of prowess at the range. During the first world war, the Maréchal Foch of France stayed with the Meekers on his visit to Chicago. To receive him the hosts thought it necessary to do over the best bedrooms in early American maple. The little Frenchman took this as no more than his due, and posed for a photograph under the famous "right side" portrait of Washington by Gilbert Stuart in the Meeker library. In addition to the entertainment of famous guests, Arthur recalled among other things the "miles and miles of red carpet" and the way he and his sister would turn out lights on each landing as they went up to their rooms after parties, leaving the great silent darkened house below.

The Meeker outpost was an important house, but those owners of Chicago who valued fashion and form had mostly gathered in the near North Side and the streets called the Gold Coast. "Don't live north of North Avenue," a society woman said to a questioner gathering material for a study by the University of Chicago. He was Professor Harvey W. Zorbaugh, in process of writing *The Gold Coast and the Slum* in a series of neighborhood studies sponsored by the university's diligent and renowned department of sociology. In surveying the selected territory, which was north and east of the river, west of the lake, and south of the barrier the fashionable woman had mentioned, Mr. Zorbaugh observed some traces of the old early spacious living of the Newberrys, Ogdens, and Arnolds in houses along Ohio, Ontario, Erie, Huron, and Superior Streets, and he noted that the name of McCormickville clung to Rush Street below Chicago Avenue because an enclave of McCormick mansions still stood there. From Oak Street up to Division Street, and further north on Scott, Goethe, and Banks Streets, and East Burton Place, with Astor Street and North State Parkway running north and south, Zorbaugh saw blocks of handsome houses and fine apartment buildings, the latter especially notable on Lake Shore Drive where the rent for seventeen rooms in No. 1200, at Division Street, came to a thousand dollars a month in 1925. Hereabouts lived Chicago's largest concentration of rich, educated, influential people. And when these men and women appeared on the streets of their agreeable neighborhood, they looked to be very healthy, and altogether unacquainted with the ordinary vexations of life.

So they were: yet no farther west than Clark Street, one encountered an abrupt change like entering a foreign country. Here one began to see what the English visitor H. G. Wells had described as "cheap base-looking people hurrying uncivilly by." Wells had been a good reporter so far as he went; but there were reasons why the people west of Clark seemed base, and hurried along without dispensing charm to others on the sidewalks. They were poor, and had to work at mean jobs for small pay, or else they were fourth-rate thieves or prostitutes, barely making a living and in constant danger from fiercer thieves and the police. In and around upper Rush Street were the low-class hotels, dubious lodging houses, and furtive nightclubs that set the metropolitan scene for the men and women who mostly looked down as they walked, not eyeing Mr. Zorbaugh with the frank interest the Gold Coast people showed. The professor didn't know it, but at first many a Clark Street pimp took him for a detective; later he became known in the district as a harmless collector of information, and he picked up some interviews that would have been a credit to Henry Mayhew. In her room on the top floor of a soot-begrimed old house on North La Salle Street, for example, a girl from downstate told Zorbaugh that after four years of college, she had decided against returning to Main Street and marrying a Babbitt, thus moving Sinclair Lewis's character from his bustling home city of Zenith to a small town. Zorbaugh offered no correction, for he knew how to listen, and understood what the girl was getting at. Disobeying her father, she had come to Chicago determined to study music, having less than a dollar left in her purse when she applied for lodging at the Harriet H. McCormick Young Women's Christian Association on North Dearborn Street. While living at the YWCA, she had met girls like herself from small places in Alabama, Indiana, Michigan, and Illinois. Then she found work waiting on tables and somehow managed to pay for music lessons while moving from one to another of a succession of lodging houses that were "old, gloomy, bleak, and base." The landladies were "queer-looking and dowdy, tight-lipped and suspicious, ignorant and coarse." The young woman went on, "I had no friends—a girl brought up on the Commandments does not make friends in rooming houses or as a waitress very readily." Then she met a girl from Tennessee at the music school, and they shared a room in a reasonably good house on Dearborn Street north of Division Street. After a year of work, saving every possible penny for music lessons, the girl was told by her teacher that "there was no chance of realizing her ambitions." The girl had never felt so desolate: she looked at her life in Chicago "and asked herself what is it, really." That Sunday night she went to the fashionable "McCormick" Fourth Presbyterian Church on North Michigan Avenue in the heart of the Gold Coast, and like many other unwary visitors to that church, was repelled by the "ostentatious and half-hearted civility" of ushers who seemed like undertaker's men without the sympathy. She said, "I never went back." Working now full time as a waitress, the young woman met a lonely man from Oklahoma who had some money in his pocket, derived from petty thievery. They "took a little apartment" until his money ran out and he returned to Oklahoma. Unable to pay apartment rent, the girl returned to rooming houses, amid what Zorbaugh described as "isolation, loneliness, and a tendency to personal disorganization." The sociologist closed this chapter by noting that a bridge over Lincoln Park Lagoon had become known as Suicide Bridge, and the Commissioners tore it down.

Continuing his study of dreariness so close to the gold of Lake Shore Drive, Zorbaugh talked to a homeless ruined man who slept in a basement by arrangement with a tenement janitor, over near Sedgwick Street, where Little Hell neighborhood began. This man, who had once held an office job, made occasional entries in a diary: "Hit the dope Jan. 1, slept all day. Nowhere to go. No money. No friends. . . . Jan. 29, went to bed with my thoughts. God! It's awful." Concluding his first survey of Little Hell, one mile inland from the Drake Hotel, Zorbaugh found that those who lived in this Italian enclave had one social factor operating in their favor that no other ethnic group enjoyed. This was the pervading sentiment called *campanilismo,* a term from the old country that meant unbreakable loyalty to all who lived in the shadow of the same church tower. The powerful feeling made it possible for immigrants to call on one another for help in the close-knit community, and guaranteed that any men of the neighborhood who joined the racketeering gangs would be safe from incrimination. No one under *campanilismo*, for example, could have done what O'Banion did to Johnny Torrio in the matter of the brewery. The custom was to have great influence in the social structure of Chicago crime; throughout Little Hell and the adjacent rooming house district, Zorbaugh found no trust in the law, and no respect for its servants.

Having laid bare so many dismal lives that utterly lacked hope, and having uncovered so much corruption and crime, Professor Zorbaugh might have despaired for Chicago, and the country as well. He had observed the disorganization of social life in the rooming houses and cheap hotels; indeed, throughout much of the territory, the people seemed to be living the lives of tenants in one tremendous dreary hotel, sometimes meeting but never knowing one another. It added up to a dissolution of social opinion, and a breakdown of theoretical democracy, due to utter lack of confidence in the city government. Nevertheless, Zorbaugh expressed the belief that Chicago might some day function as a rational social organism providing a chance for every citizen to lead a tolerable life. Extraordinary as the conclusion may seem today, he thought the residents of the Gold Coast formed the element in Chicago life that would make rational "social politics" a reality. He wrote that these fortunate people were the only group that could "see the city as a whole, and dream dreams for it as a whole." As Zorbaugh saw it, they had not only the money and power, but the necessary disinterested good will to make Chicago the place it ought to be.

During the period in which Harvey Zorbaugh studied the Gold Coast and the slums, Chicago was enjoying the most prosperous boom times in its history. In 1923 the University organized a Committee on Social Sciences to investigate all aspects of American life and make certain that no serious errors should be committed in the future. No one happened to recall that they had now reached the year of Infanta Eulalia's prediction that Chicago would be the grandest place on earth. But one didn't need recollections of World's Fair visitors to see how splendidly things were going in the Middle West and the country to which it gave sustenance. It was true that minor complaints could be heard in 1923; the members of the Chicago *Blossom Time* company, for example, were not happy at being compelled to move from the new Appollo Theater on Randolph Street to the old Great Northern on Jackson Street, where they encountered a tribe of rats that ate their make-up sticks and eyebrow pencils. Still the troupers were lucky to have a Chicago stand, with good audiences and the management paying salaries on the dot. There was work for actors not only in the Loop but in the theaters of the "satellite loops" that had developed along Wilson Avenue and Sheridan Road on the upper North

Side, and also along Milwaukee Avenue out that way; and on Ashland Avenue in the west; and around Sixty-third Street and Cottage Grove Avenue on the South Side.

Out of the South Side came music called jazz, that had started before the war, and now went to the entire country by way of spinning disks on the hand-wound Pathé, Brunswick, and Victor Victrola phonographs that only very poor people failed to place in their living rooms. Like the mansions of Lake Forest, the Chicago jazzmen and their works would require a thick volume merely for a preliminary index, and many books have been written about various aspects of their art. As it happened, Lake Forest sheltered one of the greatest jazz musicians when Leon Bismarck (Bix) Beiderbecke attended the academy in 1921 and 1922, during the reign of headmaster John Wayne Richards. Tradition goes that when he was a child in Davenport, Iowa, Beiderbecke heard the pure New Orleans jazz played by Negro musicians on Mississippi River showboats. Whatever his first inspiration, Bix was a natural musician, and had mastered the cornet before he reached Lake Forest Academy, although it was said that having been self-taught, he played it all wrong. But the music he drew from his horn was enchanting, and young Beiderbecke absented himself from the academy night after night to play with jobbing dance orchestras up and down the North Shore. Convinced that Bix was wasting his time in school, Mr. Richards released him on May 21, 1922. Beiderbecke burnt himself out in his brief career, which ended with his death in 1931. As a white man, Bix agreed with the musicologists who state that Chicago jazz was founded by Negro musicians. In the 1920s, young white Chicagoans like Eddie Condon, Bud Freeman, Jimmy McPartland, Benny Goodman, and Art Hodes among others, though scarcely out of knee pants, were listening to black jazzmen in the cabarets on the South Side. Audiences worshiped the Negro piano men—Teddy Weatherford, Thomas (Fats) Waller, and Earl (Fatha) Hines, along with Ferdinand (Jelly Roll) Morton, who came to town in 1922 and composed "Wolverine Blues," "Milneberg Joys" (generally called "Milenberg"), and "Chicago Breakdown." People traveled miles to hear Johnny Dodds on the clarinet; and Kid Ory playing his trombone could silence a roomful of drunks when he poured out a chorus of "Careless Love." These were only a few among Chicago players whose recorded performances receive serious study today, and are still a pleasure to hear. The music these men played had become oriented to the improvised solo, and some of the most remarkable passages were produced by Louis Armstrong and Joe (King) Oliver, New Orleans Negroes who played the cornet and trumpet as nobody played them before. But some say that when it comes to playing the horn, Jabbo Smith has been overlooked; the product of an orphanage band in South Carolina, he could turn out chorus after chorus in a singularly pleasing fluent style. Whatever it was, Chicago jazz was music of the middle valley. It contained something of the concert in the courthouse square, the cornetist hitting high notes with the assurance of absolute control, and it had an element of New Orleans marching bands that played for funeral processions, mournful and slow on the way to the cemetery, then after the interment stepping off to "Didn't He Ramble" with its chorus telling how the decedent had rambled around the town until the butcher cut him down.

During the 1920s, the gilded youth of Chicago often patronized South Side Cabarets, drawn by the power of the music and the thrill of participating in rowdy night life. If they stayed on the North Side, they had agreeable parties to attend during the winter social season, with music a mild version of jazz. The Casino was the favored place for debutante dances, and those who regularly attended such affairs became accustomed to the menus, the decorations, and each other's faces in a way that encouraged some to slip out and head for a speakeasy, such as Quigley's elegant place in a Rush Street mansion. Here the young people would have a few drinks and replenish their flasks before setting out for the South Side to hear "Room Rent Blues," "High Society Rag," and "Working Man Blues." Mr. Quigley was a handsome dignified man who looked like James A. Farley, the Democratic national political leader. He saw to it that nobody got bad liquor at his place, and he took the number of every cab that carried patrons from his door.

Equal pains were expended on the privileged youth of Chicago by Miss Eliza Campbell, an arbiter who scheduled the dances at the Blackstone ballroom and the Casino, and maintained a list of young extra men who could be invited to save hostesses from violating the custom that there must be more men than girls at dances. A young man on this list who got drunk or misbehaved in any way received no more invitations. It seems that the girls and men of secure position looked down on these extras, and referred to them as "The Hall-Room Boys" after characters in a comic strip of the period, and said that when not answering Miss Campbell's summonses, they lived under the Casino floor. And one does wonder what became of the hall-room boys, after the ball.

Near the Casino, in the radius of a quarter-mile around the Water Tower at Chicago Avenue, Mr. Zorbaugh had investigated an area known as Towertown, where artists lived and maintained studios, along with the delegation of eccentrics that a colony of working artists always seems to attract. Ernest Hemingway of Oak Park lived there, home from the war, and writing stories about the Charlevoix lake country where he had passed the summers of his boyhood. The Aldises had sublet their apartment to an advertising man named Y. K. Smith, who provided quarters for Hemingway. Like Carl Sandburg, Ernest had taken a trade paper job, but his friends were already thinking of him as a man of superior talent, perhaps a genius. They had observed, too, that Ernest had his own way of doing things. Smith said of his lodger, "Hemingway had organized a club in his head, and, having absolute power, he was constantly taking in members and casting out those who failed to meet his standards at a given time." Sherwood Anderson was established now by the success of his stories gathered in a book called *Winesburg, Ohio.* He took an interest in Hemingway, who accepted his friendship and advice. What Anderson didn't know was that at some point, his young friend expelled him from that private club. Notification did not come until a few years later, when Hemingway published a savage burlesque of Anderson's work. Meanwhile, Anderson's marriage to Tennessee Mitchell had ended in divorce, and she had begun to establish a reputation with the works of sculpture that issued from her studio on East Erie Street in Towertown. During these years a Chicago writer superior to Anderson, though at first considered to be no more than an entertainer, was beginning to reach a national readership that welcomed him as the people had welcomed George Ade. Ring Lardner came from a small town in the Chicago hinterland, and he followed Ade in the tradition of writing natural speech. Traveling as a reporter with the White Sox in the American League, Lardner listened to the talk of the baseball players on the sidelines and over their meals and card games in trains and hotels. From this material he produced a gallery of characters who spoke in a way that made the reader forget the writer while marveling at the reality he achieved. Lardner's first major creation was Jack Keefe, a ballplayer of overpowering ignorance and vanity. The sarcastic manager, modeled on Kid Gleason, says to Jack, "Don't work no harder than you have to or you might get hurt and the league would blow up." At this Jack remarks to other players, "I guess he thinks pretty well of me." As the cycle of stories developed, Keefe married the empty-headed Florrie, whose sister Marie was the wife of Allen, a left-handed pitcher. Allen, not Jack, was the father of Florrie's baby, born eight months after the wedding, which had been preceded by only three days of courtship. The ballplayers were a sinister crew, attended by the sardonic chorus of Kid Gleason, and Cary the pitching coach, the latter an invention speaking with Lardner's voice. The most alarming of the ballplayers was the homicidal maniac Buster Elliott of "My Roomy," who ended his career in an asylum for the criminally insane. Whether or not his characters played baseball, Lardner wrote mostly of losers, depicting them in the unsentimental manner that George Ade used for his Indiana farmers and book agents, the approach of Edgar Lee Masters to the Spoon River pioneers' descendants, sleeping on the hill. Going beyond the baseball parks, Lardner created hundreds of recognizable people from among the success-seekers coming into Chicago from its empire of farms and small towns. The boom atmosphere of the 1920s, with its pervasive greed for easy money, had corrupted these people, whose mean backgrounds afforded them no way to develop sources of inner confidence, so that they attempted to impress the world with brag and bluff. Among them were the empty old man of "The Golden Honeymoon" who recorded the exact time of each departure from a station by his train on the way to Florida; and the surly oaf of "Three Without, Doubled" whose sense of inferiority impelled him to ruin his wife's chances of joining a card club in their South Side apartment house. Among Lardner's few characters having some degree of self-knowledge is the narrator of the stories called "Gullible's Travels." Although he has made money in the boom, this man realizes the futility of his wife's ambition to gain a higher position on the social ladder. They are staying at a hotel in Palm Beach, and in the corridor outside their suite they encounter the famous Mrs. Potter of Chicago. The narrator records that the great lady spoke to his wife:

> "Are you on this floor?" she says.
> "Yes," she says, so low you can't hardly hear her.
> "Please see that they's some towels put in 559," says *the* Mrs. Potter of Chicago.

Another great American writer examined Chicago, in 1927, but stayed away from Towertown. When John O'Hara came to the city in September of that year, he was twenty-three and footloose, having just returned from Germany, and now willing to settle in Chicago for a time if he could find a job. He took a room at 600 West Madison Street and started out to investigate the city while looking for work. But nobody offered employment. In later years, John O'Hara recalled that he formed a lifelong impression of Chicago as a very cold place to be without an overcoat. He applied for a job as a groom, and the man who had the job to give asked, "What's a young fellow like you trying to get a job as a groom for?" O'Hara said, "To eat." The man didn't believe him, and would not take him on. John O'Hara went back to New York and the *Herald Tribune*, and the rest is history. Forty years later, O'Hara said, "In Chicago I never had any hope. It was not my town. I was too much of an Easterner for it." That is understandable, but the time came when O'Hara would stop in Chicago on his way to or from California, and he said a great deal about the city in one of his stories called "Common Sense Would Tell You" which takes place at "the Chez" —a nightclub called Chez Paree that was frequented by moving picture stars and racket people. O'Hara also placed some episodes involving his famous character Pal Joey in Chicago. This unprincipled little night club singer introduced himself to a delighted audience by writing a letter to his "Friend Ted," explaining "How I Am Now in Chi."

The Chicago stop-over was a recognized stage on the journey between New York and California. Each morning the Twentieth Century Limited delivered its passengers for the west coast in a car that went on in the later afternoon over the Santa Fe line, and every afternoon the Century added the "New York car," with passengers returning from California, to its Chicago manifest. Established in 1902, the comfortable train ran eighteen hours overnight between Chicago and New York on specially maintained roadbeds, arriving at each city in the morning, and leaving late in the afternoon, which allowed time for a business day. Such important Chicagoans as Albert Lasker and Emerson Foote, the advertising men, or the ironmaster Seymour Wheeler would sometimes spend successive nights on the Century with a New York day between. Passengers of this kind paid $10 extra fare plus the cost of tickets and Pullman staterooms. A pair of stewards known as the Gold Dust Twins, Tommy O'Grady and Tommy Walsh, looked after them in an expert manner and never forgot a name. As the years went by, the train became such a favorite with the moneyed public that the New York Central Railroad had to schedule additional Centuries which would leave at intervals of a few minutes after the first section and arrive with the same leeway at the other end. These additional sections carried the same equipment down to the napkins under the cocktail glasses, and the greatest day in the Century's history was January 7, 1929, when a fleet of seven identical trains left Chicago for the East with 822 passengers aboard. Tommy O'Grady, Tommy Walsh, and five other Century stewards directed forty-two attendants in the fourteen club cars as they opened Apollinaris water and the Cantrell & Cochrane Imported Dry Ginger Ale to mix with passengers' liquor while the trains loped across Indiana in the winter dusk. As the Century patrons drank from immaculate crystal Pullman glassware, they agreed that 1929 was going to be the best year yet.

Nineteen Twenty-nine started out as a good year, but carried a sting in its tail. Chicago population had continued to rise, approaching three and a half million as the decade neared its end. Building activity had been immense: from the beginning of 1925 to the end of 1928, the value of construction in Chicago came to $1,390,000,000 in tangible property. The

Michigan Avenue bridge had been completed, and although it released a torrent of automobiles each way, it had also made possible a new development of fine stores and offices, and completed the reach of the avenue from the Blackstone to the Drake. The new buildings near the start of Wacker Drive at Michigan Avenue made an especially good showing. The Wrigley Building just north of the river had been completed in 1924 from designs by the firm of Graham, Anderson, Probst, and White, successors to the Burnham organization. Its white terra cotta baroque contrasted to the *Tribune* tower across the avenue, which Raymond Hood and John Mead Howells had clothed in Gothic dress. Generations of etchers have made studies in black and white depicting this building on a snowy day. But more than one person having a sensitive eye has found himself troubled by the tower's top, supported by what appear to be flying buttresses in the sky. One could ask an architect like Dr. Black's grandson Gilmer, an encyclopedia on Chicago construction, what loads the perpendicular elements were supposed to be supporting up there, and would get the answer, "I'm sorry, but I don't know." The *Tribune* building stands today like an assured old actor with a good part, but never looks quite the same after one has read Louis Sullivan's comment that the designers crowned the tower with a monstrous spider. He was so right: in any light at any time of day, one can see that spider with its eight legs dangling down. Such considerations did not keep the new buildings around the river from arranging themselves in impressive groupings as one passed by or crossed the bridge, which was not for the nervous walker when high winds were coming off the lake. But safe on either side, one could admire an eclectic architectural display in the Willoughby Tower; the thrillingly slender forty-one-story Mather (now Lincoln) Tower; the elegant London Guarantee Building at the start of Wacker Drive; and across the way No. 333 North Michigan Avenue, designed by the new firm of Holabird and Root, partnership of the famous architects' sons. Farther down the river at Wells Street stood the Merchandise Mart, another gigantic structure by Graham, Anderson, Probst, and White, which remained for many years the largest building in the world, with a floor area of four million square feet. And along the south branch, the new *Chicago Daily News* building rose in a clifflike wall, with a forecourt reaching to the waterside, the grand conception inherited from the parent firm and completed in 1929 by Holabird and Root. This plant was a contrast to the Wells Street warrens which had housed the great newspaper before 1929. Facing the *Daily News* across the river stood a new landmark, under sponsorship of the biggest man in Chicago: Samuel Insull had built his Civic Opera House on the entire block at No. 20 North Wacker Drive. Mr. Insull had organized hundreds of public utilities into holding companies, and had shared the benefits with 600,000 stockholders. He had taken over the Chicago Opera Company when its chief patron Harold McCormick ran out of money, and had uprooted it from the Adler and Sullivan Auditorium to put it into the huge building on the river. Obviously Insull meant the new opera house to be his monument, and he engaged Graham, Anderson, Probst, and White to design the forty-five story building. One would have felt no surprise to read as its motto, "Look on my works, ye Mighty, and despair."

Two blocks south, west of the river, a new Union Station had replaced the smoky train shed of Scott Fitzgerald's youth. And around on the lakefront at Balbo Street and Michigan Avenue, the firm of Holabird and Roche had piled the entire block twenty-seven stories high to make the world's largest hotel in 1927, the year of Martin Roche's death. By the summer of 1929, his inheritors were completing the Palmolive Building, a handsome stone structure, thirty-six stories high, across from the Drake Hotel on Walton Place.* The building had a list of tenants waiting to move in, with choice locations reserved for the old Chicago advertising agency of Lord and Thomas, now headed by the dynamic Albert Lasker, who had personally tailored the Palmolive sales message in such a skillfull manner that all concerned got rich.

As citizens admired it in 1929, the new skyline spelled money; what made the idea of riches all the more pleasing was the *reality* of the great buildings, their solid presence. This undeniable steel and stone caused almost everyone to believe reality also existed in the billions of dollars of notional money that had been created on paper by the supposedly rising values of securities traded in Chicago and New York. People thought they were acquiring wealth by speculating in the ownership of stock certificates which they bought with partial payments, thinking to make big profits by selling to someone else. It was the old game that land gamblers had played in Mr. Ogden's time, but on a national scale, with the little men believing in the boom market, the big men issuing statements about permanent prosperity, and the economists scanning the heavens and consulting their charts. But down in the South Side, something didn't feel right. Although Bronzeville had expanded to eight square miles, and Negroes were making more money than ever before, the *Defender* published a warning early in the year. The paper said that in recent weeks, its reporters had observed signs of disaster on the way. Therefore readers were advised to make sure of jobs, and to save as much as possible against hard times. The white people got the bad news on October 29, 1929, when

*It is now the Playboy Magazine building.

panic hit the New York exchange, paper profits disappeared, and the experts started to explain what had happened. It was plain enough in Chicago, New York, Boston, and Philadelphia, where the big banks operated: the speculative stock-market economy had blown up, and the economy of actuality that had supported it was coming to a halt in miserable disaster as people started to hide their money, wild with the panic of greed and fear.

For some months, Chicago continued to function though in a state of economic shock. The promoters of the Palmolive Building, for example, had crowned the tower with a sixty-five foot aviation beacon, named for Charles A. Lindbergh, the Midlander who had flown the Atlantic alone in a single-engined airplane. Continuing with their plans to light his beacon and start it turning, they held ceremonies on the night of August 27, 1930, when President Hoover pressed a button in Washington and turned on a two billion candlepower light in Chicago. That was impressive, but by the following year the city's employees were taking their pay in home-made money called scrip. By August 1931 Chicago wallowed deep in trouble; it was true that Mayor Thompson had lost the election in April of that year, and he had operated a corrupt political machine; unfortunately, his successor was Anton (Tony) Cermak, who brought in another corrupt political machine. No gainers were to be counted among the people of Chicago, and in the poor neighborhoods, now well into apparently permanent hard times, there was suffering and rage.

On the South Side many Negroes who had followed the *Defender's* advice to lay something by for the hard times found themselves broke after two years of heavy financial weather, and out of jobs as well. The result was that when landlords came for their money, the tenants reported themselves in a condition that Bronzeville called "empty rent-handed." This brought evictions, which the bailiffs carried out against increasing neighborhood indignation. At the end of July, Mayor Cermak went to Mackinac Island for a period of rest and relaxation that ended on August 3 when he got news of rioting on the South Side. Next morning the *Tribune* headlined eight columns: RED RIOT; 3 SLAIN BY POLICE. The paper reported that three rioters had been shot and killed, and that three officers and one rioter had sustained serious injuries, "when 3,000 Communists, mainly colored, abandoned a parade and started a battle to prevent the legal eviction of a family from quarters at 5016 South Dearborn Street." The account continued that all those killed were Negroes, and Mayor Cermak had sent orders from Mackinac Island for police and city officials to make certain that nothing endangered law and order. The *Tribune* man wrote that "The policemen engaged in a melee with thousands of shock troops of the Reds who have been holding daily meetings in Washington Park and have been instructed by leaders in Moscow to resist efforts of their landlords to put them out for non-payment of rent." It appeared that these Moscow-instructed deadbeats had become surly a few days before, when bailiffs moved the possessions of a seventy-two-year-old woman. Next the *Tribune* reporter quoted from an interview with Detective Sheridan A. Bruseaux, a Negro who had formerly served as "Red-watcher" for Samuel Gompers of the American Federation of Labor. Bruseaux said that at least twenty-five Chicago agitators had been trained in Moscow. These agents used many smart tricks to throw police off the scent: for example, they had all been taught Esperanto, "and this language is used in their frequent gatherings." On the following day the *Tribune* brought the story down to one column with a three line heading: HALT EVICTIONS/TO CALM UNREST/ ON SOUTH SIDE. The story said that "leaders of the colored race" claimed they were in need of relief. Then, while demoting Sheridan Bruseaux from "detective" to "investigator," the *Tribune* man repeated the information Bruseaux had given the day before. And on August 6, the *Tribune* editorial page had this to say: "That American society should be subjected in the midst of its efforts to meet its problems upon its own terms and with its own resources to an invasion of foreign mischief making is an intolerable affliction deserving more efficient measures than have as yet been adopted. . . . The Communist regime, centered at Moscow, has declared war against democratic America and its invasion should be met and defeated."

The dead victims of police bullets received almost no attention, but this was not so much the result of callousness as of a fear that had frightened Chicago's rulers even more than their fear of agents from Moscow. What most disturbed them was the thought that they would have to accept Federal aid, administered from Washington. Many of the leaders were unselfish in trying to make it possible for Chicago to care for its own. In 1930 and 1931 they raised a kitty of $14,000,000 by public subscription, and organized the charitable agencies into an Unemployment Relief Service to care for immediate needs and reduce paper work. But the insoluble problem of evictions showed how completely the economy had broken down for those who no longer drew wages. The relief agencies posted signs in their offices: WE DO NOT PAY RENTS and PLEASE DO NOT ASK US TO PAY RENT. Landlords began asking for just a part of the rent: paid for one month, they would try to carry indigent families for three months more. Maybe times would get better in three months. But in January and February 1932, Chicago relief agencies would pay something on account to landlords only when the family had experienced eviction.

Social workers would say to threatened tenants, "Wait until you're on the streets." It amounted to a moratorium on rents in poor neighborhoods, with hardship for the families on relief, many of them moving over and over, and for the landlords, mostly small property owners who often had to go on relief themselves. The landlords frequently saved eviction fees by turning off gas and water to force non-paying tenants out. The unemployed man's dread of the street, with children and sick elderly parents to care for, can scarcely be imagined. To get their clients some sort of shelter, agency workers colonized them in abandoned hotels without electricity, gas, water, or plumbing, where the people lived like animals in a cave. Edmund Wilson observed them in January 1932, huddling at the gutted Angelus Apartments, now called the Hoover Hotel, and in the Ozark Hotel, which afforded seven unheated and unlighted floors, sheltering sixty-seven Negro families whose breadwinners had formerly worked as servants, porters, millhands, stockyard men, Baptist preachers, barbers, chauffeurs, and clerks. Prostitutes and hoodlums also lived here, joining in the plea to social workers: "Don't condemn the building, it's the only place we have to go." On his way back to the Loop, Wilson passed the Harrison Street Hooverville of tarpaper shanties, and saw that it was flying a black flag. Next he traveled along "interminable straight miles of streets" to the Oak Forest poorhouse, known to prospective inmates as the Graveyard. In spite of its bad reputation, the Graveyard had turned away 19,000 applicants in 1931 for lack of room. Wilson left this grim place to visit Halsted Street and talk to Jane Addams at Hull House. On the way he observed the bombed-out aspect of many blocks on the West Side: "gray limestone, red brick, windowless slots, hollow steel beams, Romanesque, brownstone, a pretentious doorway from under which, like a lower jaw, the flight of front steps has been knocked." Hull House seemed a fortress of sanity and decency amid black factories under a sky that was gray like pasteboard. Edmund Wilson saw "the old big square high-windowed mansion embedded in dormitories, eating halls, gyms, nurseries, and laundries." Inside Mr. Wilson walked through the "high Victoriam rooms that open into one another through enormous arched and corniced doorways." The rooms were scantily but servicably furnished, and still contained mahogany tables, sofas, and faded Turkish rugs. In a little study with its walls and marble fireplace painted white, Wilson met Miss Addams. It struck him that at the age of seventy-two "Jane had combined the authority of a great lady with the humility of a saint." Miss Addams had received the Nobel Peace Prize in 1931, sharing the award with Nicholas Murray Butler of Columbia University. She was still doing practical work, continuing after fifty years her basic idea of simple response to human appeal, which she had called "that old healthful reaction resulting in *activity* in the mere presence of suffering or helplessness." Acting on Jane's suggestion, Wilson visited a Hooverville that about three hundred people had set up next to the garbage dump at Thirty-first Street and Cicero Avenue. He found that they had established rules for fair turns at the garbage when a fresh dump came in. He also visited the Harrison Street dump, where one hundred people controlled the pickings; they would scald bad meat and sprinkle it with soda, make soup from chicken claws, and devour the pulp on slices of cantaloupe or honeydew.

The Meeker family had moved from the big house out on Barry Avenue in 1925, and taken an apartment at 1100 Lake Shore Drive. Here they enjoyed such conveniences as an insulated wine room, water from a private filtration plant, and a gas flame attachment for instantly lighting the logs in fireplaces. But there was one drawback to living at No. 1100, because the residents had to share the place with Samuel Insull, who made himself disagreeable both to fellow tenants and the building staff. The British-born Insull had been an official in the Chicago Edison Company. Although seventy years old by 1929, he seemed as vigorous and domineering as ever, and while it was not possible to like him, public opinion accepted Insull as the most important man in Chicago. He had managed to get control of three electric railways, and hundreds of utility companies that sold electrical current, gas, water, ice, and heat to more than four thousand towns in Maine, New Hampshire, Vermont, New York, New Jersey, Pennsylvania, Delaware, Maryland, Virginia, West Virginia, North Carolina, Georgia, Florida, Alabama, Tennessee, Louisiana, Mississippi, Texas, Oklahoma, Arkansas, North and South Dakota, Indiana, Illinois, Wisconsin, Michigan, and Ontario. Insull gathered the ownership of all these plants into fantasies of bookkeeping that he called holding companies. Next, he used every device of salesmanship to sell his holding company shares to large and small investors, with particular attention to the civil servants, office workers, teachers, and local merchants of the country. It took a sort of genius to make these shares worthless, for people had to have electricity and gas; nevertheless, the Insull empire started to fall apart after the panic of October 1929. A month later, Insull was taking bows at the grand opening of his opera house; but for all his talk, the utilities holding companies were dead and worthless. Insull held on through 1930 into 1931, borrowing some $90,000,000 from the banks, one third of that sum coming out of Continental Illinois National, known as the Field bank, and $16,000,000 from First National of Chicago. By 1932 the big creditors had shaken down Insull's books, and discovered appalling things. To put it charitably, Insull had invented a new way of keeping accounts, in which expenses were entered as assets. In the three years of 1929 through 1931, during which his investors had lost their money, Insull had taken out $1,400,000 in salary. Samuel Insull was declared bankrupt, and he left the country thirteen days later, much to the relief of tenants and employees at 1100 Lake Shore Drive, where Arthur Meeker, Jr., looked out and saw mountains of Insull luggage blocking the front door. Later on Insull was forced to return and face trial on charges of fraud in bankruptcy, mail fraud, and embezzlement. Acquitted of the legal charges but scarcely restored to public confidence, Insull then went to Paris, where he died in 1938. It still seems incredible that such a commonplace mind could have attached itself to so many useful concerns, and cause such widespread and irrevocable financial disaster. Insull made a substantial contribution to the great depression; he was probably not a thief in the sense that a burglar was a thief, but essentially only a crashing bore, who numbed people's brains with his incessant ciphering and figuring. A rational society would have entrusted Insull with nothing more important than reading the gas meters.

The great bore's victims included poor and rich: Arthur Meeker said his father had "pounds and pounds" of Insull paper in his safety deposit box. As a result, Mr. Meeker had to fire his chauffeur, lay up his town car, and ride taxicabs to the office. The Insull collapse also caused an esthetic loss to the community by impoverishing an insurance man named Albert Mussey Johnson, who had commissioned Frank Lloyd Wright to build a skyscraper for his National Insurance Company on Michigan Avenue near the Water Tower. Johnson had invested $20,000 in the completion of Wright's designs for a tower of opalescent copper-bound glass. It would have been a marvelous building, something like the Price Tower that Wright built later in Oklahoma; but he had to give up the Chicago project when Johnson told him that Insull had made off with his fortune of $14,-000,000, and there was no more money in sight.

Samuel Insull may have experienced one satisfaction in the Chicago depression, from the thought that he had served as model for Solomon Imbray, the defaulting stock promoter in James T. Farrell's fictional panorama. One of the few encouraging events of 1929 had taken place when Farrell, a student at the University, brought a short story for criticism to Professor James Weber Linn. The story told of William Lonigan who had such a fine time on Armistice Day, and Mr. Linn's comment could be reduced to two words: "Write more." Farrell accepted this advice, and by the late 1930s had produced the three novels, describing life among the South Side Irish from the First World War through the depression, which we read today as a trilogy called *Studs Lonigan*. This remarkable achievement was the climax of Chicago realism deriving from Major Kirkland, *The Pit, The Jungle*, George Ade, and Ring Lardner. The trilogy presents many an unforgettable scene, such as the Knights of Columbus initiation, the sermon on the infinite time spent by the damned in hell, and the party at which Weary Reilly earns a penitentiary term by smashing a girl's nose and raping her; another example of Farrell's narrative that stays in the reader's mind like life experienced is the account of Studs's search for work on a cold rainy day in February 1932. There is nothing for him to do. Even the promoter of a scheme to sell from door to door is a swindler out to get the last dollar from Studs's pocket as a deposit on worthless merchandise.

As days went on in the misery of depression, Americans became convinced the only hope for the suffering country was a change of administration at Washington. And it was decided that Chicago should entertain the Democratic National Convention, which would select the next President. The leaders liked Chicago with its geographic and emotional centrality, excellent communications, and memories of Populism, the old faith still in Democratic keeping. Only a little over a third of a century before, William Jennings Bryan had defied the money barons on behalf of the plain people, and had thrown down his challenge in Chicago. Now the plain people feared worse troubles than in Bryan's time, and the money men had gone on the defensive, in the face of the disasters that their failures had brought on. It was clear that this time, Chicago would hear a call to victory. And it seemed certain that the candidate would be Franklin Delano Roosevelt, the governor of New York. But first the managers must set the stage, and in June 1932 they went through the preliminary motions that brought delegates into Chicago, ready to deal for votes and shares in the coming power. Chicago loved these spectacles, and this gathering gave them the antics of buffoons like Texas Jack Garner and Alfalfa Bill Murray, who could take men's minds off their troubles. There was a certain amount of business to go through, for Mayor Tony Cermak was a big boss, and the Roosevelt people had to take care of him. The derbied former New York Governor, Alfred E. Smith, desired the nomination; he was not to have it, for the party men preferred a sure winner, and Mid-America feared that behind Al Smith there lurked the Pope of Rome. The preliminary bargaining continued, with Jim Farley acting for Governor Roosevelt in a suite at the Congress Hotel, under supervision of Louis Howe, the governor's political aide, a gnomish man so small that he could take a nap curled up on top of a chest of drawers. He needed the rest, because balloting for President failed to get under way until 4:28 A.M. on the fourth day in convention. Alfalfa Bill called out his band of pretty girls in kilts to wake the delegates up, Senator Tom Walsh of Montana pounded his gavel, and the voting began. Many eyes rested on Mayor James J. Walker of New York City, who had accompanied his delegation although under a cloud for misconduct in office back home. He voted for Al Smith. But on the fourth ballot Roosevelt got 945 votes to 190½ for Smith, and James Farley put in an Albany call. It was the most important political choice to be made in Chicago since Joseph Medill and his friends secured Lincoln's nomination in the Wigwam. And Franklin Roosevelt immediately showed that he had the imagination to make an effective entrance, sending word that he would come to Chicago and that he would travel by air, still a novel and almost daring means of transport. Next day, while the delegates absorbed this news, the managers nominated Texas Jack Garner for the Vice-Presidency, and to celebrate this decision, the band tore into "Turkey in the Straw" as rural types sashayed around the hall in a buck-and-wing that looked like a Russian folk dance as they kicked and capered, hands on hips. In the press box, local and national reporters were scribbling, or hammering portable typewriters, while H. L. Mencken enjoyed the show, grinning from ear to ear. A little later, Chairman Walsh beat a tattoo with his gavel and read a message: "PLANE TEN MILES WEST OF SOUTH BEND. WILL BE IN IN FIFTEEN MINUTES." At 4:27, the chairman quieted the crowd so that they could hear the broadcast of Governor Roosevelt's arrival. They heard the sound of engines as the airplane rolled to a stop; and out at the airport, Mayor Cermak got a good place next to Governor Roosevelt when the dignitaries posed for photographs. Then within half an hour Franklin Roosevelt was addressing the convention. The two-party nominating system had never looked better or seemed more responsive to the wishes of the people. And the men and women listening reacted with warm approval to Mr. Roosevelt's confident bearing and clear voice. It was an important scene in the Chicago story, for the Democratic candidate was speaking to a frightened nation from one its most discouraged cities. His opening set his tone: "The appearance before a national convention of its nominee for President is unprecedented and unusual, but these are unprecedented and unusual times." Roosevelt used the phrase that was to name the first years of his administration when he said, "I pledge myself to a new deal for the American people."

It could hardly be questioned that when the New Deal became a reality, it benefited both high and low. Even those who feared or distrusted government intervention accepted it as the only way out of otherwise insoluble difficulties in 1933. The first government rescuing party to reach Chicago originated not with incoming Democrats but with the departing Mr. Hoover, who had set up the Reconstruction Finance Corporation for the purpose of pumping government funds into private companies that were failing because they could not get money from banks. Indeed, the banks themselves were collapsing, and Jesse Jones at the head of the RFC attached his emergency money hose to the biggest of them. Mr. Jones, a Houston financier, had seen the signs of Chicago's fear and agony on his arrival to attend the convention that nominated Franklin Roosevelt. There had been a week of runs on the downtown banks, while scores of suburban and "corner" banks had given up and closed their doors. Attending a secret meeting called on Sunday by Charles G. Dawes, Jones heard alarming confidential news about the Central Republic Bank. Mr. Dawes, a former Vice-President of the United States and a respected oracle, said he felt responsible for the Central Republic, as he had been a letterhead official for years, and had founded its parent bank in 1902. Facing all the other important Chicago bankers at the secret meeting, Dawes said his conscience was hurting because he knew the big men were taking money out of the local banks by what he called "clearing house transactions," and squirreling it away, leaving the banks unable to take care of the little men after the runs started. Sending up a shower of sparks from the strange-looking pipe he affected, Charley Dawes said he was not going to allow the Central Republic Bank to open its doors on Monday morning. It was hard to figure Dawes's angle in this; he may have been thinking of an attempt to save something for the bank's creditors. At any rate, Jesse Jones said he would telephone Mr. Hoover in Washington and try to work something out. Jones told the President that if Central Republic closed, all the Chicago banks would shut down, to be followed by every bank in the country. Jones qualified as an expert, since he had already put RFC funds into 4,100 banks. Mr. Hoover said to take a marker for the foreign securities held by Central Republic, and pump in enough cash to prop it up for a while. Thus they kept the staggering Dawes bank alive until its reorganization five weeks later as the City National Bank and Trust Company.

Franklin Roosevelt retained Jesse Jones as head of the RFC, and Mr. Jones came back to Chicago in September 1933 to address the American Bankers Association convention. Speaking at the concluding dinner, Jones failed to please his audience by saying that they well knew half the banks represented at the festive table were insolvent. His blunt advice was, "Be smart for once and go partners with the government." Though his speech was not well received, the listeners who acted on Jones's suggestion never had reason to regret it. Continental Illinois, for example, had taken a serious wound from Sam Insull. They had to write off his loan plus $110,-000,000 in losses for 1932 and 1933. Jesse Jones said, "After the Insull collapse, I don't know who in Chicago is broke, and who isn't." He put in his own man at the head of Continental Illinois and bought stock in the bank with $50,000,000 of U.S. government money. The day this transfusion flowed through the veins of Continental Illinois, its common stock was selling for $25 a share. Four weeks later this stock sold at $225 a share, the increase in value of the entire issue ammounting to $150,000,000. The First National Bank of Chicago also got help from the RFC, in the form of $10,000,000 out of the government's till in time of need.

The banks got their help in a hurry, but the minor civil servants and schoolteachers of Chicago had to wait for their pay. By August 1934, the 16,000 teachers and 3,000 Board of Education office workers had received no salary checks since May of the previous year. What they *had* received, with great celerity, was a 26 percent pay cut; and then the maimed salaries were not paid. The Chicago banks did not care to lend money to the Board of Education, and going to Springfield was hopeless; grafters and city-hating rural politicians had nailed everything tight down there. At last Representative Adolph J. Sabath introduced an amendment at Washington to enable the RFC to pay Chicago teachers. The bill became law in the summer of 1934, and Jesse Jones came once again to Chicago, this time for a conference with the president of the Board of Education. After two days of struggling in red tape, Jones got $26,300,000 of Washington money into the board's bank account, and word went out for the teachers to come and get it. Some stood in line all night at the tumbledown building on North Wells Street where the checks were given out. In the following week, as teachers dispersed the back pay among creditors and landlords, there was a noticeable improvement in Chicago's economic health.

In 1930 and 1931, buildings that had been financed before the panic, to an aggregate value of $125,000,000, were completed to fill in the Loop and near North Side skyline that stood thereafter with scarcely a change for a third of a century. These structures included the Board of Trade, with Ceres at the top, and the La Salle-Wacker Building, both from Holabird and Root; and the Field Building at 135 South La Salle Street, by Graham, Anderson, Probst, and White. In 1933, the value of an entire year's building operations in Chicago fell to $3,700,000. One hundred times that much had been constructed in Chicago during the twelve months of 1926, seven years before. Chicago had now settled into the relatively quiet, almost contemplative silver decade which would carry it to the Second World War. The victims of depression accepted fate, which had been made tolerable by the New Deal and measures that followed it, many of them conducted under the rule of a peppery Chicago lawyer named

Harold Ickes, who had formed his social philosophy at the University and at Hull House. As Colonel McCormick of the *Tribune* observed Ickes's career in the position of Secretary of the Interior, and wielder of government money power in public works, he developed a strong dislike for what he saw. Earning McCormick's disapproval would have been a prelude to oblivion for the average Washington official, but Ickes welcomed McCormick's enmity, and remained in highest favor at the White House as long as F. D. Roosevelt lived.

Yet one might have supposed Colonel McCormick to be an influential foe in early 1933, from the tone of his letter to President Roosevelt dated May 6 and headed, "Dear Frank." It appeared that "Mr. President" was not needed from one graduate of Groton School to another, especially when they were Grotonians of the same vintage. The colonel went on to say that it would give him and his wife great pleasure to have the Roosevelts stay at their house that summer when the President came to Chicago to open the Century of Progress Exposition. McCormick became chatty: "My house was a present from my mother, who held all the mansion ideas of her generation, and is therefore so much too large for us as to contain room for you and at least a considerable part of your staff."

Mr. Roosevelt, too, had a mother with "mansion ideas," so he understood very well. But as things turned out, he wrote back to "Dear Bert" that plans had changed and he was not coming to Chicago. The Century of Progress Fair was supposed to cure the city's financial depression, but hardly accomplished that, although it was a good show and played a second season the following summer. Visitors found the exposition in newly created Burnham Park, on a neck of land filled in to make a harbor and the new downtown airport called Meigs Field. There was much to see, and a display of contemporary architectural design, though the managers had failed to include Frank Lloyd Wright on the list of consultants. It still seems a deplorable omission, as Alexander Woollcott complained at the time; however, Woollcott did all he could to promote the fair, reporting that he had seen Helen Hayes and Thorton Wilder riding in the same rickshaw, and that when he inspected the Chalice of Antioch among the exhibits, he felt certain that he was looking at the veritable Holy Grail. In part of the grounds reserved for popular entertainment, the fan dancer Sally Rand was Little Egypt for the Century of Progress.

The 1933 fair copied the Columbian Exposition in importing famous works of art: perhaps best known was the painting usually called "Whistler's Mother," which came on loan from the Louvre under careful supervision. This picture by James Abbott McNeill Whistler, grandson of an early military Chicagoan, caused some confusion in the mind of a guard who said he understood that the valuable canvas was a painting called "Hitler's Mother."

A portrait of a mother had stirred feeling in Chicago not long before, while furnishing an example of change in official taste. In the late 1920s, the director of the Art Institute had given a prominent position to a work by the Jugoslav sculptor Ivan Mestrovic, whose reputation was high. The Institute people hoped their acquisition, a seated marble figure called "My Mother," would achieve something like the renown of Whistler's picture. This it failed to do, and many who saw "My Mother" felt compelled to take it as a mannerist work because of the insistent archaism of its drapery. Their unhappiness was increased by the disappearance of an old favorite which had first gone on view in 1912, the sculptured memorial to Florence James Adams called "Inspiration." This allegorical work had been carved from two tons of Carrara marble by Kathleen Beverly Robinson. It represented a seated woman in flowing robes, whose hands are supported by a similar figure who appears to be whispering in her ear. With its appealing composition and clear meaning, "Inspiration" had apparently earned a permanent place as a well loved work of art. It served as inspiration on its own account, suggesting the one act play *Overtones* to the Chicago dramatist Alice Gerstenberg, in turn giving Eugene O'Neill the idea for *Strange Interlude*, with the characters hearing words of secondary selves who dwell in the subconscious.

And "Inspiration" memorialized a remarkable woman. The wife of Milward Adams who managed the Central Music Hall, Florence James Adams taught control of the speaking voice for thirty years prior to her death in 1910. She had given instruction to Sarah Bernhardt, the Barrymores, Emma Calvé, Geraldine Farrar, Édouard de Reszke, and Marcella Sembrich, in addition to Chicagoans who came to her studio in Orchestra Hall. Mrs. Adams had much to do with the pleasing speech of educated Chicagoans today, for as Arthur Meeker recorded, she toned down many a voice, removing the rasp and whine of the prairies. Meeker wrote that for years the Middle West had provided a refuge for exiled Rs from the eastern seaboard, but Mrs. Adams hunted them down while improving the speech of an entire city. Sometimes parents would bring a young girl destined for a place in society but handicapped by a voice like those George Ade described as sounding like the pulling of shingles from a roof. Mrs. Adams would say, "My dear, poor child. It is almost too late—but not quite. Go home and promise me not to speak a word above a whisper for six whole months. At the end of that time return to me and we shall see what can be done to save you." Although few if any of them had ever needed such drastic measures, a committee of Mrs. Adams's friends subscribed for the memorial statue at the time of her death. It is easy to imagine how these Chicagoans felt when "Inspiration" vanished into a storeroom, from which it has yet to emerge.

Mrs. Milward Adams was typical of the famous Chicago voice, dramatic, and dance coaches whose pupils came from all over the world. When the Century of Progress Exposition opened, Edna McRae, for example, had long been established as one of the country's leading instructors of professional dancers. Sometimes Mrs. McRae would ask visitors for instruction, as when she studied tap dancing with John W. Bubbles of the Buck and Bubbles vaudeville team. On another occasion she paid a visiting musical comedy dancer $125 for a tap routine. When they were little girls in the First World War, Edna McRae and her sister had upheld American morale by "interpreting 'The Star Spangled Banner' with gestures and feeling." Fifty years later, the dance critic Walter Terry said that Mrs. McRae had been "a one-woman ballet Mecca to generations of dancers, local and visiting." Another innovator and educator was the internationally famous Ruth Page, who had made her debut in Chicago as a child dancer, and later toured the world with her own group of artistes, keeping Chicago as her base and acting as principal choreographer for the local opera companies. Miss Page trained many professionals in addition to her own people, and carried ballet instruction into forty Chicago high schools with a demonstration troupe.

A leading citizen lay very ill on the morning of May 17, 1934. Propped in a couch at Hull House with a book in her hand, Jane Addams waited for the ambulance that was to take her to the hospital for an operation. Mrs. Bowen came in and said, "They'll be here in fifteen minutes." Jane said, "Then I can finish this novel." It was a story by the Canadian author, Mazo de la Roche. The surgeons found cancer, and Jane Addams died on May 20 at 6:15 in the afternoon. Not a voice remained from the malign chorus that had expressed hostility throughout her life: the city and the world began to praise her without reservations of any kind. Her nephew said, "Jane was Friday's child, loving as well as giving. . . . Representative? If Jane Addams were truly representative of the human race, we would all now be living in the Kingdom of Heaven."

Chicago gently settled into its silver decade with the realization of what had passed when Jane Addams died. There were people on the North Side who called themselves the new poor, and invented an inexpensive way of settling social debts in the cocktail party. Mr. Meeker was growing old on Lake Shore Drive, and he shook his head when Arthur described a function of this sort that he had attended around the corner on Cedar Street. The Assemblies occured less frequently, and ultimately ceased. The members of the Chicago Racquet Club abandoned court tennis. Theaters played shorter runs to smaller audiences, while people stayed at home and listened to the radio. Broadcasting was one industry that grew healthy in depression soil. And the largest audience listening to network stations throughout the country tuned in, every afternoon, to a feature originating in Chicago.

This radio show that chained the nation to Chicago was called "Amos 'n' Andy," its gruesomely apostrophized title a substitute for "Sam 'n' Henry," the act's original name. An interminable continued story about two Negroes, "Sam 'n' Henry" originated late in 1925 on WGN, the *Tribune* station, and moved to WMAQ of the *Daily News* when a chance to go on national networks came along. The *Tribune* claimed ownership of the original names and so the actor-authors, Freeman F. Gosden and Charles J. Correll, changed the leading characters to Amos and Andy. Gosden had come from Richmond, Virginia, and was directing home talent shows around Chicago when he met Correll, also a home talent impresario, who had come from Peoria looking for a partner to help him work up a radio act. They decided they would try "a comic strip adapted to radio," and made the further decision that they would play it in black-voice. The act went well on a week to week basis, and the *Tribune* signed Gosden and Correll to a year's contract in February 1926. At the end of this contractual year they took a vacation trip, tired from producing 586 episodes of the story. On returning to Chicago they left WGN for WMAQ, and took the air as Amos and Andy on March 19, 1928, to continue for twenty years. Albert Lasker of the Lord and Thomas agency arranged commercial sponsorship for the show.

A man of persuasive presence, Lasker was acquiring one of the few Chicago fortunes that increased throughout the years of financial drought; his chief associate, a sales genius named Claude Hopkins, had discovered the simple underlying secret of successful advertising.* Mr. Lasker made so much money from commissions, and from investing in his clients, that he was able to give up advertising, turn Lord and Thomas over to employees, and set up as public oracle along the lines of Bernard Baruch. As for the author-performers of "Amos 'n' Andy," their act gave fifteen daily minutes of relief from worry to an incalculable number of people whose only entertainment was furnished by the new branch of show business called broadcasting. One could walk down any street in the summer when Gosden and Correll were working and the windows open, hearing the entire program block after block without missing a word. What one heard

*Those wishing to learn the secret can find it in Claude Hopkins, *My Life in Advertising.*

was hardly memorable, for it is not possible to give any idea of the utter and absolute banality of the characters and story: but Gosden and Correll were masters of broadcasting, and extraordinarily good radio actors, playing every part in a large cast, and handling scenes of action with faultless microphone technique. They wrote one lasting line in a scene that has Amos and his partner examining an insurance policy: "The big print give it to you, and the little print take it away."

The white audience found nothing wrong in the Negro characters that these entertainers had made familiar figures in the national consciousness. Old Man Lonigan, Studs's father, never missed a broadcast: "They're so much like darkies. Not the fresh northern niggers, but the genuine real southern darkies, the good niggers. They got them down to a T, lazy, happy-go-lucky, strutting themselves out in titles with long names and honors, just like in real life. . . ."

Actual life gave some encouragement in the summer of 1935 to those Chicagoans who had the price of admission to the Cubs' baseball games at Wrigley Field at Clark Street and Addison Avenue, or followed the descriptions by announcer Ronald Reagan on the radio. Far down in the National League standings, the Cubs had reached a point where the mathematical chance of their taking the pennant lay in going through the remaining twenty-one games without defeat. The learned men of baseball, analyzing the situation in newspaper sports departments and saloons, took this to be an impossibility. Nevertheless, the Chicago Cubs started a winning streak, and by the time they reached their sixteenth successive victory, there was intense excitement among the fans, not only in Chicago but around the country, where people saw something symbolic in the Cubs' closing sprint. And although such a thing had never happened in all the ages of baseball, the Cubs finished the season by winning the last twenty-one games without a break. But the post-season World Series brought disappointment to Reagan and the fans when the American League Detroit Tigers won it, four games to two. This too might have symbolic value: Chicago seemed to have become habituated to failure. In spite of all Mr. Ickes could do for his home town, the city lay like a ship becalmed on its lake.

Chicago burned to the ground in 1936, but the fire took place in California, on the back lot at Twentieth Century-Fox. Seven acres of carefully scaled miniatures went up in a blaze that could be seen from Culver City on the south and Santa Monica on the west, to make the 1871 fire sequence for *In Old Chicago*. Producer Darryl Zanuck spent three million dollars on this film, which had been suggested by the novelist and screenwriter Niven Busch. The city had come to the attention of Mr. Busch, a transplanted New Yorker, through the tales of petty Chicago racketeers who had migrated to Hollywood after the repeal of Prohibition in 1933, trying to sell story ideas or get work as bit players. Dismissing these people and their ideas as worthless, Mr. Busch nevertheless found himself thinking about the great fire, and went to Chicago in the winter of 1935 to do some research on that catastrophe. Soon he was able to tell Zanuck, "There really was a Mrs. O'Leary, bless her black Irish heart, and she was a hell of a woman, keeping that family and giving them milk—milking that lantern-kicking cow right in the guts of the city." Zanuck cast the Busch movie with Tyrone Power as Dion O'Leary, modeled on Big Jim; the heroine was Alice Faye, and Alice Brady won the Academy Award for her performance as Mrs. O'Leary. The night they burned down the miniatures, eleven cameras mounted on fireproof steel towers recorded the scene. But the fullscale four-block Chicago Street on which the actors performed had cost too much to burn, and remained standing until the late 1960s, when the company got in trouble and sold that part of its real estate to developers.

Chicago had supplied the scene and the antagonists for the battle that started industrial labor unions on their way to power, and during those days in the 1890s, George M. Pullman had done as much to organize industrial labor as Clarence Darrow or Eugene V. Debs, although his intention had been to defeat the union men so badly that they would never fight again. In 1937, another George Pullman appeared on the scene. He was Tom M. Girdler, an industrialist who treated labor disputes as warfare, and he handed the union people an advantage they never relinquished, on Memorial Day 1937 at the South Chicago plant of Republic Steel.

At this time the United States Steel Corporation had come to terms with the Steel Workers' Organizing Committee, but Tom Girdler and the group of companies known as Little Steel rejected the agreement and continued to fight. Little Steel included Girdler's outfit, along with Bethlehem, Inland, and the Youngstown Sheet and Tube Corporation. In the spring of 1937, the Youngstown plant bought eight machine guns, 369 rifles, 190 shotguns, 540 revolvers, and 10,000 rounds of ammunition, plus 109 gas guns with 3,000 cartridges. But of all the companies in Little Steel, Republic was the largest buyer of armaments, having paid $79,000 for tear gas alone. On the morning of May 30, strikers from the Republic South Chicago plant gathered at a nearby meeting hall to hear speakers. After the meeting about three hundred people started walking across a field toward the plant gates, where a detail of police had formed in line. White clouds rode the blue sky as the people came across the field by twos and threes, an unorganized crowd. What followed could scarcely be believed, but the newsreel cameras recorded it: the police opened fire and in half a minute ten people were dead and thirty wounded. After the fusillade, the police ran into the fleeing crowd and knocked down twenty-eight more victims, beating them so badly that they were taken to hospitals. Three of the police also went to hospitals, injured by stones. The investigating committee found that seven of the dead had been shot in the back, three in the side, none in front; and this could be seen in the newsreels. Although the Republic strike failed, this May Day massacre started an undertow of public opinion in favor of John L. Lewis's organizers. Chicago and the country knew by instinct that organized labor was coming in, and the implacable Girdler was on his way out. Four years later, the National Labor Relations Board recognized the United Steelworkers of America.

Another event took place at Chicago in 1937 that had much to do with shaping history, and deciding the question of life or death for people far from the immediate scene. With help from Mr. Ickes in Washington, the Commissioners had completed the outer driveways of the Burnham plan, and linked them by a bridge over the river where it joined the lake a half mile east of Wacker Drive and Michigan Avenue. Commanding a fine view across Grant Park, the new bridge lay within sight of the *Tribune* tower. President Roosevelt himself was coming out for the dedication ceremonies, but no Dear Frank and Dear Bert letters passed between Washington and Chicago. Some time before, when the *Tribune* reporter John Boettiger submitted a question that Colonel McCormick had raised about Communists in the government, Mr. Roosevelt had drawled, "Oh, now, John, tell Bertie he is just seeing things under the bed." This made it certain that no bed at 1519 Astor Street would ever again be offered to Franklin Roosevelt. But Roosevelt took full advantage of the opportunity that dedicating the Outer Drive Bridge presented for a major speech. The surroundings were dramatic with the lake stretching to the sky and the long city sleeping on the shore, surely to wake one day soon. Here Franklin Roosevelt delivered the speech in which he told Chicago, the nation, and the world that America was going to be placed in readiness to "quarantine the aggressors." He was saying that it was no longer inconceivable that the United States would go to war against Hitler's Nazi Germany and the Fascist Italy of Benito Mussolini.

Next day a *Tribune* editorial said: "The crowd which gathered at the new bridge yesterday heard Mr. Roosevelt deliver what may well prove to be the most important speech he will ever make. Mr. Roosevelt announced a new foreign policy for the United States. It would be more accurate to say that he readopted the foreign policy of Woodrow Wilson, the policy which brought the United States first into armed conflict with Mexico and then into the World War, the policy which was overwhelmingly rejected by the American people after the war. . . ."

People throughout the country received the Roosevelt speech from Chicago's new Outer Drive with varying degrees of enthusiasm, and some with no enthusiasm at all. Among the latter were the German saloonkeepers along Milwaukee Avenue, who had been displaying pictures of Mr. Roosevelt on the bar mirrors side by side with photographs of Adolf Hitler. They now banished the Roosevelt portraits to the urinals, leaving Hitler to reign by himself among colored glassware beside the cash registers. And all through the city, many educated young men began to investigate what the Army and Navy had to offer in the way of reserve commissions. At the same time, an isolationist movement started to take form among respectable Chicagoans, including some of the young men going into the reserves. They were pulled two ways, for blind patriotism, the secular religion of nineteenth-century America, was still very strong; at the same time, common sense had not altogether vanished, and Chicago, without the direct European connections of New York, had a certain suspicion of foreigners, and even of the English who had set styles for the commercial aristocracy of the United States since the first big money came in after the Civil War.

Nobody in town better exemplified the Chicago dilemma than Colonel McCormick himself: as he showed by retaining the title, he considered himself a military man, having seen action with field artillery in the First World War. Indeed, McCormick went so far as to claim that he had introduced machine guns into the American Army. This was "incomparably absurd," according to his sympathetic biographer Frank C. Waldrop. The colonel's claim was a gross exaggeration of services that he had rendered prior to the First World War by trying to persuade Washington bureaucrats to accept the Lewis gun, invented by an American and used in the armies of England, Belgium, and France. And so it was that Chicago had in McCormick a man of the sword, ready to take the field, though fifty-seven years old in 1937, who also lived in profound suspicion of foreign governments; indeed, he mistrusted any government, including our own, and this great Chicago original, though not always rational, was not always wrong.

Robert Rutherford McCormick was the grandson of Cyrus's brother, William Sanderson McCormick, and of Joseph Medill who had made the *Tribune* a powerful paper before the Civil War. One of Medill's daughters married Dr. Patterson's son, as we know; the other daughter Katherine married Robert Sanderson McCormick, William's son. This Robert S. McCormick was a man who asked nothing from life other than a soft job with good pay. The family got him appointed Ambassador to Russia, but he made a wrong move with the grand dukes over there, and the English diplomat Cecil Spring-Rice fingered him to President Teddy Roosevelt, who gave him the boot. Resentment at this may have colored Robert R. McCormick's personality; it undoubtedly affected his mother, who showed much confidence in his brother Joseph Medill McCormick, but seems to have had little belief in the abilities of the younger son. Robert received affection and encouragement from his grandfather Joseph Medill until the old man died in 1899, and Joseph Medill Patterson succeeded him as editor of the *Tribune*. Thus the McCormick-Medill-Patterson family connection remained in control of the Tribune Company, but when Robert R. McCormick emerged from Yale in 1903, he did not go to work for the paper, but started a course of law at Northwestern University, and then in 1905 gave the impression that he might devote his life to public service, by becoming president of the Chicago Sanitary Commission, the municipal body in charge of the Sanitary and Ship Canal.* There had been a succession of attempts to complete this venture, whose object was to make the north and south branches the Chicago River's main channel, drawing with their waters an inflow from Lake Michigan along the connecting branch that ran from east to west. The system of locks, commenced in 1892, had just been brought to completion when McCormick took charge. His responsibility was to oversee the work of opening South Chicago to feeder channels running between the lake and the main canal. Although the Canal Administration was a notorious source of graft, and a dumping ground for political hacks, Robert R. McCormick put in five years of efficient and honorable service, and while he was at it, learned about his city. By 1910, he was no longer "the unknown, unwanted younger brother of the maternally designated family star." In 1911, the *Tribune* family connection received a shock when Robert W. Patterson suddenly died. They were even more astonished when it transpired that Patterson had been on the point of selling the *Tribune* to Victor Lawson. The heirs vetoed this plan, and after some discussion installed Robert R. McCormick as president of the Tribune Company. He soon became editor as well, and reigned in the two positions as the country's most independent press lord for the next forty-four years.

In the silver decade preceding World War II, fast-moving Chicago time seemed to have slowed down, or perhaps suspended its passage and ceased

*Chamber of Commerce literature has hailed this canal as the greatest feat of hydromechanics since the parting of the Red Sea. While scarcely that, as a sanitary measure it did wipe out the cholera death toll, and is now the first reach of a waterway system that extends to the Gulf of Mexico.

to have movement at all. Sometimes an event would appear to glide up, pause for a moment, and dissolve, leaving Chicago to consider it at leisure, or allow it to vanish from the mind. So it was when the newspaperwoman Doris Lockerman described the dancing teacher Alvar L. Bournique as he appeared at the annual graduation exercises of his Fortnightly Academy on March 18, 1938. It was to be the last class held by the "frail, courtly little man" and his wife who greeted the adolescent pupils at a costume party which marked their completion of the course, and his retirement. The pupils who had dressed as "assorted Bengal lancers, cowboys, sandwich men, and Snow Whites, glided and bounced through waltzes and fox trots, or skipped and bowed in the Virginia Reel. As usual, there were more girls than boys. And, as usual, most of them were taller and heavier than the boys. Even in their flat heels they towered, self-consciously, above their white-gloved partners and looked painfully ahead at the row of parents who sat on the sidelines and nodded encouragement. Colonel Bournique, looking like a child in a white wig, danced every dance. The girls of his choice seemed even less poised as they looked over his head and slid carefully along to his supple leading. When each dance was finished, he, like all his boy students, bowed gravely as he escorted the Snow Whites to their seats. For all its proud correctness, the dance ended in a snowball fight, a free-for-all. The Bourniques, who had furnished tissue paper for the missiles, expected it and left the ballroom. They had seen the same thing fifty-seven times before." Four months later, the old dancing master died in his sleep.

As the city wallowed along through the 1930s, gradually righting itself with the help of ballast that Washington put aboard, William Randolph Hearst began to feel increasing financial agony because of his attempt to compete with the *Tribune* in the Chicago morning newspaper field. There seemed to be no room for two large morning papers in a city that increased its population by only twenty thousand in the decade, and its area by only five square miles. The Hearst *Examiner,* which had named itself Monarch of the Dailies, called for help in its battle against the World's Greatest Newspaper in 1918, and combined with the *Herald,* which had been part of more consolidations than any other paper in town, to form the *Herald-Examiner.* A sensational and occasionally entertaining sheet that never gained the confidence of advertisers, the *Herex* went tabloid for a few months in 1929, then merged with the *American* as the afternoon *Herald-American;* and Chicago was left with only one morning paper.

There was no lack of headlines: the excellent foreign staffs of the *Daily News* and the *Tribune* spent a lot of money on cable tolls to keep Chicagoans informed of how the European countries were lining up to fight again. Journalists referred to the coming hostilities as the Second World War, although it would be just as accurate to speak of the second section of the original war. Chicagoans read of Hitler's oration in which he screamed that he had decided he must put on his old soldier's coat from the war of Germany's betrayal, not to take it off until the Fatherland was respected again as a world power. When politicians start talking that way, people are pretty sure to be killed, and generally the wrong ones. Sure enough, the Germans invaded Poland on September 1, 1939, which was a lovely day in Chicago, with the lake smooth in the late afternoon, showing long purplish violet ripples as the sun went down.

England and France went in right away, and the Chicago isolationists began having a harder time. However, the Chicago committee to keep American out of the fighting brought Charles A. Lindbergh to Soldier Field on August 4, 1940, and he told 40,000 people that we were in trouble if the government could force us into a fight that was none of our business. Then the nation's rulers put through a conscription law, and men of military age obediently entered their names on October 16, while Mr. Roosevelt burbled about the restoration of "the old American custom of the muster." A politician without a big army is like a snake with a broken back; there was something decent inside McCormick that made him hate the idea of press gangs and conscript armies, and he spoke bitterly against the draft. There was warfare between Roosevelt and McCormick; and the President's adherents supported Marshall Field III in establishing a new Chicago morning paper to challenge the *Tribune.* On December 4, 1941, Chicagoans saw Volume One, Number One of an impressive full-sized newspaper called *The Sun,* and bought 896,000 copies. On the same day the *Tribune* published a secret U.S. Army document giving the plans to oppose Germany with 10,000,000 American soldiers in Europe. Some of McCormick's Washington enemies thought they had him now: Mr. Ickes felt it might be possible to shoot or hang the Chicago colonel for treason, or at least throw him in jail. But it turned out the Army Air Force had leaked the document for the purpose of undercutting the ground forces. The heat came close to General Hap Arnold, head of all the flyers, and the White House said to drop the matter. Until the time of Mr. Roosevelt's death, McCormick and his Patterson cousins pursued him like three furies: Eleanor Medill Patterson with her *Washington Times Herald,* her brother Joseph Medill Patterson with the *New York Daily News,* and Robert R. McCormick firing away from his Michigan Avenue tower.

When the Japanese attacked Pearl Harbor, three days after the birth of the Chicago *Sun,* the local anti-war committees closed shop. The young men among the isolationists went into uniform, Hitler's picture disappeared from the Milwaukee Avenue saloons, and Mr. Roosevelt's confident countenance came into display on every hand. Correspondents for the *Daily News*, the *Tribune*, and the *Sun* set out for England, Africa, the Pacific, China, India, and Burma. But the most significant event of the war, and perhaps of all history, occurred on the South Side of the city they had left.

The scientists whose task it was to make a bomb using atomic energy had chosen the University of Chicago as the place to run an experiment to see if the thing could be made to work. They selected this university because of its reputation in science, and the quality of its staff. Chicago was well located in the center of things for the coming and going that the secret project made necessary, and the shipping of materials for the test frame, which was called an atomic reactor. Also, there may have been an instinctive feeling that this was the city where the country's shaping events took place, and all its energies came together. Dr. Enrico Fermi said he thought everything could be kept under control, and on November 7, 1942, he started putting together an experimental structure in the racquets court under the football stadium at the university. This room was about ten times the size of a squash court; like the little-used stadium, it was a relic of days when the university had planned to play intersectional football and cater to sporty undergraduates who played indoor court games with racquets. Today the authorities were using this space to start Chicago Pile One (CP-1). Assisted by Walter Zinn and Herbert Anderson, Fermi began building the pile, which was made out of lumps of uranium spaced eight and a quarter inches apart by graphite blocks. Of these there were forty thousand, each 4⅛ by 16½ inches long, alternating solid blocks and those with holes for the uranium. They got started and then Fermi called in thirty graduate students, the coolies of research, and put them to work piling up blocks until they had filled the court. At 9:45 A.M. on December 2, Fermi ordered the control rods taken out. The neutron counters began clicking. They took out some more rods; by twenty minutes past three the counters had gone crazy, recording so fast that the ear could not separate the clicks. Fermi closed his slide rule and said, "The reaction is self-sustaining." The work on CP-1 done under the cover name of Chicago University Metallurgical Laboratory was a success.

Further experiments on the reaction of atomic masses lay ahead to get atomic energy under sufficient control for use in destroying life. That phase of work reached successful conclusion at Hiroshima on August 6, 1945, when the first atom bomb killed 80,000 men, women, and children. Three days later, Americans exploded a second bomb, over Nagasaki,

[393]

killing 40,000 civilians without warning. On August 14 the *Tribune* said, "The peace upon which the world is entering presents mankind with what may well be its last opportunity to practice the virtues of fraternity and reason." Those virtues had been absent at Hiroshima and Nagasaki, but the *Tribune* made no mention of that, continuing in a tone of moral exhortation: "If the old hates persist, if nations nurse their animosities and await the opportunity of vengeance, if men allow their minds to dwell upon the grievances of the long past, instead of turning with hope to the future, then it may yet be that this earth will become a barren waste, in which the survivors of the race will hide in caves or live among ruins."

The return of soldiers to Chicago after World War II did not cause the city-wide displays of emotion that greeted the men of World War I, but they received adequate welcomes and dispersed to homes and jobs with considerable hope for the future. One thing was certain, war could be ruled out from now on, because of the destructive power in atomic weapons. And in any event, it was clear that Americans would never attempt to fight a land war in Asia. Even the generals could see it wasn't practical, and no politician would try to get away with it. Little Harry Truman in the White House looked harmless, although he had turned the A-bomb loose on Japanese civilians. But wise men in saloons said that served them right for being Japanese, and you had to hand it to Truman, he had saved American lives.

Chicago had made money during the war, but in 1946 seemed to be settling again into a sort of drowsy calm like that of the silver decade. However, there was a noticeable increase in population, which would amount to 230,000 more people in town by 1950; and there were enough houses going up to accommodate these people, except that the Negroes usually had to accept poor housing and crowded rooms.

The fortunate Chicagoans, the cultivated ones, heirs of the early owners, felt a dreamlike quality in the first years after the war. The pull of the past was strong. Old Mr. Meeker died. His wife died soon after, and Arthur and his sister had the task of clearing the apartment at 1100 Lake Shore Drive. They found enough pictures, glass, china, silver, and linen for five households. They unfolded twenty-foot Italian tablecloths, and took the flannel coverings from enormous indescribable silver gilt *décors de table*. There were sets of Crown Derby, Wedgwood, Rookwood, Russian enamels, and Byzantine mosaics. There was a billiard table and a grand piano and scores of fragile little Buhl tables loaded with silver and ivory snuffboxes, music boxes that played waltzes, and framed signed photographs of Foch, Robert T. Lincoln, Ambassador Myron T. Herrick, the Graf von Bernstorff, Marie of Roumania, and Edward of Wales. More than five thousand separate items the appraisers made of it, including one trunk filled with Mechlin lace, and another that was stuffed to the lid with ostrich feathers.

Business kept up in an encouraging way as Chicago entered the 1950s, for the long run of inflation had started. There was money to spend, the banks were handling paper at a gratifying rate, and although there were too many automobiles on the streets, most of the white people felt comfortable in their jobs and homes. Some of the substantial men in Lake Forest ran a private railroad car, called the Deer Path, on the North Western line in and out of Chicago. Younger men who went to town earlier started a similar car and named it the Cow Path. Then a group of prosperous Winnetka commuters, many of them psychiatrists, put on a car which they called the Psycho Path. Bridge was the card game of the private cars, the term "station rubber" indicating agreement that the score rode on the tricks played and quitted when the train slowed at either end of the run. This term also got into the private language of Lake Forest as a signal between husbands and wives that it was time to leave a party. There were not more than four or five fully staffed great houses in Lake Forest now, but in smaller houses—still quite large to most people—the residents of this beautiful town continued to enchant visitors with easy-mannered hospitality that could hardly be matched in any part of the country for generosity and charm. Howard Shaw had left his mark on Lake Forest, and his daughter Sylvia Shaw Judson had adorned many of the community's quiet places with garden sculptures of children and animals that captured the viewer with their honesty and grace. After Shaw's time, the architect David Adler had designed a number of elegant moderate-sized houses, and William T. Priestley, Jr., a student and associate of Meis van der Rohe, achieved gemlike simplicity in the design of his own house on Negaunee Lane. Down in the city, Meis had altered the lower Gold Coast skyline in 1952 with the famous apartment buildings at 840 and 860 Lake Shore Drive. Except for Meis's apartments, there was little change in the main Chicago skyline until 1955. In that year the Prudential Building appeared on the northeast corner of Randolph Street and Michigan Avenue; it was a structure having perhaps more economic than architectural significance, for it meant that after a quarter of a century, downtown Chicago was building again.

Along with the other papers, the *Tribune* welcomed the Prudential Building, and predicted boom times ahead. But Colonel McCormick probably knew nothing about it, for he was dying at his estate near Wheaton, which had once been the farm of Grandfather Joseph Medill. Robert R. McCormick had not worn well in old age. His friend and associate Frank

[395]

Waldrop wrote that in those years the Colonel "had fallen far in self-indulgence at invective, exaggerated language and grandiosity of manner." And yet when McCormick died, on April 1, 1955, Chicago felt that the last link to the old owners was broken, and that this was not an entirely good thing. "And so in his native city," Mr. Waldrop wrote, "McCormick was finally recognized as a citizen who had done much and done it very well indeed. . . . And as for the newspaper that was the center of his effort, any institution so embedded in a city's life has also perhaps, even in spite of itself, acquired merit." One thing more came from Robert McCormick's death: it seemed to restore to the passing of Chicago time that quality of national significance that so often attached itself to occurrences in the city's life. Chicago had again started to nominate Presidential candidates: Roosevelt had received two more nominations there in 1940 and 1944. Thomas E. Dewey accepted a Chicago Republican nomination in the latter year. Now Chicago was at it again, sending out both Eisenhower and Stevenson in 1952, and Richard M. Nixon in 1960 to lose a close election to John F. Kennedy.

If Henry Adams could have returned to Chicago in the late 1960s, he would have found even more sources of education than those of the Columbian Fair. This student of energy would have immediately felt the revived cadence of construction in the city, and would have taken time to examine the Inland Steel Building with its tower in appropriate stainless steel; the Hartford Insurance Building, its glass deeply embedded within reinforced concrete frames; and the twin towers of Marina City, designed by Bertrand Goldberg, on the riverbank opposite Wacker Drive.

Henry Adams would have looked for a mighty courthouse square with something like Hunt's Administration Building at its center. And looked in vain, for all one could have found to show him would have been the new Civic Center, whose plaza gives an impression of meanness, and supplies the setting for a large work of sculpture by Pablo Picasso which bores on sight. And it would dismay Henry Adams, surely, to walk west to Halsted Street and see the Hull House complex ripped off to make room for the concrete Chicago campus of the state university.

Adams might then head for the Academy of Science, to walk through a presentation of the rain forest that preceded Lake Chicago, and enjoy a green thought in a green shade as he contemplated horribly lifelike walking fish and huge-winged insects. This was education, and the kind that he valued; turning it in his mind, he might walk back through the near North Side, and approaching the Michigan Avenue bridge this veteran viewer of architecture would line up the Wrigley building in perspective, and note that there was something to say for it as a descendant of the

World's Fair. Across the street, a new Equitable Building would excite some curiosity in Adams's mind, but he would observe again a public meanness, expressed this time in a pavilion having all the grandeur of a suburban train shed. Adams would pause at a nearby monument to read a list of twenty-seven names, presumably the worthiest of memory in Chicago history to the present time. Jane Addams is there, and Charles H. Wacker, and the enlightened manufacturer Richard Teller Crane. There are noticeable omissions, for Burnham and Jenny are there, but no John Root. Omitted are the names of Harriet Monroe, Vachel Lindsay, John T. McCutcheon, and George Ade. One would try to explain how this could happen, and then would have to let Henry Adams go, perhaps to walk up St. Clair Street past two elegant brick hotels from the 1920s, the Eastgate and the St. Clair, and stroll around the corner to Seneca Park, a patch of green preserved in front of the Pearson Hotel, and see a gigantic black metal structure looming over that section of Chicago, one hundred stories high. Did it have meaning? Adams had long studied architecture as the expression of force; why was this sinister building just so high and no higher? A group of Chicago high-school students had appealed through the newspapers for discarded bottle caps. They were going to save the caps until they had 1,000,000 of them, to see what a million of something looks like. In what way did their project differ from the raising of the ominous tower? It was the kind of question that Adams liked to ask, and his answer would have been that there is no difference between number for the sake of number and size for the sake of size.

In the summer of 1968, one had various ways to feel the energy that was racing through Chicago. One could breathe it on any corner when automobiles stopped for traffic lights and poured out unconsumed energy in the form of poison gas. One felt it on the South Side where a plan was made to run additional auto roads through Jackson Park and kill hundreds of trees. One read about schemes to put an airport in the lake, and to throw up walls of buildings along the river to cut off the view, the light, and the air—economic energy on an open throttle. One could see animal energy in the strength and agility of the alley rats, known as "jokers" on the South Side, where young Negro gang leaders showed sport by organizing joker hunts with twenty-two calibre guns. And an outburst of energetic noise struck the town in July when the Nobles of the Mystic Shrine came in for a convention. If there were an international award for bands that produced noise but no music, the only question among the Shriners would have been which of their bands should accept it. There was something terrifying about these middle-aged mid-Americans on a frolic: they never smiled, they never laughed, and under each red fez, the face was exactly the same. On their big day, they marched up Michigan Avenue for hours, still without any expression of joy, executing the drill, inherited from Colonel Ellsworth's Zouaves, the folk dance of Middle America. Chicago tolerated these people, for they brought money into town, and would be gone in a few days. The police warned dive-keepers that terrible penalties would follow if anyone drugged or damaged a Noble of the Shrine. And with a roar of brass and drums the Shriners went away; not one had been heard to laugh during all their time in Chicago.

The next large crowd of visitors was not entirely welcome: the National Democratic Convention was to meet in Chicago in August, and hotelkeepers and restaurant men expected to make something out of the delegates. But the convention was drawing an additional crowd of people—some said half a million—that was coming to town for the purpose of demanding the nomination of a candidate who would take us out of the war in Vietnam. It was reported that these persons were rabid revolutionaries who had no respect for Mayor Richard Daley. A man of limited education and understanding, Daley had inherited control of the Chicago Democratic machine from the successor to Mayor Tony Cermak, who had been shot in 1933 at Miami when only a few feet away from President-elect Franklin Roosevelt. It had been assumed that the gunman intended to assassinate Mr. Roosevelt, but plausible theories have been advanced that Cermak was the target because of some villainy in Chicago. At any rate, the ignorant and vain Richard Daley was an embarrassing anachronism in 1968. He was Studs Lonigan's old man.

As the opening date for the convention drew near, Daley's security measures brought an ugliness into Chicago that men who had traveled over the world recalled having seen in Moscow, Fascist Rome and Berlin, and in banana-republic capitals when one gang of generals turned another out. Yet one can imagine the feelings of official Chicago toward the longhairs, the agitators, and the irreverent who were expected to descend on the city five hundred thousand strong. This proved to be an overestimate, but when the convention opened on Monday, August 26, the visitors to Chicago who had dissension or disturbance in mind numbered about one hundred thousand. Some of the officials believed that the invaders planned to assassinate Hubert Humphrey and poison the water supply. But in addition to the shaggy, unkempt "hippies," there were detachments of neat, polite college students who planned to "work within the system" for candidates opposing Humphrey. These young people were the sort described by Jane Addams as believing "that somewhere in Church or State are a body of authoritative people who will put things to rights as soon as they really know what is wrong." The college students

[398]

stated their case in a manifesto: "People are being asked to spend their taxes and blood supporting a government in which, it becomes clearer day by day, they have little voice. The supreme insult will be the 'choice' between two candidates supporting identical policies which are destroying our country's potential for decency."

Throughout the convention week, demonstrators pelted the police with sticks, stones, bathroom tiles, and obscene words of a deliberately provocative nature. The cops in most cases were all too ready to be provoked, and a series of battles between police and crowds took place. Sometimes running berserk and flailing at anyone in their path, police inflicted injuries that required first aid or hospitalization for 1,126 persons. The officers reported from their own ranks 192 injuries, some of which would not have passed sick call at a children's camp. Still, the police had a trying time of it, and the truth appears to be that they were put under a greater emotional than physical strain. These were six-pack, blue-collar men of the sort who stand in reverence to the National Anthem before a wrestling match or the first race at a dog track, and choke with anger when they think of a dirty Red showing disrespect to Our Flag. We have two ways of looking at policemen: we expect them to risk their lives for us, and yet we have reason to fear them as men of prejudice and limited understanding, armed with clubs and guns. In Chicago, one may recall that policemen climbed out on the *Eastland*'s side. It must be especially hard to be a policeman in Chicago, where judges get up on call in the night to arrange the release of Mafia hoodlums from custody. And in August 1968, a great many of the Chicago force added to the energies contesting there the seething energy of hatred.

Before the week ended, uniformed cops and plainclothes men burst into the headquarters of Senator Eugene McCarthy, and assaulted young people on his staff. In the streets and parks outside, police were equally brutal. Nora Sayre reported in the *New Statesman:* "Such blood: released from bruised and broken veins, from foreheads, scalps and mouths, from eye-sockets, shattered wrists and skulls. Broad bloodstreaks on the pavements showed where bodies had been dragged. We all bleed inwardly from the particular atrocities we witnessed. I saw seven policemen clubbing one girl—long after she had fallen; a row of sitting singers whose heads were cracked open by a charge of running cops; a photographer's camera smashed thoroughly into his eyes. Each day, scores staggered bleeding through the streets and parks, reeling or dropping. . . . Outside the Hilton, a nice little old lady . . . and I were suddenly hurled against the wall when 100 policemen seized their blue wooden barricades to ram the crowd (mainly onlookers and the press) against the building with such force that many next to me, including the old lady, were thrust through plate-glass windows. People sobbed with pain as their ribs snapped from being crushed against each other. . . ." The television cameras sent these scenes to millions of viewers, and Jimmy Breslin wrote: "For anybody who was on the streets of Chicago, it must always come down to a cop with a gun hitting a 16-year-old girl with a McCarthy button." Richard Daley made the defense that the ugly scenes on television had been selected, and probably staged, to discredit his city. Breslin commented that Daley, "talking of assassination plots and God-blessing his family and pulling out all the old Irish in him, seemed to have the country believing that what they saw on television never really happened. Investigate the press, not the police."

The hostility expressed by the mayor toward press and broadcasters was an especially frightening aspect of convention week in Chicago. The police and National Guard troopers smashed cameras and beat newsmen in the streets. In the convention hall, private cops hustled and hindered television men, sometimes while cameras showed the bullying. The viewers also saw Mayor Daley like an enraged gnome, giving signals to bring this man on and push that one off; they saw at last a commitment of Daley reserves when he summoned a crowd of municipal employees for a gallery demonstration. No casting director could have assembled such a collection of pitiable serfs, waving their signs that read WE LOVE DALEY.

These people were sufficiently grotesque, but the cameras in Chicago sent out an even more stupefying spectacle when they covered the grand climax, the unveiling of Hubert H. Humphrey. Surely this grinning, guffawing man had escaped from a novel by Sinclair Lewis, to represent the great city of Zenith in the great State of Winnemac. Yet when one began to take in the feebleness, the inanity of his acceptance address, he became real enough. The tragedy was that in the line of Presidential candidates who had addressed the country from Chicago, some had spoken well: Roosevelt II in crisp clarity, Roosevelt I with his call to Armageddon, Bryan with his silver plea for the plain people. And the last fires of Populism went out under Humphrey's damp verbiage. Once again this city had given the country a message—and it was a message that the Republic had fallen desperately ill, and the pains were felt with torturing intensity at Chicago, the country's heart.

Henry Adams had said, "Chicago was the first expression of American thought as a unity. One must start there." In August 1968 one finished there with depressing conclusions. And yet as it stood in high summer, between the prairie and the lake, the city had never looked more beautiful. Chicago still had its old meaning, its old necessity for the country as a whole, and one hoped that it might survive. For if Chicago cannot be what it ought to be, the United States will fail to reach the destiny so many orators have promised through so many years. All we can now write with certainty is that Chicago was wonderful in its time, and its story will be often repeated, until Lake Chicago comes back to cover the ruins, and the land falls silent under the sky.

Acknowledgements and Bibliography

I am endebted to Barbara Black Dunbar, L. Ellsworth Laflin, Jr., William T. Priestley, Jr., and Christabel Wheeler Priestley for much kind assistance in gathering material for this book. However, the conclusions and judgements recorded are entirely my own. I also wish to thank the staffs of the Chicago Public Library, the Newberry Library, the Library of the Chicago Historical Society, and the New York Society Library, for the services and facilities they have provided me, over the years, in those venerable and civilized institutions.

A survey of published work on Chicago could be expanded indefinitely: the library at the Historical Society, for example, contains about 90,000 books, pamphlets, and manuscripts. In writing this personal history of Chicago, I depended first of all on my own impressions and feelings about the place, going back some fifty years. For information on what happened before I had a chance to see for myself, I turned to files of the newspapers with which Chicago has been singularly blessed since earliest times. The lighted screens of the microfilm reading devices in the Newberry Library and the Historical Society have been magic lanterns through which I looked, hour after hour, on the town's recorded and pictured life, the doings of criminals and politicians, and, what was of equal interest, the advertisements showing the state of commerce and retail trade.

Much early documentation was destroyed in the Great Fire, but I found material ample for my purposes in the Historical Society, where notes based on lost papers regarding early Chicago are preserved. One of the storehouses of information is *The History of Chicago* (1670–1885) by E. T. Andreas. The three volumes, running to 2,304 closely printed pages, are fascinating in their detail. But the modern researcher will note that Andreas is uncritical in his handling of material. Nevertheless, Andreas is vital to an understanding of the city, as may also be said of Major Joseph Kirkland's *Story of Chicago*, which is cited in the text.

It is not possible for me to recall and list everything about Chicago that I have read in some twenty years of preparation for the writing of this book, but the sources from which I have taken quotations are identified in the text. Further reading by interested students is recommended in any or all of these sources, and I feel that some of them have sufficient importance to be listed again in this bibliographical note. My method has been to present the story of Chicago both chronologically and by topics, such as politics, art, literature, business, and building. My interest in the building of Chicago is obvious, and I would like to suggest that all interested persons read a remarkably fine study, the *History of the Development of Building Construction in Chicago*, by Frank A. Randall, a structural engineer who was also a special lecturer at the University of Illinois. Mr. Randall's history is detailed and complete, and includes the Rand, McNally *Bird's-Eye Views and Guide to Chicago*, published in 1898. The line engravings showing the downtown district of the time, block by block, repay examination with a magnifying glass, which will cause seventy-five years to melt away, and give the student a sense of standing on the street in late nineteenth-century Chicago. Another look at that period is afforded by the two volumes of *Industrial Chicago*, published in 1891. To get the feeling of the Gold Coast (where the Meekers lived), in more recent years, I recommend two brochures of real estate firms, the *Directory to Apartments of the Better Class on the North Side of Chicago* (Pardridge & Bradley, 1917), and the *Portfolio of Fine Apartment Houses* (Baird & Warner, 1928). In addition to the writings of Montgomery Schuyler on the Monadnock Block and other buildings, the serious researcher should read *The Chicago School of Architecture*, by Carl W. Condit, *Louis Sullivan, Prophet of Modern Architecture*, by Hugh Morrison, and Harriet Monroe's biography of her brother-in-law John Wellborn Root.

When we take up crime in Chicago, other than that of politicians, we find one book which stands as a model of historical writing—*Gem of the Prairie: An Informal History of the Chicago Underworld*, by Herbert Asbury. Coming at Chicago crime from the political angle, Lloyd Wendt and Herman Kogan give a fascinating account of Aldermen Mike (Hinky Dink) Kenna and Bathhouse John Coughlin in *Lords of the Levee*, one of the most interesting books ever written on any aspect of Chicago. William A. Stuart tells the story of Mayor William H. Thompson in *Twenty Incredible Years*, and A. J. Smith gives a rewarding study of Chicago crime in general under the title *Syndicate City*. Sociologists at the university included *The Professional Thief* among their objects of study, and the confidence game has been described to the last detail in *The Big Con*. There are many studies of specific crimes available—for example, the report on the Jake Lingle murder by John Boettger, Franklin D. Roosevelt's son-in-law. The gutter journalist Shang Andrews wrote the sensational novel *Wicked Nell* to portray commercialized vice in the 1880s: I had the privilege of reading a copy of this work—perhaps the only one in existence, and falling apart—at the Historical Society, where I also examined a rare and fragile copy of *If Christ Came to Chicago*, by the English journalist W. T.

Stead, from which I quoted in the parts of this book having to do with the bad times following the World's Fair of 1893.

For the Fair itself, whole libraries are available; I found a fresh point of view in a novel of the period, *Sweet Clover*, by Clara Louise Burnham. The collection of books and pamphlets on Chicago social organizations at the Historical Society gave me a glimpse of The Argonauts and their voyages to the Fair. Many excellent photographs of the Fair, again calling for the magnifying glass, can be found in the multitude of souvenir books published for visitors. One of the best, the *View Album of Chicago,* was printed in Columbus, Ohio, by the Ward Brothers for Exposition trade. A book of value from several points of view is *A Poet's Life: Seventy Years in a Changing World* (1938), by Harriet Monroe. I learned much from Miss Monroe about the Fair in addition to what she revealed of her interests in architecture and poetry. Perhaps the most important writer on the Chicago Fair is Henry Adams, whose impressions of that event in 1893 remain fresh and vivid.

The question of how useful fiction may be to a writer of history is an interesting one. I found that many fictional Chicagoans struck me as absolutely real and trustworthy. There were not only Wicked Nell and Mrs. Burnham's Clover, two girls of the South Side, but a gallery of convincing men and women in the works of Theodore Dreiser and George Ade; and Henry Blake Fuller's people have existence for the historian like the New Yorkers of Edith Wharton and Henry James. I believed in the profane truck driver of the Rev. E. P. Roe's *Barriers Burned Away,* the Lake Forest heroine of Hobart C. Chatfield-Taylor's *An American Princess,* and the grain speculators of *The Pit,* by Frank (Benjamin Franklin) Norris, and I saw truth in the picture that was drawn by Arthur Meeker, Jr. in *Prairie Avenue.* The greatest work of realistic fiction about Chicago is, I feel sure, the Studs Lonigan trilogy by James T. Farrell, on which I have made extended comment in the main body of this book. The pages of these novels tell even more about Chicago than the studies from the university, which is saying a good deal, for the studies, such as *The Gold Coast and the Slum,* are eminently worthwhile. But Studs and his friends and enemies are alive, and whenever a historian can touch life, he has a chance to make of his history something that lives.

Writing the lives of actual men and women in Chicago has long been a recognized industry, because of the remarkably vivid and various characters the city has provided for biographers both foreign and local. Many fine books have resulted, and I was especially grateful to James Weber Linn for *Jane Addams, a Biography,* which he wrote as a labor of love about the saintly woman who was his aunt. Miss Addams's own accounts of the Hull House years are part of American literature; I also found much to think about in a less well known book by Jane Addams, *The Excellent Becomes the Permanent.* Ishbel Ross wrote a reliable biography of Mrs. Potter Palmer, which gives a convincing portrait of a woman who was kind and intelligent as well as beautiful and rich. This excellent biography throws light on a number of matters, including the women's movement of the 1890s and its effect on the World's Fair. The evangelist Dwight L. Moody was an important Chicagoan, and his impressions of the place are recorded in the *Life* written by William R. Moody. A Chicagoan of a later time, who studied the city as carefully as Dwight Moody did, but from a different point of view, was Edith Abott of the university, whose *Tenements of Chicago,* published in 1936, showed what happened to the poor and uneducated subsequent to the money panic of 1929. This is a necessary book for anyone who wants to find out about Chicago. One must also consider Frances Willard of Evanston, who left her diaries and memoirs, and one is obligated to read *Julia Newberry's Diary,* which I have quoted in the text. The *Diary* should be read at full length so that the student may know the story of this young Chicagoan, told in her own words which retain their singular charm after one hundred years. A valuable autobiography is *Stormy Years,* by one of the city's best mayors, Carter Harrison, II. There are important biographical elements in the account of the Field department store, *Give the Lady What She Wants,* by Kogan and Wendt; these historians give much information on Marshall Field and Potter Palmer. Another authoritative account of the Field family may be found in *Marshall Field III: A Biography,* by Stephen Becker. The Field and McCormick families receive masterful treatment in *Battle for Chicago,* a scholarly and immensely fascinating and readable history of the city's newspaper wars by Wayne Andrews. There have been many books about the Chicago press lords: two of the most rewarding are *McCormick of Chicago,* by Frank Waldrop, and *Victor Lawson, His Times and His Work,* by Charles H. Dennis, who was managing editor of the *Daily News.* George Ade's life is a Chicago story in itself: there is much to be learned in his biography, written by Fred C. Kelly, and in *The America of George Ade,* edited and introduced by Jean Shepherd, a book that contains some of Ade's most important writing. I also found a number of revealing sidelights on Ade's life and character in the material from the Sigma Chi Fraternity on file at the Newberry Library. The biography of another writer associated with Chicago and the Middle West, which has useful passages about the city, is the story of Vachel Lindsay's life by Edgar Lee Masters. But the most useful of all Chicago biographies from the historian's point of view, because it concerns a man completely concerned with the city, is *John S. Wright, Prophet of the Prairies,* by Lloyd Lewis. John Wright's own prodigious commercial study of Chicago struck me as remarkable for what might be called a poetic and inspired presentation of statistics, in addition to its call for the green belt of parkways which has become a reality of life in Chicago.

An enormous official literature has gathered around the merchants, bankers, and businessmen of Chicago, generally to be found in heavy, gilt-lettered volumes such as *Chicago and Its Makers,* and *Notable Men of Chicago* (1910–1925). Historians need not reject such publications because the biographies are invariably complimentary to their subjects: there is much to be learned by anyone who reads these puff-sheet biographies with an eye for detail and comparison, and a feeling for period. A critical but affectionate view of the greater magnates can be found in *Giants Gone,* by the Chicago novelist Ernest Poole. His family was based in Lake Forest, the old suburban town, on the bluffs above Lake Michigan, which must be considered part of Chicago. A complete and fascinating account of this suburban community is written in *Lake Forest, Illinois: History and Reminiscences, 1861–1961,* by Edward Arpee, from which I have quoted in the text. Another book of value in calling back reality from the past is Caroline Kirkland's *Chicago Yesterdays,* which presents some of the ladies on the near North Side who had their portraits done by G. P. A. Healy. Such a lady was Janet Ayer Fairbank, whose collected newspaper pieces have given us a place at the tea tables of Division Street and Lake Geneva. Frederick Cook of the *Chicago Times* left in his memoirs a general record of the feel of Chicago life from the post-Civil War period up to the 1890s. Like Mrs. Fairbank, he used a gift for characterization that kept life in the people he wrote about long after the newsprint began to decay. In considering the racial groupings of Chicago population, one could devote a lifetime to the material now available in print. I should mention *The Jungle,* by Upton Sinclair, as a work of interest not only in the matter of Chicago meat packing in the early twentieth century, but for what it reveals about the Slavic and American Negro laborers in the stockyards. I found information about the Chicago Negro surgeon, Daniel Hale Williams, in *The Lonesome Road,* by Saunders Redding. The classic work on Negroes in the South Side is *Black Metropolis: A Study of Negro Life in a Northern City,* by St. Clair Drake and Horace R. Cayton.

Anyone attempting a survey of Chicago runs into the problem of describing the engineering achievements of the harbor, the river, and the drainage canal. He could not do better, as I discovered, than begin with *The Chicago,* Harry Hansen's contribution to the *Rivers of America* series. Waldrop on McCormick is also helpful here. Chicago demands treatment as a magnet for visitors, and the researcher will find a trove of information on these people, from the earliest times, in *As Others See Chicago*, compiled and edited by Bessie Louise Pierce and Joe L. Norris. The violent disturbances of Chicago's life have been covered by the newspapers, by official investigators, and by numerous writers. It is bewildering to attempt a summation of the Great Fire, until one finds that Robert Cromie has spoken the final word on that disaster in *The Great Chicago Fire*, a highly readable scholarly book of conviction and authority. In the matter of the Haymarket bombings and their aftermath I followed the classic *History of the Haymarket Affair*, by Henry David (1936), together with contemporary newspaper accounts. Clarence Darrow's memoirs are useful in re-creating the Pullman strikes, and I added my own studies in the daily papers to this section of the text. For the race riots of 1919, I followed the *Chicago Daily News*, including Carl Sandburg's feature stories, plus the reports of investigating commissions, and the activities of Studs Lonigan. Concluding research for this history in the summer of 1968, I used newspaper and magazine accounts of the disturbances accompanying the Democratic Convention, along with *Chicago Eyewitness*, by Mark Lane, and *Rights in Conflict*, the report of 101 investigators to the National Commission on the Causes and Prevention of Violence. I should like to add that for occurences in Chicago, rough or peaceful, there exists a remarkable typescript, *Historical Events of Chicago (Chronology 1673–1936)* compiled by Charles Spaulding Winslow, a high school teacher, which may be examined at the library of the Historical Society.

I was privileged to examine material in all sorts of collections in the Historical Society, and was especially grateful for the opportunity of looking over the notes from John Kinzie's account books; the letters of many survivors of the Great Fire; the early dance programs and material on the dancing masters, including Louis Sullivan's father; the reports and annual books of all the Chicago clubs, including the *History of the Chicago Club*, by Edward T. Blair; many portraits by Healy; the papers of George M. Pullman; the account books of John Van Osdel, survivors of the Great Fire; Daniel Burnham's beautiful book of plans; all sorts of family diaries and papers of various periods; and several issues of the State Historical Society *Journal*. In the Newberry Library, I looked at papers and letters concerning Ring Lardner, Burnham, Victor F. Lawson, Wallace Rice, Theodore Thomas, and Charles H. Dennis; and here I also had the privilege of examining a facsimile of the first Chicago directory, and the memoirs of Lyman J. Gage, along with a number of social directories, bluebooks, and statistical abstracts having to do with various chapters in the story of Chicago.

Index

McGraw, James, 128
McGregor, Mrs., 117
Mach, Ernst, 315n
McKenney, Thomas L., 34
McKim, Charles Follen, 172, 181, 194, 358
McKim, Mead, and White, 172, 173
McKinley, William, 154, 224, 225, 310
MacMonnies, Frederick, 180
MacMonnies, Mary Fairchild, 184
McNarry, Jim, 262
McPartland, Jimmy, 366
McRae, Edna, 384
McSwiggin, William H., 348
MacVeagh, Franklin, 120, 121, 141
McVeys, The, 26
Madison, James, 19, 22
Maeterlinck, Maurice, 316, 317
Mahor, 69
Main-Travelled Roads, 187
Malloy, Snapper Johnny, 131, 296
Malott, Capt. D. M., 68, 69
Manitou, 328
Marcosson, Isaac F., 287
Marie of Roumania, 394
Marina City, 396
Mariners' Temperance Society, 51
Marlowe, Julia, 260
Marquette, Father Jacques, 12, 13
Marquette Building, 284
Marsh, Pink, 255, 258
Marshall, Benjamin Howard, 325, 342–344
Marshall Field's Department Store, 288, 405
Martin, John, 192
Martine, J. Edwin, 125–127
Martineau, Harriet, 41, 42
Mason, Mayor, 111, 112
Mason, William, 304
Masonic Temple, 283
Masters, Edgar Lee, 18, 285, 319, 327, 328, 333, 369, 405
Mather Tower, 371
Matson, Sheriff, 150
Matthews, Brander, 260
Matz, Otto H., 114
Maurier, George du, 320
Mayhew, Henry, 200, 363
Mead, William Rutherford, 172
Medill, Joseph, 67, 69–73, 77, 80, 82, 83, 87, 100, 112, 114, 139, 275, 357, 379, 389, 390, 395

Medill, Katherine, 357, 389
Meeker, Arthur, Jr., 315, 361, 362, 376, 377, 383, 384, 394, 403, 404
Meeker, Arthur, Sr., 326, 361, 362, 377, 384, 394
Meeker, Mrs. Arthur, Sr., 394
Meigs Field, 382
Mellody Farm estate, 359, 360
Memoirs of an American Citizen, 279
Mencken, H. L., 379
Merchandise Mart, 371
Merchant's Club, 292
Merlo, Mike, 349
Mestrovic, Ivan, 383
Metropolitan Hall, 57
Meyers, Henry, 332
Michelson, Abraham, 278
Michigan Central Railroad, 272
Michigan Southern Railway, 272
Michigan Transit Corporation, 328
Miles, Gen. Nelson A., 178, 183, 185, 187
Millard, George W., 316
Millard, Zoe, 300, 306
Miller, A. H., 90
Miller, Daisy, 109
Miller, Kid, 131
Miller, Samuel, 30
Milner, James W., 113
Milwaukee Female College, 132
Minot, Edward J., 93
Mirandeau, Victoire, 17, 20
Mirasole, Monsieur, 125
Miss Porter's School, 162
Miss Whiting's School, 56
Missouri, 328
Mitchell, John J., 356
Mitchell, John J., Jr., 360
Mitchell, Lewis, 174
Mitchell, Tennessee, 318, 319, 327, 368
MIXED DRINKS, The Saloonkeeper's Journal, 320
Modjeska, 260
Monadnock Block (Tower; Building), 163, 173, 283, 403
Monet, Claude, 181, 192
Monon Block (Building), 40, 218
Monroe, Harriet (Mrs. John Root), 162, 163, 173–180, 197, 198, 294, 321–327, 333, 397, 403, 404
Monroe, Henry Stanton, 162, 175
Monroe Building, 342
Montauk Block, 162, 163

Rotary Club, International, 289
Rothmere estate, 359
Rudkus, Jurgis, 281, 286, 287
Rush Medical College, 49, 50
Russel, Lillian, 260
Russell, Bertrand, 315n
Russell, R. H., 260
Russell, William F., 353
Ryder, Albert Pinkham, 181
Ryerson, Martin, 283
Ryerson Building, 342

Saarinen, Eliel, 192
Sabath, Adolph J., 381
Sable, Jean Baptiste Point du, 14, 15, 23, 55
Saddle and Cycle Club, 362
St. Clair Hotel, 397
St. Denis, Ruth, 360
St. Gaudens, Augustus, 180, 181, 184, 192–194
Saleslady, The, 278
Salisbury, Rollin, 138
Salter, William M., 150
Salvation Army, 323, 324
Salvation Nell, 256, 316
"Sam 'n' Henry," 385
Sandburg, Carl, 33, 319, 320, 324, 336–338, 407
Sandburg, Lillian Steichen, 319
Sands, the, 55, 56
Sanitary and Ship Canal, 390
Sankey, Ira, 140
Santa Fe Railroad, 280, 370
Santayana, George, 315
Saturday Evening Post, 258, 268
Sauganash Hotel, 31, 32, 36–38, 63
Sawyer, Professor, 56, 57
Sayre, Nora, 399, 400
Scalisi, John, 350, 351
Scammon, Jonathan Young, 39, 40, 89, 92, 105, 106
Schiller Tower, 284
Schnitzler, 318
Schoolcraft, Henry Rowe, 27
Schulman, Joseph, 354
Schultze, Carl Emil, 258
Schuyler, Montgomery, 121, 163, 192, 282, 403
Schwab, Michael, 148, 149, 151, 208, 209
Science of Mechanics, 315n

Scientific Method in Philosophy, 315n
Scott, James W., 265, 266
Scripps, John T., 67
Sears, Roebuck, 295, 299, 300, 321
Select Dancing Academy, 125
Selfridge, Gordon, 288
Sellers, Col. Mulberry, 40, 42
Sembrich, Marcella, 383
Serritella, Dan, 354
Seward, Sen. William H., 72, 274
Seymour, Ralph, 322
Shaw, Frances, 317
Shaw, George Bernard, 315, 316
Shaw, Howard Van Doren, 317, 344, 395
Shaw, Victoria, 170, 300–302, 306
Shea, Cornelius, 288
Sheldon, Edward, 256, 316
Sheldon, Ned, 323
Shepherd, Jean, 405
Sheridan, Gen. Phil, 93, 111, 112, 326
Sherman, F. C., 47
Sherman, John B., 161, 162
Sherman House, 47, 103, 104, 122
Sherman Stock Yards, 272
Shortall, John G., 105, 106, 113
Shortall and Hoard, 105, 106
Shrigley, John, 44
Shriners (Nobles of the Mystic Shrine), 397, 398
Sigma Chi Fraternity, 405
"Silence," 90, 91
Sill, Anna Peck, 137
Sinclair, Upton, 286, 287, 406
Sister Carrie, 252, 316
Skinner, Otis, 260
Smith, Dr., 15, 16
Smith, A. J., 403
Smith, Alfred E., 378, 379
Smith, Gen. Arthur A., 76
Smith, Byron Laflin, 358
Smith, F. Hopkinson, 185
Smith, Franklin C., 76
Smith, George V., 62
Smith, Gen. George ·W., 76
Smith, Gen. Giles A., 76
Smith, Gipsy, 307
Smith, Gen. Gustavus A., 76
Smith, Jabbo, 366, 367
Smith, Gen. John C., 76
Smith, Gen. John E., 76
Smith, Mary Rozet, 157–160
Smith, Gen. Robert F., 76

[424]

Walsh, Tommy, 370, 379
Walters, Bancroft, 254
War of 1812, 19–22
Ward, Ella Bradley, 110
Ward, Mrs. Joseph Frederick, 56
Ward, Montgomery, 282, 294–296;
    Montgomery Ward and Company,
    295
Ward, Col. Philip R., 335
Ward Brothers, 404
Warren, Nicole, 361
Washington, George, 14, 63
Washington, Mrs. J. A., 63
Washington Park Race Track, 127,
    252
Washington Times Herald, 392
Washingtonian Home for Inebriates,
    272
Waste, 279
Water Tower, 96
Watson, Carrie, 170, 204
Watterson, Col. Henry, 179
Wayman, John E. W., 309
Wayne, Gen. Anthony, 19
Wealth Against Commonwealth, 154,
    217
Weary World, The, 320
Weatherford, Teddy, 366
Webster, Daniel, 47, 76
"Webster's Reply to Hayne," 88
Weiss, Ed, 303
Weiss, Hymie, 349, 350
Welles, Mrs. Susie, 117
Wells, H. G., 315, 318, 363
Wells, Capt. William, 20, 21, 26
Wendt, Lloyd, 403, 405
Wentworth, Elijah, 31
Wentworth, John, 43, 44, 52, 55, 56, 72,
    76, 78, 272
West, Rebecca, 318
West, Roy O., 325, 326
West Side Saloonkeepers' Ball, 309
Western News Company, 106
Wharton, Edith, 404
What Maisie Knew, 315
Wheeler, Seymour, 370
Wheeler family, 119
Wheeleretta, Eleanora, 57
Whistler, George Washington, 15, 26
Whistler, James Abbott McNeill, 15,
    281, 382
Whistler, Capt. John, 15–17
Whistler, John, Jr., 16, 17

"Whistler's Mother," 382, 383
White, Stanford, 172, 194, 358
Whitechapel Club, 263–266
Whitlock, Brand, 257, 258, 263
Whittier, John Greenleaf, 176
Whittlesy, Effie, 256
Wicked Nell, 170, 205, 403
Wigwam, the, 71–73, 379
Wild, Jonathan, 130
Wilde, Oscar, 131
Wilder, Thornton, 382
Willard, Frances, 74, 131–135, 137, 161,
    163, 165, 174, 183, 200, 345, 405
Willard, Mary, 74
Williams, Charlie, 255
Williams, Dr. Daniel Hale, 339–341,
    406
Williams, Minnie, 219
Williams, Nannie, 219
Willoughby Tower, 371
Wilson, Edmund, 375
Wilson, Capt. John, 68
Wilson, Woodrow, 276, 312, 330, 331,
    388
Winesburg, Ohio, 368
Winnetka, Ill., 395
Winslow, Charles Spaulding, 407
Winter, Dale, 345, 346
With the Procession, 320
Woman's Club, 200
Woman's Temple, 161, 163–165, 173,
    284
Women's Christian Temperance Union
    , 131, 132, 134, 135, 161, 163–165
Women's Medical College (Philadel-
    phia), 138
Women's Trade Union League, 139
Woods, William Allen, 214, 216
Woollcott, Alexander, 382
World War I, 326, 327, 330–335, 389,
    394
World War II: era prior to, 388–392;
    war years, 392–394; post-war years,
    394–401
World's Columbian Exposition of 1893,
    165–198, 200, 283, 396
Wright, Frank Lloyd, 173, 341, 355,
    377, 382
Wright, John S., Prophet of the Prairies,
    406
Wright, John Stephen, 36–38, 40, 63–
    67, 80–82, 84, 93–95, 108, 115, 116,
    154, 155, 206, 292, 406

Wright, Mrs. John Stephen, 88
Wrigley Building, 371, 396
Wrigley Field, 386
Wyatt, Edith, 322

Yeats, William Butler, 315, 317, 318,
322, 324, 325
Yerkes, Charles Tyson, 175, 250, 251
Young Lonigan, 335n
Young Men's Christian Association
(YMCA), 75, 98

Youngstown Sheet and Tube Corporation, 387

Zanuck, Darryl, 386, 387
Zinn, Walter, 393
Zorbaugh, Harvey W., 362–365, 367
Zorn, Anders, 183, 185
Zouaves (Berber troops), 77, 398
*Zury, the Meanest Man in Spring
County,* 26
Zuta, Jack, 353, 354